A FATHER'S VOICE

STEVEN D. PARENT

First Edition

NEWMAN SPRINGS PUBLISHING
320 Broad Street
Red Bank, NJ 07701

First originally published by Newman Springs Publishing 2020

ISBN 978-1-64801-987-6 (Paperback)
ISBN 978-1-64801-988-3 (Digital)

Printed in the United States of America

No judicial decision in our time has aroused as much sustained public outrage, emotion, and physical violence, or as much intemperate professional criticism.

—Ronald Dworkin

1

Yesterday, another time…

A simple black ledger, its spine torn, creased from use, was removed from a box stashed beneath the bed and thrown onto the untidy blanket of flowery pastels. A small length of frayed blue ribbon tied in a perfect bow was unraveled, and the flimsy book fell open to page 1. A young girl's hand, pale and white, gently swept over the handwritten text of the mostly blank page, feeling the dry texture of the page with emotion. A longing search for an escape between the lines.

The Book of Torture

Melissa's diary.

Slowly thumbing through the pages, she stopped to read a few words here and there, dark memories mostly, things she'd rather forget, tried to forget. Finally, she stopped at a blank page and tentatively put pen to paper, slow at first…

Dear diary,

As no one else is listening again, I turn to you, the blank page of my diary, to be my salvation. I call you friend.

Today was another dark day in my meaningless existence. A journey through a world that is empty and devoid of anchors to reality. Darkness is creeping into my world and slowly taking over all the light and hope, which is all that matters to me. It was just another day teasing me with false hopes, lies, and broken dreams.

It happened again today, and it came in the form of pain and everlasting torture, just as it did yesterday and the day before. The mental picture won't leave my head, which is about to explode with all the images that flash across the screen of my mind. Is this a cruel joke to test my faith, my sanity? Is this my dark, gothic poem?

I'm at my lowest point, God. The life-sustaining dreams I once counted on so strongly to get me through my dark days are dead, just like me. I can't take another day. This is not supposed to happen to a girl my age. Please stop the hurt. Please stop the pain. God, please let this end today. Give me this on my birthday. Please let me close my eyes this night and let me wake to death. Please…

Mel

2

Tomorrow, six months from now

Santa Monica, California

With the epic Pacific Ocean spreading out with panoramic splendor less than a mile away on this pristine, sunny Southern California day, the scene from the air was ominous at best as thousands upon thousands of people were gathered and tightly packed in front of the Santa Monica courthouse. The crowd was alive, moving and swaying back and forth like a jugular vein pulsating with a rapid heartbeat ready to implode at the core of the heart. An implosion was imminent, no doubt. The LAPD and LA county sheriffs were there in force to make sure the disobedient plebeians remained calm and orderly and without any violent tendencies.

Helicopter blades roared over the crowd. Their blades cut the salty air and thumped their menacing presence to the surging crowd below. There was a massive traffic jam of circling and hovering helicopters, both police and news helicopters. At least twelve at last count. This was an event that was to not be missed, "film at eleven" on your local news. An FBI helicopter was also hovering, and a US Coast Guard chopper came cruising in for a glance at the event.

The handheld news camera held tight on the two opponents verbally jousting in front of the crowd that was on the verge of sheer chaos behind them. Yelling and screaming, pushing and shoving, cursing and crying all around them did not stop the two from preaching their side of the issue. Come hell or high water, they were each going to have their say in front of the camera.

"Sad," Troye started above the roar of the crowd. "As morals, when not attached to religion, are based on the value of life, the humane way to treat people. Without valuing the lives of others, everything is okay." This discussion, which was but a sidebar to the "breaking news" and the mayhem that was going on behind them, had mostly been drowned out by the rattle and hum of the crowd. Troye and his sparring partner Betty Goldsmith was becoming louder to match the electric pulse that surrounded them.

"If our democracy fell, fighting to get it back would supersede everything else," Betty replied curtly. It was no secret that Betty did not like Troye or anyone else who carried the torch for his side. She was a patriot, and her opinion was all that mattered. If you did not agree with her, you just did not exist in her eyes.

Troye followed Betty with his eyes as the camera waited, trained on his dark face. The crowd continued surging. Pulsing. Vibrating with a dull roar dancing on the sea air.

"I imagine we have different definitions of what constitutes a fall," Troye said. He wanted to find out exactly what she held behind her dark eyes.

"Maybe, but the key word is *democracy*, as in democratic republic, as in our representative form of government. If due process and/or our ability to choose our leaders and vote on laws ceased, then I would believe our democracy fell—as in martial law or the president claimed emergency powers, the scary drawback in our constitution." Betty held her victory smile in check.

Troye grinned smugly. He knew he could take this foe with his tongue tied behind his back. But he wanted to play it out, egg her on, and see where she was going. "Extremely rare and not supported by the cause. Your ant hill isn't exactly the mountain you make it out to be," he replied with a taunting smirk.

A roar exploded through the crowd, and the heated emotion grew. The two sides continued yelling and screaming. Venom in the eyes of strangers gathered for the cause. Their spiteful and bitter words hurled across to the other side. A gaping scare would forever taint the soul of everybody involved.

"I see you carefully trimmed the subject, Troye."

The smirk remained on his face. He knew it was getting under Betty's skin. "If abortion were the entire choice issue, this nation would fold."

"Choice is a much bigger issue that covers political economic systems," she shot back quickly. "Abortion is one of the choices available to pregnant women."

"Which hardly means it covers the entire issue of choice," Troye quipped back.

"Yeah, and that's irrelevant."

"You don't like the term because you don't like to appear to be against a choice no matter what the choice is," Troye lashed out, raising his voice to match the crowd's bellow.

Something was happening in the crowd. A frantic commotion spread like wildfire. The cameraman held his steady shot on the two mouthpieces still in debate.

"Exactly, and this appearance is backed by the true meanings of pro-choice. Anti-choice equals pro totalitarianism, which is not the antiabortion stand," Betty said in a single breath. Her face was flushed.

Wow, Troye thought, *this chick is actually keeping up with me.* But that wasn't much of a surprise to him; she had always been quite the foe in their many debates in front of the camera. "The so-called antiabortion position is, in reality, a no-choice position," he said with a mocking smile.

"No, it isn't! Totalitarianism is a no-choice position," she shouted. "Many choices exist even if abortion weren't an option."

"Exactly what choices exist for a pregnant woman," Troye started with a bite of sarcasm, "as far as her pregnancy is concerned? The question is restricted to a woman who is pregnant. It does not include any factors whatsoever before she was pregnant nor any factors after she is no longer pregnant."

Betty was momentarily dumbfounded. That was a big question that required an equally big response, and as she was about to respond in some condescending manor, the crowd exploded with anarchy. The camera followed Betty as she was shoved to the ground and trampled by people who were running with wild abandon. Fistfights were breaking out everywhere.

Troye helped Betty to her feet and escorted her to the outskirts of the fray.

Pro—and antiabortion signs were flying through the air in every direction, hitting people in the head and face. People were swinging the signs at one another. Others were throwing water bottles, shoes, hats—whatever they could throw was in the air, aimed at the other side. One lady was hit in the face with a rock, and blood came quick down the side of her face.

People were scared and running for cover; some fell down and were trampled. There was no telling what was going to happen next. They wanted out of there now, and they were going to get to safety any way they could. And if it meant squashing some poor bastard deeper into the grass for traction, then so be it. At least they would be safe.

Police in riot gear made a massive surge into the crowd. Sirens roared, and cops on bullhorns shouted orders. People ran. Police dogs were barking ferociously as people scattered in all directions. Cops on horses moved fast into the crowd as panic set in.

3

Today, present time

THE HAND-CARVED wooden sign that read *Chaos Manor* should have been an indication of things to come, at least for the next few hours anyway. But is chaos only this night? Is it this house? Or is there something else he should know? Is it a manifestation of events, past, present...future? Those two words instantly tattooed his mind as he focused, almost hypnotized by the sign, waiting for someone to snap their fingers, count to three, say the magic word. An answer! What did it mean?

Walking into the beachfront condominium was like being transported into a surreal David Lynch film on hallucinogens, pushing the dimension of the subconscious, morphing the normal boundaries into mind-altering shapes and images right out of a Salvador Dalí masterpiece: a spontaneous method of irrational knowledge, causing one to rethink his own beliefs in normalcy.

A bizarre array of clutter adorned the room and walls, and it took him by shock. He wasn't sure how to react. Chaos Manor sure fit this place, he thought. Two wall posters really piqued his psyche and left him unable to think of anything else. The first one read EVE WAS FRAMED; and the next, a much larger black-and-yellow poster, almost shouted FUCK THE POLICE.

He tried to shake off the bizarre confusion. This was not the normal house. But it was too late. The needle had already pierced the veins, and the opiate was beginning to run its tainted course, tearing through him, altering his mind with a psychedelic landscape he could not understand.

Confusion!

Inconspicuously concealed on one frenzied wall, nestled between the FUCK CENSORSHIP poster and the numerous stolen vanity license plates, hung a precariously twisted frame with what turned out to be a diploma. This stood out most amidst the audacious interior simply because it was the one thing which just did not belong. Surprisingly enough, it was a law degree from the State of California.

Michael Bishope was floored, utterly astounded with the attitude of the room. He found it hard to believe that this joint belonged to an attorney who was conspicuously absent from the scene. The owner's absence seemed appropriate somehow. This whack job of a house was one he was not accustomed to living in the upscale neighborhood of Brentwood, California, with all the snobby, holier-than-thou, gossip-hungry neighbors.

Michael was one of the youngest entertainment executives in charge of the eleven o'clock news for KNRQ television in Los Angeles. This allowed him to reside in any neighborhood, but he was not born into a pampered life. He grew up in the valley, not far from the gangs, pimps, prostitutes, and drug dealers on Van Nuys Boulevard. This was home, where his parents struggled to keep a roof over their heads when Michael was a child. They never had the means for life's luxuries. They knew the meaning of hard work and tried to instill that in Michael.

Approaching thirty-two, Michael's well-toned athletic build and rugged features, topped by wavy brown hair, made him an unrivaled magnet to women of all ages—his soft voice and caring manner, so polite, and above all, that irresistible air of ingenuous audacity which was so much a part of him.

"So where's your buddy, the guy who lives in this…place?" Michael asked Nick Vach, his closest friend and the best man at Michael's forthcoming wedding.

As they lived next door to each other, Nick's home, for all intents and purposes, became a second home for Michael after his parents died. Nick's parents, acting as unofficial surrogates, played an intricate part in shaping Michael's character.

A little taller than Michael's six-foot-two frame, Nick was built for football, though he never played. His dashing good looks appealed to women. But women saw him as their big brother, not their lover. He was a teddy bear to them, too loveable to actually love. Nick would always be labeled as just one of the guys.

Nick smiled. "Relax. It's your bachelor party. Have a beer and enjoy the festivities," he said, handing Michael a bottle of beer.

Michael looked around at the cluttered walls. "You know what this place reminds me of?" he asked.

"Yeah, our frat house," Nick replied. He smiled in reminiscence of their exploits in college. "Shamma a-lamma ding dong."

"Is this guy really a lawyer?"

"You wouldn't think that looking at this joint, would you?" Nick replied. "But it's great. You got the beach right out the window."

The mere thought of this place was tripping Michael up with confusion and unanswered questions. It was a perplexing riddle he couldn't solve. Before he could ask a riddle-solving question, the front door swung open as if it were kicked, and in walked the guy—the lawyer, Tyson Nash. An Eastwood moment ensued—music, beady eyes, and all—as he eyed the startled faces staring back at him.

At first glance, Nash appeared dirty and unkempt. He appeared to be an offensive, foul-mouthed, swinish brute. He was the sort, it seemed. The fact was, Nash was a wimp. His rough facade was just that: a facade for the outside world. In actuality, he was conflict-adverse. He hated to fight and thought if he made himself look tough and talked a good game, nobody would openly oppose him. And for the most part, he was right.

Tyson Nash appeared to be anything other than a maverick lawyer. Wearing a torn flannel shirt and a do-rag bandana on his head, coupled with his tall, wiry frame and goatee, he looked as if he belonged in prison. His appearance made Keith Richards look like an unsodomized choirboy.

Nash stood poised, sizing up the situation with a look of amusement on his chalky-white face. "What's up, Nick?" he said with a cool-guy nod as he shook his buddy's hand. He nodded around the room "what's-up?-I'm-cool" type nods to acquaint himself with the unfamiliar faces. "So where's your bud?" he asked Nick.

Nick nodded, and with a sheepish grin on his face, he addressed Michael, "Welcome to the cave," he said extending his hand to Michael.

"Thanks," Michael said, still not sure this guy was really talking to him. His visceral reaction was to take cover. Nash's dirty grin reassured him. Michael looked around once more. "You have an interesting place here." He held his sarcasm just under his breath.

"I like it," Nash replied, posturing for the small group around him. "It's home." Nash continued his wide-eyed grin. He felt an instant liking to Michael. Most people did. "I call it controlled chaos." He pointed to various things on the walls. "A carefully crafted statement of my fucked-up life that reflects on the ever-increasing dismantalazation of the state of society as we know it."

Michael cocked his head and smiled. Yeah, this guy belonged here. "That must be lawyer talk." Nash broke out in laughter. "It sounds rather cynical, though, especially coming from a lawyer."

Nash embraced Michael's straightforwardness. "We live in a cynical world, my friend. A world controlled by big brother, big industry, and big government wanting to know every detail of our private lives. What fucking business is it of theirs what I eat, drink, or who I fuck?" Nash said in a single breath.

Michael smiled. He knew it was going to be an interesting party.

* * * * *

A CHILL RAN through Michael's body as a gust of wind pushed across the beach, where Michael sat in the early-morning darkness pondering his future. The lucent stars, brilliant overhead, held their own magical stories. Michael became bitterly aware of his humanity as the wind chilled him to the bone.

Staggering across the soft sandy beach with a beer in each hand, Nick cautiously approached Michael and sat quietly beside him.

"Silence is sometimes necessary," Michael said as if talking to himself, though he was keenly aware of Nick's presence. He continued staring out at the moonlit Pacific Ocean.

Nick glanced toward him and studied his face a long, silent moment. He knew Michael's words held a deeper meaning, but in his inebriated state, he had no clue what the hell he was talking about. He didn't need to ask. Nick simply nodded and shared the peaceful silence spreading over the beach.

Letting the night slip deeper away, they sat and began a silent ascent into their own private thoughts. But as a powerful burst of wind momentarily cleared the night air, Nick looked back at Michael. "Are you okay, man?" he asked softly. A concerned tone quivered in his voice. He cared deeply for his friend; and this emotion, this epic silence, troubled him.

Michael returned the look and placed his hand on his friend's face. "Yeah," he simply replied.

Strangely, Nick understood the moment and said nothing. Instead, he let his thoughts mingle with his friend's as they remained in the darkness as the night slipped away toward the oncoming dawn.

4

THE COLD LIGHT OF DAY had long since faded into the eerie silence of the witching hour; the time of night where silence is no longer considered welcome. Paranoia strikes a primal chord, tainting the mind's eye, triggering the cause and effect to intensify the slightest sound, movement, thought into the most vial creation imaginable.

Allocating the collective subconscious was another person sharing Michael's profound thoughts of the future. Susan appeared more anxious and uneasy than in deep thought. Her gaze pitched far into the night, past the clear picture window she was staring through. She gazed past the gathering of clouds that obstructed her view from a deeper meaning.

Frustration!

A peculiar expression crossed her face as she sat, uneasy, on the drab white couch. Looking up, she felt like a cliché, small beneath the high vaulted ceilings, the walls moving further apart, as she grew smaller through the looking glass in her mind. The cool air of the hour wrapped around her like a cloak of mist; its icy fingers clawed around her throat. A spooky shiver spread throughout her body.

Susan took note of how perfectly in order everything appeared. Michael was going to be happy of how hard she worked, she thought. Pleasing him always made her happy. The hardwood floor was a deep mahogany that gave flavor to the room. There were two quarrel windows on the high wall along the staircase, where Michael hung his UCLA momentums, plaques, frat logos. A German flag hung above a large chunk of concrete with faded paint of various colors. There were photos of Michael's travels, pictures of him at the Berlin Wall with thousands of cheering people.

Michael had a deep fondness for European culture, especially for Sweden, and it showed in the decor of his home: Viking helmets and swords, a little red Rättvik's Hestin placed on the mantle, little mementos from all over Sweden.

Susan held her gaze through the clear glass window, as if beckoning the gods above with her power of persuasion. Her face was abstract as though she were standing in another reality altogether. She was looking for something that was yet to be found.

What would it be like to stow away on the back of a star and go for the ultimate ride? Oh, the stories she once heard. What were they? How did they begin, end? Why couldn't she remember those beautiful childhood stories? Stars in the night sky, dreams, hope a chance. What was it? She closed her eyes in a moment of inner searching.

It was nights like this when she found herself alone, her mind altered and twisted reality. Now was the time she needed Michael the most. When she needed the sheer proximity of another human soul. She began rocking slowly, gently, back and forth, like a scorned child banished to the corner of the room.

The uneasy expression aside, Susan was—of course, indeed, still was, no doubt—something of a beauty. She was naturally poised, talkative at times, and then fluently silent with the next breath. Her pale-white porcelain skin gave light to her natural strawberry-blonde hair she wore down past her shoulders. Her petite figure belied her appearance smaller than her five-foot-five frame.

Only on this night, she did not have the appearance of a woman who was about to live what was supposed to be the happiest day of her life. On the surface, her beauty masked the anguish that appeared to be brewing in her heart. Her eyes became lifeless as an inner pain crippled her. By her actions and erratic body movements, she looked like a caged animal growing enraged at the bars keeping her from freedom.

As she gathered herself, she settled into a comfortable position on the couch, her legs folded demurely to one side. For a brief untainted moment, she had a great simplicity about her. She resolved herself to relax and be calm, not panic. Her posture loosened slightly, though she could never completely relax and let her guard down, at least not here, not now.

Cerberus, the hellhound, the mythical watchdog of the underworld, was back, scratching at her mind's door. The fact was, he never left. He skulked silently in the shadows of her mind, somewhere off in the distance, waiting, always ready to pounce at the first sign of weakness. He's the unseen entity, the hot breath on the back of her neck. It was that sickening feeling she always felt when you just know something is inevitable.

Her heart quickened as a sudden sound broke in the silent room. She clutched the throw cushion and pulled it to her chest as her eyes frantically scanned the room.

Nothing there!

Her pulse came rapid. Susan tried to stave it off, but it was too late. She began crying into the weft as she buried her head into the cushion to muffle the sounds of her sobbing. She could feel it coming like a runaway freight train picking up speed on its downhill run. Fear took over her trembling body and shook her to the core. She could feel the steel wheels on the tracks coming closer, faster! Faster! The horn blowing, clearing a path! Old number 9's coming through, and she's a hot one, boys!

She stood quickly and covered her ears and forced her eyelids shut.

We got a runaway heading for disaster! We ain't bringing this one in! Clear the tracks ahead!

Susan screamed!

Her eyes flashed open in an instant and scanned the room, searching for any signs of her echoes.

All was quiet.

She blew a sigh and sat a long, silent moment, as if in a trance, searching for answers that could not be explained, at least not to her. Not now. Not here.

Susan pensively wiped another tear from her face with the back of her hand. Her gesture was like a child's hand tearing roughly at the stinging tears, removing that awful wet stuff from her face. Susan set the cushion back on the couch and slowly rose to her feet. She glanced toward the bathroom and peered head-on into the oncoming freight train. She took a deep breath and started across the cold hardwood floor toward the bathroom.

Old number 9, you're on a collision course! There's debris on the tracks! You're approaching disaster!

5

PIERCING RAYS from the early-morning sun shone through the louvered blinds and painted the dark room with wicked threads of dusty light.

A sleepless night was clearly visible on Susan's face. Her waking mind felt collapsed beneath the burden of her palpitating visions. A throbbing pressure was building in her head as she sat, drenched in silence. Tear tracks marked her cheeks. Crumpled white tissue paper scattered around the couch and floor, surrounding her like patches of new snow dotting the landscape.

She was not entirely conscious of her own presence in the large room. Her movements were slow and involuntary, almost mechanical. "You can do this," she said aloud as she started for the bathroom.

The fluorescent light illuminated the dark room as Susan walked into the bathroom and opened the medicine cabinet and removed another home pregnancy test. It was the last one. Four empty boxes were piled up in the trash can near the toilet. Again she carefully read the text on the box, then methodically opened the flimsy cardboard and removed the test. Her disconnection was lost in a flash, and a confident look was reborn on her face, something new. This new look fit her; she wore it well. She was born to be confident, proud, and strong.

Denver, this was a test of the inner psychosis network. It was only a test! Do not adjust your television screen. Old number 9 was just a test…

* * * * *

The crisp scent of early morning flooded the house as Nick almost smashed the door in. The fresh scent of morning was followed by the acrid odor of alcohol. Nick pulled the keys out of the lock and entered the house with his arm supporting Michael, who was semiconscious. Michael's mumbling words were scarcely audible, the usual drunken dialect. Nick helped him up the stairs to the bedroom.

Throwing Michael onto the bed, Nick left the room. He moved ever so quietly down the stairs, trying not to make any noise and to not fall on his drunken ass. He heaved a sigh of relief as he reached the bottom landing of the stairs.

"Nicky!" Susan called out suddenly from across the room.

Nick was caught off guard by the sudden throw of her voice. He stumbled and fell backward toward the hardwood risers. He tried to break his fall by grabbing the handrail, but the wooden knob he instinctively tried to grab broke off in his hand as he fell back onto the stairs.

He quickly jumped to his feet. "I'm cool. I'm all right." He turned toward the voice and caught sight of Susan exiting the bathroom. She looked so small and strange to him. Nick shook the cobwebs out of his head, hoping to clear his impaired vision. He took a second glance. Ah, now that's much better. You are real!

"Are you all right?" she asked, moving across the room toward him.

Nick smiled, trying to nonchalantly hold himself up against the broken handrail. "I broke it," he said as he sheepishly handed her the wooden knob. He shrugged and made an odd gesture.

Susan loved the mischievous look in his eyes. She knew he was tanked. The look was like that of a ten-year-old boy who was up to no good. He felt as though he had been caught in the midst of some dastardly, adolescent prank. He smiled and felt the guilt wash over him.

"It's okay, Nicky. Michael will fix it." Her eyes passed over him slowly, lingering slightly as he swayed. She held her warm smile. This was the Susan everybody knew and loved. She was smiling, warm, and happy, a breath of fresh air and very approachable. This woman who was glowing with radiance was an altogether different version of the person who came all too close to her loneliness just a few hours ago.

Nick smiled and searched for an icebreaker, something to divert her attention away from his mishap, but his thoughts were drowning in a sea of alcohol. They held each other's gaze in the heavy silence. "So how's your friend Kerstin?" he said finally. "She's from Switzerland, right?" A longing, boyish smile came over his face. It was clear to see that Nick had somewhat of a flame for Susan's absent friend. It was clear to Susan that Nick seemed to have a crush on every woman he met.

"She's from Sweden actually, and she's there for the summer. So you'll have to wait, Nicky," she said with a smile. "That's why I'm taking the summer off as well. With her gone and the wedding and all, I'd just rather not work right now," she finished. "I had no idea how stressful planning a wedding really is."

Again Nick smiled as he tried to focus through blurred vision on her tired, drawn face. "So how you doing, kid?" he asked.

"Oh, Nicky, I'm so happy," she said with a genuine smile. "Things look so much better now. So much better." she repeated and paused for a moment. She studied his face, still smiling as she pursed her lips.

"You should be. You're about to take me best friend away," he said jokingly.

Susan threw her arms around him and embraced him for a moment. "You'll always have him, Nicky. I'll never take away what you two have together," she replied and again pursed her lips. "I'm just going to borrow him for the rest of my life." She held her great smile. "Oh, Nicky, I'm so happy. It's so good to see you." She paused for a moment and glanced upstairs. "So how is he?" she asked.

"He's pretty lit up."

"I can imagine."

Nick chuckled to himself.

* * * * *

Opening the front door of the typical Brentwood house, big and lavish, Michael's silhouette cast a long dark shadow back into the room from the torrent of sunlight rushing in. Michael reached down and picked up the Sunday morning paper and moved back into the house.

Michael's eyes widened as he focused on the *Los Angeles Times'* cover story. He tried to shake last night's bender out of his head and then refocused on the paper. HATE CRIME: MURDER IN TEXAS. His face showed the horror of the story as he read. Michael shook his head in disbelief. "Unbelievable," he said aloud as Susan walked down the stairs and entered the room behind him.

"What is it this time?" she asked. "Another wild car chase?"

Michael lowered the paper and turned around as she reached down and kissed him. "Morning, baby," he said. They kissed.

"Morning," she replied. "Want some coffee?" she asked and walked out of sight into the kitchen.

"You read my mind, baby, thank you." Michael returned his attention to the paper. Susan shouted something from the kitchen, but it went unheard as Michael's full concentration was on the gruesome story.

Walking out of the kitchen, Susan placed the hot cup on the table in front of him.

"Honey, listen to this," he said, reading from the newspaper. "'A man in Texas is being held for the murder of a black man, Roger Lucian.' Apparently, he and another accomplice, who was shot and killed by Texas police, beat this guy with tire irons. And as this guy lay there dying, they tied him up to the train tracks and watched as the train tore him to pieces. They actually filmed it. Says here 'they found parts of his body up to two miles away.'" Michael lowered the paper. "We're going to be all over this at work."

BOOM! BANG! FLASH!

White hot light! Hazy focus.

Susan stood frozen in time. Her eyes frosted and lost. Chains clanked and dangled from the ceiling in the dark misty basement. It was the underbelly of pure-white trash. The steady drip of water heard coming from somewhere in the darkness, probably near the stairs. Humming? Was that a child humming? A nursery rhyme? Yelling and screaming from the bad place above where the light is. Bottles breaking. Moaning. Pain. The smell of alcohol held heavy in the damp darkness. Crying. Blood. Broken glass. The smell of urine. Heavy footsteps. The door to the basement opened and quickly filled the room with grainy light. A dark, ominous presence loomed!

Evil was here…

*****

Susan flashed back to the present, to the here and now, and her facial expression had drastically changed. "We live in a godless world that is quickly falling apart and is becoming a disgusting place to live!" she said. Her voice filled with venom. "It really makes me want to throw up sometimes. I mean puke my guts out!" She finished with a sick, jaded look on her face.

The intensity in which she spoke threw Michael for a loop. He had never heard her so ruthless before, so blunt. She was always so calm, so polite, a quiet little church mouse, never said a harsh word about anything or anyone. He knew she had a little fire in her somewhere, but he was surprised as hell to see it come out so directly. "How can you say we live in a godless world? How can you say any of that?"

"Because if there was a God, he would not allow his children to suffer like he has." Her eyes narrowed. "If there was a God, I'd blame him!"

"Whoa. Come on, Susan," Michael protested.

"How could a merciful God let something like this happen? Look around you, Michael. Look at the news. You of all people should know—you see it every day. All the pain and violence and war and suffering in the world is becoming more and more prevalent. We can't avoid it. It's doubling every damn day! There are starving children, murders and rapes, holy wars. And what about everything you told me about the atrocities in Germany? How all those people were killed and held hostages in their own country? Where was their

God to protect them? Don't you think if there was a God, he would not let this happen?"

Wow! She was pissed, and that was something he was not used to. Something set her off, and he didn't like that she was so bothered by the article. They never really had any kind of argument before, nothing that amounted to much, so this was way out of character. This was not like Susan at all, and he wondered if something else was bothering her.

"God gave us free will, Susan."

"Bullshit!" she yelled.

"Look, things are going to happen, Susan. They've always happened, and they always will. There is nothing you can do about it. There are people out there who are hell-bent on destruction. There's hatred and racism that you just can't stop, but that doesn't mean there isn't a God." Michael had no idea, until now, that she felt this way. He was quite shocked.

"Michael," she said, holding his gaze through narrowed eyes, "God would not have let your parents die and leave a small child alone in this world. That's a terrible thing!" she finished. Her face glared a burning anger.

Michael was too shocked by what she said and by the striking way in which she delivered it to offer a response. The mere mention of his parents caught him completely off guard. He held silent for a moment. He was too shocked to respond.

"If there were a God, I'd blame him for everything that happened in this miserable world! More shit happened than you could ever imagine, Michael! That's just a fact of life."

Michael looked at her in stunned silence. A dumbfounded look struck his face deeply. He knew not how to respond. Surprised by everything she said, Michael was speechless as he watched her walk out of sight into the kitchen.

6

As he walked through the dimly lit corridor at the KNRQ television studios, Michael's footsteps echoed through what seemed to be an abandoned building. It was the walk he knew was the calm before the storm, same as every other night. But as he pushed through the glass doors at the end of the hallway, he entered into a room full of noise and chaos as men and women frantically performed their daily ritual to make the night's deadline for the eleven o'clock news telecast. There was never a moment's rest.

There was a buzz here, something extraspecial, an energy Michael had not seen in some time. He loved it. This emotion, this atmosphere, it was the reason he entered the news game in the first place. He stood silently a moment and watched. The smell of energy flowed around the room with excitement. He loved the rush and the quickened pace that came with the job; it was intoxicating to his senses.

Michael made his way through the maze of people to his office, greeting people as he moved. He stopped at the assignment desk a moment and spoke to an older lady with beady eyes and glasses. She smiled and handed him a sheet of paper. Michael turned and reentered the tangle of moving people.

Michael's assistant, David, a wide-eyed kid of twenty-five, rushed over to his side. He looked as if he had not slept in a week, but that was his every day appearance. "What's tonight's lead?" Michael asked his eager assistant.

"The Texas murder," he replied and followed his boss into his office. "All the major networks are leading with the story." He looked

Michael in the eyes as he sat behind his beautiful oak desk. "It's been national all day, Mike."

"I didn't hear about it until this afternoon," he replied. "Did the bachelor-party thing last night."

"Yeah, sorry I couldn't make it."

"No worries, bro."

"So how was it anyway?" David asked. "Better yet, how was the stripper? I'm assuming there was a stripper, right?" The young kid looked on, eagerly awaiting the juicy details.

"Yeah, there was a stripper," Michael said, but his thoughts were on the night's call sheet for the telecast. "This story…in Texas," his eyes still on the paper. "It's going to be a horse, isn't it?" He spoke more or less talking to himself.

"Oh, yeah," the kid said quickly. "The media is covering it like stink on shit. We've got two crews on the way there now."

"Two crews? Who sent them?" Michael asked, lowering the paper. He had a hunch who sent the news teams.

"Chandler sent Tecate and Jefferson's crew as soon as it hit the AP wires," David replied with a worried tone quivering in his voice. "They tried to call you, but…but…"

"It's all right, David," Michael said. "Have Tecate call me the moment he checks in. I want to see where he's going with the story. I want Jefferson on the Vic. I want the back story, family, background. I want blanket coverage. Where he went to school, where he worked. His wife, kids, child support, anything. I want absolute coverage."

"You got it, boss," the kid replied as he left the office. Michael returned to the night's call sheet, which held his interest.

Michael flipped to the second page, and something caught his eye. He then reached for a stack of papers on his desk and started sifting through the mess in search of a similar article. As he found the page he was looking for, the door to his office swung open, and David moved across the room. "Mike, you're wanted in Edit One. We've got breaking news!"

Michael looked up from the article. "What is it?"

"The Texas thing, man. There's been a bombing," David replied.

Michael's eyes widened.

David smiled. "Yeah, I thought you'd like that"—he paused for effect—"and we have it on tape."

Michael moved out from behind his desk. "I'm on my way."

* * * * *

Michael walked into the frenzied newsroom and caught sight of his nefarious boss entering his office. Michael frowned. He was not usually in the office on Sundays. Come to think of it, he hadn't really been in the office much at all lately. The fact that Chandler was absent from the station on most days and nights suited Michael just fine. He was annoying and full of himself. In Michael's opinion, he was a pompous ass.

Michael never broke stride and held a sheet of paper above his head and addressed the production staff. "Breaking news, people!" he chirped quickly.

Silence washed over the room for a brief moment. The silence was almost deadly, as if waiting for a time bomb to go off. It did. The production staff began moving about like unruly children looking for trouble. Michael continued through the newsroom and handed the paper to the lady at the assignment desk as he passed.

As Michael stepped into the edit room, a voice yelled out to him.

"I'm one step ahead of you, chief," said Gabriel, who was pushing the keys of the AVID computer, manipulating the coverage on the screen.

Michael walked over and stood behind him. "Is this it?" he asked.

Gabriel was the computer nerd, the video-playing teenager who never grew up. He was a tall, thin man in his midtwenties, with long stringy hair and thin glasses. His scruffy face looked as though the razor missed a few dozen spots. "We got it in real time. Tecate was on live remote when the fireworks started," he explained.

"Very nice." Michael patted him on the shoulder. "Stay on this. Let me know when it's ready for air." He started walking out.

"You got it, chief."

Before Michael reached the door, he stopped and turned back. Michael thought for a moment and shook his head. "This is going to be our white elephant," he said quietly to himself.

"Yeah. How'd you like to be the poor bastard who's going to be at the center of all that media coverage?" Gabriel said jokingly.

"Being at the center of that sort of insanity would be the last place I'd ever want to find myself. That's why I'm on this side of the camera." Michael spun on his heels and walked out.

* * * * *

Sitting back at his desk, Michael's head began swimming in the alcohol consumed during last night's festivities. He should have just stayed at home, he thought. He threw his feet up on the windowsill. He reached over and grabbed a small piece of concrete off his desk and started rubbing it in his hands. It was something he did often.

He looked out the window at the city lights, endless in their flickering glare. He folded his arms behind his head and drifted into thought. Michael conjured up the fading memories of his parents. With the wedding only a few days away, his parents were on his mind a lot lately. He wished they could have been there for his wedding. His mother would have been so proud that he was married at the church she attended as a child.

As he sat there trying to figure out what the hell his mind was doing to his thought process, he felt exquisitely simpleminded. With a quiet laugh to himself, he played it off to work stress, his upcoming marriage, and his tired, alcohol-absorbed brain. He had a lot on his plate lately, and he was seeing the signs.

Michael swung his chair around with a slight smirk on his face. He placed the small piece of concrete back on his desk. A thundering wrap on the door echoed through the office. His boss, Frank Chandler—Mr. Ivy League, vice president of the Los Angeles affiliate—walked in and approached the desk. Without saying a word, he sat across from Michael. He frowned.

"This is going to be a big one, Mike." Chandler spoke with an effeminate tone in his delicate voice. Chandler was in his fifties, and

Michael never cared for his ass-kissing practices. Chandler was nothing more than a business associate to him, one he could barely tolerate. "This is the second such killing in Texas in the last two years. It's a hot bed for murder. The whole world is going to be watching. The NAACP is already in an uproar. We better not drop the ball," he said in an intimidating manor.

Michael smiled. He was not threatened by this spec sitting across from him. Nothing Chandler said meant anything to Michael. Michael was his own boss. Chandler couldn't touch him, and they both knew it. Chandler's boss was grooming Michael to replace Chandler, and he resented Michael for it.

"We're preparing to cut into programming within minutes. The suspect's mother's house was just bombed, and we have an exclusive," Michael said with a dubious look.

"This story better be solid!" Chandler paused to keep his blood pressure from imploding his heart and filling his chest cavity with all that blue blood. "I don't have to tell you about our ratings over the last quarter. We need to pull a rabbit out of our ass to save jobs around here, even mine."

Michael smiled. "Don't worry, Frank, it's a solid story. We knew about it before the police did. Tecate was in the right place at the right time."

"Good thing I sent him, huh?" Chandler said, patting himself on the back.

No response from Michael, just a cold, hard stare. Then finally a sarcastic smirk.

Chandler felt it. He rose from the chair and strutted toward the door. "I'll see you in editing," he said without turning around. He left the office.

Michael shook his head.

7

Frantically scanning the room, Susan was in a desperate search for her keys. She was in a hurry and didn't have time for lost keys. She ran into and back out of the kitchen. Looked under the living-room table. She ran upstairs into and back out of the bedroom. Checked under the sofa. Then finally stopping in the middle of the living room, she blew a sigh of frustration. "Where the hell are my keys?" she said as she lifted her hand to her forehead, smashing the keys into her skin. She gave herself a brief laugh. "I must be losing my mind," she said and ran for her purse on the table.

Moving swiftly across the room, Susan fumbled with the car keys and looked up at the clock. "Shit," she mumbled and made her way to the front door. "I'm so late," she said to herself as she opened the front door and screamed!

A shock wave washed over her. Her mouth remained slightly parted. "Oh my God!" she said. Her face went flush. "Oh my God!" she repeated. "Macy?" she asked. "Is that you? Is that really you?" Susan's heart quickened.

Standing at the doorway, with her hand still up in the air, ready to knock on the door, she too was startled when Susan quickly opened the door. Macy returned Susan's sincere smile. "Surprise," she said with a wonderful hand gesture. Macy was wearing a cute Gingham sundress with tiny orange sunflowers splashed throughout the thin material. Susan smiled. She always loved the way Macy dressed. She looked so natural and innocent, so beautiful. Oh, how she loved and missed her.

"What are you doing here?" Susan asked, obviously still in shock.

"I told you I would look you up when I got to LA."

"Yeah?"

"Well, I'm here." Macy smiled. "I just moved here. Like yesterday," she finished.

Susan let out a roaring smile and embraced her long-missed friend. Susan couldn't have wished for anything more. Macy was family to her, like the sister Susan never had, and she loved her dearly.

"I sent you an email," Macy said, parting from the embrace.

"I haven't been online in like a month," Susan replied. "Oh my God, come in," she said and hugged her again as she entered. "How long has it been?"

"Since we left school," Macy replied.

Susan led her to the sofa, where they both sat. "Can I get you something to drink?" Susan offered.

"No, I'm fine, thank you."

"Has it really been that long?" Susan asked.

Macy thought a moment. "You took off as soon as we left school. You never came back, and I never left. Well, until now," she finished with a smile.

Susan couldn't help it. She reached over and embraced her once more. Susan moved back and took her all in. Macy smiled. She had grown up well, Susan thought. She still had a hint of freckles on her cheeks and nose, not as much as when they were children, but they were still there. Her teeth were perfectly straight, and Susan had always been jealous of how perfect they were. She had the same hair, only much longer and much less red, more of a strawberry blonde now. Her hair was swept up at the sides in a half ponytail and tied with an orange bow that Susan found so adorable.

"It's so good to see you again," Susan said. "You were always my best friend growing up. You know that."

"I was your only friend growing up. We were inseparable," Macy replied with a bright smile.

Susan looked a bit perplexed, but the smile remained on her face. "I had other friends, but none like you. You're right. You were my only friend. My only true friend," she said with a laugh they both shared.

Macy's smile lit up the room as she glanced around. "You have such a beautiful home," she said and stood up. She began walking around the room, looking at various things. Susan followed her with her eyes. It appeared as if Macy were floating in the air with her graceful walk. Susan held her smile. Macy stopped at the wall, where she focused on a framed picture.

"It's my husband's house. Well, we're not actually married yet," Susan said as Macy turned to face her.

"It looks like a man's house," Macy replied.

"What's that supposed to mean?"

"Nothing. It's just not you, Susan. This isn't how I remember you. Your soul is not in this house. You have nothing personal here. Nothing belongs to you," Macy said. "It's like you're a renter or, even worse, a roommate." Macy knew exactly how to push Susan's buttons; it was a game to her as a child.

Susan looked like she had been hit in the head with a hammer.

"I'm sorry. That didn't sound right, did it?"

"Michael and I love each other, and this is just as much my house as it is his," Susan started. "I just never thought about changing anything. You know I didn't bring much with me when I left home, and I certainly didn't acquire much after that either," she said, searching her eyes for understanding. Pleasing Macy and winning her acceptance was always so important. Susan felt the same feelings come rushing back to her.

"I didn't mean anything by that, really. I don't know what came over me," Macy said and smiled, hoping she didn't offend her friend. It took a minute, but the smile returned to Susan's face. But that comment hit her hard. She was confused by it. "Can you forgive me?"

"There's nothing to forgive you of," Susan said.

Macy hugged her. "So when is the wedding?" she asked. Her bright smile disarmed Susan. She always knew how to ditch the subject at the most convenient time, always switching gears on the fly.

Susan smiled. "What are you doing this Saturday?"

Macy again embraced her dear friend. "I'm so happy for you, Susan. You always needed someone good in your life, someone to love and shine for you. I'm so happy for you," she said again in a soft whisper.

That hit Susan. She lowered her head. "After all that..." She paused. "You know...back then. I thought nobody would ever love me," she said with sad eyes.

Macy looked at her intently and nodded. She too had thought Susan's prospects at a decent future were bleak. But that was long ago. Susan had grown up, and Macy was genuinely happy that her beloved friend had finally found her knight in shining armor.

Susan shook her past right out of her head and brought that special smile back to her face. "So can you make it? To the wedding, I mean."

Macy always remembered Susan's beautiful smile and how wonderful she felt just to watch her beam as she did now. A sudden change of expression on her face answered Susan's question. "I'm sorry," she said. "I won't be in town. I'm still moving my stuff from back home." Macy's frown darkened the room. Susan felt smashed. "If I would have known sooner, you know I would have come."

"It's okay, Macy. I couldn't expect you to come on such short notice," Susan said with a saddened heart. Macy sensed the sadness and hugged her friend. She missed her so much, missed these moments of closeness with her dear friend. They both missed it. They remained there holding each other for a long, timeless moment. It was magical, this reunion, something they both needed.

Parting from the embrace, Macy looked deep into Susan's eyes. "Hey, listen," she started, "I don't have a lot of time. I actually have to run now. But I want to pick up where we left off," she said. "Just like it used to be."

"It will be exactly like it was," Susan replied without thinking. They embraced once more. Susan walked her to the door and saw her out. She turned and walked back into the living room. Moments later, after she had picked up her belongings, Susan was walking out of the kitchen when the doorbell rang.

Susan smiled as she opened the door. "You're still forgetting things," she said, opening the door.

"I never forget anything," Renee said as she walked in past a questioning Susan. "Were you expecting someone else?" Renee asked as she walked over toward the kitchen.

"Yeah, uh, no," she answered, shaking her head. "My friend Macy just left, like five minutes ago. I thought you were her."

"Uh, no, Susan, I'm me. She left, remember?" Renee said with playful sarcasm.

"Smart ass," Susan replied and then smiled. "That's why you're still single," Susan said with a sarcastic smirk.

"Kiss my ass." Renee shot her a dirty look, then smiled. "So who's Macy?" Renee asked with a quizzical glance.

"A friend I grew up with. She just moved to town and came by to see me. We had so many good times together." The bright smile remained on Susan's face, but a slight hint of confusion clouded her vision.

"Great, now I'm going to have to compete with her for your attention," Renee said jokingly as she peeled off her dress jacket.

Susan glanced up at the clock. "I'm sorry I didn't get to the store. Macy was here longer than I expected," Susan said.

"Don't worry about it. We'll get a pizza or something," Renee replied. "So tell me about Macy. Is she coming to the wedding?"

"She can't. She's going back home to move the rest of her things out here. It's too bad, though. I would have loved for her to come," Susan said softly as she recalled old memories with Macy.

Renee sensed that something was troubling her but couldn't quite figure out what it was.

* * * * *

Sitting with her leg folded beneath her, casually sipping red wine with her closest friend, Susan appeared quite at ease. Renee loved coming here. She loved the casual, laid-back feeling she got each time Susan entertained in the warm kitchen.

Renee was exquisite with ice-blue eyes and blonde Nordic features. Though she was born and raised in the States, she had roots in the Old World. Her mother named her Runa, but she preferred Renee to the proper Norwegian name. "I can't believe your wedding is less than a week away. God, I envy you. I'm so jealous."

Susan was genuinely touched and smiled. She felt lucky to have a close friend like Renee, someone whom she could always turn to. Susan hesitated a moment as she looked across to her friend. Their eyes met, and Renee sensed something else was on Susan's mind. Her mood was a stranger, one Renee had never seen.

"So tell me, how do you feel? And I mean all the details, because I may never know what it's like. Lonely and bitter party for one," declared Renee with a hint of sarcasm. She reached for the bottle of wine and realized it was empty.

"You will never have to worry about being alone. Just relax and quit looking," Susan chided.

*****

The once-dark living room was now illuminated softly with scented candles. Their glow danced off the hardwood floor, breathing life into its surface. A glance at the clock on the wall told Susan it was quarter past one in the morning as she sat alone on the couch, awaiting Michael's return.

The silence of the room, combined with a mixture of wine shared earlier with her friend and passing the dark side of the witching hour, Susan began feeling tormented by the animal within, which awakened and started to snarl inside her mind.

She knew the name of the animal. It was not panic or fear; it was, in fact, herself. A "self" whom she thought was long behind her, buried so deep her subconscious couldn't dig it up. Would never dig it up. If she didn't control it, she might do something that would destroy everything she had built since her move to Los Angeles. It could jeopardize her upcoming marriage.

Panic and fear struck her face as visions and thoughts of her past flooded her mind. "Not now—not now!" she said. "Don't do this to me," she said aloud in the empty darkened room. Nevertheless, the animal was yammering louder. The maddening silence of the room and her slight intoxication only added to her fear. "You're not here!" she yelled. "Not now! Not here, not like this! Go away!" she screamed. Her echoing voice came back to her in rapid fire, bouncing images off the walls. And in the fleeting moments, she swore she heard laughter.

Realizing she was alone in the house, her panic doubled and overshadowed her mind. Susan did the only thing she could think of to stave it off. She reached for the light as—

*****

A hand reached for her, waking her from her terror-induced dream. She woke up in a sweat of confusion. A bloodcurdling scream rebounded off the wall.

Michael jumped slightly as the scream tore through him. "It was just a dream, honey," Michael said in a calming voice. He held her close to his chest. "It was just a dream," he reassured her.

Susan cried in his arms and knew that it was more than just a dream. The rational part of her mind took over her thought process, and she knew that her past, for some reason, had been pried open. It was now visible to her conscious mind, and the thoughts and feelings she once buried could come flooding back at any moment. She lay there terrorized in Michael's arms, crying in the ominous light of the room.

8

As Michael's brother Matthew arrived late on the red-eye from Boston, he rushed past the ushers' attention and crossed the vestibule. He was so worried that he would be late for his baby brother's wedding that he was barely aware of the marble columns and the brilliant gilt mosaic in the vaulted ceiling. His ears were almost deaf to the soft organ music that engulfed him, one subtle chord slowly dissolving into another.

Matthew's focus was to let his brother know that he made it to the most important day in his brother's life. Nick's parents, Dale and Lisa Vach, warmly greeted Matthew, and he sat with them as Susan joined Michael's hand. Michael's eyes caught his brother's brilliant smile. Relieved to see his brother, Michael returned a joyful smile. Everything was going to be fine now.

Out of curiosity, Matthew turned and scanned the room of people in attendance at Saint Rose of Lima, the Roman Catholic Church in Simi Valley where Michael and his brother were baptized. It had always been their mother's dream that her sons would be married there. That was the one thing Michael remembered from his mother and honored her wish. He felt her presence there with him.

Nick found himself looking past Michael and Susan and staring at Renee, whom he had met on a few occasions, but he had never thought of her the way he was thinking about her now. Perhaps it was the sentiment of the moment and the whole wedding thing. Whatever the reason, Nick had been caught by a muse.

As Renee glanced to her left, she smiled at Nick, who was blatantly staring at her. Renee's heart skipped a beat as she quickly shed eye contact and focused back on the celebrated couple. Her smile lingered.

The smile sent shivers through Nick's body as it was more than the average polite smile. He wasn't expecting any reaction whatsoever, but the smile his stare generated set his mind in motion. Nick turned back toward the priest, who began to speak. Nick's mind continued racing with thoughts of Renee.

"Dearly beloved," the priest started, "we are gathered here today to partake in the union of holy matrimony between two of God's children." The great mosaic figure of Christ, arms outstretched, hovered ominously above the priest.

"We are gathered here to join together this man and this woman in holy matrimony." He paused and looked on with a fatherly smile. His peaceful face held the stark promise of hope. It was reassuring to Susan.

Michael and Susan looked on, both smiling.

"Into this holy estate these two persons come now to be joined. If any man can show just cause why they may not lawfully be joined together, let him now speak or else hereafter forever hold his peace." The priest looked up from the Bible at the gathered crowd, then back at the couple in front of him.

"Michael Douglas Bishope, wilt thou have this woman to be thy wedded wife, to live together after God's ordinance in the holy state of matrimony? Will thou love her, comfort her, honor, and keep her in sickness and in health and, forsaking all others, keep thee only unto her so long as ye both shall live?" He made perfect eye contact with Michael.

"I will," Michael responded. His heart pounded. He loved her and was so happy to be her husband. Oh, how he wished his parents could have been there.

The priest fixed his eyes on Susan, who was visibly shaken, her face even more flushed.

"Are you all right?" Michael asked quietly.

Susan nodded awkwardly and continued smiling.

A reassuring smile from the priest momentarily comforted her. The priest nodded. Susan returned the gesture, letting him know she was ready.

The priest started, "Melissa! Susan Carriere—"

Boom!

She was not ready for that—not here, not now! That name, why did he have to say that name?

A nuclear bomb went off in Susan's mind, sending rapid-fire visions of terror flashing through her head like cannon fire. Roaring thunder exploded all around her. Twisted reality. It was an out-of-body experience. Her ascent was a high-speed crooked journey through a vortex of tainted, suppressed memories that choked her from within. It tore apart the inner walls she built up against the attack. Those scary faces, the ones she long feared, came at her through the gaping holes of her crumpling fortress.

Her legs turned to jelly as a sheet of white instantly covered her rosy cheeks.

The priest stopped as Susan stumbled, almost losing consciousness, and fell over, leaning heavily onto Michael. She lay motionless in his arms. A concerned groan wavered over the seated crowd.

* * * * *

The door to the basement swung open in a burst, as if kicked open with a heavy blast. The patter of tiny feet belonging to a young girl hurried down the old wooden steps leading to the basement. The child landed hard on the cold concrete floor and dove for the narrow opening near the wall. Quickly, she crawled through the dark opening and moved toward the very front and wedged herself into the dark narrow space under the stairs. A place only a small child could fit into. Her heart pounded, and her breath came hard and rapid as she waited in the cold dark place.

She could hear the sound of approaching footsteps coming through the kitchen above her. The footsteps came heavy and strong, with a purpose. A man's rough voice called for her in anger. The child began hyperventilating and rocking back and forth as the footsteps reached the basement door. Time was running out! Again she held her breath as the basement door swung open. She could not understand why she was tormented like this.

Dust fell on her head as the deep voice crept down the wooden staircase. The child froze like a statue, her exhaled breath stuck in her lungs, choking her, waiting to be set free. She wasn't about to do anything to give away here position.

The evil voice reached the bottom landing and peered through the darkness. "Melissa! You in here?" he shouted with a strange Southern accent. "Melissa… Melissa, you get out'cher now, girl!" He waited, listening, looking for a sign, a slip, a breath. "Come on now, you get on out'cher right now!"

She could see his old stinky boots through the steps. The smell of fish and dried blood and the hard corn liquor almost gagged her. She always hated that stink on his breath, hated when he drank, which was every day. He was only an arm's length away, and he was out for blood. "MELISSA!" he shouted. "MELISSA!"

* * * * *

"Melissa?" the priest called to her. "Melissa?"

"I'm here," she said, confused as she looked around the room and gathered her bearings.

"Are you okay, honey?" Michael asked.

"Yes… I guess I got a little dizzy," she replied.

"Are you all right, my dear?" the priest asked.

"Yes. I'm fine," she replied. Hearing her given name *Melissa* threw her for a loop. She was flooded with misery and pained by the sudden images from her past. Her name echoed and pounded in her mind even still. And in this life-renewing day, her first and foremost thought was death. Her second thought was to run as fast and as far away from here as possible. But she knew that no matter where she ran, her demons would follow.

"Are you ready to continue?" the priest asked.

"Yes, I am," Susan said with a shaken look on her face.

The priest nodded and smiled, trying to bring the focus back to the ceremony. Susan returned the nod with a forced smile. The priest looked back down at the Bible and began.

"Melissa Susan Carriere, wilt thou have this man to be thy wedded husband, to live together after God's ordinance in the holy estate of matrimony? Wilt thou love him, comfort him, honor and keep him in sickness and in health and, forsaking all others, keep thee only unto him so long as ye both shall live?" The priest looked up, awaiting her response.

Susan appeared frozen as she stood next to Michael at the altar. Her face was pale, and her eyes were cold and empty. She felt dizzy.

The priest waited.

Michael continued holding her in his gaze. Waiting.

"I do," she said finally without any emotion, as if the words were rehearsed. She blew a cold sigh of relief.

Bright sunlight washed over them as they approached the narthex of the church. The huge mosaic of the Saint Rose of Lima ascended above them on the church's stucco wall. The saint's head was cast downward, as if saying a silent blessing over the newlyweds.

Sweeping her up in his arms, Michael looked deep into her glazed eyes. "I love you, wife," he said and smiled. "We did it. We're married."

Returning his smile, she kissed his lips softly. "I love you, Michael. I will do everything I can to make you the happiest husband in the world," she replied.

Michael and Susan held on to each other as a prolonged silence fell upon them. They stared into each other's eyes as cars roared by on Royal Avenue. Their love for each other came through and spoke volumes on the warm California day.

Their serenity was prematurely shattered as their guests followed them outside. Michael's brother was the first one out, hugging and congratulating his brother. Nick followed Matthew in wishing his close friend the best of luck.

Renee took Susan's attention for a moment as they also hugged and celebrated the joyous moment. Susan appeared reborn and uplifted from her earlier lapse as she engaged in a timeless embrace with her friend.

As Renee parted from the embrace, she backed up a step, and as she did, she backed straight into Nick as he stepped away from Michael. They both turned apologetically and faced each other. Realizing whom she had stumbled into, she swiftly shed eye contact, leaving Nick smiling at her innocence. Laughing off her awkwardness for what it was, she turned back and returned a bright smile. Nick held out his hand. Renee shook it, performing her half of the ancient ritual. The smile remained on her face as Nick held on to her hand a little longer than expected. There was a long pause and a hot spark that seared them both.

* * * * *

Crossing the threshold of the hotel room with Susan in his arms, Michael entered and pressed his lips against hers in the dimly lit room. She let a soft moan escape past her lips as their passion built. Michael slowly walked her across the floor and held her close.

Abruptly, she broke away from him and walked to the center of the room and looked over her shoulder back at him. She stopped and stood by the bedpost, inviting his approbation. Michael could only stand in silent awe of his beautiful wife and her beguiling beauty.

All was yet a mirage as Michael's gaze fell upon her. Nevertheless, within the intimate and mysterious recesses of his soul, he felt power to make his dream exist. Making love to his wife, not two halves of a whole but two souls joined by God with the common interest of each other, forever as husband and wife.

Painted in the shadows of the room, Susan ever so slowly shed her wedding dress, revealing a white satin-and-lace teddy with garters and matching stockings.

Michael broke out in a cold sweat. In his imagination, pleasure fought with virtue, and lust stood reveled in the shape of a prowling beast. He felt his pulse began to quicken. His breathing came heavy. He turned pale and became light-headed, perhaps from the consumed spirits at the wedding reception.

Misreading his dilated eyes, Susan hung her head with a shiver, then with blatant coquetry, came toward him.

Taking her into his arms, Michael gazed deep into her hypnotic green eyes. He felt as though he were falling, pulled into the depths of her inner being, some enchanted nymph he never had the chance to encounter before.

Returning her smile, Michael eased her onto the bed. Their lips met in a touch of souls, sharing the wine of their love. A moan escaped from within her as Michael's hand caressed her stomach and breast.

Their embrace became furious, almost animalistic, as they tore at each other in a desperate race to consummate their love. A supreme harmony flowed between them. Shedding Susan's sexy teddy, leaving her naked on the bed, Michael paused a moment to take in the voluptuous canvas of her body.

As Michael maneuvered his body on top of hers, parting her legs with his, an uneasy look crossed her face as she winced at the weight of his mass pressing against her body.

A flash…

An explosion blasted through her mind and brought back memories of a past life. All the life drained from her eyes.

Michael's lips pressed against hers, moving onto her cheeks. She could feel his manhood pressing against her body, pressing against the folds of her opening, seeking entry. She was unresponsive and became frigid. As Michael continued, she became more disenchanted, tormented by the demons haunting her mind.

A thousand surreal images violently flashed through her mind: a galactic explosion, three candles burning an old church, brilliant stars shinning against a black sky—vast empty fields, a young girl kneeling, a three-headed dog with glowing red eyes, a man yelling in anger.

"No," she whispered in a barely audible voice. Her soft words fell upon deaf ears. Tears welled in her fear-filled eyes as more images came at her with rapid crushing blows: a Catholic priest, the Gulf of Mexico, a gun, famine, her mother, an exit sign—a young girl in the presence of a doctor, funny-looking birdlike people with long pointed noses, the mighty river, a "Dead End" sign.

An uncomfortable feeling swept over her body. She became frantic, as if fighting him off. "No!" she said with a sharp blast.

Michael stopped and looked into her eyes. "What?" he asked with confusion on his face.

"No," she repeated.

"I don't understand."

"I can't."

"Susan—"

"Don't call me that!" she replied abruptly. Then realizing what she had said, she covered her mouth and began crying. Before Michael could respond, Susan bolted out of the bed and ran into the bathroom, slamming the door behind her.

Dazed, Michael remained on the bed. His eyes fixed on the bathroom door, confused by what lay beyond.

Troubled by the events, Michael walked across the room to the door. "Susan?" he called again. But the only sound coming back to his ears was that of a pill bottle being pried open. Pills dropped into the porcelain sink and onto the floor. "Susan, are you all right?" he asked.

No reply…

9

The soft muted voice of the spring shower sang in the early morning outside the slightly opened window. The closed blinds muffled the sound. Runoff dripping from the rooftop outside danced, dimpling puddles below. The sweet fragrance of morning rain filled the room. A gray day lay awake, waiting to peddle its wares. All is magical under my spell. *You will be lifted and start anew*, the new dawn said out to all in its new embrace.

* * * * *

A single beam of sunlight pierced the gray sky, cutting through the raindrops, between the slivers of the blinds and onto Renee's pale, white face. Her hair glowed with a halo effect in the sun's paint. Her sleepless nights were a distant memory as she lay peaceful, nestled in Nick's shoulder. His burly arm around her promised security in her tranquility. Her brilliance was captivating as she lay innocent with the dawn promising a new day, a new beginning and time for lovers.

Nick lay awake with his gaze on Renee's sun-painted hair, not wanting to move, to lose this dream, this illusion, that lay before him. This is what the dawn promised him, but fear slipped through the crack of his shell as he thought of her waking up and ending the illusion. He remained still, silent, almost breathless, pasting this moment into his memory, hoping against hope that she would not regret waking up with him. He wanted to possess this mirage, keep it, and hold it forever. But things never last. They break, they leave, run away, he told himself over and over again.

Renee hastily turned in her sleep. A late passion-filled night of romance lying behind her added to her utopia. A content look was etched on her angelic face. Nick moved in time with her, not wanting to disrupt her sleeping rhythm.

The black sheet fell with the move of her trim arm, pale, glistening in the sun of a sculptor's chisel. Her breast became exposed to Nick's gaze. Her nipple firm, erect, piercing out of the light-colored brown of her aureole. Nick added this to his gathering memory and gently lifted the sheet to cover her naked breasts.

"No," she said, still with her eyes closed. Lifting her arm, she pulled the sheet back down, exposing her breasts for his eyes.

"I didn't want to wake you," Nick said softly.

"Last night was not a dream, Nicholas."

A long hush hung loose in the air as Nick tried to understand the meaning of her words. What happens the next morning? Had there ever been a next morning? One-night stands were the norm for him. Had he ever had a relationship? One he longed for. A place of understanding and comfort. Would the new dawn with her beautiful promise allow this to come true?

Her soft Nordic-blue eyes opened and laid into his gaze. Her face said yes. Yes to a new day. A resounding yes to a promise of happiness carried by the new dawn. Yes to an unanswered thought swirling in Nick's mind.

"My heart's pounding," Nick said softly.

Renee traced the length of his arm, from the shoulder to the end of his fingertips with her long fingernails, painted shell pink to match her bridesmaid gown. Taking his hand in hers, she lifted it and placed it on her breast.

"My heart is pounding with yours," she said in a whisper. *Take me. Take me again and again*, said the whisper as it danced throughout the folds of his memory.

"Love is a stranger to me," he said in shame and lowered his head slightly.

"To me as well," she replied, lifting his eyes to meet hers. "A promise was made last night when we were lost in the magic of a fantasy." She paused briefly. Their eyes remained transfixed on each other. She craned her neck and softly kissed the sweetness of his lips, reassuring his doubt. "It came with understanding, Nicholas. It came with emotions that we both have buried in our hearts. The promise was—"

"That we would finally know the beauty of waking to a new day with the person who has captured our whole being," Nick said quietly, finishing her sentence with an eloquence he never thought he could muster.

A smile beamed across her face as a tear found its way into her soft blue eyes. Finally, at that very moment, they both felt as if they had found something they had been searching for: a place of comfort and irrefutable acceptance. They understood each other without any further words.

The long gaze was broken as their lips met like lightning and metal, exploding with passion, each clawing at the other, two naked bodies frantically searching for each other in a sea of lust, both wanting to once again consummate their illusion of each other before they woke from the dream they were both sharing—if, in fact, it was a dream.

10

THE FLIGHT from Frankfurt to Berlin, the city whose division symbolized the polarized world of the Cold War, was a little over an hour and breathtakingly exciting to Susan as she neared the end of the journey, her first abroad.

Exhaustion filled her eyes from the long flight originating in Los Angeles, but the life all around her, strange life, lifted her spirits and heightened her curiosity. It was like a dream from another time and place. It was a dream where nothing was understood; things were so different and confusing. She had been here before, or to a place just like it. It was a feeling she just could not shake.

As she passed through the terminal, all the different languages and the thousands of travelers resonated in her memory. A vision of unknown people, clearly European, tall, blond, blue-eyed Nordic features all rushing to make their connections. Beautiful languages spoken like a song, a rhapsody, Swedish perhaps. That was her first impression. Maybe they were descendants of the great Vikings Michael had spoken of so many times. Pagan blood pumping through their veins. Odin watching over them as they made their journey back to the Northland with their treasures. Their poetic voices stayed with her, lingering softly.

Susan absorbed every nuance, every face. The cobblestone street that ran for miles. The way the car felt driving on the stones, sending warm vibrations, smooth like the strumming of heavy rain through her body. Buildings, the ruins. She was swimming with images and information pouring into her senses. Everything new, alive. The Old World exceeded the limitations she set for herself in her imagination.

They pulled up just outside the hotel on the Kurfürstendamm, an enormous upscale shopping street in the center of Berlin, with its large open area and shops, big and small, and brightly lit cafes with well-dressed people. These splendid people sat outside in the cold, sipping coffee and other hot drinks with steam rising from their cups. Watching the people was synchronized confusion to Susan's eyes, happy confusion. She smiled inwardly as she gazed. She had seen nothing like it before, so many people walking and interacting. Such a large rich promenade. She couldn't get over it. So many faces.

*****

Brandenburger Tor, the gateway to the West, standing majestic in its splendor, rose above the blond-and-dark cobblestone street. Heavy, dark clouds hovering above the gate gave the illusion of a secret significance. The statue of Winged Victory stood atop a fifty-meter column, celebrating Germany's military victory in the 1890s over Denmark. One hundred years later, it became the focal point of one of the most powerful events in recent history, where another war victory was celebrated, a victory of freedom over tyranny. A profound time and place that captured the world and renewed the hope of millions of people held prisoners in their own homeland.

Wow, she said without any words, just the movement of her pouty lips. They began walking the length of the street toward the massive gateway. "It's beautiful. You never see things like this in the States."

Michael's eyes remained fixed on the gate. Images came rushing back to him. Faces. Massive crowds. Crying and joyful cheering. Fireworks. He had returned, keeping the promise he made to himself all those years ago.

Michael explained what he learned about Berlin's history, pointing here and there. Susan's face showed the joy and horror of his story as they walked. Michael told her the story and significance November 9 had with Germany. It was at Reichstag on November 9, 1918, that a fellow Social Democrat declared the ill-fated Weimar Republic. Its weakness would let the Nazis win power fifteen years later, and history was rewritten. He told her of Kristallnacht, the Night of Broken Glass. It was on November 9, 1938, when Adolph Hitler's Nazi thugs smashed shops and synagogues, killing at least ninety Jews and rounded up thousands more in a prelude to the Holocaust.

Michael continued telling her of the war and the aftermath. How it all ended here in Berlin, when the Allied forces destroyed Hitler's headquarters. He told her how Berlin was sectioned off after the war, with the Russians occupying East Germany, and how they eventually built a wall around the city—and how freedom was literally cascading over the wall as it buckled with the surge of humanity and the fall of Communism. Tears of joy rained as brother reunited with brother. The night's popular pressure forced Soviet Allied East Germany Communist leader to open the checkpoints in the Berlin Wall and set their people free on November 9, 1989.

Despite the numbingly cold night, the exotic streets were full of life as Michael and Susan approached their hotel under the cover of darkness. Decadent people remained out and about, milling around as if it were midday on a hot summer afternoon. Most of them were well-dressed young adults and teenagers.

Their day of sightseeing left them worn out. Michael showed Susan all the sights of the historic city. Potsdamer Platz, which used to be the center of Berlin. Nearby was the mound, which was the remains of Hitler's bunker, from which he commanded Germany into total defeat. The castles. The tomb of Count Alexander von der Mark in Berlin. The concert hall of the Berlin Philharmonic on the opposite side of the Tiergarten. Susan loved it all.

They approached a street performer sitting in the semidarkness tuning his guitar. Susan stopped, frozen before him as a single note sounded from the guitar. It was as if someone had suddenly called her name. She had to stand there, waiting for the resolve. Michael's motions to leave went unnoticed by her as she focused on the man sitting on the ground in front of her. His long blond dreadlocks were curious to her.

The man's face remained unseen, concealed in the shadows as he began picking the guitar and singing in the night air. The music floated, and the words danced in her mind. She was compelled by the sound, even though she could not understand the words; she knew she had to be here. It meant something; there was a purpose, a reason. His voice was deep and scratchy as the intoxicating German words resonated from his lips. There was something she needed to hear in the music; it was talking to her.

Michael tried pulling her away, but she was hypnotized by the music. This man, this bohemian man, knew her. He somehow knew her. Knew her life. Knew her past, her present, and future. It frightened her. She knew she was meant to come here, to Berlin, at this very moment just to listen to and try to understand the meaning of this music, this rhapsody.

Abruptly, the music stopped; and in the darkness, Susan watched as the man packed up his guitar. Michael took the opportunity and led her toward the hotel across the promenade. Turning back to the spot where the musician created magic, she found the spot well lit and nobody around. He disappeared completely. Did this really happen, or was it a figment of her imagination? She wondered. She shook it off to the long day, to the jet lag, to the memories of this place and how it infected her.

*****

The long day came to a close as Michael and Susan entered their elegant hotel room. A dazzling spread of flowers, compliments of the hotel for their honeymoon, were on the desk. Complimentary champagne chilled in the silver bucket filled with ice.

Susan's eyes held still, fixed on Michael's aura glowing in her sight. Her breathing felt exquisite, lusting for his touch, making love to him with her eyes. Chills covered her body as he reached over and removed the bottle from the ice. She confirmed her chills with a heavenly caress of her skin, running her hand softly down her chest, between her breasts, craving his touch.

Take me!

Michael remained deep within his private thoughts. Susan studied him closely. She has never felt so close to him, to the emotion he revealed, witnessing his heart in its purest form. Never had she felt an emotion such as she was feeling now.

She wanted him, here, now. Waiting. Silence. Her body felt delicious and anxious for his touch. She wanted to finally, on the second night, consummate their bond.

Take me now! I want to feel you inside my body. I want to cover yours with warmth. Enter me. Yes!

She watched as he caressed the glass, his fingers stroking the crystal stem. There was something sensual about his demeanor.

Take me! Fill me with your passion.

She longed to be him, to enter his skin and live his passion.

Her eyes followed his movements, subtly and without thought, another shade of himself. He could feel her eyes on him through a looking glass.

Take me now, Michael. Invade my body.

Her knight had swept her up in shining armor, and inside him was her castle, her safety. There was nothing that will destroy this sanctity she had longed for her entire life.

I want to be you, Michael.

Approaching the bed where Susan lay, Michael handed her a flute of golden champagne. She grasped it gently in her hand, caressing his fingers, a touch without words. He sat quietly on the bed next to her and watched her sip from the glass.

Yes, Michael. Yes. Her eyes continued talking to him. *Take me!*

Her head fell back as he reached out and gently stroked the skin on her neck.

Now, Michael, now. Take me. Yes!

Michael traced his way to her face, soft and angelic. Michael's fingers felt wonderful on her skin. Her eyes closed, taking in the fantasy, feeling his touch with her soul.

Yes, Michael. Take me, love me, fill me with your passion. Let me be the canvas of your last supper, paint me like Dalí. Paint me like Ann Rice paints her romantic vampires, beautifully decadent and forever young with perfect white skin, enchanting eyes, and full of lust. Paint me with passion, with lust. Paint me with your carnal hunger. I am forever yours. Take me, paint me as the pure white snow paints the virgin landscape.

His hands moved in silent harmony with her skin, possessing her essence with his touch. With the friction building, her passion grew.

Take me. Yes, Michael. Yes.

Removing her top, he found her nipples erect, poking, prodding, searching for a way out of the confines of her satin bra. A breathless moan was let slip and shared between them. His hand moved down toward her old faded jeans and unbuttoned the first button.

Yes!

The second.

Yes!

She moaned in silence. Her body arched and heaved like the sea's great rolling dunes.

The third, fourth button.

Yes! Yes!

Her breathing escalated.

Take me! Yes, Michael, yes, my love. I am your promise, and you are mine.

Their lips pressed together, sharing the passion of their love.

Yes. Yes. Yes!

Her eyes opened as the love for him choked her. Michael looked into her beautiful eyes. But something was left unsaid.

"Honey, I want to explain about yesterday—"

"Shhh," he said softly. "There are no yesterdays. Only now, today, and the future. The past is gone. Let it be gone, my love."

Her eyes filled with tears as they remained long in a deep gaze. "Make love to me, Michael. Make love to me now," she whispered.

Their lips met, tasting each other's wine.

11

Entering his office, Michael sat behind his large oak desk. He removed the small chunk of concrete he took as a souvenir from the Berlin Wall. He needed to feel it in his hand, to relive the memory one more time. He'll be back again someday, and he will never forget, especially now that he shared it with his wife.

He returned to work rejuvenated and ready for the fast-paced news world, though he was not ready for his boss, who almost kicked down the door as he entered Michael's office.

"Where the hell have you been?"

"Fuck you too, Frank!" Michael said with a raised voice. "I see you're still working on your people skills," he said sarcastically. "Not that it's any of your business, but I've been on my honeymoon!"

"We'll talk about that later," Chandler said with his eyes ablaze. Hatred hung heavy on his breath. "We've got a mess in Texas. A real media circus." Chandler turned and started moving back out of his office. "I want you in editing now!" he said just before he slammed the door.

* * * * *

Craning his neck, Gabriel turned to see the latest intruder barging into his cutting room. He was relieved to find that it was Michael approaching him. "Dude, the savior has returned," he said, extending his fist for a fist-pump. Gabe appeared weary, racked with an edgy tension. "It's been a fucking madhouse without you here. People in and out, get me this, let me see that. And Frank, man, I don't even want to start on that dude! Man, it's like he's got PMS twenty-four hours a day. What an asshole!"

"Tell me about it."

"He's all over us, man," Gabriel said with a rough sigh. "I'm just tired. I haven't been home in two days. He's been working us like big hairy dogs."

Michael smiled. Gabe sure had a unique way with words. Michael broke off and pondered the situation a moment. "We'll get you out of here shortly."

"Naw, it's cool. I mean, it's not like I have a life anyway."

Michael grinned.

The cool air from the air-conditioning pushed over Michael's hair as he looked on in disbelief as the video played. He shook his head as an inner thought baffled him. He felt the old familiar feeling of despair once again touch him. It was a feeling that came to him on occasion when certain news stories brought the emotion with unwanted convictions. "Stay on this, Gabe. And don't let Chandler rattle you," Michael said as he started for the door.

"Taking off? It's not over yet."

"I'm going to see if I can lose my job," Michael responded, walking out of the room.

* * * * *

Michael burst into his boss's office, showing him the same respect. "It's later, Frank. What exactly do you have to tell me?"

Chandler's eyes narrowed and appeared as bits of dark onyx. "I don't like your attitude!" he objected, pointing his almighty finger at Michael. His voice was hot, letting Michael know exactly who he thought he was.

"I don't care what you like, Frank! You're an asshole! You treat people like shit."

Chandler protested and quickly stood behind his desk. But before he spoke, Michael shut him up. "I put in for my vacation time six months ago, Frank. I get married, and you call me during the actual wedding, wanting me to come in. What kind of shit is that, Frank? Are you insane? And when I'm on my honeymoon, you threaten my assistant with losing his job. Who do you think you are?"

Chandler remained speechless with his mouth agape. He knew even if he wanted to, he couldn't fire Michael. If he did, Chandler would be fired before Michael made it to the front door of the building. Chandler's direct boss, Larry Moranville, hired and loved Michael. He was grooming him to take over the Los Angeles station. Chandler knew it and hated them both for it.

"You treat people like hell and expect them to jump just because you said so. That's not the way to manage people, Frank." Michael was still hot. He spoke fast and was very harsh. "So what's it going to be, Frank? You want to fire me? You want to grow a sac and see exactly where you stand with your boss?" Michael held up his cell phone. "I've got his number on speed dial! It's your move," Michael finished.

Chandler remained silent and seething with venom. His face was turning red. And then nothing. He slowly backed up a step. Even though he was technically Michael's boss, he always felt intimidated by him. And seeing this side of Michael for the first time made him even more intimidated. He didn't know what to say or do.

"That's what I thought," Michael started. "Stop being a little bitch and let us do our jobs." Michael spun on his heels and slammed the door, leaving Chandler dumbfounded behind the desk.

One month later

SILENT FALLS THE NIGHT in the scope of her mind. Susan leaned against the large maple dining-room table with an absent stare in her empty eyes. She peered into the living room, looking at the walls and ceiling with an intense interest. She spent so many nights in here waiting for Michael to return from work in this sheer solitude. She didn't care much for the fact the he worked nights—the time she needed him the most. But, alas, she was once again all alone. Alone with her old friend—the here and now—the maddening, mind-altering silence.

A tall glass of milk sat on the table next to her. It had been there for a while; she meant to drink it but never did. She had other things on her mind. She continued staring at the walls with empty eyes.

Susan turned quickly as if startled by a noise. Then in a strange gesture, she turned back again and looked at the same wall. She turned again and hit the table and knocked over the glass. The white liquid bled over the table as it raced toward the edge. Susan watched and made no attempt to pick up the fallen glass. She just watched as the milk reached the edge and fell like a white waterfall over the side in a thin stream. A milk puddle on the hardwood floor. Susan turned as if nothing had happened and walked through the kitchen and into the garage. After a moment, she returned with a large cardboard box.

All of a sudden, Susan heard Macy's voice repeating in her head. She had heard it all day—certain things, nothing in particular, just her voice over and over again.

It looks like a man's house.

Susan shook her head, trying to stave off Macy's voice from driving her up the wall. Susan loved her, but this was too much.

Your soul is not in this house.

They were stabbing her in the heart. Her face became dark and angry. Her head turned from side to side as she surveyed the space in the room.

You're a renter. You're a roommate.

"No!" she exclaimed under her breath.

Roommate. Renter. You have no soul here!

Susan turned in circles trying to fight off the maddening voice poking at her resolve. She had such a love for Macy. So why were her words tormenting her? They were tearing her apart. Why?

Suddenly Susan slammed down her fist on the table. The glass jostled and rolled a short distance. "I am not a roommate!" Susan yelled. Her echo bounced off the walls and shot back at her. She winced with a peculiar facial expression and crooked her neck. Suddenly it came to her.

* * * * *

A short while later, Susan found herself frantically working on the house. It appeared as if she was redecorating the joint in some bizarre manor. Open cans of paint in various colors lay open on the hardwood floor. Absent was the drop cloth and the sanity it took to partake in such an endeavor. Indeed, Susan appeared to not have all her wits about her as she worked frantically with a paintbrush.

Splatters of red, yellow, blue, and black paint dried and drying on her face. A white smear of paint across her forehead. The pristine hardwood floor was hastily becoming dotted with various-colored drops.

Susan stood at the base of the extension ladder looking up at the ceiling. She raised her arm, stretching it above her head in a nonsensical gesture, as if measuring something from a distance. Her other arm dangled at her side like a broken wing. Keeping her arm stretched above her head, she spun in a complete circle. She looked like a gawky kid trying to ride a gust of air into the atmosphere. She paused a moment, then repeated the peculiar movement. "You're stupid," she said as if a different person were speaking altogether.

"I am not," she answered in her own voice. The room held still. Susan was motionless in the interpretation of the aftermath. Her eyes danced on the walls, searching the shadows.

Nothing.

Climbing the ladder, Susan made it to the ceiling's high mahogany beam, which spanned the entire room. Her hair was pinned in two pigtails like a young girl, her face sweaty, no makeup. A childlike expression altered her face as she worked the wood with fervency.

Below her, the buildup of excess paint was growing on the hardwood floor. Wood chips floated to the floor.

A drip echoed. Then another. Susan's internal alarm embraced the sound, and her breathing stopped in a moment of fear. She turned and scanned the room with radar eyes. All was quiet. Another drip. Her eyes latched onto the glass still on its side. Another drip of milk fell from the table and splashed into the pool formed on the floor. Her breath returned with a sharp sigh.

Susan continued working on her masterpiece at a fever pitch, poking, prodding, stroking, and smoothing with a final, delicate touch. An accomplished smile swept across her face. Pride flared in her eyes. She made her way down the ladder. She looked up and smiled. Michael was going to be so happy, she thought. Her pixie smile lit the room as she gazed at her work.

Susan sat alone in the darkened room. Paint stained the planks of the hardwood floor. Yellow smears and drops stood out on the once-beautiful floor. As she began to nod off, her ears tinged with the vibrations of a car door shutting nearby. She became alert and responsive. Her heart quickened. She sat bolt upright as she heard the bell tones of Michael's keys jingling together like an alarm.

She ran across the room to the door as the key hit the tumbler. Turning the dead bolt, she opened the door to find Michael standing surprised before her.

"What are you doing up?" he asked. His eyes fixed on her, not quite knowing what she had done to herself. With his lucidity in an information meltdown, he wasn't able to grasp the changes in her appearance.

"I have a surprise for you," she said, beaming with joy.

Michael looked on with curiosity. Something strange in her voice, very different—eerie, in fact. It was a dissimilar tone, as if somebody else was talking. "Your hair," he said, smiling. "It's in tails. Looks cute." He took a closer look at her face. "What's with the paint?"

"That's part of the surprise. Close your eyes," she said. She jumped into his arms with the enthusiasm of an adolescent and planted a passion-filled kiss on his lips. "Okay, now close your eyes," she said with excitement.

Michael smiled and obliged. Susan led him through the doorway and onto the tile floor in the entryway. Taking his hand, she led him down the three steps into the sunken living room. "Stay there and don't open your eyes," she said, walking over to the candle and blew it out. The room was shrouded in complete darkness. "Just hold on," she called out in the darkness. He could hear her moving across the room.

"Okay, are you ready?" she asked.

"I'm ready," he replied.

"Okay, open your eyes."

"I can't see anything. It's pitch-black."

"Ta-daaa," she said as she flipped on the lights.

Michael's eyes bugged out of his head! His chin hit the floor. "WHAT THE HELL HAPPENED!" he shouted.

His eyes were on fire as he frantically scanned the room. He took a few steps forward. Shock, disbelief, and anger etched onto his face as he took in the horrific scene. He glanced at the floor. "And what's this? There's paint on the floor—it's everywhere!" his hot voice ricocheted off the wall and hit Susan in the heart.

Susan cringed inwardly and instinctively took a few steps away from Michael. It was a natural reaction when she was in the proximity of anger. Fear gripped her. His sudden display of anger brought back frightening thoughts and images of the past flashing through her mind with vivid clarity.

Looking up, Michael couldn't fathom what he was looking at. He was dumbfounded when he found their initials carved into the splendid mahogany beam. The deep grooves were painted in a brilliant yellow. "My God, Susan, what the hell did you do? What were you thinking?"

"I wanted to surprise you," she said, lowering her head.

"By destroying the house?" His voice held just below a yell. "Well, you surprised me, all right!"

"But—"

"You trashed the house! My God, we have to live here!"

Susan began pacing, almost in one place, turning in full circles around herself. Michael stood and further peered around the room. He was so consumed with the disaster around the room he was unaware of Susan's peculiar behavior as she turned in circles on the floor. His mind was trying to unfold this bend in reality. "You carved our names in the beam," he said, pointing to the ceiling.

"Just our initials," she spoke in a child's pout. She wore strange body movements as she paced. Odd hand movements and a strange twitch.

"There's yellow paint all over the beam!"

"You're mad—"

"Hell yes, I'm mad! Look at the wall!" he said, pointing to the bizarre paintings she attempted on the far wall. It looked like two red-and-yellow stick men, a child's attempt at art. A blue stick-man dog next to the artwork. "And what the hell is that!" he asked, pointing to the new colors on the wall. "Ronald McDonald? And is that a donkey?"

"It's supposed to be us," she said softly. His rage didn't allow his ears to hear her murmur.

"Fuck!" he said as he sat on the sofa. He took a deep breath and rubbed his eyes with the palms of his hands. Perhaps if he rubbed long enough, hard enough, this would all just go away. He'd wake up from this surreal nightmare. This just wasn't happening!

He placed his hands on the couch next to his legs. Feeling moisture beneath his fingertip, he looked down to find yellow paint splattered all over the sofa. "Unfuckingbelievable," he said. He took no notice of Susan, who was moving closer to the wall, still turning in circles. He stared in silent wide-eyed disbelief, slowly shaking his head.

Susan paced herself into the wall, where she stood with her face pinned against its texture, cold against her face.

Michael turned and realized where she was. "Susan, what are you doing?"

"You…you…like pretty things," she said in a slight stutter. What could she say to make him understand? How did she used to explain it away? She tried to remember.

He stood in confusion and grew concerned over her behavior. He had never seen her act so out of character. "What are you doing, Susan?" he asked again.

"You always liked when I painted. And you…you…you always liked when I painted pretty things. Pretty things," she repeated in a stuttering childlike tone, a tone Michael had not heard before. He was disoriented as he watched Susan.

Susan began tapping her head against the wall, gentle at first, then harder and harder.

"Susan, stop that!"

"You liked it...you always liked it," she said, working herself up. "You were good to me then. Nothing happened. Good to me. I was good. You liked it. You liked it," she rambled.

Michael held himself from any further comment. She was in the middle of a slow-speed come-apart, and his face was still in utter shock as he watched. Something was seriously wrong with her, and he didn't want to provide more fuel to the fire.

After hitting her head repeatedly on the wall, Susan abruptly stopped and turned to face Michael for a brief moment. Michael looked on with morbid curiosity. He feared her next move.

Susan began to spin in a tight circle, slow at first, just as a child might do at the playground. Michael was beside himself as he watched her start to spin faster and faster. She stopped suddenly and tried to focus on his face, but her head was swimming in a sea of silvery blackness. Her vision started to blur. That's when it went black. She slipped silently to the floor and lay motionless.

Michael rushed to her side. "Susan!" he called out. "Susan!" He checked for a pulse, strong and rapid. Kneeling, he gently picked her up in his arms and cradled her.

Susan opened her eyes and glanced around the room and finally focused on Michael. Her awareness was keenly alive and well in her new vision. She was, or appeared to be, back to normal. She smiled. "You're home," she said as if nothing out of the ordinary had occurred. "I must have fallen asleep."

Michael was horrified by her comment. "Susan, you fainted," he informed her. His eyes were narrowed. He had no idea what the hell was going on.

"Huh? What are you talking about, Michael?" she asked with confusion. The voice he was used to returned with resounding clarity. "I was sleeping, Michael," she said, closing her eyes to what she thought was the night's late hour. She appeared to have no recollection of the events that played out only moments before.

Michael held her gently, letting her drift to sleep. Something just wasn't right, and he was concerned. He took one last look around the room and shook his head in disgust. He carried his wife up the stairs toward the bedroom.

12

A TRAITOR'S MOON crested the parched summer sky. The last of the day's light glowed on the distant horizon, casting protesting reddish-orange rays that were disappearing over the great Pacific.

Red-hot and white coals smoldered in the barbecue pit. The charred smell lingered in the evening air. Michael and Susan left their twisted night behind them, but Michael held the memory very close to him. Her actions profoundly bothered him. He thought about the episode often. He even started doing research on the internet, though he didn't really know what to look for.

"I love the flowers. They just seem so perfect out here," Renee said to Susan as she refilled Renee's wineglass.

"I just love sunflowers. They're so, I don't know, happy, I guess. I mean…"

"I know what you mean," Renee replied and sipped from the glass.

"Yeah," Susan replied with a smile and looked up at the sky.

Craning her head, Renee overheard the conversation Michael and Nick were having as they approached the backyard table.

"You're not the one who has to live with her! She's just a fat cow and doesn't get along with anybody," Nick said in protest.

"They're talking about Jody, Nick's roommate," Renee said to Susan, who nodded. "Have you ever met her?"

Susan shook her head.

"There's no dealing with this woman. She's been everywhere, done everything. No matter what story you tell, she's done it, been there, or has seen it," he said in a huff.

"Look, Nick, you're going to run into people whose personalities don't mesh with yours, and you gotta deal with it. It's called life, man," Michael said as he sipped his beer.

Sitting next to Susan, Michael leaned over and kissed her softly on the cheek. Michael made sure that he was more attentive to Susan. An extra touch, an extra smile, an extra kiss to make her feel special and keep her mind on the positive vibe around her.

"She keeps getting fatter—"

"Nicholas!" protested Renee. "That's not nice."

"If you're so unhappy, then move out," Michael replied.

Renee looked at Michael with a spark in her eye. It was something he had said that snapped her mind to attention. Renee leaned forward closer to Nick, then stopped herself and pulled back. Then she decided to shoot for the moon. "If you dislike it so much, why don't you just move in with me?"

Roaring silence descended on the backyard. All eyes turned to Renee with utter shock. Especially Nick. Her statement floored him. Was she serious?

Susan smiled as she watched her friend squirm uncomfortably. She couldn't believe what she heard. Michael didn't know how to react. He still couldn't picture the two of them together, let alone living together.

Nick remained speechless and held his gaze on Renee's eyes. He wasn't exactly sure of what to say or do.

"Maybe we should talk about it later," Renee finally said quietly.

Nick nodded with his gaping mouth stuck wide open.

The four friends shared a moment of uneasy silence in the cool night air. Renee watched as Susan leaned her head on Michael's arm; it looked so natural. Susan cast her head upward and looked at the sky, but her thoughts were with Nick and Renee and their blossoming love. She hoped they would move in together. It was such a wonderful idea.

* * * * *

How many worlds remain undiscovered, untouched by human eyes? How many people, aliens, other beings are looking down at me, the same moment I'm looking at them? How many dead or lost souls are watching from the celestial bodies above?

Sitting in the bedroom beneath the large picture window, Susan's eyes remained fixed, looking past the clear picture window to the heavens above. The stars always fascinated her. Brushing the goose bumps from her shoulder, she felt Michael walk into the room and approached her from behind like a phantom. She couldn't take her eyes off the stars.

"You're in the backyard every night looking up at those stars, and now you're in the house looking out the window at the same stars," Michael said jokingly.

"Every night for week there's been nothing but fog. I couldn't see a thing. But tonight it's crystal clear. It's strange, don't you think?"

"Maybe it's the calm before the storm," he said in jest as he nudged her arm, nodding for her to come to bed.

At that very moment, something snapped inside her. She forced her eyes tightly shut. Her forehead wrinkled as she fought through the gray matter of strange visions she had in her mind. Maybe he was exactly right; maybe it was the calm before the storm. But if this was the calm, what was the storm going to bring to the dance?

Emotion swept across her face. Her eyes relaxed, but they remained closed. She was privy to something else that came fast to her mind. They were beckoning the gatekeeper of her conscious being, *Let me in. I demand it!*

Susan's eyes opened with striking brilliance, like a burst of lightning. She looked around the room slowly. Everything in this new surrounding looked magical through these new looking glasses. Her dark pupils were portals to another vessel. Her luminous-green pigment was missing, leaving two dark spots in her eyes.

Craning her head, she turned toward Michael lying in the bed. A strange sigh passed from her lips. "I'm out," she whispered. The voice carried an eerie, maligned tone, one not associated with such a beautiful young woman. Its tone was deep and scratchy, like that of a heavy smoker. With a sinister grin, she started slowly across the room to the bed.

She stood at the foot of the bed and shed her clothes, letting them fall loosely on the floor. It was an act Susan wouldn't normally do, not so boldly. She looked upon Michael, whose body was outlined by the sheets. Glancing at her own body, a freakish, sadistic look washed over her face.

Her hands moved up to her breasts, when, in an odd gesture, she roughly grabbed them tightly, nails digging into the skin. She shook them violently between her fingers. Her head fell back in rapture, and her mouth parted with a silent moan. Letting them lose, she looked upon them as if they were an annoyance intruding on her body. Taking her nipple between her fingers, she squeezed the sensitive flesh with all her might. Again her head fell back as she let the pleasure sweep over her body. "Does that hurt, bitch?" she asked quietly.

"What did you say?" Michael asked as he removed the sheets from his sight. A curious look struck his face.

"I didn't say anything," she replied with an evil glare.

Michael held his eyes on her naked body. He was sure he heard something odd, but he shrugged. "Well, don't you look yummy," he said, sitting up on his elbows.

"What, you like this body?" she asked with a disgusted look, mocking her skin as if it were rented flesh.

"Yeah, baby. Come over here and let me get a closer look."

"This body makes me want to puke!" Her voice was loaded with venom.

Not used to her harshness, Michael glared at her with a questioning look. This was not like her at all, he thought. What was she up to? What a strange voice.

Leaning down at the foot of the bed, she ripped the sheet off in one motion, leaving Michael naked on the bed.

"You don't tell me what to do! You're going to do what I say," she said in a hot voice.

"Oh, really," he replied, thinking she was playing around. "What exactly are you going to do to me?" He smiled, playing along.

"I'm going to teach you the meaning of respect," she said as she knelt on the bed at his feet.

"Respect, huh?"

"You've been a bad boy, and I'm going to punish you for it! I'm going to put a stop to all your evil deeds." She brushed the palm of her hand over her chest. Her ivory breasts now welted with red marks. Michael looked upon her naked body, not exactly sure of her intentions. She had seemingly lost her inhibitions and was becoming somewhat adventurous.

Moving farther up on the bed, she straddled his body and sat on his groin. "Tell me what you've done, Michael."

"Let me guess," he said with a smile. "I've been a very bad boy—"

She slapped him with the palm of her hands, hard onto his bare chest with all she could muster. The slap's echo rebounded around the room before he could yell.

"What the hell are you doing!"

"I'm not playing around, Michael!" she said with a roar. Her violent eyes frightened him for a moment.

"What's your problem, Susan?"

"You're the one who has a problem! And I'm gonna take care of it!" Her eyes breathed with fire and were lit by a source that didn't appear human. "Are you fucking her?"

"What—"

"Are you fucking that bitch?" she yelled in anger.

"Where the hell did that come from?" he asked as he leaned up. Grabbing his wrists, she slammed him back down on the bed. The unnatural strength took Michael by surprise. He was left with a look of utter shock.

"Answer the question! Did you fuck her?"

"Who, Renee?" The bewildered look remained on his face. It never left. This truly wasn't happening! He felt as though she were going completely nuts.

"Don't play games with me, Michael. You know exactly who I'm talking about. It's a simple question, are you *fucking* her? Answer the question, or I am going to hurt you!" Her wild eyes spooked him.

Incensed, Michael pushed her off him and climbed off the bed. "I haven't done anything with anybody since I met you!" he replied with a hot voice. "Look, Susan," he said as he stepped into his robe, "I don't know what your problem's been lately, but you've been acting nuts! You're scaring the hell out of me!"

"Don't try to turn this around on me, buddy! I don't have a problem, you do! You're the one who's fucking that bitch!"

"You need help, Susan! I don't know what's going on in your head, but you need help!" he said, jabbing his finger toward her.

"She's a disgusting slut!"

"You're circling the drain. You need help," he said, walking out of the room.

"I'm going to put a stop to it, you know!" she called after him. "She's a whore," she said in a heartless tone.

Susan lay back with one hand behind her head, the other at her side. There was a contradicting content look on her anger-laden face. A menacing giggle escaped into the room as she, no doubt, thought about a twisted little conclusion in her mind.

* * * * *

Materializing without a calling card came the rains in the dark of the night. It was the start of something all, right. The June swoon was upon us, and what it carried with it had already arrived. What it vowed was dark gray days ahead.

Susan woke to an empty bed, ruffled sheets, and a torrent of rain tapping against the windowpane, her naked body partially covered with the sheets. She pulled them up, shielding her body from the chill in the morning air. Wiping the sleep from her eyes, she searched her mind for answers to last night's events, of which she had no memory.

Holding herself against the handrail at the top of the stairs, Susan looked down and saw Michael in the living room sitting on the couch. Her gaze never left his as she cautiously walked down the staircase and across the room. She reined to a halt just beside the couch. Holding there a moment, she studied him and waited for movement, some kind of sign. She could sense nothing from him and couldn't remember anything from the night before. What had happened? Why was guilt choking her?

Michael showed no signs of approachability as he read the morning paper. She remained somewhat disoriented and grasped the lapel of her terry-cloth robe. She waited, hoping Michael would address her, say something—anything. It didn't matter.

Michael was keenly aware of her presence and made a blatant point to avoid eye contact.

"Michael?" she said quietly.

Silence.

"Michael?" she said again.

Michael lowered the newspaper and presented her with an overwhelming look of disdain. He waited for some kind of logical explanation, a response, anything that made the slightest bit of sense. He held his contemptuous glare. She felt the blade of his stare cutting through her flesh.

"Michael, I… I don't remember what happened last night," she said apologetically.

Michael held his glare, still hoping for reason, any kind of sane explanation.

Susan had no answers. She had no explanation or reason. A long, uncomfortable silence fell between them.

Finally, Michael looked up at her with softened eyes. "What is going on with you, Susan? I've never seen anything so strange in my life. It's like you're two different people."

Susan stood there wading through her thoughts—so many bizarre images as she searched the gray matter for the evil that lay and waited. She looked spent, wrung out. She thought of her miserable childhood, tried to conjure up a single happy moment. Nothing! She was unable to cast off the cloak of sadness that was spreading over her.

The silence was too much for him. "Cat got your tongue?" he said with spite. His voice rolled like thunder across the dark sky of Susan's mind. She cringed and retreated a little deeper within herself.

"I think maybe I drank too much wine last night," she murmured.

"That's bullshit, Susan, and you know it! This isn't an isolated incident. Remember the remodeling job you pulled with the finger paints? How do you explain that?" Michael asked, his voice firm and steady. He waited, but nothing came, not a single sound. "There is something seriously wrong with you, and I think we need to get you some help."

She remained in her standing position with her arms folded tightly across her chest. She began shaking her head, disagreeing with his suggestion of help. A curious look crossed her face. Michael repositioned himself on the couch as Susan sat next to him.

"I think we just need to move away. Nobody can bother us then. We could be free," she said as she took his hand into hers.

Michael's face was blistered with sudden shock. He roughly pulled his hand away from hers. That sudden move tore the rug right out from under Susan. She couldn't stand the look on Michael's face, but she continued pleading with hopeful eyes. She appeared bitterly unaware of the course of conversation. Michael wasn't! She couldn't take much more of his disapproval; it was tearing her apart.

"Who are you?" he asked in disbelief. "Because you're not the woman I married! Not the woman I fell in love with."

Susan stammered quickly to her feet as if she were hit in the chest. She was not ready for Michael's harsh reaction. A bizarre series of facial expressions and gestures tore across her flesh, as if she were suffering from Tourette's syndrome. She looked quickly to her left and shook her head.

Michael was horrified as he witnessed his wife's slow-speed come-apart.

"Shut up!" she said and caught herself as Michael's eyes darted from side to side, searching the empty room. Susan looked at him with an impish look in her empty eyes.

Michael looked upon the distressing scene with great concern. He shook his head and shed eye contact. "Susan," he started softly, as if surrendering. "I think we need to get you some professional help." His eyes remained averted.

"No!" she exclaimed vehemently. "Who do you think you are? I don't need help!" she proclaimed. "I just need time, just a little more time," she repeated as an afterthought. Susan lowered her head and began with odd head gestures.

Michael looked on as she started pacing in tight circles, 'round and around. "Tell him," she said in a voice he was not used to. Michael folded his brow.

"No!" she answered herself abruptly in another voice.

"Tell me what?" he asked cautiously. He wasn't sure if he really wanted to hear the answer.

Susan continued pacing in bizarre little circles.

"What do you want to tell me?"

Nothing.

Silence.

Circles.

Michael came up off the couch and approached her and attempted to comfort her, but his attempt was brushed off coldly. "What's going on with you?" he asked with compassion, anything to draw her back to the realm of reality.

Susan sighed deeply. Everything rushed out of her. Every odd gesture, every strange emotion, and bizarre act was gone. Michael waited in deafening silence. Her eyes moved up to meet his. "Oh, Michael." Tears roared in her eyes. "I'm pregnant," she whispered this last.

Michael felt like a crash-test dummy hitting the wall at a hundred miles an hour. "What did you say?"

"I'm pregnant."

Yeah! I get it, yeah! Michael was floored, but this answered everything for him, especially her behavior, as strange as it was. This answered everything! He knew there had to be an explanation, a reason why she had been acting so strangely. This answered everything!

Elation swept across his face. He took her hand into his. "We're going to have a baby," he said with a smile. His dream of a family of his own was about to come true. "That's why you've been acting so strange?" It really wasn't a question.

Huh? That was something she never thought about, and it threw her for a loop. *I guess it's possible*, she thought, but she knew otherwise. But with what Michael said, she wasn't sure anymore. His statement left her a little confused. "Yeah, I guess so," she muttered softly. Confusion swept across her face.

Michael pulled her into his arms and screamed with joy. His exhalation echoed through the house. He hugged her as tears rushed into his eyes. "I'm so happy, Susan. This is wonderful. I don't know what to say. This is wonderful!"

His emotion confused her. This was not how he was supposed to react. She looked at him with an odd expression. *What the hell is he up to?* she wondered.

"Oh, honey, this is the most wonderful thing you could have told me. You did it. You did it," he said with a smile as he embraced her.

"But—"

"I'm going to be a father. This is my dream come true. You know that. You did it, baby."

She had to fight a little, but she broke from his tight embrace and backed away from him. She searched his face with sadness in her eyes. She still didn't understand his reaction. Why was he acting like this? Now she was the one who stood in confusion.

"Michael…there's something I have to tell you." Her murmur fell upon deaf ears as Michael's happiness was single-tracked. He knew there was an explanation for her behavior, and he was thrilled.

"We have to take you to the doctor. Let's do it today—"

"Michael, I can't keep it," she said just above a whisper.

Michael froze, his mouth parted slightly.

"I can't keep the baby," she repeated a little louder.

Michael's face went blank. "What do you mean you can't keep the baby? Of course, we're keeping the baby. Why would you say something like that, honey?" he asked.

"Michael, you don't know. You…you just don't know enough to understand." She tried, but the words just didn't come. She wanted to say so much, tell him everything, but she was lost by his reaction.

"I know enough to know that you've been going through hell, Susan. I know enough to know we're keeping the baby."

Susan shot him with a bitter scowl. "What's wrong with you?"

"Nothing, honey, I'm going to be a father."

"No, Michael," she said with icy breath. Her words hung frigid in the air.

Michael thought a moment as he held her in his gaze. "Honey. Susan, you've been through so much lately. Let's not talk about this right now. Of course, we're keeping the baby. This is the happiest day of my life, but we'll let you rest, and we'll talk about it later, okay?"

Susan stood motionless and stared at Michael.

"Why don't you go and get some rest. We'll get you an appointment today if we can."

Her sad eyes remained lost as she searched his face. She knew right then that he would never understand—nobody would! She didn't really understand herself. Her pupils cried out for help, but her cries fell upon blind eyes staring back at her. "Get some sleep, honey. We can talk about this later, okay?"

She knew she could say nothing that would penetrate his happiness. She gave up. "Okay," she said softly. She lowered her head to cover her welling tears.

Michael embraced her warmly as a thousand thoughts raced through his mind. He wanted to start planning this whole thing out. "I love you, Susan. Everything is going to be okay now. I just knew there was something behind all this. I just knew it." He kissed her on the forehead and guided her toward the staircase.

Michael turned and moved slowly across the room. "I've got to call my brother. He's going to be an uncle." He stopped in his tracks and smiled. "I'm going to be a father!" he said to himself. Tears welled in his eyes.

Susan hesitated at the bottom of the stairs and focused through tear-filled eyes at her husband reaching for the phone. *Why doesn't he understand?* The tears came down her face, and she moved slowly up to the bedroom.

13

DENSE FOG spread inland like a blazing fire cresting the Santa Monica Mountains in the fall firestorms. It threw out an eerie effect as the thick mist sifted through the trees of the yard. She could feel the gloomy chill, which wrapped her like a cold, wet blanket. Though the stars above were obstructed from view, she continued searching the fog-laden sky for a glimmer of hope.

Susan's gaze held no meaning. The light in her eyes was dim, just like her hope. She no longer tried to figure out the great poem of the universe. The loathing fear and self-hatred had crept from its old hiding place. It was coming; she could feel it. She was on a collision course with destiny. Her emotionally torn face remained edgy and on the cusp of collapse. She sighed.

"No!" Susan called out into the darkness to the presence she felt approaching her from behind. She closed her eyes and waited for the response she knew was coming. She tensed her entire body and held her breath.

"No to what?"

Susan exhaled her breath and relaxed her body. She smiled as Macy sat across from her at the table in the spooky mist of the rolling fog. Macy's voice covered Susan with comfort and quieted her inner voice. "No to your ridiculous question," Susan chided.

Macy beamed with a great smile. "I haven't asked anything."

"Oh, it's coming."

"It is, huh?" Macy asked with a gleam in her bright eyes. "How is it you know so much, my darlin'?" Her Southern accent really broke through and reminded Susan of her childhood. When their eyes met, Susan felt an embracing air of peace. It was the calming effect Macy always had on her, and she loved it. Loved her.

"Actually," Susan started and broke out with a great smile, "I heard your car pull up. And you sounded like a bull in a china shop coming into the backyard."

Macy held her smile. "Oh well, there goes my theory that you're a psychic. Or something," she finished with a sweet smirk.

Susan smiled, but it didn't quite look right, at least not to Macy, who noticed everything. "What's with you, darlin'? You sure don't seem yourself," Macy said.

Susan continued looking at her dear friend. She felt that all-too-familiar serenity that came with Macy's presence. She wanted to reach out and touch the feeling and embrace it with reckless abandon. Susan blew a long, deep sigh. "I'm just glad that you were home when I called tonight. I missed you." Susan broke eye contact as Macy studied her face. "I needed you tonight."

"Are you okay?"

"No, I'm not," Susan replied with a saddened heart. "I'm losing control of myself…"

"Like before?"

Susan shamefully lowered her head. "I think so," she said quietly.

Come the fog now, eerie and ever so quickly, rolling like a rogue wave into the yard, splashing through the trees and smoking the pool with steam. This was more than just a coastal eddy making its way inland.

Macy nodded. "I had a feeling you were," she said with concern.

"Why?"

"You've been on my mind like never before lately, and it's troubling, you know."

"Yes, I do," Susan replied and sank a little lower within herself.

Macy nodded as if she were privy to something only she knew. "I know what's going on, darlin'," Macy said with concern in her eyes.

Susan perked right up, like she had been challenged to a fight. "Oh! And what is it?" Susan asked with a questioning gaze.

"Darlin', it's me! You can't keep things from me. You know that."

"If you think you know me so well, then tell me what I'm going through," Susan replied, almost as a challenge.

"I can't, not right now."

"Why not?"

"Because you're not ready," Macy replied.

"What do you mean I'm not ready? Ready for what exactly?"

"You're not ready to face your fears," Macy replied.

"What? Are you a shrink now?" Susan shot her a quick laugh. "Maybe we don't know each other as well as we think we do because that certainly was a load of crap," Susan replied. "A lot can change in ten years, Macy. People move on. They grow up. Life continues."

"Yes, it can, but the way you and I feel about each other can't change, darlin'." Macy moved a little closer to Susan. "I was the only one there, Susan." She lowered her voice. "I know how you felt then. I know how you feel now."

"This is different than before," Susan said. "So much different."

"No, it's not. It's just a different time and a different place."

Susan squirmed in the wooden yard chair. She was rapidly becoming uncomfortable in front of her lifelong friend.

Macy could sense the discomforting vibe growing between them.

"Look. I really don't want to talk about this right now." Susan broke eye contact and lowered her head, but not out of shame this time. She was angered. Macy could only imagine what she was thinking.

A long pause lingered and mixed with the fog that was creeping heavier in the air. "Okay, Susan. You know I'll be here when you need me," Macy said. She touched Susan on the shoulder. Her hand remained there for a moment, letting her know that she loved her. "You know how to get a hold of me. I'll be around, darlin'." Macy turned and slowly walked off into the soupy night.

* * * * *

Several hours later, Susan found herself in the backyard, where the trees were barely visible as the thick fog transcended on the yard.

Steam rose from the pool. The steam further added to the eerie effect of the scene.

Susan sat motionless in the same chair. She never moved from the chair after Macy left her. A blank stare was frozen in her timeless face as she endeavored to find hope in the stars in the sky beyond the fog.

Go away. Please go away.

Her hair hung limp and wet from sitting in the fog. A fine veneer glowed on her bare arms in the dim light of the yard. Not even the ringing of her cell phone on the table in front of her could wake her from her trance.

A crackle in her throat gave birth to sound for the first time in her long hours of silence. It was the sound of humming, some far-off ditty she held in her psyche. Her head and body remained motionless; strings from above had control of her body, a marionette in the powerful hands of a master puppeteer. It was something she was used to, waiting for the next move from the master. *I will obey you, master.* She always did.

Her face remained motionless as she hummed the familiar tune she had heard before. But from where had she heard it?

* * * * *

Rushing down the stairs with a panicked expression, Michael glanced and took notice of the clock: 2:26 a.m.. He stood still in the living room holding a clutch of videotapes and gathered his thoughts. Where the hell could she have gone all night long? He held a long thought, and as he was about to sit on the couch, an idea flashed in his mind. He set the videotapes on the coffee table and turned toward the backyard.

Michael walked onto the backyard deck where he found Susan sitting, almost frozen in the chair. She was soaking wet and shivering. Her eyes appeared as black coal, staring at the soupy fog, as if hypnotized by the heavens.

Whatever Michael said as he approached went unheard. She was catatonic, lost to the world. Michael swept her up in his arms.

Her head fell back, and her eyes remained on the poisonous fog, trying to get one last glimpse of the stars before Michael took her into the house.

*****

Stale air hung heavy, like a damp towel around the cruel morning. Michael sat on the couch contemplating the unusual events—the elations he felt knowing he was going to be a father, his lifelong dream, and the hopelessness he felt over the turmoil his wife was experiencing. Hot and cold mixed emotions tore at his shell.

Holding his face in his hands, his elbows rested on his knees for support, and his eyes wandered aimlessly and finally stopped on the stack of videotapes marked KNRQ Field Report with a series of numbers. Michael let his eyes dance over the tapes a moment.

He picked up the tapes and walked over to the television and placed the first tape into the VCR and picked up the remote. He took a quick glance up the stairs before he sat back down on the couch. He watched as the reporter interviewed a group of local psychiatrists, throwing out words such as the *mentally ill*, *paranoia*, *paranoid personality disorder*, *delusional*, *schizophrenia*.

"Are you kidding me?"

Michael jumped out of his seat at the sudden throw of her voice echoing through the room. "You startled me," he said as he looked over and found her standing at the bottom of the stairs with a hot look in her malicious eyes. Her mouth became ridged and bitter. Her appearance was so unnatural to his eyes. He had never seen her like this, not with such anger.

"How dare you! I know what you're trying to do, but this is my life!" she shouted.

Michael was mute with shock. He wanted so much to find a referee and call time-out, go back to the beginning, and start over. "If you haven't noticed, Susan, we're in this together. We're married, remember? I want to help you get through this, whatever the hell this is."

"I don't need your help! I can do this on my own," she said, pleading with her eyes as she moved into the room. Michael felt a wave of chills sweep over him as she approached.

"You're not doing a very good job of it, Susan. What was that shit last night? You call that getting through this? Or do you even remember what went on last night?" His quip darted her skin.

Susan began moving around the room like a caged animal. She held her arms folded across her chest as she paced. Michael's eyes followed her back and forth. Michael spoke to her, but she heard nothing. She searched her mind for a way to get out of this situation. "If you love me, you won't do this," she said weakly.

"Oh, don't try to lay your guilt trip on me, Susan! I don't play that game, and you know it," he replied.

"Why can't you just let me deal with this on my own?" she shouted. Her eyes quickly returned and remained submissively on the floor.

"I won't let you do this alone, Susan, because I love you. You're my life, and there is something wrong. Don't you get it? I know you're hurting," he replied, lowering his voice an octave. He wanted to approach her, wanted to reach out and hold her in his arms, but he wasn't sure what to do anymore.

"Just let it go, Michael," she yelled. She continued like a wildcat, back and forth, trapped in a cage.

"Since we got married, Susan, you haven't been yourself," he said. "Did something happen to you, something I should know about? Did I do something? I need to know, Susan. I love you, and I want to help you through this. For God's sake, let me."

Susan continued pacing but stopped herself in the corner of the room, her face to the wall. Strangely, she started humming the same familiar tune that struck her chords the night before. As the sound formed in her throat came louder into the room, she began rocking with the innocence of a child.

Michael looked on. He couldn't begin to fathom what was going on in her mind. Louder and louder came the sound into the room. "See? This is what I'm talking about, Susan. Look at you. What the hell are you doing?" He was agitated, frustrated, and worried. "And you're telling me you don't need help, huh?" He shook his head with a sour smirk.

Susan continued humming the tune over and over again as if she were alone and without a care in the world. Her sound was beautiful as it filled the room with innocence.

Michael noticed the change in her disposition with the melody and let her continue. He needed the time to think anyway. "What do we do now, Susan?" he asked finally.

Susan suddenly stopped. She stopped humming. She stopped rocking and stopped pacing. She pulled her head up, but her eyes remained on the wall. "Maybe I'm not capable of feeling what you want me to feel," she said. Her eyes never left the surface of the wall.

"It's not about feeling one way or another, Susan. It's about the strange way you've been acting. I think it's time for help."

"Well, thanks anyway, but I don't need any help."

"Susan—"

"Life is very painful, Michael!" Her voice rose but leveled off just below a scream. It was her survivor's instinct. Strike first, no questions. Just strike first; then there will be no more questions. "It's not always how you want it to be, believe me, I know!" In her defensive mind, Michael was just an outsider, somebody who was trying to learn her secrets, somebody who was trying to harm her and take her off to some awful place she had always been told about.

He followed her with his eyes, trying to understand. Inwardly, this was killing him. Rising up off the couch, he cautiously walked across the room. He had to try another approach, a last-ditch effort to somehow reach her. She never looked at him. Her eyes remained on the wall and moved to the floor with his touch. "We're going to have a baby," Michael said as he took her into his arms, trying somehow to reclaim his wife.

Susan abruptly parted from his clutches, and her eyes lifted off the floor enough to look at his chest. "Michael, I know how much you want to have this baby, but I can't have it. I just can't. Please, just trust me."

Michael's heart sank as he tried looking into her eyes. Susan's head remained lowered in a subservient pose, waiting for the puppet master to guide her next move with his skillful hands. The master was hard at work with this veiled metamorphosis.

"I'll trust you if you can give me an explanation that makes sense. 'Just because' doesn't really work for me!" he roared. He was on the verge of explosion.

"I can't explain anything to you, Michael. I just can't have this baby. You'll have to accept that!"

His frustration got the better of him, and he yelled. He wanted to explode and break things. He was human, after all, and so was she.

Susan returned to pacing the floor in much of the same patterns Michael had come to recognize. They made no sense to him. None of this did.

Michael turned back around and watched as she swept the floor with her feet, back and forth. He shook his head slightly. "You have wonderful ability to create life, and now you want to destroy it!" he said, following her with his eyes.

Nothing!

He waited.

Though she never made eye contact, she could feel the force of his gaze knifing into her skin. Susan felt small at that moment, like an insect crawling between the cracks of the floor. That's where she wanted to go, somewhere, anywhere away from his hurtful glare. She never meant to hurt him. She never meant for any of this to happen. Her worst fear was now confronting her with absolution.

She stopped in her tracks and slowly turned her head toward him. Their eyes met. Michael felt a chill sweep over him. If felt so unnatural the way she looked at him. There was something in her eyes. "You can't make me have this baby!" she said in a malignant voice. "It's my body!" She abruptly broke eye contact and continued pacing.

"What? Don't I have any right? It's my baby too!" he replied with a hot snipe. Then, as she said nothing, Michael roared, "That's bullshit, Susan!" He pointed his damming finger in her direction.

"It's my body!" she yelled, pointing with an almighty finger of her own. She was so callous and heartless. Michael never imagined his wife could be so ruthless. It wasn't like her; none of this was.

Finally, she looked him in the eyes, but only long enough to destroy his world. "It's my body, and I'm not having this baby! End of story!" she said and returned her eyes to the floor.

"I guess what I want or feel doesn't matter, right? After all, I'm just a man. I had no part in the creation of anything!" he said as sarcastically as possible. He wanted her to feel his indignation. Deep down, he had the disgusting feeling that no matter what he said, Susan was going to hold strong and never give in to his protests.

And with the shrug of her shoulders, Michael had his answer. Not the one he would have liked but an answer nonetheless.

"You're not going to abort this baby!"

"Yes, I am," she replied and started walking toward the staircase. "And there's nothing you can do about it!"

"What about my rights?" he called after her. "I'm the baby's father!"

She ended the conversation with the slam of the bedroom door.

"Fuck!" Michael yelled in the empty room.

14

Came the rains still on a summer's breeze. The June swoon held heavy like a new moon cresting the night's blackness on a Friday of the thirteenth. Friday the thirteenth was beginning to feel a lot like every day in the labyrinth of his mind. So many bizarre twists and turns, new rules to the game. Echoes of madness loomed ominous and cruel, and the clock was ticking. There were no time-outs in this psychosis, no second chances, no turning back. The wheels were in motion, and Michael was spinning his hamster wheel, trying to stop this insanity.

Michael stood quietly outside the open bedroom door, carefully contemplating this reality that lay before him. Nothing he had experienced could have prepared him for this situation, which had been thrust upon him with such harsh cruelty. He was disoriented, beside himself, overwhelmed with the sheer brutality of her firm stance. What could have led her to such a formidable conclusion?

He found her sitting on the edge of the bed looking down at her bare feet dangling just above the floor. He mused at her childlike innocence as she examined her feet—funny-looking things. She felt him standing in the doorway, felt him scrutinizing her, probing for answers she wasn't about to impart. No longer able to look him in the eyes, her head remained lowered in a subservient pose. *Dance with me, my sweet lullaby*, said the shadow to the ghost.

"Is it me, Susan?" Michael asked softly. His voice quivered slightly. Michael couldn't bring himself to look at her either. He couldn't take the chance of looking into her striking eyes. "Have I done something to hurt you? Because I just can't figure any of this out. It's crazy." Mixed emotions and a bewildered look etched his face. "I feel like I'm caught in a surreal dream that I just don't want any part of. There's crazy visions of all sorts of confusing shit, and… and…it's truly bizarre. I want off this ride!" He took a chance and let his gaze fall in the vicinity of her eyes, but they were still looking down upon her feet.

"No, Michael, it's not you. It's me," she said softly. "It's always been me," she said very quietly, almost as an afterthought. His emotion struck her heart and appealed to her better judgment. She had never seen him so vulnerable. Michael was the one star she always reached for in the dark night sky. He had always been there for her, pulled her through the toughest times, and she would do anything for him. Anything but this.

Wishing to choose his words carefully, Michael thought for a moment in the impending silence. "Then if it's not me, why are you so unwilling to work this out?" he asked, beseeching her sense of fair play, right and wrong, her humanity.

"I can't," she stated quickly. "Michael, I don't want to talk about this anymore. I am going to have an abortion, and you're going to have to get over it. I'm sorry. I know this isn't what you want. I know you must hate me and think I'm a monster, but I have to do this for me." A long pause. "I only wish you could understand."

"I can't!" he shouted. He did everything he could to fight back the urge to reach out and throttle her, shake some sense into her stubborn, self-centered state of mind, but he calmed himself with a deep breath. "You know," he started, his teeth slightly clenched to keep from a total meltdown. "You've asked me to understand this fucked-up situation, but how can I? You don't want to give me a reason, yet you want me to act as if nothing has happened, like you're not pregnant." His anger started boiling. "I'll never forget that you're carrying my baby, Susan. My baby! It's part of me! And if you kill it, I'll never forgive you!"

Nothing he could say would change her mind. She was determined, though mute with her unspoken reason.

"It's not going to happen today or tomorrow, Michael, but I am going to do it soon."

Michael's eyes narrowed. He could not believe she had the balls to make such a statement. He was beside himself. Susan felt her skin blister from his burning glare. "You've got a lot of nerve, sister!" He was pissed! It was checkmate. He knew the game was over, all because of one little insignificant fact—because he is a man. He shook his head, shot her with yet another intense glare, then turned and walked out of the room.

* * * * *

Michael came into work early that night, hours before he needed to. He wanted the solitude behind his closed office door. He needed to get away from the house and away from his wife for a while.

As he settled in behind his desk, he took the chipped piece of concrete he took from the Berlin Wall and clutched it in his hand. And like Aladdin rubbing the lamp, his finger stroked the rough texture of the concrete, over and over again, hoping for one last wish. It was something he did often when the world appeared overwhelming. It was his worry stone.

Turning toward the computer, Michael punched up an abortion site and began reading in an effort to gather more information on the subject. Abortion had never been a subject he thought much about. It was always somebody else who had to deal with it. He wasn't sure what his stance was before Susan's blatant declaration. But he sure knew now; and the only question in his mind was, What could he do about it? As he read, he made notes of his own on a yellow legal pad.

Michael knew there was not much time. The vivid image of his child he had in his mind was beginning to fade with the slow passing of time. If they remained on course, if Susan held strong, his image would disappear altogether.

He had no course of action. He had no rights. Where did our system fail? Michael had been turning the wheels all day, trying to make sense of it all. Why is it generally understood, and accepted, that a man had absolutely no rights and no say in any of the controlling decisions about whether or not to have or even keep a baby? It has always been about the woman and what she wants. What rights does the biological father have beyond that of a mere sperm donor, whose apparent interest in the project terminates simultaneously with his ejaculation?

It was driving him insane as he searched for a new avenue to travel, one that would lead to Susan's altered stance regarding the abortion.

Michael sighed and reached for the phone. He dialed. "Hey, want to meet for dinner? It's on me," he said into the mouthpiece. "The Palm. Yeah. Six sharp."

*****

With an unsettled feeling in the pit of his stomach, Michael pushed his plate aside. His steak was untouched. He finished telling Nick what was going on with him and Susan as they sat in the crowded restaurant. Michael found it hard to hold eye contact with Nick, choosing instead to focus on the table's surface, tapping it with the worry stone still in his hand.

Nick appeared stunned, appalled, and confused. He could clearly see the stress etched onto Michael's face. It was hard for Nick to grasp the enormity of the situation, but it wasn't enough for him to lose his appetite as he reached for Michael's steak. "Jesus Christ, Mike. What are you going to do?" he asked as he shoved a large chunk of steak into his mouth.

"I don't know," Mike replied. It was the look of defeat in Michael's eyes that really got to Nick. "What can I do? I don't have any rights." His eyes remained on the table in a cold stare, his hand still working over the worry stone.

Looking up at all the painted faces on the walls of the famed restaurant, Michael wondered if any of them had been in a similar situation. What would they have done, all these famous people? How would they have handled it? But the mocking faces told no tales.

"I've known you all my life, and I've never seen you like this. I don't like it," Nick said, looking at Michael. "This is really fucked up! I don't know what else to say." Nick finished his food and sat back, rubbing his stomach. "I can't believe this could be the end of you two. That is something I don't want to see happen. You guys are like two peas in a pod. You were born to find each other and live happily ever after."

"We can work it out somehow. I know we can," Mike started. "Splitting up or divorce is not an option in my mind. But first we have to somehow get past this."

Nick nodded as he studied his friend's troubled face. "How are you going to get past this, Mike? This will no doubt drive a major wedge between you and Susan. It'll always be there," he said. "I mean, whatever the outcome, it's going to be devastating to one, if not both, of you. There's going to be scars for years," Nick finished.

Michael held still as a long, uncomfortable silence fell between them. Michael sipped from the water glass. "I know," he said in a deep, sorrow-filled sigh.

Nick pondered the situation a moment, searching his mind for a new direction. He wanted to snap a smile onto his friend's face. Then it hit him. "Fuckin' sue her, man. We're in California. Sue her," he said with a straight face.

Michael locked into his cold stare. "What?"

"Stranger things have happened," Nick replied, shrugging his broad shoulders like a silly gesture from a stand-up comic.

Was it that simple? Michael thought for a moment and bolted out of his chair.

"Hey, where you going? I was only kidding," Nick called after him as Michael walked past the questioning eyes of patrons and straight out of the restaurant.

* * * * *

It took no time for Michael to make it back to the KNRQ studios. He had a burning thought in his mind, and he was on a mission. Michael walked into the edit room. He was thankful to see Gabe still sitting in front of the edit machine. "I've got a project for you," Michael said as he approached him. "Are you busy?"

"I'm running Tecate's tape now for the eight o'clock teaser. Chandler's all over me about it."

"Don't worry about him. Can you do something for me?"

"You're the boss, absolutely. And only because you're not a dick."

"I need you to pull tape on this," Mike said and handed him a slip of paper.

Gabe looked it over. "Abortion? Court cases?" he said with a scowl. "What the fuck?" he mumbled to Michael, but his boss was already walking out the door.

*****

Sitting on the couch in his office, Michael took notes, still trying to formulate a plan of action as he watched the taped court proceedings on the monitor. But after a few moments, he paused the tape and placed his palms over his face. With the circumstances surrounding his life, he found it difficult to concentrate on the video. Instead, his mind traveled off in another direction. It was in a direction of another injustice of humanity.

He imagined the East German people lingering behind the wall, waiting to die, each hoping for a stray bullet to finally, once and for all, put an end to their suffering at the hands of tyranny. *Of all the times,* Michael thought, *why can't I get that off my mind?*

But his thoughts pressed on and asked the difficult questions. *Did they lose their will to live? How does this relate to my situation? Get off the subject, dammit!* So many souls longing to escape the imminent peril and unspeakable torment at the hands of their so-called leaders. How many died in silence, their bodies decaying in dark alleys and ditches? When did the rebellion begin against the Stasi and the Russian government? How did it start—with a rock, a gun, a word? He thought long and hard for the answer to his burning questions.

Then it struck him like a bolt of lightning spreading its crooked fingers across the dark sky. Survival! That's it! It's the basic human instinct: the will to survive.

Somebody took the first step, cast the first stone, and questioned the system. One voice questioning the system, saying, "This is not acceptable." Rosa Parks exclaiming a resounding *no*. It all started with one voice. One defiance. One *no*.

Struck by an epiphany, Michael rose to his feet. This was his East Germany, his war. He knew now what he must do! He was so in tune with his thought he was unaware of his own presence and the end of the tape rolling black-and-white snow on the monitor.

That's it!

That's what he was going to do—say, *No, that is not acceptable!* He was going to stand up for his rights as a father of an unborn child—his unborn child. He would become the voice unrecognized, unheard for decades by society—the voice of man.

The more he thought about it, the more he began to realize how little a man's voice was taken into consideration. Why does a man's voice mean so much less than a woman's when it comes right down to a fetus's right to life? Why is it only a woman's choice? It is not a life she created alone. So why does she have that innate right to pass sentence on something that she alone did not place there?

* * * * *

Standing in the doorway, Michael hesitated a moment as the last of his thoughts raced across his mind. He carefully weighed them out. Though confused and utterly disturbed by her actions of late, he let a brief smile crease his face when he found her looking out the window at the night sky. "Rain or shine, you're still looking up at the stars," he said softly.

Susan never turned, never flinched, at the sudden voice piercing the stillness of the room.

Michael waited, but she remained in silence. She knew his heart was shattered, but she was fighting with her own demons and continued searching for a way out, a parting in the clouds, any portal in the universe she could crawl through.

As she never turned toward him, he could not see the tears welling in her eyes.

"Where does this leave us, Susan?"

"I don't know, Michael. That's up to you, I guess." Her words were barely audible.

"Nothing is up to me. Remember, you're the one making all the decisions. You have this idea that I have no say in anything," he said rather calmly. "Not even the fate of my own baby," That last part started his heart pounding. He could feel the rage begin to scratch the surface. "Don't you think you should have told me before we got married that you didn't want to have kids? You knew I wanted a family. You knew how important it was to me!"

With the heartless shrug of her shoulders, he knew it was a lost cause. He wasn't going to get anywhere, not with her mind so set on a course of destruction.

"Will you at least wait a month and think about it?" he said pleadingly. Anything to buy more time. Anything that will give him time to figure out a way to stop her from going through with her awful plan.

She shook her head. "What will that do, Michael?" she said softly.

"This isn't a rational decision, Susan. Perhaps it will give you time to think and clear your mind," he said. "Susan, it's a life that you're taking away."

"I'm not going to change my mind, whether I wait a month or two months. I'm still having an abortion," she said in one long sigh. This was getting old to her, and she was growing tired of his attempts.

Michael felt it again, rage boiling just beneath the surface, ready to come out in a burst. "Why are you so insistent about this?" The cruel sound of defeat filled his voice.

"It's my body, Michael. And it's my right, my choice what I do with it," she said almost mechanically in a monotone voice. Then she shrugged her shoulders. That gesture almost sent Michael over the edge.

"You can't take my baby away!" he protested.

"You can't stop me."

"Fuck!" he yelled.

"I don't want to talk about this anymore, Michael," she said. Her face remained in a trance, her stare out the window, focused on some false hope in the sky.

An angry frustration seized him. "Yeah, that's right, sweep it under the rug. Maybe he'll forget about it," he said with blatant sarcasm. "Well, guess what, sister, I won't forget about it! And if you do this, I'll make your life a living hell, Susan!" Shit, he thought, he shouldn't have said that. But it was too late.

She craned her neck, and her eyes shot him with a look that brought shivers throughout his body.

Michael held her cold stare a long moment, trying to find some lucidity in her eyes.

Nothing.

Nothing at all. He nodded. "Okay. Okay," he repeated. "If that's how you want to play it, we'll go it your way." He stopped himself before he said something else he would regret. He turned and walked out of the room.

15

THE CENTURY CITY office was perfumed with the aroma of rich leather and dark rosewood. Hundreds of leather-bound lawbooks lined the shelves in open bookcases. Leather chairs and a matching couch added to the rich flavor of the room. This was how Michael had always imagined a high-end lawyer's office would look like.

Michael was speaking with animation, explaining his situation to the high-priced lawyer sitting across from him. The lawyer stopped him. "You want to do what?" he asked. He really didn't believe what he was hearing. An original smile swept over the man's face as he looked across at Michael. "I don't think I can help you. Frankly, you don't have a case. You will continue to hear that if you choose to pursue this. The courts are prohibited from placing an undue burden on a woman's decision to abort," the lawyer said as he stood up behind his desk.

Michael knew that the meeting was over right then and there. "How do you determine what an undue burden is?" Michael asked.

"That's the question the courts have been arguing about since this debate started. Sorry, Mr. Bishope, you just don't have a case here."

Dejectedly, Michael stood and extended his hand. "Thank you for your time."

* * * * *

Crossing off another attorney's name, Michael built a picket fence of red ink in the phone book. Moving down the list, he dialed another number and told the attorney of his case. Michael quickly held the phone away from his ear as bellowing laughter screamed into the earpiece. Frustrated, Michael hung up the phone.

Frustration slipped from Michael as he contemplated the consequences of his next move. Was there going to be a next move? All the doors appeared to be closing around him. Tapping the worry stone on the desk, Michael knew time was of the essence if he were going to take any action. Then it struck him, and he decided to roll the dice and take his chance. Placing the worry stone back on the desk, he started toward the door. Once there, he quickly turned and moved back to his desk, where he picked up the stone and left the room. This time, it was for luck.

*****

The crisp sound of the ocean-driven wind pushing through the palm trees snapped like a leather whip cracking in the air. Michael spun his head and looked up from the paper in his hand toward the sound breaking in the air as he walked out of the Santa Monica Courthouse. Seagulls swarmed, swimming in the salty air. Some landed on the green grass, scavenging as a homeless man tossed bread crumbs near busy Main Street.

Traffic noise flooded his hearing and mixed with the stagnant emotion lingering in his mind. A lawnmower roared nearby, and he felt it hard to concentrate with so many distractions. He needed to understand what he was about to endeavor. He took another deep breath, sucking in the salty air and exhaled his frustration, a momentary release as he sat on the bench.

"Last time I saw you, you were on your hands and knees, crawling out of my house," the voice said.

Michael looked up to find a dark shadow peering down at him. Though it was cloudy, he had to strain through the glare to make out the face. "Yeah, at the bachelor party, right?"

"Yeah. Tyson Nash," he said. "How you doing?" he asked with a nod.

This must have been the brother of the guy Michael met at the party. Lost was the gangbang attire. This guy was clean-shaven with the same slick sunglasses. He was as different as day and night, Michael thought. He still looked like he dabbled in mind-altering stimulants; not even a five-hundred-dollar suit could hide that.

"Michael Bishope," Michael said, holding out his hand. "I've been better."

"I remember. I never forget the name of someone I like," Nash replied as he shook his hand. "So what are you doing on my stomping grounds? Traffic ticket?"

"Nothing that simple," he said with a shallow sigh. "It's a long story."

Nash could sense the frustration in him and glanced at his watch. "I've got some time before court."

Michael studied him a moment and figured what the hell. He had nothing else to lose. "Why not? It's not like I haven't already been laughed at by a hundred other attorneys." He paused. "Why not one more."

Peering over his shades, Nash said, "You lost me there, bro." He sat on the bench next to Michael.

"I need a lawyer. And I need a lawyer now," Michael said with a heavy emphasis.

Michael started, slowly detailing his situation. Nash's facial expression was drastically altered. He interjected here and there with questions but let Michael do most of the talking. It didn't take long for Nash to grasp the enormity of Michael's desperation.

* * * * *

Sitting on the couch still littered with colorful paint splatters, Susan held her knees to her chest. Her face was pasted with an emotionless stare of a thousand dead souls. Her eyes held no life. She was born on an evil promise she kept so dear to her fearful heart.

Susan looked up, and her expression changed to one of curiosity as she tried to remember exactly why she came down stairs. She was truly lost, even when the doorbell echoed through the living room.

When the doorbell rang for the second time, Susan finally got up off the couch and walked into the kitchen. A moment later, she came back out holding a tall glass of ice water and a large butcher knife.

Susan sat back down on the couch. The doorbell rang again. Even when Renee called for her behind the door, Susan remained still and silent. Renee continued calling for her, but Susan was not about to move. "I know you're home, Susan," Renee called out. "I'm worried about you."

Again the doorbell rang. Susan was in no mood for company. She knew there would be so many questions she didn't want to account for nor had the answers to.

Susan leaned over the side of the couch and placed on her lap a white photo album. She opened the album and found her wedding photos. She tried to force a smile, but it didn't come. She continued through the photo album, slowly turning page after page. She wasn't really looking at the pictures; it was the mere physical act of turning the pages that seemed to fascinate her.

Suddenly she shouted in the empty room and slammed the butcher knife deep into the photo album. She threw the album onto the coffee table and ran toward the staircase and up into her room, slamming the door behind her.

*****

Blown away by Michael's story, Nash, probably for the first time in his life, was left speechless. He just stared at Michael. "Whoa! It sucks to be you," Nash said with a snipe before he continued, "This could go one of two ways. One, it could be one of the biggest cases since *Roe vs. Wade*. Laws could be rewritten, courts would be bombarded with new abortion cases on an hourly basis." Nash thought a moment. "And two, the judge denies your case, and I'm sorry to say, you lose your kid and your wife too, most likely," he said bluntly.

"I just want my baby to live." Michael's eyes begged for help. "Family has always been so important to me, and she knew that when she married me." Tears welled in Michael's bright eyes. "I lost my parents when I was a kid, and having a family of my own is the only thing I have dreamed about since I was a child."

Nash studied him for a moment. He wanted to tell Michael what he wanted to hear, that he was going to win the case—that he, in fact, had a case—but he couldn't lie to him. "I know I'm going to hate myself for this," Nash started, but his wide eyes betrayed his voice. Nash knew the potential grandeur of a case such as this, and he really didn't want to watch from the sidelines. He wanted to be at the helm, front and center of the numerous cameras he knew would clamor to such a case. Nash wanted the spotlight.

A perfect position indeed, one to promote his name and likeness across America's television screens. "You should know, I am a criminal lawyer. Your case does not fall into my expertise, but I think I can present an argument for you." Nash paused. "I'm great at research, and my motions are, if I do say so myself, brilliant," he said, brimming with confidence.

It was exactly what Michael needed—hope, a chance. A glimmer of light glistened in his eyes. "I go into court tomorrow," he said, holding up the paper in his hand.

"Tomorrow, yeah. You're going to have to go it alone, but that shouldn't be a problem," Nash said. "I have court myself tomorrow. Day zero of ten on a drug case, but it looks like the DA is going to accept a plea. If he doesn't, then I'll see what I can do about postponing the trial. Your case is a little more important than a two-time drug loser," Nash finished. He tried to build some hope within Michael, but inside Nash knew that Michael did not stand a chance.

Michael smiled. "Thank you."

"Nobody wants to argue an abortion case. It's a loser. It's probably the most difficult of cases. There's always a way in the back door. The trick is finding it," Nash said with a confident smile. "But I can do it."

It was exactly what Michael needed, someone blurting out total confidence and support. The life rushed back into his eyes.

"Why don't you give me a call tonight, and I'll walk you through your argument: what you will need to say in court tomorrow. The judge will deny your injunction, but make sure he sets another date, and I'll be there," Nash said as he glanced at his watch. "I have to run. Call me tonight."

"I will," Michael replied and shook his hand. He watched Nash walk into the courthouse.

16

Walking into the courtroom, Michael took no notice of the only other person sitting in the gallery, a young man with wire-rimmed glasses sitting on the aisle. Michael passed the man as he approached the plaintiff's table. The man took notice of Michael and jotted down a short note on a writing tablet.

Cameron O'Brian, the lone man in the gallery, looked bored to hell. He glanced at his watch. This was nothing—a big, fat nothing story, and he knew it. He knew his being there was a colossal waste of time.

Holding his breath a moment, Michael stood silent before the imposing room. He was greeted by voices of the past that still lingered, trapped in the space he was sharing. These walls held secrets, nasty lies, and judgments. Michael's blood ran cold as the strange visions entered his mind. He snapped himself back to the here and now.

Not exactly sure of what to do, Michael asked the bailiff, who pointed him to the clerk, a saucy older broad with dirty-blonde hair. She was sitting to the right of the judge's bench. She pointed Michael to the plaintiff's table, where he took a seat. He tried to remember everything Nash told him to say, but he was already lost. With this being a very private matter, Michael wondered if there were going to be more spectators in the gallery. He hoped not. He was embarrassed enough as it was.

The burly bailiff soon stood and addressed the courtroom in a rather demure voice, not a voice that matched his massive frame. "All rise. The Superior Court of the County of Los Angeles, the State of California, is now in session. The Honorable Harrison M. Fields proceeding," the bailiff called to the courtroom. "All who have business before this court step forward and make yourself known."

On cue, the judge entered from the side door. Michael's vision took in his entrance in slow motion. He noticed every detail of the judge's honest face, his thinning hair and glasses. He watched the way his black gown flowed like liquid silk.

"You may be seated," called the bailiff. He moved over to the side of the room and stood sentinel by the judge's entrance.

Michael watched as the judge glanced through some papers. His pulse came rapid and strong as he waited. He had no idea what he was going to do. Momentarily, he questioned his own sanity. He fought hard to remain in his seat. He lost his train of thought as the clerk approached the bench. The judge was probably in his late fifties, Michael thought. His face held wisdom and compassion. Michael was relieved to see such a sincere-looking man behind the bench.

Looking up from the paper, Judge Fields dialed in a quick focus on Michael as he shifted slightly in the tall leather chair. "Bishope versus Bishope. Mrs. Bishope is not present?" he asked, looking directly at Michael. Michael was surprised by the heavy tone of the judge's voice, strong and steady. The sound commanded respect, and Michael almost instinctively snapped to attention.

"No, Your Honor. She is not," Michael replied.

Judge Fields nodded slightly. "All right." He looked back down at the papers in his hand. He quickly refocused on Michael with a questioning pause. "You're seeking an injunction to prevent your wife from having an abortion?" he read aloud with a skeptical glare.

Hello, O'Brian said to himself. He was now awake and paying attention.

"You can't be serious?" the judge asked, looking at Michael. The judge thought he had heard it all, thought there was nothing that would surprise him. But, indeed, he was surprised, and he couldn't wait to hear this one. He began twirling the pen between his fingers like a baton with perfect rhythm, never missing a beat, a finger or a twirl. It was a trick he had been doing for years behind the bench.

"Hoooo-leeee-shit! Now that's a story!" O'Brian said. He thanked his lucky stars for the mysterious phone call from an old buddy that directed him here this morning. He became suddenly alert and alive with a bright spark reignited in his hazel eyes. He pulled out his minirecorder and waited for more.

"Yes, Your Honor. I am quite serious," Michael replied. All of a sudden, he felt like the enemy wearing a target on his back. Michael swallowed hard before he drew his next breath.

"On what grounds do you bring this before my court?"

"Your Honor," Michael began, "my wife and I have been married less than a year, and we just found out that she's pregnant. Now instead of informing me that she was pregnant, she informed me that she was having an abortion—"

"That's her right, Mr. Bishope. It's her body," the judge interjected firmly.

"Yes, Your Honor, but my question is, Does she not have to gain my consent if we're married before she has an abortion? Do I not have any say in the matter? Do I not have any rights?" he asked.

The judge peered over his glasses and smiled. "I commend your convictions, Mr. Bishope. Most men would welcome her decision."

"Not when having a family is the most important thing to him," Michael replied. "And she knew that before we got married. She knew how much I wanted a baby."

"I don't know if you are aware of the enormity of a judgment in a case like this. It would be groundbreaking," the judge said.

"If it helps the biological father have the slightest say in the matter of his own unborn child, it would all be worth it, don't you think?"

"My opinion is not relevant here."

"Yes, it is, Your Honor. It may be the only relevant voice to stop a child's murder," he said, pleading with his eyes.

An enormous smile swept across O'Brian's face as he held up his microrecorder. Quietly, he moved three rows closer and sat directly behind Michael, who was unaware of his presence.

"There always has to be a first voice, Your Honor," Michael continued. "Someone to stand up and challenge the system. Abortion was illegal before *Roe vs. Wade*, and now look at our value system. It's used as a form of birth control. That's not what *Roe v. Wade* was about," he said with a pounded fist. Michael was suddenly alert, alive, brimming with passion that came out of nowhere. Having come into this with no clue, no idea what the hell he was going to say, he felt as though he were presenting a strong argument. "I'm not for or against abortion. I can see both sides of the issue and all the morality and humanity that comes with it. But I think in certain cases, an informed consent that of the legal husband and father of the unborn child should be required."

The judge reached for a book on the bench and never broke rhythm with the shiny pen, still twirling it between his fingers.

The clerk gave Michael the once-over, but he did not notice her eying him. Nor did he see the wheels turning in the bailiff's head, trying to put himself in Michael's shoes. What would he do?

"Again I applaud your convictions. Unfortunately, ideals alone will get you nowhere, certainly not in my courtroom," the judge said, looking directly across at Michael. But Michael wasn't deflated by the stern look the judge gave him. It was somehow encouraging to him, though he did not know why.

Judge Fields was beside himself with the case before him. Having sat on the bench for the better part of twelve years, he had never heard of such a case. He had always wanted something different than the everyday, run-of-the-mill divorce and custody battle, and this was it. But he knew there was no way this could go any further than it had come now. Inside, he wished there would be precedence for him to hear a case such as Michael's.

"Abortion was illegal before somebody did exactly what I'm doing now—standing up and fighting for my rights," Michael said with verve. "The laws changed then, but they neglected to include the voice of the other participant in the pregnancy."

"Are you trying to make a stand against the system or just showing me what you have learned from the internet?" the judge asked. A slight smile spread across his face.

"Your Honor, right now you can call me selfish. I'm fighting for me, for my baby. The baby I helped create, a part of my body. It was not her alone who gave it life. After all, that's what it is right now, life—"

"We're not debating that, Mr. Bishope."

"But if it helps other men, other potential fathers, gain equality, the rights that none of us have presently, then yes, I guess I am standing up against the system," Michael said. "But my baby first!"

O'Brian was giddy with joy, soaking up Michael's misery, recording his passionate plea. He couldn't believe the case he was hearing and the story it was going to create. He always dreamed of a page 1 story. He knew the ramifications of the story and knew this was his best chance at a page 1 column.

Judge Fields smiled. "I think you would make one hell of a lawyer, Mr. Bishope. Your arguments have potency, and that, I assume, is without any professional training. I think with a little digging, you just might attain what you're seeking. What you need, Mr. Bishope, is an injunction, and I am not going to grant that here today." Judge Fields pulled off his glasses and peered in at Michael. "Abortion is a very difficult subject to argue, especially from the angle you're attempting, and that's with the most seasoned attorneys. I'm not saying it can't be done, mind you. You will need to hire a lawyer, Mr. Bishope. This is far too complex to argue this yourself."

"Tyson Nash, counsel for Michael Bishope," Nash called out to the judge as he made his way down the aisle of the gallery.

Cameron O'Brian nodded to Nash as he walked by. *Oh, how the plot thickens,* he thought, as he watched Nash saunter over and stand next to Michael. He was relieved to see Nash. Michael wasn't sure if he had anything left.

"You work fast, Mr. Bishope," the judge said with a smile. "Nice of you to join us, Mr. Nash," he said sarcastically. "My court started twenty minutes ago!"

"I apologize, Your Honor. Won't happen again," Nash shot back quickly and flashed his glistening yellow smile.

"Your client was doing one hell of a job, but you're going to have to come in here with a presentable case I can rule on," the judge said, looking at them both.

"Your Honor, at this time," Nash started, "we would like to request under expedited schedule, due to the nature of the case, forty eight hours for discovery."

The judge held his gaze on Nash a moment, trying to figure out how the hell they were going to approach this. "I'll bite," he said, nodding. Looking down at his docket, the judge glanced back at the duo. "I'll see you back here Thursday at 10:00 a.m."

"Thank you, Your Honor," said Nash.

"I feel for you, Mr. Bishope. It's a sad thing when the biological father has no say in this type of matter. And it's a sad fact in this country that men just don't have any rights in a case such as this. But it is her body, and thus renders outside interference by government null and void. Come back and show me something, Mr. Bishope. Put your convictions to work, and I'm sure you will find an avenue for your attorney to argue a case before this court," said the judge, slamming down the gavel. The look he gave to Michael was encouraging.

The judge was gone in an instant, out of the room like dust in the wind.

"You impressed the shit out of him. That's good. This guy likes you," Nash said.

"He probably like's me because I'm not a bloodsucking, scumbag lawyer," Michael replied with a bright smile.

"That's good, Mike. I gotta write that one down," Nash said. Nash looked over his shoulder and nodded to O'Brian, who got up and walked outside into the corridor. Nash turned back to Michael. "You and I are going to have to pull a rabbit out of thin air, my friend. And we're going to have to do it within two days. Still remember where I live?"

"Yes, I think so."

"Be there at eight. I have to meet another client now," Nash said and shook Michael's hand. "We'll talk about money then. You know what bloodsuckers are going for nowadays," he said with a smile and walked out of the courtroom.

Michael was slow to gather his things. His heart was pumping adrenaline through his veins. He sat for a moment and took in the courtroom. He felt good. He wondered a moment what it would be like to be a lawyer. Would he have the patience for such an endeavor? He felt proud that he stood tall in the face of adversity.

Walking down the corridor, Michael had a little extra hop in his step. He stopped a moment and took a drink from the water fountain. Looking up, his eyes fell upon Nash talking to O'Brian at the end of the long hallway. Thinking nothing of it, Michael turned and walked out of the courthouse.

* * * * *

THE DAMP WEDNESDAY-MORNING paper lay on the wet grass like a soggy rag. The June sky held its gloom, blanketing Los Angeles with a gray layer hovering overhead. No rain, just a shitty day. No sun in days.

Walking out of the house in his bathrobe, Frank Chandler's bony, white, chicken legs dangled beneath his faded-blue terry-cloth bathrobe. Chandler looked up at the sky and smiled. Gloomy, rotten days did it for him; it was his sunshine.

Chandler reached down and picked up the morning paper and glanced around the neighborhood—nothing new; he didn't have to keep up with the Johnsons today. With a shit-eating smile, he flipped open the paper as he started walking toward the house. Suddenly he froze in his tracks. A look of utter shock spread across his white face.

As he looked at the small page 1 column with the byline "LOS ANGELES MAN SUES WIFE OVER ABORTION," a glimmer of light flickered in his beady eyes. His smile became broader and brighter than any kids on Christmas morning standing in front of a tree full of colorfully wrapped presents. Sinister thoughts danced in his mind. This was his lucky day. There was to be no more biding his time. He had his ammunition, and Michael was his target. He quickly scurried his way back into the house. Needless to say, old Frank was going to be in the office early on this glorious day.

* * * * *

It was only when Michael was away from the house that Susan dared to venture out of her room; only this time, she stopped halfway down the stairs when she laid eyes on Macy sitting on the couch as if she owned the joint.

"What are you doing here?" Susan asked.

Macy craned her head and looked at Susan. "Waiting for you, honey," she replied.

"How did you get in?"

"Your husband invited me in as he was leaving. Said you'd be down in a while."

"What did he say to you?" Susan asked as she entered the living room and walked directly in front of Macy.

"We really didn't talk much. For obvious reasons, he's not too happy right now," she said.

They stared at each other for a long, uncomfortable moment. "So?" Susan asked abruptly.

"Don't shut me out, Sussie. You need me," Macy started. "We're in this together."

"What do you want, Macy?" Susan was short and harsh with her words.

Macy was taken off guard by the severity of her friend's tone. She paused a moment and looked deep into Susan's eyes. She knew it would not be long before Susan broke eye contact. "You know what I want, Sussie."

Susan huffed and walked over to the table and dragged the wooden chair across the floor and sat face-to-face across from Macy. "If you've come to talk me out of this, you're wasting your time."

"Honey, you're never a waste of time," Macy replied. She reached for Susan's hand, but Susan pulled away from her attempt. "Come on, Susan. We're as close as two people can be. We grew up together. I was always there for you, just like I am now," she said with a daring plea.

Susan studied her a long moment before her eyes went cold. "You're a friend I had long ago, Macy. I haven't seen you in years," she started and paused. "That was a long time ago, Macy. Things have changed. I've changed, and so have you."

"No," Macy replied. "Nothing has changed. You're still the same person."

"Not quite," Susan quipped.

"You still have the same fears."

"No."

"They haven't gone away, Susan."

"Whatever."

"And I am still here for you."

"Where were you for the past ten years?" Susan asked. She was becoming heated. She was in no mood for any of this.

"I never left, Susan. You did," Macy said as she got up off the couch and circled around Susan. Susan's eyes never came up off the floor. She felt as though she was about to explode. "And when you left, yes, things changed, but nothing changed between us, Susan. What you are confusing with change is all your past you tried to bury. All the things you don't want to remember. But that's all you did, honey, is bury them. They're still there, and you know it."

Susan sat there in abstract silence, staring into the nothingness that lay in her field of blurred vision. Macy moved into Susan's line of sight and smiled. Her piercing green eyes stared into Susan's mirrors of green. They were sad eyes, and Macy hurt deep inside. "Susan, nothing about you has changed." Her voice sent shivers through Susan's body.

Susan continued her somber stare, just waiting for Macy to leave. She wanted to be alone so she could embrace her infinite sadness without interference. "This is bigger than both of us," she said in a long sigh. "It's not about the past, Macy, or what you think happened." Susan stopped and lowered her head. She clenched her teeth. She had had just about enough.

Macy had already started pacing in circles in front of Susan. "Susan, I was there. I remember everything." Macy began making odd hand gestures as if she were rapidly counting on her fingers. Suddenly she turned and came toward Susan. "I was the only one you could turn to," she said quickly. Susan appeared startled by Macy's deliverance. "Do you think your husband will understand your past?" Macy held her gaze into Susan's absent eyes.

Was that a threat? Susan thought, but it faded quickly. Macy was frustrated as she held her stare, but then she couldn't resist. She reached in and stole a quick kiss from Susan.

Susan didn't so much as move. It wasn't the first time Macy had kissed her friend. She used to do it quite often way back when the curiosity of youth was too much to bear. Susan never minded then, and she suspected she didn't now.

Macy smiled. She knew she got away with it once again. She moved a few steps away from Susan. "They don't make friends like me anymore, Sussie," she said as she again started pacing. "Appreciate it, Susan. Appreciate what I am to you. Be thankful that I love you, Susan. Embrace me and let me help you through this."

Macy stopped and waited, hoping for a certain response she knew wasn't coming. There held a poisonous silence that shook the air. Susan exhaled slowly. "Why did you kiss me?" Susan asked quietly.

Macy held her slightly twisted smile a moment longer than needed. "'Cause I wanted to." Her reply was childlike and innocent. "I wanted to feel you again like I used to. You're just not there anymore, Sussie. I wanted to feel you enter my heart and dance inside my thoughts like you used to," Macy said as she knelt at Susan's feet. "I've been dead without you in my life all this time. But you have brought life back into my eyes and allowed me to see what really matters," Macy said, trying to stop Susan's inner voice from breaking all the rules.

"Why?" Susan asked. Tears continued pooling in her eyes.

"Because I love you, Susan. I always will." Macy tried to embrace her friend, but Susan brushed her away. Macy felt the harsh rejection that almost broke her heart. She held her gaze a moment. She couldn't believe Susan would push her away so abruptly. Frustrated, Macy started for the front door. Her posture and gait were twisted and full of dejection.

Tears came fast and hard to Susan's eyes. "I love you too," she said softly to herself as Macy exited the house.

* * * * *

Walking into the beachfront condominium, Michael was reborn into the surrealism known as the home of Tyson Nash. A little less messy and a lot less intoxicated than the night he first experienced it long ago but still a psychedelic landscape nonetheless.

The same twisted thoughts and visions returned to him as he glanced around the cluttered room. Unanswered questions that lingered from his first visit still haunted him. It again reminded him of the surrealist artist Salvador Dalí, whose art was created after a horrific vision of this apartment, as if the artist was trying to poke out his own eyes. But nothing could recreate the image of this chaotic apartment; not even the confusing movements of Dalí's paintings could do this place justice.

With the midnight hour rapidly approaching and the court appearance just a few hours away, Michael and Nash continued formulating a plan to take into court and shock the world.

Michael took notes as Nash read aloud from a lawbook and mumbled incoherently. Nash was sitting in a tall captain's chair he rummaged out of the dumpster. Nash looked up from the book and sighed dramatically. "I need to know it all, bro—your relationship with her, your sex life, the life you had before you were married. I want to know your habits, her habits. Does she drink, smoke? Does she have any skeletons in her closet? Does she have a criminal record?" Nash asked promptly.

Michael looked confused. He was not sure he wanted to divulge any information that wasn't necessary. Nash could sense his reluctance.

"Hey, look, do you want to keep your baby or not?"

"Yes, I do."

"Then I need to know everything."

Michael searched Nash's chalky-white face. Michael sighed. "I think she needs help," he said finally.

"Psychological help?"

Michael knew Nash was sharp, but when he saw the gleam in his eye, he knew he was on to something. Nash swung his chair around and moved for a lawbook on the shelf. Nash smiled as he opened the book and read a moment. Michael waited and tried to understand what the hell was going on. "And with that, the gates of Oz will be a lot easier to breach."

"What do you mean?"

"That, my friend, means this is possible," Nash replied. "What has she done to make you think she needs help? What have you seen? What have you heard? What has she said?" Nash asked quickly in a salvo of questions. He was on a roll. "Does she hurt herself? Does she sleepwalk, talk to herself? Does she see people who aren't there—"

Nash's comment struck Michael's face with certain conviction. Nash caught his facial expression and knew it hit a chord. "That's it, isn't it?" Nash asked.

Michael lowered his head and thought a moment.

"If you want to win this case, you need to tell me everything, whether it hurts or not. Look, we don't have much to stand on here. We need everything we can get."

Michael nodded. "She talks to people as if they were there, imaginary people. She holds conversations. She's had a few episodes like that," Michael said quietly. "She destroyed the house, the couches, and the floors."

Nash continued writing notes on a yellow legal pad.

"We were in bed…" Michael's voice trailed off.

Nash waited. He could see that this deeply troubled Michael.

"It was like she had supernatural strength. Like she was somebody else. He voice, her mannerisms, everything about her was completely different," Michael said as he looked at Nash.

Nash wasn't looking for answers to her twisted psyche. He was looking for a way to stop her from having an abortion. That's all he cared about: winning the case. He agreed to handle Michael's case without a clue on how to approach it. He was thrilled by the challenge it presented and for the notoriety he would gain from such a case, win or lose. He didn't care much about what Susan felt or how to find help for her. This case was special, and he knew it.

"We're going to go with the mental issue then," Nash said as he shelved the book. "From what you've said, it sounds like she's schizophrenic, and if that's the case, it's possible that the judge will allow for a psychological evaluation."

"What good will that do?" Michael asked.

"That, my friend, will buy us time," Nash replied.

17

Gray skies above showered the landscape with a light coating of warm summer rain. Not the enchanting rain of summers past. This was a dark penetrating rain that announced its presence and foretold of gloom on the horizon.

Michael noticed the two satellite trucks when he pulled up to the courthouse but thought nothing of it. Perhaps they were there, he thought, for the handful of protesters, perhaps one hundred, gathered on the wide thatch of grass near the street, yelling at horns blaring from the passing cars. "Honk if you're for this or that." From his moving vantage point, Michael couldn't quite see what their signs said. He continued into the rear parking lot.

A handful of people, reporters mostly, and cameras were gathered at the end of the corridor. Michael heard the commotion as he entered the courthouse and glanced ahead with curiosity. He had been in the business long enough to recognize the boom mics and the Sony Beta cams and bright lights. Once the reporters caught wind of Michael's footsteps echoing throughout the hallway, they swarmed him, coming at him all at once, a giant mass with their questions, microphones, lights, and cameras.

"Michael, do you hate your wife?"

"Mr. Bishope, are you trying to change the laws set by the state?"

"Do you think your case will have any effect on *Roe vs. Wade*?"

"What right do you have to tell a woman what do with her body?"

"Why are you doing this, Mr. Bishope?"

"Are you gay?"

"Are you willing to take your fight to the Supreme Court?"

"Which men's group do you represent?"

"Are you pro-life?"

"Do you believe in God, Mr. Bishope?"

Michael stood there dumfounded; he was floored. This was the last thing he wanted. How the hell did the media find out? This was a private matter. He felt he was doing the right thing and didn't want to bring any attention to the case. Michael tried to push his way through the reporters but stopped in his tracks as another question came from somebody he recognized very well.

"Mr. Bishope, Samantha Rain from KNRQ," she said halfheartedly. It was clear she wanted no part of this story. Michael felt like he had been shot in the chest. He shook his head bitterly and shot her with a distasteful glare. He felt betrayed by his own people. And he had a pretty good idea of who sent her. "Do you think this trial will affect your job as vice president of news programming at KNRQ?" she asked with a shrug, like she was forced to ask that particular question. A disgusted look remained on her face as she waited for his response.

"I have nothing to say," he replied with a contemptuous glare. He roughly pushed his way through the crowd and entered the courtroom.

Walking into the courtroom, Michael again stopped in his tracks as his eyes fell on a packed room, not an empty seat. There was a buzz in the air. People spoke to one another with an extraspecial feeling of excitement. It was just one of those rare stories that had the potential to explode into a wildfire. A hush fell upon the room as the spectators in the gallery became aware of Michael's presence and held him in their sights. Their faces blurred and melded together in his state of shock.

Michael wasn't ready for this. He stood motionless in the aisle. His eyes were frozen in thoughts of flight. He felt the scrutinizing eyes on him. He was paralyzed with fear.

As Michael's legs began shaking, the silence broke in the room, and people began muttering quietly. Michael snapped out of the trance and started walking straight for the plaintiff's bench where his lawyer awaited him. Michael felt numb and disoriented, like he was in a drunken stupor. He glanced back at all the blurred faces and immediately recognized the angelic face of Nick's mother, Mrs. Vach, standing in the front row, directly over his shoulder. She held the best smile she could manage. It was a smile for his comfort, letting him know that she was there for him.

Michael approached her. "Lisa, how did you find out about this?" he asked.

"Michael, it was in the newspaper yesterday and again this morning. Haven't you read it?" She looked at him apologetically, as if she were sorry for knowing his secret.

Michael looked on, all the while weighing the consequences in his mind. But the look on his face rendered him speechless.

Michael gave her a look that thanked her for coming. She understood and smiled as Michael turned back to the bench. But something once again caught Michael's eyes. Turning his head, he found his boss, Frank Chandler, standing also in the front row with a shit-eating grin. Michael passed through the knee-high gates and approached Chandler. "What's going on, Frank?" he asked with a questioning look.

"Just reporting the news, kid," he blurted. "And guess what, you're it!" he said with malice and his best evil smile.

"Frank," Michael started, "this is a very delicate situation. You have no idea what's going on here. It doesn't need to be publicized." Michael glanced around the gallery.

"Somebody had to cover the news," he said casually. It was a bit too casual for Michael's taste. He knew Chandler had it in for him. "That's what we do, report the news. And I made sure it went out on the AP wires this morning," he said with a smile.

"You smug, arrogant son of a bitch! Where's your loyalty? We work together for Christ's sake!"

"You're on your own agenda, kid. You've always been a loose cannon, and I knew one day you'd fuck up." Chandler moved a little closer and lowered his voice to a whisper. "We're going to make you a star, Mike," he said with a grin. "We're going to make you a household name."

Michael was floored. Even as Nash placed a hand on his shoulder, Michael glared at Chandler with contempt. "You know, when I'm through here, no matter if I win or lose, I'll know that I fought for something I believe in."

"What's your point? Because you're starting to bore me."

"My point, you pretentious prick"—Michael started with fire raging in his narrowed eyes—"you do what you think you have to do because when all is said and done here, I'll be able to live with myself, and you'll still be an asshole!"

Chandler smiled and turned to sit in the gallery seat, where he held his unblinking stare on Michael.

Michael watched him with evil intent dimming his pupils. Again Nash pulled at his shoulder, trying to gain Michael's attention. When Michael turned to face Nash, his eyes were lit with anger.

"You need to calm down and not listen to these pricks. You're going to get a lot of shit throughout this whole process because it's become news—"

"And how did it become news?" Michael asked, accusing him with his eyes. He was throwing daggers into the wind, and he didn't much care where they landed.

Nash didn't care for the accusation, even though he was most likely responsible for leaking it to the press. "Hey, reporters know everything that goes on with the courts. They have plants in every courtroom, and this happens to be a major news story. The press is not going to let this go by without coverage," he said, leading Michael to the plaintiff's table. "So just chill, okay? If anything, the media could be a good thing for us."

"Oh yeah? And why is that?" Michael asked as he reluctantly sat next to Nash. He still wanted to tear somebody's eyes out.

"Because it will build sympathy. Not to mention, the pro-life advocates will jump all over your bandwagon and ride you for the duration."

"I don't give a shit about that!" Michael felt himself becoming more disgusted by the whole situation. "I'm only here because I want my baby to live! Nothing else," he said in anger, almost yelling the last part.

Nash shot a concerned glance toward the gallery, then back to Michael. "You need to calm down. Court is about to start, and this place is filled with reporters. You don't need to be misquoted, you got that?" Nash was becoming upset himself. "You have any talking to do, it will be done through me. You say nothing to nobody. You got that?"

Michael turned toward the bench and sighed. He wasn't ready for this. He always felt bad for the people who were at the center of the media storm, but never really knew how they felt until now. Michael knew how the game was played; he fanned the telltale flames many times. He had sent out reporters to hound the "newsworthy," the latest "poor sap" caught in the media blitz. He sank slightly in the leather chair. He could feel the reporters' eyes dancing off his back. He could hear them punching the keys of their laptops. Oh, how he wanted to stand up and shout, *GET THE FUCK OUT OF HERE AND JUST LEAVE ME ALONE!*

Nash placed his hand on Michael's shoulder in a comforting gesture. Michael heard the clicking shutters of cameras exploding behind him. He could only imagine what the papers would say about him the following morning. *DON'T YOU PEOPLE UNDERSTAND? THIS MIGHT BE MY ONLY SHOT AT A FAMILY OF MY OWN!*

Again he wanted to run and forget the whole thing. But the thought of holding his child in his arms kept him focused. He had to follow through with this. He felt sad for the fact that he had to go through this sickening process just to become a father. It was going to put Susan through hell. He prayed for her forgiveness.

Michael's heart quickened as the bailiff entered the courtroom through the side judge's entrance. The bailiff paused a moment and looked at the crowd. He wasn't expecting such an audience. He moved into the courtroom and moved directly in front of the judge's bench. "All rise," he shouted above the dim roar of the spectators. Silence fell upon the room as the audience drew to attention. The harvesters of gossip were gathered with their mighty pens poised, awaiting all the juicy tidbits. "The Superior Court of the County of Los Angeles, of the State of California, is now in session. The Honorable Harrison M. Fields presiding," the bailiff called to the courtroom.

Judge Fields entered with his head down, but he glanced up before he sat in the leather chair. He was taken aback at the number of people gathered for his only court case of the morning session. “You seem to draw quite a crowd, Mr. Bishope,” Judge Fields remarked as he sat behind the bench.

Michael wasn’t sure how to react.

“You may be seated,” said the bailiff.

Judge Fields addressed the courtroom first. He lashed out at the numerous reporters and announced that this court will be closed to the press.

When the judge made that statement, Chandler stood up in the gallery. The man next to him, Timothy Doria, dressed in a spiffy black Italian suit also stood.

Doria was the lead attorney for KNRQ Television and somebody Michael knew very well. He was a maverick in his own right. He had always gained television access to closed trials for KNRQ exclusives. He knew the law and how to slip through the cracks. He was the absolute best in his field. That is why Michael hired him.

Doria and Chandler appealed to the judge for a separate hearing to allow cameras in the courtroom.

Judge Fields was a bit upset by somebody challenging his decision, but he glanced at his schedule. He was somewhat beside himself. He was not used to having a crowd such as the one before him. “Seeing as this case will be under an expeditious schedule, you have today at four o’clock.”

“We’ll be ready, Your Honor,” Doria said. Both he and Chandler returned to their seats. Chandler wore a look of confidence whereas Doria was somewhat apprehensive about the whole situation. He, for the first time in his illustrious career, felt dirty, felt as though he just now earned the reputation so bestowed upon lawyers: a scum-sucking bastard. He slouched slightly in his chair.

“I’m going to allow this circus until I have a chance to hear arguments. I will not, however, tolerate any outbursts. This is a court of law,” Judge Fields said. He looked down and flipped open his laptop on the bench. He looked across just as he had done a thousand times before. Never was it on a scale of this size, and never before was there this much at stake for all parties involved, even for him. "*Bishope versus Bishope*," he started and paused a long beat. "Mr. Bishope. You are seeking a preliminary injunction to prevent your wife from having an abortion," Judge Fields said, looking directly at him.

"Yes, Your Honor," Michael replied with encouragement from Nash.

"You do understand the enormity of a case such as this. In doing research, my clerk and I have not found precedence, so whatever the ruling, this would be a first." The judge paused for a moment, then leaned back in his chair. "Mr. Nash, blow me away."

Tyson Nash stood up. "Thank you, Your Honor." A flurry of cameras flashed in the gallery.

Slamming his gavel down, Judge Fields silenced the spectators. "Let me remind you," he said, "this circus will not continue! I will not tolerate any further outbursts in my court! That means no more photos. If this circus continues to be a distraction, I will have you all escorted from my courtroom. This is a court of law. It is not a forum for demonstrations or inappropriate conduct. There will be order in my courtroom, or it will be closed." He shot his stern look around the room. "Now you may continue, Mr. Nash."

"You Honor," Tyson started with a thank-you nod, "life…when does it begin?" He paused for effect. He knew the reporters would eat it up. "Is it when the child is born and takes its first breath of air, or is it as the point of conception? And if there were two people present at the time of conception, then why, with respect to the unborn child, is it the choice of one sole individual? Is that not playing God itself?"

A buzz spread through the gallery of reporters as the judge took his own notes. Nash knew he had the attention of the reporters; they were the jury he was trying to win over.

"We believe—and our argument will attempt to show—that life begins at the very moment of conception."

"And how exactly will you show that, Mr. Nash? That's been the stumbling block of the entire debate since 1973."

"Because the fetus grows!" Nash replied without respect, which surprised the judge. It wasn't an answer he was expecting, and he certainly wasn't expecting the condescending manner in which it was delivered. "From day to day," Nash continued, "the fetus grows. Because it does so, it, like every other living thing on earth, can and should be considered life. This life already has its own unique set of DNA, which contains a complete blueprint for its whole genetic makeup. Its whole psychical future will be determined—short, tall, fat, or thin. The sex of the fetus is already determined at the time of conception, eye color, everything."

Michael was shocked to hear this come from Nash's mouth. He had no idea he was so articulate. Michael was impressed beyond words, and his hope was slightly gaining momentum with each spoken word.

"We know it is life because it is growing and changing—every day." Nash paused to read his scribbled notes. "Your Honor, simple morality dictates that unless and until someone can prove the unborn human is not alive, we must give it the benefit of the doubt and assume it is alive. Thus, it should be entitled to life, liberty, and the pursuit of happiness."

Judge Fields flipped through a lawbook on his desk, glancing at the text a brief moment, but never missed a beat.

"Throughout history, we as a society have a sad legacy of dehumanizing those who get in our way or have something we want. Once a group of people is dehumanized, it is very easy to justify their mistreatment and destruction. Such is the plight of the unborn child." Nash paused a moment to catch his breath. A few chuckles were fired off in the gallery, but the stern look from the judge silenced them.

"Abortion will continue to be trivialized as the lesser of two evils. Perhaps even a necessary evil, as long as it is allowed to remain an invisible obstruction. In this case, Your Honor, we ask that you make it visible and let the two people involved each have an equal say with regard to the pregnancy as it was, in fact, created by both parties and not solely by the mother, who holds all the cards. It was a choice they both made at the time of conception—an unwritten agreement, if you will." Nash had no time to pause; he was throwing down the gauntlet.

"Consenting adults who engage in sexual intercourse, each know the possible consequences of the act and also know that the whole physiological purpose of intercourse is to get the woman pregnant, even if there is a slew of other reasons they are consenting to have sex. The fact is, each person consented. A stranger did not rape Mrs. Bishope—her husband impregnated her. They consented to the physical act of sex. They consented to any consequences that might lie thereafter, including becoming pregnant. The mother and father, in this case, consented to the woman getting pregnant by having sex."

"You're becoming redundant, Mr. Nash."

Nash held up his hand as if to apologize. "They consented to having a child and to care for that child until it is old enough to take care of itself. This is the agreement my client and his wife—his wife, Your Honor," he repeated for emphasis, "made when they both consented to have sex." He paused, but not for the reporters. For a brief moment, he forgot about the news monkeys behind him as he was lost in his own passion. Perhaps he didn't realize the power of what he had just blurted out to the world until he actually said it.

"Your Honor, we ask that you let God be the invisible stranger and not give his power to the person carrying the child," Nash said. He turned toward the reporters. He knew his argument was going to make the news, especially after clashing church and state. He knew this taboo subject was going to be the start of his fifteen minutes of fame, and he was going to make it last as long as possible.

Judge Fields motioned for his clerk to approach the bench, where he leaned over and handed her a slip of yellow paper. Nash waited for the clerk to leave the bench and watched with lustful eyes as she walked out of the courtroom.

"So you're saying that they should both have the innate power of God?" she said with a smile. "What exactly are you grasping at, Mr. Nash? Because right now you're shooting blanks."

"I'm saying in a democracy, the power of many outweighs the voice of one. Why should one person's voice be the final say in anything, especially when there are two people invited to the party, when each was a willing partner?"

"Three people, Mr. Nash."

"Yes, Your Honor, but I was referring to the time of conception when an unwritten agreement was reached between the two parties."

Nash folded his brow as a thought dashed into his mind. "And if in three people, you mean the unborn child, Your Honor, then isn't that an answer as to where life begins?" Nash looked on, waiting for a response, but then thought better of it. "Strike that, Your Honor. I was just thinking out loud," he said.

Judge Fields held his stern glare on Nash. It was a loaded question. The reporters waited anxiously for his answer, but they knew he couldn't answer it. Judge Fields wasn't quite up to speed on the ramifications on his answer, though he had a pretty good idea of the backlash that would rain down no matter what kind of educated answer he gave.

Nash flipped through his notes and read a moment. Judge Fields continued his heated glare. He was not happy with that question, and everybody felt his uneasiness. "Your Honor," Nash said, looking up, "in today's society, there are two sides to this topic. Why is that?" Nash asked with a confused look etched into his face. It was a baited question, and he wanted him think about it. He really wanted to belittle him, to see just how far the leash was, but Nash held his gaze short of cutting him.

"Because there are only two sides to the issue, Mr. Nash." His voice was heavy with displeasure, and the thickness of it lingered and choked the air.

"Wrong! And I mean no disrespect, Your Honor."

"Make your point," Judge Fields said. Indeed, he felt Nash's glare; and combined with his loaded question, the judge wanted to throttle him with a contempt order. But deep down, he admired Nash, admired his passion, and he was actually buying the argument. Judge Fields was once a passionate young attorney himself and saw a lot of himself in Nash. That's why he allowed Nash to walk on the knife-edge.

"We have pro-life fighting for the birth of the child, that's one side. We have pro-choice fighting for the rights of the mother, that's the other side. What about the third side? There is a third side—it's the side of the forgotten person. Who, Your Honor, is out there fighting for the rights of the father? Why was he left out of the equation? Where are his rights? Who is there to fight for him? Were his rights lost with his ejaculation?"

"Unfortunately, he does not have any when it comes to a woman's body and her choice to do what she wishes to do—with her body."

"Why not? He created the life that is in her body," Nash said and watched as the clerk reentered the courtroom carrying a stack of lawbooks to the bench, where she placed them to the judge's left. The judge leaned back in his chair, thought for a moment, and said nothing. The festering seed of anger was planted deep by Nash, and he could see it working on the judge's mind.

Silence strained through the courtroom. All waited for the judge's answer. It never came. Nash held his gaze upon the judge with hopeful eyes.

"For the very fact that you cannot answer the question is the reason we are here."

"You're not going to push me into a public answer, Mr. Nash, no matter how clever you think you are. I never said I cannot answer the question," Judge Fields said sharply. "It was a very loaded question, Mr. Nash. You seem to be full of them this morning."

"It's a loaded question for the politicians wanting to choose the side with the most voters."

Judge Fields leaned forward and peered over his glasses. The glare he gave told Nash that he was coming dangerously close to cutting himself on the blade he was dancing on. Nash quickly changed his tone.

"But here, Your Honor, we are not buying votes. We are not running for political office. We are fighting for the life of my client's child. Though it's not breathing air, the fetus is a living and growing entity. Its blood is already coursing through its tiny veins. Please, Your Honor, base your decision on the merits, better yet, the morals presented here and not the uproar and ramifications that such a decision could lead to. This is a life. I implore you to respond to it as such," Nash said with the last of his breath, the last of his passion. Michael was so impressed, so inspired, he wanted to stand and applaud him.

Glancing up at the clock, the judge nodded to his clerk. "This would be a good time for us to break. I would like to explore a few points of interest that were brought to my attention," he said. He looked down at his docket, then back up and addressed the court. "Court will resume at one o'clock." With that, he slammed the gavel and moved from the bench and walked out of the courtroom.

Reporters rushed, almost tripping over one another out of the courtroom to get a head start on their story, to be the first in line to interview Michael and Nash as they exit into the corridor where the reporters would be gathered for the feast.

*****

Chandler felt especially joyful. This was good stuff, better than he expected. He knew this would destroy Michael, something he had been waiting to do since he was first hired at KNRQ. He never had the power to fire him, but did his best to make his life a living hell. A proud smile creased his face as he watched the reporters multiply. This was going to be a media horse, and he was going to place his best reporters on Michael's back day and night.

Chandler caught a glimpse of Samantha Rain, sitting on the stoop outside the courthouse. Bloated with entitlement, he walked over to her and huffed. "What the hell are you doing?"

"This isn't right, Frank. Michael is one of us," she replied. "He's family."

"I really don't care about your personal feelings. You're a reporter, and it's your job to report the news," Chandler barked. He moved in closer to her. "He's the news. Make him famous."

"I want to go on record that I am against this. I want off this story," she said sharply.

"I don't care what you want. I am in charge of this station, and if you want to keep your job here, you will report what I tell you to report when I tell you to report it," he threatened. "I want your report on the midday news. I don't care what you have to do to make it happen!"

"I'll file your report, but I'm not going to bury Michael. Whatever this personal thing is you have against him, that's between you and him. You have no right to make it public!" she said, returning his spite before she turned and walked away from him.

"You can't have scruples in this business," he shouted after her. "You gotta go for the throat!"

* * * * *

The pack of reporters were poised, chests expanded in full pride when Michael and Nash exited the courtroom. That's when the blood hit the shark-infested water, and the feeding frenzy started. Rapid-fire questions nailed Michael's ears. Camera bulbs exploded in his face. Screaming voices echoed, mixing into a confused blob of noise in the corridor. Nash tried his best to shield Michael. He tried to place himself between the cameras and Michael, exactly where Nash wanted to be. Nash looked forward to the press corps. He longed for the attention and the praise he knew he would receive. Back in law school, he always dreamed of trying a case in the media.

"Michael, do you think you have a chance of stopping your wife?"

"What gives you the right to think you have any say in this? It's her body!" a woman reporter shouted.

"Mr. Nash, what do you think your chances are? Do you think you will win an injunction?"

Playing it up for the cameras, Nash smiled. He held up his hands to quiet the noise before he spoke. "I think we have a good chance—"

"How do you think this will effect *Roe v. Wade*?"

"Mr. Bishope, do you hate your wife for putting you through this?"

"Whoa! Let's stop this now. For the duration of the court process, please direct all your questions to me. Michael Bishope is a private person. I have directed him not to speak to reporters, not even his own reporters. If his reporters don't have a chance, neither will you, so don't ask," he said with a smile, trying to gain the side of the media. "Mr. Bishope is an unwilling victim here, and we're trying to stop a great injustice of humanity from incurring. Mr. Bishope has chosen to stand up and fight for what he believes in. He has chosen to try to stop a murder. Because when it comes right down to it, it is, after all, a murder. It's a murder of an innocent living person."

The gathered sharks ate up the gospel by Nash. Tyson Nash had a hunch that he was on national television at that very moment. He wondered if it was worldwide yet. Then he wondered how long this case would take to go global.

"Mr. Bishope is a stand-up guy. He is a respected member of the community, and believe me, this is the last place he wants to be. All he ever wanted was a family. All he ever wanted was a child of his own with the woman he loves dearly," Nash said. He knew he was giving them great fuel to fire the debate. This was the start of something, all right, he thought, an explosive debate with major ramifications; and Nash was going to be just where he had always wanted to be—front and center of the media storm.

"Mr. Bishope, how do you feel about your wife?" a reporter asked.

Michael looked at Nash, who nodded.

"I love my wife. She's my life," Michael replied.

Nash stopped any further questions. "I'm sorry, but that's all for now. We have a case we need to prepare for. We'll have a statement later," Nash said as he led Michael through the gauntlet of reporters and past a flurry of unanswered questions that hung in the air. Michael and Nash entered a private attorney's room and shut the door.

* * * * *

Judge Fields briefly glanced at the notes he made in chambers. "Mr. Nash, on your argument regarding the unborn child's state of, quote-unquote, life, which has not been proven by science, do you have case law to back that up?" He asked.

"Yes, I do, Your Honor," Nash started. "But that's not our only citing. We have another argument, and we believe it's vitally important to this case."

"We'll get to that," Judge Fields stated with a hand gestures.

Nash nodded and retrieved a sheet of paper from the desk in front of Michael, who looked wrecked from the day's wares.

"*Aka v. Jefferson Hospital Association Inc.*," Nash started. "The Arkansas Supreme Court ruled that a fetus *is* a person in a wrongful death lawsuit brought by a man whose wife and unborn child died during birth procedures. In reversing a lower court, the Supreme Court cited a 1999 law that altered the state's criminal code to include a living fetus of twelve weeks gestation in the definition of a person. The case stemmed from the December 13, 1995, death of Evangeline Aka and her unborn son."

"How far along is Mrs. Bishope?" Judge Fields asked.

Nash looked at Michael and nodded. "She's right at fifteen weeks, Your Honor," Michael said firmly. "This has been a tough decision for her." A buzz spread through the room of reporters. Michael heard the jostling of papers and pencils. Lead against paper clandestinely filled the room.

"She's quite a ways along," Judge Fields said to himself and wrote a note.

Nash continued, "'Given this amended definition of 'person,' the legislature plainly affords protection to unborn fetuses,' Chief Justice W. H. Arnold wrote for the court," Nash stated while reading from his notes. "A circuit judge ruled in early 1999 against Aka's claim, citing a Supreme Court ruling that a fetus was not a person in wrongful death actions. Later that year, the legislature approved a law specifying that an unborn fetus could be considered a person for some purposes in criminal law.

"'The relevance of the legislature's response, by statutorily defining person in the criminal context to include a fetus, cannot be understated,' Arnold wrote. In a dissenting opinion, Justice Robert L. Brown said he agreed with the lower court ruling that viable fetuses are not considered persons for purposes of wrongful death cases. 'The majority's reasoning is inconsistent and extremely hard to justify,' Brown said. 'A decision of this magnitude requires clarity and direction and not a patchwork quilt woven from desperate statutes, constitutional provisions, and Supreme Court decisions.' Brown said he believed the public policy shift didn't occur until this year with the passage of another law specifically amending the wrongful death statute to include a viable fetus in the definition of a person. The act was approved April 4, 2001." Nash finally looked up from the paper and searched for a sign, but Judge Fields was a rock. He knew not to show any such emotion, especially when he was on the horizon of a media blitz.

"Also, *Webster v. Reproductive Health Services,* 1989. The Supreme Court said a Missouri law that declares 'the life of each human being begins at conception' and that 'the unborn child at every stage of development holds all the rights, privileges, and immunities available to other persons' was unobjectionable as long as Missouri did not use this to restrict abortion."

Nash could sense that he was on to something. He knew he was at least wowing the reporters with shit they didn't understand. But what he needed was the prize trophy: the judge himself.

Nash decided to shoot for the moon. "A woman was convicted and sentenced to twelve years in prison for killing her unborn child by using crack cocaine during her pregnancy," Nash started. His eyes were unblinking as he looked up at the judge.

"Granted, hers is an entirely different situation than that of which we are arguing, but ponder this," the lawyer said as his eyes returned to the page. "'The verdict marks the first time a woman in the United States has been found guilty of homicide for taking drugs during pregnancy.' Now I ask you, Your Honor, if she was, in fact, convicted of homicide for killing her unborn child, then wherein lies the question as to whether or not the fetus is alive? If it is not, then why was she convicted of homicide?" Nash said, looking up at the judge. "I can cite the whole case for you if you like." Nash held up a stack of papers.

Michael shot him with a look of confusion. He knew Nash was holding a stack of blank papers.

"That's not necessary, Mr. Nash."

Michael smiled. Nash played his best poker hand and won.

"Case law, state law, federal law—this unborn child is alive!" Nash said dramatically for emphasis.

Judge Fields ignored Nash's dramatics. "You had something else?" Judge Fields asked.

"Your Honor, the reason for the ubiquity of abortion is, in part, its universal availability. Abortion is legal through all nine months of pregnancy in all fifty states. *Roe vs. Wade*, 410 U.S. 113, 1973, established the right to abort, but *Doe vs. Bolton*, 410 U.S. 179, 1973, ruled at page 192 that no abortion could be prohibited if sought to terminate a pregnancy which threatens a woman's health. The court defined *health* so broadly as to include 'emotional, psychological, familial, and age-related factors,' which made it functionally impossible for any government to prohibit any abortion. It should also be noted that the supremacy clause of the US Constitution nullifies state law to the contrary."

"And this is in reference to what?" Judge Fields asked.

"We don't believe that Mrs. Bishope has the mental capacity to make such a choice."

Judge Fields peered over his glasses. "You just stated federal case law, Mr. Nash. 'Impossible for any government to prohibit an abortion, etc., etc.," Judge Fields stated.

"Yes!" Nash started with a bang. "But the statute fails to address a third party from stopping her."

The gathered crowd looked on with a collective look of confusion. A few reporters smiled.

"We believe Mrs. Bishope to be psychologically impaired and grossly lacking the mental capacity to make a clear and concise choice with regard to her pregnancy. We further request that she be ordered held for a 730 psychological evaluation until such matter can be resolved," Nash said as he reached for a sheet of paper, which he immediately held up. "Your Honor, this is a petition to declare Mrs. Bishope incompetent and to declare Michael Bishope her legal guardian."

"I'm not hearing any petitions at this time, Mr. Nash," Judge Fields said quickly, then paused, looking down at the bench. He had a feeling Nash might pull that card. Hell, that's what Judge Fields would have done himself if he were arguing the same case. He admired Nash's fire and passion and was impressed at the depth of his argument. Nash seemed to have covered his bases very well. And with a few more years behind him, he's going to be one hell of a lawyer, Judge Fields thought.

Michael and Nash held their collective breath. Nash had a feeling that he just pulled a rabbit out of the hat.

There was a long pause in the courtroom as the reporters waited for the judge's response. They had already formed their stories they were going to file and couldn't wait to hit the computer and get in front of the camera. This story was becoming bigger and bigger with every spoken word.

"I am inclined to give you the benefit of the doubt, but not for the purpose of stopping Mrs. Bishope from choosing her right to choose what she does with her body. It is her choice and will always remain so," Judge Fields said and paused briefly. He returned his eyes toward Nash. "What you have given me, Mr. Nash, is a passionate argument and a lot of unanswered questions. And quite frankly, they are questions I feel need to be answered. This issue is far too important and complicated to not have clear and succinct answers, and frankly, I am sick and tired of this topic being bandied back and forth while so many victims suffer with horrific consequences. I want this issue to come to a head, not only here but also nationally and worldwide. Therefore, Mr. Bishope, until one week from today, when I have a chance to hear from Mrs. Bishope, you have your injunction."

The courtroom erupted with anarchy, which the judge quickly halted with the slam of his gavel, slamming it repeatedly on the bench to quiet the crowd.

"I am appointing counsel for Mrs. Bishope, and the week should give new counsel appropriate time to become acquainted with the case."

Another buzz spread across the courtroom. This story was going to explode across the country within minutes, and every reporter knew it. And soon the Santa Monica courthouse was going to be the focal point for the hottest legal topic of our time.

Judge Fields sounded off with his gavel, ending the day's court session.

Not quite sure what just happened, Michael looked at Nash, who was beaming. This was an epic decision, and Nash knew it. He was already counting the future money that was surely coming his way. He leaned over and told Michael what had happened, which brought a smile to his face.

Chandler was already on his cell phone, making sure this story instantly went nationwide with breaking coverage. Michael was about to become the most famous person in Los Angeles, and Chandler would soon have his vengeance. Michael could not, would not, survive this media blitz that Chandler was about to throw down on him.

Nash was anxious, glowing with giddy anticipation to give a statement to the throngs of media. He was going to be the new poster-boy lawyer for the pro-life movement, and the rewards were sure to follow. He said a parting word to Michael and left him alone at the table. One of the few remaining reporters left in the courtroom began taking photos of Michael sitting alone, head down at the table.

Michael's happiness was not long lived as a thought crashed into his thoughts of fatherhood. He became disgusted for a moment with his chosen career. Up until now, he never had to face what the other guy had to face: the scrutiny of the camera and the ruthlessness of the relentlessness of the reporters. He never knew what it was like to have his life seen through a fishbowl. He never really thought of the other guy before, the guy his own ruthless news crews hounded day and night just to get the story. That's all that mattered back then, the big story. Now Michael was doing something most people had never done: he was walking in the other guy's shoes, and he was having second thoughts and feeling sick of what he did for a living.

18

A MELANCHOLY CLOUD of emotion lingered in the stagnant air of the living room as Michael sipped Johnny Walker Red from the clear highball glass. He could still hear the lingering crowd, reporters mostly, gathered on the street outside his house. He could only imagine how his neighbors were filling the crimson-color gossip mill, another freaking media circus in their righteous neighborhood. They had been through it before with that football player and wanted to stay away from any further bullshit in their backyard.

Michael glanced up now and then with sad eyes. He could hear Susan moving about in the room above. He was sure that she had no idea what had transpired in the courtroom. She hated watching the news on television, and he was sure that she hadn't watched television at all lately. He wanted so much to run upstairs into the room and embrace her. He wanted so much for this to be just a bad dream, the worst. No matter how many times he tried to understand her reasoning, he just couldn't come close to her train of thought.

Michael became startled as the doorbell shattered the silence. He turned toward the door and moved stealthily from the couch and walked across the room like a burglar on the prowl. He felt foolish for having to creep around within his own house. Nevertheless, he continued his clandestine movements across the room and stopped quietly behind the front door and peered through the peephole. He blew a sigh. Unlatching the door, he quickly ushered Nick into the house.

"It's a fucking zoo out there!" Nick said. "Reporters are everywhere. CNN is out there—in front of your house, man."

"It's been like that since I came home from court."

"You've opened a major can of worms here, bro," Nick said. "I saw my mom on TV! What's up with that?"

Michael nodded. "It was good of her to come," Michael replied in a subdued tone Nick was unfamiliar with. Michael tried to smile, but it just didn't come out right. "Thanks for doing this," Michael said with a deflated sigh.

Nick sensed his frustration, and he knew this was killing him. "You know you can always count on me, no matter what it is."

"I know," Michael replied as he walked over to the table and flipped open his briefcase and handed the subpoena to Nick. "She's upstairs," Michael said in a slight murmur.

Nick followed his gaze. "Yeah," Nick said halfheartedly as he grasped the document. This was the last thing he wanted to do. He loved Susan and felt a rush of guilt that trembled throughout his body. But Michael was his brother. He had to be there for him; he had to do this deed. "So where you sleeping these days?" Nick asked for lack of something better to say. He was trying to delay the inevitable.

"Spare bedroom," he replied with a nod. "Guess I should move out until all this is settled."

"Might be a good idea," Nick said as he looked up again. "Well, I guess it's gotta be done. I just feel so dirty," he said with a shiver.

Michael nodded as Nick started walking up the stairs.

* * * * *

Drinking from the dark long neck bottle of Pete's Wicked Ale, Nick looked disgusted as he stared at the television. The evening news showed Michael and Nash walking out of the courthouse with a bevy of reporters in tow. Flipping the remote, Nick found that every channel was locked onto Michael's court case. He knew the blanket coverage of another highly publicized court case would only heighten America's trivial resolve.

Renee walked briskly into the house and slammed the door behind her. She was in a huff and tossed her dress jacket on the floor as she kicked off her heels. "Have you heard about Susan and Michael?" she asked as she approached Nick and kissed him on the cheek. "I heard it in the car, and I couldn't believe it. This can't be true, could it?"

Nick pointed to the television screen and flipped through all the channels that were covering the story. Various photos and videos of Michael were on every news station, even his own. "Oh my God," she said with a gasp and covered her mouth with her hand.

"It's been on all day," Nick said.

"I can't believe this," she muttered.

Nick sighed as he drank the bottle of amber ale. He held up the bottle. "Wanna drink?"

Renee only stared at the screen. "I better get over there. She'll need somebody to talk to," Renee said. "I can't believe Michael is doing this. It's not like him at all."

"What's that supposed to mean?" Nick asked with an inquisitive glare. He wasn't in the mood for anything tonight. He still felt sick to his stomach for serving Susan with the subpoena. "She's the one who wants to have an abortion."

"Yeah, and she has every right to," Renee replied.

"What about his rights?"

"It's her body, Nick. She can do what she wants with it. It's her choice."

"Is he or is he not the father?" Nick roared.

"So what if he is?" she shouted back. "He has no grounds to stand on here, Nick. This is a joke. It's her body. It's her choice! He's gonna lose his ass in court."

"With her stance, Susan is using abortion as a birth-control method, and that's fucked up."

"That's a bunch of crap," she said angrily. "Wait, what do you mean with her stance? You knew about this?" Renee asked with a questioning glare. She never did miss much, and Nick had a feeling she wouldn't let that one slip by.

Nick lowered his head and sighed. "Mike told me last week." He looked up at her with soft eyes, trying to somehow avoid the brawl he felt coming on. "Look, Renee, there's a lot more to this than you might think. It might not be a good idea for you to go over there right now," Nick said quietly.

"I don't understand you, Nick. You knew about this, and you didn't tell me! How could you keep something like this from me?"

"Michael came to me in confidence. What could I do?"

"You son of a bitch!"

Nick broke eye contact and shook his head. He knew this was not going to get any better. He took a long drink from the bottle.

"Susan is my friend too, Nicholas!" Renee was pissed. She was on the verge of a total meltdown. "Don't you think you should have told me?" she said, shooting him with a blistering glare.

"No, I don't! Michael had a problem, and I was trying to be a good friend and be there for him when he needed me. You think he wanted the whole fucking world to know about this?"

"Her problem is much more important than his," she said.

"Oh, and how is that? Her problem is his problem!"

"Because she's the one who is pregnant, not Michael! It's her body that has to go through hell, no matter what she does!"

Nick was at a loss for words. He wanted to knock her out with his response, but nothing came to him. Then he remarked, "You women are such hypocrites. You bitch, moan, and cry for equal rights, and not only do you get them but you also take rights away from us men."

"That is bullshit, Nick, and you know it! Men have just as many rights as women do," she said.

"Okay, so where are Michael's rights?"

"He doesn't have any."

"Why not?"

"Because he's a man!"

Nick folded his brow. He knew she had slipped. He jumped on it. "You just said that men have just as many rights as women!" he shouted. "Make up your mind. Do you understand what you're saying?"

"Men have the same rights as we do, but not when it comes to a women's pregnancy! It's her body!"

"But it's his child."

"So what!"

"Isn't he entitled to rights too?"

"Are you not listening? It's her body!" she shouted in anger. She was pissed. She quickly looked around for something to throw, but she thought better of it. She seared him with a scowling glare.

"It's his baby she's trying to kill! Michael's baby."

"How can she kill something that is not alive in the first place?" she asked.

"It is alive."

"It hasn't been born yet, therefore, it's not alive, Nick!" Nick hated the way she said his name with such spite and hatred. "It's just a blob of mass." Renee threw up her arms. "You'll just never understand any of this."

"Why? Because I don't agree with your point of view?"

"Yes!"

"You don't make any sense, Renee." Nick said. "Like I said, you're a hypocrite. Your argument is not only bullshit, it's downright stupid."

"You're impossible," she shouted as she started for the front door.

"You shouldn't go over there," Nick called after her.

"Fuck you!" she shouted before she slammed the door behind her.

* * * * *

Tyson Nash opened the front door like a vampire emerging from his dark resting place. His eyes lit up with the clear blue sky and the salt air. But looking across the sandy beach and the rolling tide, the horizon held its gloom, only hours away from its arrival. Again it was coming: the June gloom coming to cover the city with its dark presence. *I am the darkness of the creeping mist. I come to you with not a hand but with a fist.*

Living on the beach, Tyson Nash was becoming tiresome of the June swoon. The gray skies were lingering a little too long this year. Reflecting on years past, he could not recall a clear June. It seems as though every June had been gloomy in the past since he had lived there.

Nash started out of his house, turned left, and began walking up Speedway Avenue toward Washington. It wasn't long before joggers, roller-bladers, and bicycle riders were craning their heads as they passed Nash. They recognized him but couldn't quite place from where they knew him. He must be famous, perhaps an actor. Others knew he was at the center of the courtroom storm. Nash knew it too, and it was for that very reason he ventured out of his domain this early in the a.m., so that he could soak up his newfound fame, or at least see what it generated.

Turning the corner onto Washington, he walked into the Coffee Hut, or as Nash affectionately called it, "the stink hut," where tragically hip people gathered and considered coffee to be a hobby: it was the hip and cool thing to do. A place where everyone dressed the same to show what an individual they want to be. Nash wasn't really into the latest mocha, half-double twist sensation with a splash of this and a hint of that crap. He thought it was a joke and couldn't believe how the coffee companies fool the general public into spending $9 on a cup of crap. He didn't even like coffee; the mere smell of it made him want to puke. He found it quite humorous that all these "individuals" paid a small fortune for something that stinks so badly. But he knew this was the place to be in the morning, usually very crowded. Just as it was when he walked into the joint.

If it wasn't for Nash's driving passion to be seen as a quasi-celebrity, he would have never ventured down here; it just wasn't his thing. His agenda on this day was the morning paper to see just how big a celebrity he had become.

"Aren't you that lawyer?" a young blonde girl asked him. She was a stacked vixen, plastic everywhere and legs up to here. "You were on TV this morning. The abortion guy, right?" She spoke with an accent that he couldn't place, but he could care less; he was hooked like a fish.

Nash was instantly in love with his fifteen minutes of fame. Never before, as far as he could remember, had a woman like that even given him the time of day. He decided then and there that he was going to slowly sail his fifteen minutes of fame for as long as the boat would stay afloat. "Yes, I am. Tyson Nash," he said as he extended his hand for hers.

"I watched you yesterday, and wow—I mean, wow—you sure are a good lawyer," she said with a sincere, bright fuck-me smile as she playfully batted her baby blues.

Some of the other patrons sitting in and around the stink hut, out-of-work actors and the highly insecure, took notice of Nash standing in line. Some approached him and offered their two cents on the case. One lady was visibly upset with Nash over his defense of Michael, saying that he had no right to tell her anything: it's her body, and it is her choice. Nash informed the lady that, that was her opinion and that the freedom of speech gave her the right to spout it off. He also added, rather bluntly, that he didn't give a shit about her opinion.

"I'm not in this for who's right and who's wrong," he said to the lady. The crowd was growing around them. He knew this was another stage for his voice, and he made it loud. "I'm in this because my client's baby is about to be killed," he said loudly, playing to the crowd. A few people cheered and applauded. Some shouted, "Right on!" "You tell her!" and other nonsensical gibberish.

"Michael Bishope's dream is about to be sucked out and sent out with the trash," he said. Again the lady tried to speak, but Nash cut her off with a bitter scowl. "Have you ever seen a photo of an aborted fetus?" he asked. "Do you know how developed it is at ten weeks? How about twenty weeks? Do you know how bloody it is when the doctor throws it into the trash can? That's where it goes, you know, in the trash like a stinking diaper."

"It's her right. She's a woman in control of her own body. Nobody, not even the government, should have the right to tell her otherwise."

"For your information, it is not legal to kill a baby in the United States." Remembering that he had not brushed his teeth this morning and his dragon breath was thoroughly offensive, Nash moved a little closer to the woman as she spoke. He wanted to rub her the wrong way, more than he already had—wanted to push all the buttons on this little insignificant spec of a person.

"At this stage, it's not a baby," the woman responded. "Our semantics at play again. *Baby* is a relative term. I don't believe that a few ounces of cellular matter makes a person. If you do, I wonder why you're not clamoring over the lack of research into the mind-boggling rate of spontaneous abortion."

"Spontaneous abortions, when the woman knows she is pregnant, are grieved. I know that those who want to believe that abortion doesn't cause emotional pain do not understand that it does. Maybe it is less painful for a woman who didn't want her baby to believe it is not a human being, but when you wanted a child, then a miscarriage, even an early one, hurts because this is a human baby even though it's not fully formed," Nash said in one long breath.

Nash knew he had the upper hand, especially with the growing crowd seemingly behind him. Nash was in an invincible mood and wanted to shoot for the moon just to see what his newfound fame would let him get away with. "How many abortions have you had, lady?" he asked. The woman gasped along with the crowd. "How many babies have you killed?"

"That's none of your business! You're a sick man!" she said with venom.

"Maybe I am, but you're the one who wants to glorify another woman's abortion. You want to turn her into a murderer. What does that make you?" Nash glanced around the crowd. They appeared to still be on his side. Nash continued, "Did you feel guilty when the doctor threw your baby into the trash can? Or should I not be speaking in the singular?"

She raised her hand as if to slap him but stopped herself as she looked around the room and the crowd awaiting the outcome. She shook her head. "I hope you lose," she said and was confronted by another stink-hut patron.

"Look, lady," said a young man in a dark suit, "abortion is murder. God gives life to us. If you choose to have sex, then you must be ready to face the consequences. God has given you the miracle of life and the blessing that baby could be to you. If you kill it, then that baby's life is on your hands. You are now a murderer. Why is your side so blind to the fact that taking a life of an innocent fetus is murder?"

Oh, this is beautiful! Absolutely fucking beautiful, Nash thought inwardly. He could see the flames of the debate growing right in front of his eyes. This was going to grow minute by minute with giant leaps and enormous bounds. Emotions and heartstrings were going to rise and fall like the stock market. He was so thankful that he once hosted a little insignificant bachelor party.

The lady looked around at all the faces who were all talking down to her. She knew she was outnumbered and wasn't going to get her voice heard. She turned without saying another word and pushed her way through the crowd.

"I guess she didn't like the coffee," Nash said with a smile. His comment generated laughs from the crowd. People began shaking his hand, one after the other.

The national debate was born in the media and now living on the streets and on the breath of John Q. Public. Nash could sense the eye of the storm coming with a furry, and he loved every minute of its anticipated arrival.

* * * * *

Glancing toward the window by the front door, Nick could see the gray skies coming inland, blanketing the landscape with its darkness. He too was growing tiresome of the gloomy weather and longed for the customary Southern California sunshine.

Nick couldn't find much coverage on Michael's court case, though CNNs morning show had a brief comment on the subject, which held his attention for a moment. Nick quickly sat up on the couch as the front door opened quietly.

Renee walked over and stood above Nick on the couch.

"Where have you been?" Nick asked.

Renee looked at him a long silent moment before she answered. "I've been with Susan," she replied and continued staring at him.

"I take it you're not very happy."

"What the hell were you thinking, Nick? How dare you do something that underhanded," she said with a raised voice.

"Michael needed my help. I couldn't say no," he replied. "I'm sure you would have done the same thing for Susan."

"That's beside the point," she said.

"No, it's not, Renee! You would have done it without thinking about what I or anybody else thought."

"But Susan is my friend!"

"She's my friend too!" he shouted. "And I feel like shit for doing it!" His voice was hot and dangerous.

"So why did you then?" she asked with wild eyes.

"Susan hasn't answered the door in weeks. She doesn't even come out of her bedroom anymore. There was no other way of serving her. Michael had to be there to let me in," he said firmly. "Didn't he let you in?"

"Well, yeah," she said quietly, but changed with the quickness of a rattlesnake. "But that doesn't change the fact that you did this to her!"

Nick threw up his hands. "Look, what do you want from me? I did it, it's done. It can't be undone, so what the hell do you want?"

Renee said nothing as she moved across the room and sat on the chair near the sliding glass window. "I want you to care," she said, lowering her voice. And for a moment in her somber softness, her eyes reminded Nick that she still loved him.

"I do care, Renee," he replied. "Susan is a dear friend of mine too, but I grew up with Mike. I was there when his parents died. I cried with him. My loyalty will always remain with him. And right now he's in the middle of something I wish he never had to go through, and I have to stand by him," he said with a compassionate look.

"What he's doing in not right."

"You can make the same argument about what Susan is doing."

"No, you can't. It's her body," she said, raising her voice.

"If you're going to stay with that stance, Renee, we are just going to get into the same unwinnable argument," Nick said. "Look, maybe you're right. Nobody has the right to tell her what to do, but there is always going to be two sides to this." Nick lowered his voice a bit. "Your opinion will always be your opinion, and mine will remain mine. Your side will always be wrong, and so will mine, and that's because nobody can agree on this issue."

Renee leaned back in the chair and curled into a ball, folding her knees to her chest. Nick tossed the blanket aside and remained on the couch, waiting as the silence wrapped around him.

"So the only thing that remains now is, where do we go from here?" Nick asked. "What do we do?"

"I don't know," Renee replied.

* * * * *

The Santa Monica courthouse had become the center of the storm that the local weatherman didn't see in his seven-day forecast. The storm had nothing to do with the June swoon. This storm had already past the horizon and was rapidly approaching hysteria. Even though court was not scheduled for the day, the place was crowded with people protesting, chanting, and carrying signs: pro-life on one side and pro-choice on the other, each with numbers in the hundreds. Religious groups protected by the cloth, mingled in the middle.

Reporters gathered for the feast, standing on the outskirts, fanning the fire. Their enticing seven-course meal was standing before them, waiting to be cooked, carved, and devoured by fat-bellied kings with their cameras and microphones. This was going to be a feast of epic proportions.

People were pushing and shoving, yelling and screaming. Cursing. Racial slurs. Chanting. This was not a civilized society in which they protested life, love, peace, and choice. This was the verge of sheer madness, hate, and promised violence. Camera crews were having a hard time trying to keep up with the fast-paced commotion between the two sides as each jockeyed to get their camera time.

A man roughly pushed through the crowd, knocking over an older man, and approached a female reporter. "Abort all the little snot-nosed brats, for all I care! The world has far too many of 'em in the first place! The human race is like a roach infestation," said the man. His face was red as he shouted his statement. Foam was gathering on the sides of his mouth. "Ya ever stop to think that the abortion of a welfare baby-to-be may prevent that child from growing up and killing someone else?" he looked directly into the camera. The anger in his eyes frightened the female reporter. "Guys, if you wanna have sex, wear a condom! Women, if you get pregnant and you know you can't support the kid, do the world a favor and get a freaking abortion. It's that simple!"

The man paused, but only long enough to catch his breath. "A fetus is no more intelligent life-form than a cow. Cows are slaughtered every day for human consumption. Is abortion murder? Who gives a damn! God knows we need some legal form of population control."

The reporter's mouth was agape as she listened to the seemingly deranged man spewing his angered stance on abortion. She could not believe what she was hearing, but before she could respond, the man faded back into the surging crowd and disappeared from her view.

People were carrying all sorts of signs: PRO-LIFE, PRO-CHOICE, PRO-DEATH, BABY-KILLERS, STOP ABORTION NOW, WOMEN DESERVE BETTER THAN ABORTION, NRLA, and NOW (National Organization for Women). There were hundreds of different signs in a wide array of vivid colors. ABORTION IS MURDER waved above the crowd. KEEP ABORTION LEGAL.

Heated arguments between the two sides continued back and forth as the police tried to keep order. Both sides lobbied shots and arguments back and forth as the camera crews and reporters tried to keep up.

19

It came to pass in the events of her mind as they caught up with her present and threatened her future. The demons she had always feared were here now, expecting her to pay homage to their cunning resistance. They were caterwauling, demanding entry to her vision. They demanded to be seen and heard.

The night was still, stagnant, and pierced with fear. Susan appeared worried; her head was bleeding with voices from within, throbbing with the pressure of so many thoughts, so many faces and so many memories. Only she knew the significance of this conundrum that was about to unfold, and only she knew (or thought she knew) just how far its lurid fingers would spread. It was playing out before her mind's eye, pouring out from her inescapable past and into the macabre dreams of her ambivalent waking present.

Events from Susan's past life, which seemed so distant, so concealed, were unfolding now. Suppressed memories came rushing back like a flashflood sweeping across the barren desert floor, destroying everything in its path.

* * * * *

Michael walked across the room as the doorbell rang for the second time. The last thing he wanted to do was face the reporters who had been hounding him all day, repeatedly knocking and ringing the bell. He had had enough. With all the reporters and satellite trucks parked on the street in front of his house, he was sure his prissy neighbors were at the lynching stages. They weren't about to have any more of this nonsense in their neighborhood, not after the fiasco with the ex-football player.

As the doorbell rang again, a voice called out, "Mike, it's Nash," Nash said from behind the door. Even still, Michael took the precaution to look through the peephole. He wanted to be absolutely sure. He knew firsthand how clever the news jockeys could be.

Michael opened the door hastily and quickly led Nash into the house, shutting the door quickly behind him. "What are you doing here?" he asked.

"I'm your attorney. That means my job never stops. Not even on a Sunday afternoon. Besides, your phone is off the hook."

"Yeah, so what do you want?" Michael asked abruptly. He wasn't really in the mood for Nash's rambling bullshit about how great he was.

Nash took a step back. "Bad mood?"

"Sorry," Mike said with a sigh. "It's this whole thing, man. It's driving me crazy."

"No worries, bro. Hey, listen, you working tonight?"

"No," Michael responded, but he was riddled with dejection. "I took a few weeks off. Well, at least until all this dies down," he finished.

Nash knew that things were not going to die down for quite a while. This hornet's nest was just beginning to buzz with anger. He knew there might be a lengthy appeal process, and they could eventually approach the US Supreme Court. Secretly, that's what Nash was hoping for, a trip to the big dance. But he knew that was a long way off, and there would be a definite resolution to the case before then. Michael's life was going to change in the most profound way, and Nash just didn't have the heart to tell him that his life, regardless of the outcome, was never going to be the same again.

"I've got something that might really help our case," Nash started. "But it's going to take a lot from you. It's going to take an open mind." Nash gave him his best serious look.

"And what is that?" Michael asked, reluctantly.

"Larry King wants us on his show. Tonight." Nash could sense Michael's displeasure. "Before you say no, just hear me out."

Michael nodded slightly.

"As much as you don't like it—I know you don't want to do it—but this is where we have to win the case, in the media, the court of public appeal. That's how we're going to get the public sympathy behind us. This is exactly what we need, Mike."

Michael sighed and sat on the backside of the couch. "I never wanted this to go public in the first place. You know that."

"It's important that we humanize you. See, right now, you're nothing more than a black-and-white photo in the morning paper." Nash began walking around. He thought better when he was in motion. "We'll let the people hear the facts straight from the source. Let them see the pain you're going through and the life you are trying to save, your own child's life. Let them see it through your eyes," he said with a lowered dramatic tone.

Michael thought for a moment and sighed. "You really think it will help the case, huh?"

"I know it will," Nash replied.

Michael moved toward the dining-room table and held on to the chair. He remained standing. A myriad of thoughts were violently colliding in his mind, a mass of contradiction and confusion. He sighed again. "All right," he said quietly.

Again Nash had his victory. He was on a roll. Doing the show would surely help the case; it certainly couldn't hurt, he thought. But Nash had his own agenda. He wasn't about to miss out on one second of his fifteen minutes of fame, and the Larry King show was big time as far as Nash was concerned. It was a huge stepping-stone into the high-rent district of lawyer land. He could finally move his office out of his living room and into one of those plush Century City high-rise offices.

With his appearance on Larry King tonight, Nash would have clients waiting at his door, waiting to throw hordes of cash in his direction. Nash smiled inwardly as he looked around. "Nice pad by the way," Nash said quickly as he started for the door.

* * * * *

"And three...two...," and with the point of a finger, the red tally light came on, and the camera started rolling. Larry King leaned forward in his seat like a frail old man leaning heavily on a cane. "Welcome to the show, America. Tonight my guests are fire and water. They are on extreme opposite sides of today's hot topic. It's a turbulent topic at best, and it's tearing the world apart at the seams. And I'll tell you something: I have seen this topic before. I have seen it explode with intensity, violence, and even murder. And if we, the most powerful nation in the free world, do not heed its screaming calling card, we will face the wrath of violence that so often shadows the name. The name is abortion, and there appears to be no middle ground." He turned toward camera 2.

"My guests tonight are Betty Goldsmith, a pro-choice activist. She is also the president and cofounder of the New York chapter of It's My Right and author of *Life, the Woman's Choice*. Also with us is best-selling author, Troye Jenkins, who is a lawyer from the pro-life committee. Troye has authored two books for pro-life," Larry said. "Welcome."

Betty and Troye nodded politely. They have met on this battlefield on numerous occasions and have been at odds over the abortion issue for years. They are both pivotal figures for their cause.

Sitting in the studio was nothing new to Michael; he had seen the chaos and hustle and bustle a thousand times. Nash, on the other hand, was in awe at the activity in the studio. It was nothing like he expected. It was hard for him to keep focus on Mr. King.

"To my right is Tyson Nash, the controversial attorney for Michael Bishope, who is also with us," Larry continued. "Thank you all for being here." Larry turned toward Michael. "You're suing your wife over an abortion—"

Michael didn't have a chance to respond to Larry's question.

"He knew the risks when he had sex with her!" Betty said, cutting in. She spoke with spite, and the severity of her harsh voice rubbed Michael the wrong way. Betty had been waiting like a savage jungle cat for the chance to tear Michael's throat out. She is a passionate, outspoken advocate, and fighting for her cause is her entire life. And at the moment, her targets sat directly across from her penetrating stare. "If he wasn't prepared to father a child, then he should have used birth control or abstained."

"Excuse me, but that's not what this is about," Nash said. He painted her with a look of contempt. The camera saw it, and she felt it. "Hey, listen, before you *choose*—no pun intended—to appear on a show like this, I suggest that you read up on the subject and know what you're fighting against," Nash said with a blistering glare and narrowed eyes. "My client wants to be a father. She is the person who wants to abort his child. And for your information, she also knew and took the same risks as he did," Nash replied through narrowed eyes.

"It's her right to abort. He doesn't have to spend all of his time caring for the kid. The mother does," Betty said.

"Why can't a father be the primary parent and spend his time caring for the child? My argument here is for a case where the father wants the child and the mother does not. In such a case, why would the mother be the one spending all her time raising the child? She doesn't want it in the first place," Nash finished.

"She's got more at stake!" Betty spat out the words with anger. "It shouldn't even be a question. It's her body, and if she doesn't want to put her body through nine months of hell, that's her choice," Betty said. She was a spark plug straight out of the streets of New York with the famous attitude. Her Jewish roots ran deep, but her strong, outspoken views and harsh criticism clashed with her parents' beliefs. They barely spoke anymore.

"She doesn't have more at stake. Yes, she carries the child—"

"Fetus!" Betty hastily replied. "Science has yet to prove with conclusive evidence that life begins in the womb," she said sarcastically, rolling her eyes in the process as if she had made the same speech a million times, which she probably had.

"That's nonsense. Where else would it begin?" Nash asked with a dumfounded smile. He quickly shot a glance toward Larry. "Jeez, where do you find these people?" he said with sarcasm.

"Hey! I didn't come here to be insulted!" Betty said.

"Then get your story straight, lady. Learn the fact before you enter into a debate, then maybe people might not be so inclined to look at you and see the village idiot," Nash said with spite.

Betty's mouth fell open. She was left speechless. Troye and Michael were as well.

"Okay," Larry said, "let's not get personal here. Let's stick to the subject."

Troye Jenkins did well to hide his smile. He had wanted to say that to Betty for years. "The fact is, we do have scientific proof," Troye said in a low articulate voice. "But your side chooses not to accept the scientific findings and facts." Troye also hails from New York and has a disposition to match Betty's, but he had enough tact to keep it in check. Troye was a tall light-skinned black man with short tight hair. His parents were very proud of what he has accomplished with his life.

"Don't give me your forty-day theory again. It's more pro-life propaganda, Troye, and you know it," Betty said. She relished the verbal encounter no matter how many people were against her. She had a voice, and no matter where she was and no matter how many people were against her, she was not going to go silent into that good night.

"Forty days?" Larry asked with a questioning glance. He actually looked interested for a moment.

"His pro-liar side believes that brain waves in the *fetus* starts at forty days," Betty replied. "It's something their spin doctors cooked up at their propaganda factory."

Larry turned and faced Troye. "Does your side have proof of this?" Larry asked.

"Yes. It's all published as well," Troye started. He smiled as Betty cut him off. She was good at it, and Troye was used to it. He waited patiently and let her have the floor.

"Oh, brother! Here we go again," she stabbed with bitter sarcasm. "Try not to bore the national audience, Troye."

"Sources for the forty days claim are John R. Goldenring's 'Development of the Fetal Brain,' a letter published in the *New England Journal of Medicine* in 1982. The pro-life advocate website quotes it along with Hamlin, 48. Goldenring, J. 1982, 'Development of the Fetal Brain,' *New England Journal of Medicine*, August 26, 1982, 564. And so does 'Abortion,' 'Questions and Answers.' 'Brain functions as measured on the electroencephalogram appears to be present in the fetus at about eight weeks gestation or six weeks after conception,'" Troye said. He turned toward Betty.

"Goldenring simply expresses his personal opinion that abortion might be banned after eight weeks based on brain-development activity. Physicians have always determined when a person is alive by measuring for the presence of certain vital signs. When it becomes possible to replace both cardiac and pulmonary functions with machines, physicians turned to measuring the functions of the only truly unique irreplaceable organ: the brain. I submit from that from this effort, the following principle has clearly emerged—"

"Lies. Lies. More pro-lies." Betty huffed.

"All facts, Betty. You have to take off your blindfold to understand the facts, to actually see them," Troye shot back. "When you hide behind your cloak of ignorance, it's hard to see or even recognize the truth, Betty."

Betty continued shaking her head. In her mind, she was right; and no matter what Troye or anybody else said, they were wrong. "Lies and half-truths—and total BS!" declared Betty.

"The presence of a functioning human brain means that a patient—a person, if you will—is alive," Troye said over her raised voice. "This is the medical definition of human life. Physicians have approached fetuses in the same way as in any other patient, seeking vital signs to determine the patient's status, hence the emphasis on the quickening in legal and medical thinking before this century."

"Pro-life propaganda written by pro-life Nazis." She turned toward Larry and casually said, "See, I told you they have a factory."

Larry cracked an abstract smile. "His argument sounds like it makes sense," Larry retorted.

That's because you're a dumbass, Betty thought to herself. She held a high opinion of herself and no one else. Everybody who didn't agree with her single-tracked way of thinking was wrong and stupid.

Larry wasn't sure if he liked her. She was a little too loud and fidgety, and the way she stabbed her point of view across was a little too harsh. But what the hell, this show was surely going to generate through-the-roof ratings.

Betty ignored Larry's response and addressed her attentions directly to Troye, somebody who knew what he was talking about, even though he disagreed with her righteous opinion.

With Betty blatantly turning away from him, Larry made up his mind: he didn't like this broad.

"They're facts, Betty. And pro-choice need to start realizing that there is more documented findings out there than just your one-sided, simple-mined rhetoric," Troye said.

"Your facts. They mean nothing outside the pro-life party because nobody outside your group will agree with you. It is what it is, ridiculous propaganda to promote your argument and build your troops." Betty snorted.

Troye smiled and shook his head. He exchanged a brief look with Nash. "Pro-abortionists everywhere are trying to deny the humanity of the unborn child," Troye started. "You people are so blind by your fight for the woman and her rights you won't take the time to read and examine the scientific findings," Troye finished.

"Listen, once a child is born, it could go either way. It can go with the father or with the mother," Betty said. She was famous for running from the facts and changing directions when she feels backed into a corner. Even in her books, she stated only one point of view—hers. She stated only one theory, the pro-choice theory. She made no mention of any scientific findings that Troye brought to the table. And when she said anything about the pro-life group, which was often in her books, it was with ridicule and harsh criticism. "As far as your proof—"

"It's all in print, Betty. It's all published and in practice. C'mon, Betty, I know you know how to read. Give it a go, maybe you'll learn something that you just don't know," he said, goading her. He knew how to push her buttons, which was not all that hard.

"Oh, please! The fact still remains that you have no solid proof as to whether or not life begins in the womb," Betty said.

"You're sounding like a broken record again. Different location, same response. When are you people going to come up with something new?"

A heated debate on his show only meant a massive boost to his sagging ratings, and Larry knew that. He was inwardly thrilled at the passion of the argument from both sides. The topic of abortion alone would surely double the ratings, and Michael's passionate plea to save his child's life would surely grab the attention of the American people. Larry's next bonus check was going to be huge.

"Okay, we're getting off the subject here," Nash said, cutting in. "We're fighting to save the life of an innocent child. And regardless of the outcome, my client wishes to somehow work this out with his wife, whom he loves very much."

"Oh, how sweet," Betty blurted out with nasty sarcasm. She was ignored by all, though her comment generated a slight chuckle from one of the cameraman.

"You don't want a divorce?" Larry asked. He was kind of surprised.

"No, I don't," Michael replied. "I want to remain married to my wife. I believe in the sanctity of marriage. I love her, but I want a family and a child. I want the child she is presently carrying, my child." Michael lowered his head a brief moment to fight off the emotion that was tugging at his heart. "I mean, who knows if she'll ever be able to have another child if she follows through with the abortion."

"That's a good point," Larry said.

"There's something wrong with her, Larry," Michael said. "She's not in the right state of mind, and I need to make sure she doesn't make the wrong decision while she is not thinking right. I want my wife to be healthy, and I want my child," Michael finished somberly.

Larry nodded.

"The child she is trying to kill," Nash said with a strong emphasis.

"That's pretty harsh, Mr. Nash," Larry said.

"It is what it is. Murder is murder," Nash said with a cold shrug and turned toward Betty. "The only thing saying the mother should raise the child is society's attitude and the legal precedent which is largely shaped by societal attitudes. There is no reason why the father couldn't raise the child," Nash finished.

"The man doesn't lose under the current system," Betty started. "He's just responsible for what he does with his own body, sex, as the woman is responsible for what she does with hers, birth or abortion. It's called freedom and responsibility."

"If he's responsible for his body, 'sex' as you say, and she's responsible for hers, 'birth or abortion,' then you are only holding him accountable for his donation—meaning, in your narrow-minded opinion, that he has no say thereafter his donation of sperm," Nash replied quickly. "And if she's only responsible for 'birth or abortion' when the choice between the two came out of sex, then why isn't she held accountable for having sex in the first place?" Nash waited for some kind of response, but Betty just stared at him. "So what you are saying, in an ignorant sort of way, is that man is just the dumb Neanderthal incapable of creating intelligent thought, feeling, or emotion, and woman is the all-knowing in the universe. She's the almighty, the one who has the final say in something it took two people to create, a man and a woman." Nash shot her with spite. "You're pathetic, lady." He just couldn't resist that last comment.

"It's the way our system works, buddy," Betty replied.

"In the grand feminist scheme of things, men get screwed! In our system, men are stripped of their rights and are essentially forced into slave labor because of something as arbitrary as a biological triviality." Then it occurred to him: this uptight bitch sitting across from him really needed to get laid. "It just so happens that for nine months, the mother carries the kid, that's just a fact of nature. Once the child has been born, there's nothing saying it can't go with the father. But in our case, that is not an option as the mother wants to abort the living child without an explanation, without regard to the biological father, who, in this case, just happens to be her husband," Nash said with passion. "She wants to kill the child," Nash accentuated his point.

"There's nothing to kill. It's not alive," Betty replied. Her face was like stone, emotionless and pale.

Nash threw up his arms. He couldn't believe that she was a mouthpiece for the pro-choice movement. He was amazed that they let her speak or say anything for their party. It was all nonsense.

Michael was a reluctant participant. He wanted to say nothing more than he had already said. He wanted to let Nash speak for him, but listening to the argument, Michael felt that this was his fight. It was his baby's life that was at stake, and he needed to be heard. "You know, I've never been pro anything. I've never had to stand on either side of this issue, because frankly, I've never had to deal with any of this. I think that before this case, I never actually said the word *abortion*," Michael started but was cut off.

"And now you're an unwilling player due to the unfortunate stance your wife is taking," Larry commented. "Can this be overcome? I mean, can you and your wife somehow work this out and go on as a happily married couple?"

Betty grunted like a canine gnawing on a bone. "What is unfortunate about it?"

Again she was ignored.

"I think we can, but it's going to take a lot of time and a lot of healing. And no offense to you, Larry, but I'd rather be living my life privately, awaiting my child's birth, than sitting here with you," Michael replied.

Yes! That was good, Nash thought. He was building points with the audience and surely winning the vote of the American people.

Larry laughed briefly. "I'd rather you be doing that too. *No* offense," Larry said with a smile.

Michael returned his smile. "The way I see it, our system is this. In a pregnancy, the mother basically gets to decide how everything is going to unfold. This has a dramatic impact on the next eighteen years of the father's life, and he is powerless to do anything about it. That's not fair. Our laws should take into account that there are two parties involved in the creation of life, and both sides should have equal decision-making power for the child's entire life, right from conception." Michael lowered his head and felt a choke building in his throat.

Larry could sense Michael's emotional pause, and he felt that a short fuse was burning between the gusts. An explosion was imminent. "We have to take a break here," Larry said, turning to the camera. "When we come back, we will have as our guests Richard Hoven, a speaker for the NRLC, the National Right to Life Committee. And also with us will be Father Samuel Becker of the Catholic Church. I'd like to thank tonight's guests for being here and for their passion. This is an explosive issue no doubt, one that has the nation on its knees awaiting the outcome of the trial that could very well make history," Larry said as he turned toward Michael. "Good luck with your fight."

"Thank you," Michael replied.

"We'll be right back, America," Larry said, cracking a slight two-hundred-year-old smile.

20

Sixteen weeks

A CHARGE OF ELECTRICITY filled the air under the thick gray skies covering Los Angeles like a glass meant to hold in all its lurid secrets. Los Angeles was once again abuzz with another sensationalized media court case. Overnight, the streets in and around the courthouse and city hall had exploded with impassioned people fiercely loyal to their cause. It quickly became a fire-breathing dragon, waiting to devour its innocent victims of the nearby village.

The Larry King show drew massive ratings, and it brought out the masses in droves. It also drew the ire from thousands of supporters, both pro and con, and they were all here now, gathered like contemptuous children playing in the street with no supervision. This was a special time for the abortion armies as both sides gathered troops and readied themselves for battle in front of the Santa Monica courthouse. Several other groups were here as well. This was going to be the battle of all battles.

*****

If one looked down on the disorderly plebeians from a helicopter, they appeared to be a mass of writhing maggots surging with activity, consuming its host. A majority of the plebs carried signs of protest or support as they jockeyed for position in front of the camera.

People wanted to hang Michael; others praised him for his courage to stand up and fight for his rights as a father. Even though the general public had never laid eyes on her, people loathed Susan for what she wanted to do, and others applauded her strength and courage.

The energized tone was loud as both sides screamed their argument from one side to the other. The NRLC was also present, along with numerous religious groups making their voices heard. Quite a few of them were screaming into bullhorns.

Hundreds of LAPD officers and Los Angeles county sheriffs were gathered in force to hold the peace between the two warring sects, both of which were known to become violent in the past. This was a gathering they hadn't seen since the O. J. Simpson murder trial in downtown Los Angeles.

The hundreds of reporters gathered from all over the world to capture the story fueled the frenzy. Satellite trucks were lined up around the block. News crews from as far away as Sweden, France, Japan, South Africa, and Australia were there to bear witness to history in the making.

* * * * *

Turning the corner, Michael stopped his car in the middle of the street. He was in shock when he laid eyes on the size of the crowd that was spilling onto the street and blocking traffic. The police had to shut down one lane. Right then and there, Michael decided to call the whole thing off and put his car in reverse. But as he turned to look over his shoulder, the cars that were backed up behind him began honking their horns and cursing him like a New York cabbie. Michael heaved and jammed his car back in drive and slowly continued past the gathered crowd.

Michael read some of the signs as he drove: BABY KILLER, ABORTION IS MURDER, CHOOSE LIFE. WE LOVE YOU MICHAEL was a sign two young women were waving near the street. KEEP ABORTION LEGAL, GOD SAVES, EVERY CHILD A WANTED CHILD, PRO-DEATH, PRO-LIES, PRO-MURDER, and the ever-present JOHN 3:16. There were large, picture-window-sized photos of aborted fetuses and embryos. The signs went on and on.

Still he wanted to turn and run. None of what he was attempting was worth all this, he thought. But something inside him knew that he couldn't run like a coward. He had come too far and had too much at stake to run now. He needed to free himself of his own imprisoning wall, or he might never be able to live with himself if he at least didn't fight to save the life of his child.

He entered the Santa Monica civic center parking lot, where he kicked the parking attendant ten bucks to let him park there. Michael pulled in and parked in the very back of the lot, clearly out of view of anybody on the street.

Exiting the Range Rover, Michael looked around before he started walking toward the back of the courthouse. The traffic on the 10 Freeway roared in the distance. As Michael approached the rear entrance, he saw what he dreaded most: legions of reporters gathered at the back entrance.

Michael did not break stride when they swarmed him, and he said nothing as he walked into the courthouse. Walking through the corridor, Michael was surrounded and harassed by another group of sanctimonious reporters; they were an infestation. Michael lowered his head and plowed through the group and entered the courtroom.

* * * * *

The tumultuous dark skies swirled and held its karmic curse, ready to strike the sinful souls below. But as Renee led Susan out of the house, Susan glanced up at the sky, only to find a slight parting of the gloomy sky. A piercing ray of sunlight broke through a slight tear in the murky clouds and onto her pallid face. She held still for a moment and let the sun paint her with its glory.

Susan momentarily bathed in the magnificent sunlight. She knew her dark days and her demons would soon be gone. And she hoped with their absence, the clouds would part, and the bright stars in the night sky would soon return for her to behold. Inwardly, she knew that her hope would not return with the stars. She knew the price of redemption, and she knew she couldn't pay it. Not this time. Her present situation had been forecasted and played out over and over again in her mind. She knew that no matter what happened in court, her fate was already chosen, sealed, and tucked safely away.

* * * * *

Walking into the courtroom, Michael was not surprised to find that the only camera in the courtroom belonged to KNRQ, and its focus was trained on him as he maneuvered past the reporters and sat at the table next to Nash. Chandler made sure that the camera had full coverage of Michael.

Michael was stunned as his eyes fell upon his number one field reporter and friend Tecate, who was probably there on Chandler's orders. And as Michael watched Chandler walk into the courtroom, his suspicions were confirmed. Chandler walked over to Tecate and put his arm around him as they both stared at Michael. Tecate did not appear to like Chandler's gesture and abruptly pulled away.

Like Samantha Rain, Tecate also did not want to be here. He liked Michael; everybody did. His boss was the only person who had it in for Michael. Tecate was scheduled to have an exclusive interview to break the Texas murder story, but Chandler pulled him away before the interview took place, and Tecate resented Chandler for it. He especially didn't want to be here, covering this story. He didn't want to bury a friend, and that's exactly what Chandler ordered him to do, or lose his job. He too was just a puppet on a string that had no leverage or say, and anything he felt or thought was inappropriate.

Michael looked at him with a questioning glare and shook his head. He knew that Tecate was relentless and was going to start digging into his world. Michael wondered for a brief moment as they exchanged looks if he had any skeletons in the closet. Because if he did, Tecate was going to find them; that's why Michael hired him in the first place.

* * * * *

Renee was shocked by the enormity of the crowd as they approached. Adrenaline began pumping through her veins. She felt for Susan. She too wanted to turn and run. She wanted to take Susan to the nearest abortion clinic and get this thing over with. Renee drove past the crowd and turned into the parking entrance and drove around to the back. There, she saw the reporters near the rear entrance of the courthouse, waiting like beasts of prey.

As she parked the car, her heart began its adrenaline-induced pounding. She was about to face the snarling beast head-on and look into its mouth and examine its many layers of sharp teeth. She didn't want to be part of this, but she invited herself when she didn't want her best friend to go through this alone. She feared this could ruin Susan's life.

Susan sat up in the back seat and glanced at the large white building and the reporters loitering around the rear entrance. "They don't know who I am," she said quietly.

Renee turned and looked at her. "What do you mean?"

"They've only seen Michael. They don't know what I look like," Susan said quietly. Renee smiled and opened the door.

Approaching the entrance, Renee had an arm around Susan's shoulder. The reporters began fighting for position with every woman who came toward them. They wanted the best shot, the best angle, to capture her image or get a quote.

"Is this where you go for traffic tickets?" Renee asked. The reporters blew a collective moan. Mumbles and grumbles came from a few in the background. They were deflated and now very uninterested in the two women entering the courtroom. As they entered the corridor, they were in the sights of more reporters standing outside the courtroom. They moved in for the kill and ran toward the two women.

"Are you Susan?" one reporter asked. That started a frenzy of questions hurled frantically at Susan and Renee.

"How do you feel?"

"Why do you want to kill your baby?"

"Do you love your husband?"

Reporters asked a bombardment of questions until Renee whistled to quiet the lot of them.

"Hey! We're just here for a speeding ticket," she said to the group. They groaned and shut off cameras and mics.

Letting Renee and Susan pass, they watched the two women walk down the hallway toward the courtroom. And as they entered, the reporters knew that they were duped and ran after them. It was too late. The women had entered the courtroom, and they were barred from the proceedings.

Entering the courtroom, Renee and Susan froze in their tracks as silence fell upon the crowded room. The world was now witness to the woman at the center of the story. Their eyes scanned the silent blurred faces staring back at them. The soulless camera focused on the two women. Slowly and quietly, Renee led Susan through the maze of muted people.

Susan's court-appointed lawyer, Warren Vecchio, greeted her as she approached the table.

Vecchio had a monumental task before him, with a mute client. But he thought he understood her stance and was ready to proceed with or without her help. Vecchio was feisty and competent and had been around a while. He wasn't the everyday court-appointed attorney without a conscience. He was a full partner in a private practice law firm on the Westside. He was appointed by Judge Fields on a favor and was taking the case pro bono at the judge's request.

Passing Susan off to the waiting hands of her attorney, Renee turned to the bevy of spectators. Renee's eyes immediately found Nick staring back at her. She wasn't pleased to see him standing behind Michael's table. He nodded to her, but she shunned his gesture and sat directly behind Susan. Nick wasn't surprised with the contemptuous glare she shot in his direction. It was meant to kill everything in his general area. He knew, though he didn't want to admit it, that this was probably the start of their end. He sat quietly behind Michael, showing his support for his buddy. His mother, Lisa Vach, sat next to him.

Susan felt the scrutinizing eyes as she sat uneasy behind the large table. The buzz came back to life and filled the courtroom, energizing it with emotion. Susan dropped her stare and lost herself in the wood grain of the table. It was all she could do. The curved lines and arches and swerving grain was hypnotic to her impressionable eyes.

Susan's eyes followed the grain right off the table and onto the floor, where she found the judge's massive bench directly in front of her. It too had grain she found so interesting, rich grain she thought must be centuries old with its timeless history. It was the only thing she could do to tune out the scrutinizing world around her.

Susan tried for the first time in weeks to find a happy memory, but her thoughts were of darkness and horror. For the life of her, she couldn't remember one happy moment, one happy thought, not with Michael, not with Renee or Macy. She could not think of one happy moment with her family or even her life before Michael. She was unable to pull herself out of this atrocious reality her mind had entangled her in. Indeed, she was caught in a tangle of webs she had long ago escaped. But now, this time, the arachnid was coming with all its raunchy crooked legs and fanged teeth.

Michael couldn't take his eyes off his wife. She sat so beautifully across from him. He longed to hold her once again in his arms. He wanted to caress her and run his fingers through her soft hair and breathe her in like air. But he knew if he didn't stop her now, she would kill his baby. He feared the weeks, days, and hours that lay ahead for her. His love was deep for her. He dreaded the fact that she had to go through this. He dreaded that he was responsible for putting her through this. He hated himself for it. He should loathe her, hope she was tormented by the choice she made, but he didn't. His marriage vows meant the world to him, and he would do anything to see them through with the woman he loved so dearly.

Michael felt his heart begin to beat a little harder as the bailiff he came to recognize stepped to the front of the bench. "Come to order," the bailiff called out to the crowded courtroom. "All rise. The Superior Court of the County of Los Angeles, of the State of California, is now in session. The Honorable Harrison M. Fields presiding."

The gathered spectators quickly jostled for position, rushing to grab their seats. As was protocol in such a case, the hefty guards positioned themselves in front of the heavy doors. Nobody was coming or going from the courtroom without going through them.

The red tally light on the KNRQ camera came on, and the cameraman peered through the eyepiece. Chandler stood next to him, ready to direct him exactly how to film. Chandler wouldn't have missed this day for the world.

Chandler was right, after all. He did make Michael a household name, and Chandler was tying the noose, waiting for it to be stretched by his sheer mass. But the public opinion was on Michael's side. He was fighting for what he believed, and the public felt for him. He was the underdog trying to save the life of an innocent child, his own innocent, unborn child.

The public was embracing Michael with every new clip the news was putting on their television screen. Michael was becoming a hero among men who previously had no rights. Men's groups were sprouting up across the country, and Michael was their hero.

Michael stood next to Nash and adjusted his lapel as the judge walked in and sat behind the bench. Michael noticed that Susan remained seated the whole time. Even her attorney's attempts went unnoticed by her. Susan held her gaze on all the delicacies of the courtroom. She was trying somehow to lay her attentions elsewhere, another state of conscious being.

"You may be seated," said the bailiff before he took his post near the judge's entrance.

Judge Fields briefly glanced at his notes and then looked across at the gathered crowd. He took a quick glance at Susan, who was looking at the floor under her desk. Her mannerisms were that of an adolescent, Judge Fields thought. The room was silent with anticipation.

"Mr. Vecchio," Judge Fields said, "have you had a chance to become familiar with this case?"

"Yes, I have, Your Honor," Warren replied. "Though I would now request additional time to confer with my client as she has been completely uncooperative up to this point."

The judge wrote a quick note as the hopeful attorney looked on. Warren Vecchio had just pushed fifty years of age and was well dressed for the occasion. He too had been following the case in the news with exuberance, and he wanted to look his absolute best for the media—well, as best as the frumpy little man could look. Vecchio was short and could do well to lose some weight. Vecchio was a sharp attorney who was great on appeal. That's precisely why Judge Fields asked him to come in on this case. Judge Fields wanted to make sure he had all his bases covered.

"There will be no continuances here, Mr. Vecchio. We're running on an expedited schedule due to the nature of the case."

Vecchio nodded and began skimming over his papers.

Michael noticed another bailiff walk briskly into the courtroom and straight over to the clerk and whispered into her ear. The clerk quickly wrote something down on a yellow legal pad and instantly walked over to the judge, where she placed the note directly in front of his face. Judge Fields glanced down at the note and then peered at his clerk.

"This court is dismissed until further notice. All previous orders are to remain. We're adjourned," Judge Fields said and slammed down the gavel. He was quickly whisked out of the courtroom by two bailiffs.

The court was stunned, and a rumble of confusion spread throughout the room. Susan barely noticed the crowd of reporters in an uproar, searching for answers. Her attorney was speechless as he looked on. Michael was beside himself, especially after Nash couldn't answer his questions. Nash too was left speechless.

* * * * *

Pandemonium reigned outside the courthouse. The sea breeze carried the aroma of fear and the bitter salt of tension. People were running and screaming in every direction, stopping cars in the streets. The frantic crowd trampled men, women, and children. Nobody knew where they were going in such a hurry; they just ran for their lives. There were no sides anymore, just the side of fear, an emotion shared, and for the first time agreed upon by both sides of the issue.

The infestation or reporters frantically tried to gather the story from hysterical people as they rushed past. One lady ran directly into the camera, knocking it to the ground as she ran. Reporters stood in confusion, speechless for the first time as they looked on the warlike images of fear and terror in the faces of the panicked crowd running for their lives.

Television stations all over the country broke into local programming to bring the breaking news from the Santa Monica courthouse. Two Los Angeles stations broke into a breaking story of a local car chase to show the mayhem taking place at the courthouse, though they were still in the dark as to what was going on. Confused news anchors babbled on without a script.

*****

The confusion in the courtroom was almost as reckless, and Chandler was there to make sure his camera captured all the action. He was the authority in his domain, directing his very capable cameraman where and what to shoot. Reporters were screaming back and forth. Most were on cell phones trying to figure out what the hell was going on. Chandler could only imagine the delirious ratings this would bring. His bosses in New York would surely put him on a pedestal. Michael appealed to Nash for answers, but even the all-knowing Nash was hard-pressed for them.

Susan was the only person in the courtroom who remained seated and appeared very calm. Renee came around and frantically started talking to her, but Susan was in an absent, hypnotic stare. She held her focus on an exact spot on the wall. All was silent to her; the world had stopped. Fear struck Renee's eyes as she watched Susan look on in a daze. Renee yelled at Susan to move, to get up, do anything, but Susan remained unresponsive. Renee took her by the arms and tried to drag her to safety.

Chandler noticed Renee pulling at Susan's arms and ordered the camera trained on them. Renee was getting nowhere; Susan was dead weight.

Three burly bailiffs rushed into the courtroom from the judge's entrance and tried to quiet the crowd. Nothing. But with a blaring whistle, silence came quick. "We're going to have to ask you at this time to, number one, remain calm. Number two, to exit the building out of the rear exit," the bailiff said, pointing.

"Why? What's going on?" asked a faceless reporter.

"We have received a bomb threat, and we have to evacuate the building," replied the bailiff.

The spectators groaned, and a few of them immediately started for the door. Nash quickly gathered papers lying on the desk and shoved them into his briefcase.

"Now, if you will all exit in an orderly fashion and head for the rear exit," the bailiff continued. "That will be to your left, ladies and gentlemen. There will be further instructions when you reach the parking lot."

Michael started following Nash out of the room, but he turned to see Susan still at the table with Renee trying to help her up in a futile attempt. Michael rushed back to the table and grabbed Susan, but she was unresponsive. Her eyes remained locked onto nothing. Michael motioned for Renee's help, and they led her out of the building.

* * * * *

Handheld signs—pro-this, pro-that, I'm right, you're wrong, keep abortion legal—littered the lawn outside the courthouse. Thousands of papers and debris and leaflets covered the lawn. The crisp sea breeze blew papers across the yard. Sirens from an approaching police car and emergency vehicles filled the air.

Police officers and court guards rushed about trying to remove any remaining civilians from the premises. LAPD and LA county sheriffs barricaded the building with yellow caution tape. Police cars blocking the intersection of Pico and Main Streets quickly moved out of the way as the approaching sirens came closer. A large black van passed through the two squad cars. On the side of the van, clearly marked in large white letters: LAPD Bomb Squad.

21

"BOMB HOAX DELAYS COURT!" was the headline in the morning edition of the *Los Angeles Times* just above a half-page photo of Michael leading Susan out of the courthouse. They were surrounded by chaos and panicked people. Michael's photo had graced most newspapers across the country for over a week, but now Susan was no longer a mystery; she was no longer just "the wife." Her photo was plastered everywhere as well. Her photo was in newspapers and on all the news broadcasts.

Most news rags deplored the Santa Monica bomb hoax and pleaded for peace during the court process. At least that was a direct quote from Michael as he left the building.

Chandler was spending most of his time in the newsroom trying to come up with more diabolical ways to bury Michael. A few chosen people in the entertainment industry are known for such vengeance, blackballing someone he or she no longer liked. Chandler had done it before, and he was doing his best to do it again.

Since the bomb threat, Chandler had spent every waking moment at work writing lead stories and deviously planning his next move. Chandler could have taken this in another direction, giving credence to the story and brought credibility to his network, but he chose to show his true colors. He thought he was invincible now that Michael was almost out of the way. He had visions of running the station with total control. This was one of the happiest times of Chandler's life.

* * * * *

Nick was so in tune with the national news broadcast of nightly America that he didn't hear Renee walk into the house. She had spent the past two days with Susan, trying to help her through this situation. She was about to speak to Nick when the sight of Tyson Nash on the television caught her eye. She stood quietly behind Nick watching the broadcast.

"Pregnancy can certainly be considered normal, but unfortunately, circumstances are often far from normal. Pregnancy does not exist as a physical condition alone. If it did, many would-be mothers would not have a problem in giving their newborns away because there would be no emotional connection," said Troye Jinkins. He and Nash had been answering all requests to appear on television shows. Nash was there simply for self-serving purposes: to preach the voice of Nash.

"But it is not a mere physicality," said Kathy Taylor, a renowned pro-choice advocate and author of several pro-choice books. Unlike the outspoken Betty Goldsmith, Kathy had a clear view of both sides of the issue. She believed in the woman's right to choose but was also able to accept the pro-life stance as well and, in certain cases, agree with them. "To properly debate the abortion issue, one should use real examples, not up-in-the-air theorem that can seldom be applied to actuality in other but inappropriate abstract terms."

"Interesting," Nash said quickly. He was learning how and when to cut into dialogue in front of the camera. "Less abstract and controversial that consciousness, as a creation for individuality, it might be the possession of gender, or any trait that can only be possessed by the whole rather than its parts. So possessing human DNA doesn't cut it because all of our parts do that."

"Yeah, that makes sense," Kathy said, nodding. Her soft voice was articulate and gave a hint of a warm New England dialect.

"Take, for instance, a comatose patient. They have no conscious thought. And at times, they have no measurable brain activity. Do you suggest that we have the right to kill them?"

"Whoa. Excuse me, Mr. Nash. I think you're taking what I am saying way out of context. That's not what I am saying at all."

"Gee, thanks! May I finish now?" Nash said with a sarcastic grin. "As I was trying to say, I'm still unsure why you think consciousness is necessary for an individual to exist?" Nash asked.

"Actually, I don't particularly," Kathy started and quickly searched her thoughts. "However, I think that where there is some awareness that can be objectively identified, it is much less controversial to argue that an entity is an individual. I think that all individually aware entities are individuals, but it does not follow that all individuals are aware."

"Indeed," Nash said quietly to himself.

"Whether some individuals are not aware is a matter of more involved debate, but I agree that awareness is itself arbitrary," Troye said.

"The life-span development of the organism can be traced back to its conception. That's true by definition," Nash said, but with some confusion pasted on his chalky face as though he didn't fully grasp what he just said. "I still don't see how pro-choice can justify their belief that a fetus is not a life because it is in the womb," Nash started. "Maybe I'm just looking for an explanation because I've heard nothing to back it up. Nobody appears to want to take a firm stance. Your side has facts, and their side has facts, but nobody seems to want to meet in the middle and shake hands," he said and paused with a sigh. "It just seems to me, and from what I've read, that life begins at conception."

"Well, that's simple," Kathy countered.

"Nothing about this debate is simple. I hope you've been paying attention, Ms. Taylor," Nash replied with a flirtatious smile.

Kathy returned his smile. "It's like church versus scientology," Kathy said. "The church says it is so based on thousands of years of belief. And scientology says show me proof. It's the same way with abortion. Show us proof that the fetus is a life prior to birth, and I'll even jump on your bandwagon," Kathy finished.

"How do you explain the growth the fetus incurs between conception and the time it's born nine months later? That's proof of life right there. It surely doesn't expand to nine pounds when it is introduced to air," Nash said sarcastically. "Are you telling me something that grows that much is not living?" Nash asked and waited for a rational answer. "How do you explain that?"

Kathy smiled. "You make it all sound so easy, Mr. Nash," Kathy said.

"Maybe it is," Nash replied. "Maybe both sides need to take a whole new approach to this subject."

"Here I was thinking the standard pro-choice party line said fetuses weren't children, weren't persons. They were, at best, potential and were nothing but tissue matter. That's how your party referred to them, is it not?" Troye asked Kathy and held her gaze. "If that's so, how can tissue mass delivered alive in midabortion at twenty weeks gestation experience torment? Or am I incorrectly characterizing your beliefs?" Troye asked with a quizzical smirk.

"It is incorrect that pro-choice has one of many basic tenets stipulating that prior to birth, it is a fetus. After birth, it's a baby—birth being the conventional point at which the law recognizes it as a baby," Kathy replied.

"Are there any other reasons to support your position beyond legal arguments? After all, a new government could change the law," Ted Knight asked. He was the national anchorman that America has known for years.

"I find that a new government will find it quite difficult to change. The right to privacy implications from Griswold, which predated *Roe v. Wade*, was, in fact, the basis behind the right to privacy, not *Roe v. Wade* as had been claimed by the antiabortion movement," Kathy stated and took a deep breath.

"Secondly, Chief Justice William Rehnquist, Justice Clarence Thomas, and Justice Antonia Scalia have all put forth their own opinion in *Planned Parenthood vs. Casey*, 1992, that they consider *Roe v. Wade* to be the wrong way to give a woman abortion rights and have their own justification of abortion rights based on the Fourth Amendment," she finished, then leaned forward.

"So no, I don't think that the law will change much in the decades to come when even the type of conservative justices the incoming president had stated he would appoint to the US Supreme Court agree that a woman has a constitutional right to an abortion.

Any constitutional changes would require such a radical cauterization of the Bill of Rights that even antiabortion conservatives would be hard-pressed to justify these changes to libertarian individuals back home," Kathy stopped a brief moment to gather her thoughts.

"Unbelievable," Nash said in a huff. He was instantly sickened. He appeared to lose his appetite for fame and actually felt, if only for a brief moment, what Michael had been feeling all along.

*****

"I can't believe you're friends with that guy. He's such an asshole!" Renee said aloud as Nick turned to face her.

"He's fighting to save the life of an innocent child. Or is that too much for you to comprehend?" Nick stopped before he said something that would really cross the line. "Don't you have a heart?" he asked instead.

"I do, but it's with Susan where it belongs."

"And if she were the one who wanted to keep the baby and Michael wanted to abort it, you'd still be on her side?"

"Absolutely! She's my friend," Renee replied. "It's called loyalty and friendship."

"Now you know my deal with Mike," Nick said sharply. "But you're a sellout, Renee. You can't think for yourself. You take the side of the people you know and let them make up your mind for you just because you know them. It doesn't matter to you whether they're right or wrong. If Mike was wrong on this, I sure as hell would tell him."

"You're right, it doesn't matter!" she replied in anger.

"It matters to Mike, and it surely matters to the baby Susan wants to kill," he said, shooting her with a spiteful glare.

Renee stood in silence, her eyes roaring with flames. Nick could see the wheels turning as she raced through her thoughts. She was searching for verbal weapons to heave in his direction.

"Look," Nick started, "you can clearly see that this is hard on both of us. We're being forced to two different sides obviously. But think about them. Think about what they are going through."

"I am! That's why I'm so pissed off at you because you just don't care about Susan."

"I do care about Susan," Nick roared. "Will you just listen to me for a minute?"

"You're not going to change my mind on this, Nick. I believe what I believe, and if you don't like it, that's just too bad!" Renee said.

"I'm not trying to change your mind about anything," Nick said. "I just want to find a way for us to work through this without tearing us apart."

"It's too late for that, Nick," she replied with wild eyes. "It's just too hard being at odds with you over this. Susan is so close to me, and she needs someone to stand by her. Michael is obviously not doing it!"

"I really don't believe you," he said. "There are two sides to this. What about Michael? Am I supposed to ditch him just because you believe what you believe? Just because we're in a relationship?"

"Yes, Nick, you are! You're supposed to love me! And in loving me, you would be able to see more of my point of view and support me. We're living together for Christ's sake."

"Are you actually listening to yourself because you make absolutely no sense," Nick said. "Maybe I would be on your side, but we are involved in this. We're knee-deep in it. If this was an outside issue and we weren't involved, I would be more inclined to see your point of view."

"The woman has the right to choose what she does with her body. That's just all there is to it," Renee said.

"Okay, who is to say that what she does is the right choice?"

"It's just the way it is, the way it should be. My body is my body, just like your body belongs to you," Renee started and moved to the center of the room. "You wouldn't want anybody to tell you that you have to have a vasectomy, would you?"

"No, I wouldn't, but that's different," Nick replied.

"Oh, how is that any different than someone telling her she can't have an abortion?"

"Because whether or not I have a vasectomy, the outcome does not impact anybody else's life, just mine. Whereas an abortion affects both parties, not just the woman."

"Bullshit! If you have a vasectomy, it affects not only you but also the woman you're involved with. What if she wanted a baby and you do not, doesn't that also affect her?"

"If you put it that way, yes, it does. But it does not include life-and-death consequences. That's what we're talking about, Renee, and you break it down to who you like better, him or her, and that's bullshit!" Nick responded.

"No, it's not!"

"No matter how you sugarcoat it, Renee, bullshit remains bullshit!" Nick said. He was becoming more animated and a lot less tactful as he went on. Now the old Nick was coming out, but at this point, he didn't care. He felt as though their relationship was pretty much over anyway.

"I don't have to take this!" she shouted.

"Then why don't you drop it?"

"Because I'm right, and you're not!"

Nick held her blistering gaze a moment. Her malignant eyes pierced right through him. Nick took a deep breath to calm himself. "Renee," he started softly, "when you look at the issue and you do not see the facts because you are blinded by friendship, blinded by the love of that person, which is what you're doing, that makes you ignorant, and your ignorance makes you wrong, or at least incapable of seeing the issue from both sides. You only see what your love for Susan will allow you to see. You can't be objective," Nick said. His eyes followed her around the room as she paced.

"Well, if I can't, neither can you because of your friendship with Michael. So how does that make you right?"

"Yes, he is my friend, but I can also see things for what they are," he said. "Since this all started, I have been reading up on the issue. I wanted to be informed so that I can make an objective decision and think for myself, unlike these fucking sheep that jump on either side of the issue. What have you been doing other than stewing in your own venom? Do you know anything about abortion, I mean other than only a woman can have one?"

Fire burned in her eyes. "You're such an asshole!" she said with bitter spite.

He really wasn't expecting anything less from her. If it wasn't over now, it sure was heading that way, and he couldn't do anything to stop it. He couldn't even shut up to save his own life, let alone his relationship, the only one he's ever had.

Renee was fuming with every word he uttered. The runaway freight train was knifing down the tracks at break-neck speed. But he didn't care. He was actually standing up for something for the first time in his life, and it felt good.

Nick smiled again. He knew their relationship was crumbling over this single issue. "I feel sorry for you, Renee. It's sad that you have all this love for your friend, but you still can't open your eyes to what's really happening. You're wrong, Renee. You're so fucking wrong it's pathetic."

When she next opened her mouth, her face turned red. "Yeah, well, I'm not wrong about wanting you out of my house!" she yelled.

Nick smiled. "I figured you would do something like this," Nick started. "It's too bad, Renee. It's just too bad that you can't see past your own ignorance. Everything was fine between us before this happened," he said and got up off the couch and walked over near the door and picked up his jacket. He looked at her a moment and shook his head. Her piercing eyes danced all over his skin, trying somehow to inject him with her venom. "Everything's eventual," he said and lowered his head in a moment of thought. "It's like I always suspected," he said softly. He felt a choke building in his throat. "Things never last. They leave, run away," he said softly, still looking at the floor. His voice held the bitter pain he tried so desperately to hide.

The fire quickly left Renee's eyes as Nick's gentle words hit her like a jackhammer.

Nick turned and walked out of the house.

"Nick?" she quietly called after him. She began crying. "Nicky?" she called again in the empty room. "I love you," she said as she fell into the couch, crying to herself in the empty room.

22

A FIERY DAWN BROKE over the City of Angels cascading its radiant heat onto a city in need of its warm shower. It was a long-forgotten sight. This dawn brought with it new hope, new life, and an ominous promise of the violent storm after the calm.

Far in the distance, deep in the western sky where the sea touches the clouds on the edge of the world, still fighting the unearthly darkness over the calm Pacific, lingered the last of the June swoon's clouds. They were no more.

This new dawn claimed victory and promised brilliant sunshine and bright days ahead. Clear vision would be the word of the day as blistering temperatures would rise throughout the City of Angels and approach the century mark.

Susan woke to a beam of sunlight piercing the thin skin of her eyelids. She strained in a sea of unyielding brightness as she walked slowly toward the window she loved so much. This light was so unlike the gray, dim color of her recent past. Opening the venetian blinds, she smiled, the first smile she could remember in weeks as she bathed in the genial sunlight. She gazed at the mysterious blue sky and listened for the dawn's whisper of a new pledge.

She felt reborn, alive, and so fresh. She saw through untainted eyes, and oh how beautiful it was to see with such vivid clarity. It felt as if the sun's reappearance had reached out and lifted the veil of darkness shrouding her. Susan sat back in the chair just below the window and tilted her head back and let the sun shine down on her alabaster face. Her smile lit the room with warmth, with the innocent beauty that Michael fell in love with.

But the wheels of karmic redemption were already in motion. The universe was on its own course with destiny, and there was no turning back. Cosmic decisions have already been made. Lives were forever going to be effected, and no matter what the new dawn promised, a dark conclusion was swiftly approaching. A soft sound broke in her throat, and Susan began humming, slowly at first, a tune that, for some reason, gave peace to her splintered consciousness. The dawn's secret promise wrapped around her softly like a longing embrace.

Eighteen weeks

The body-thumping sound of helicopters flying overhead like circling vultures was a menacing feeling to the over four thousand people gathered on the grounds of the Santa Monica courthouse. Another thousand plus were packed along Main Street, which had been barricaded by police standing guard. Thousands more were gathered at the nearby shopping mall. Police and news helicopters dotted the sky like moving stars in a sea of enchanted blue.

Shown from the eye of many airborne cameras, the crowd below was a moving sea of ants, surging and swaying back and forth, constantly moving. Satellite trucks parked back to front surrounded the block; newspeople were everywhere. This was the grandest of all parties, and no one needed an invitation. They came from all walks of life just to be here for this gathering of fire and ice, the clashing of wills, the ultimate battle of sexes.

The ominous-looking black LAPD Bomb Unit van parked on the street directly in front of the courthouse lent of sense of caution to the scene. The police were there in force. Twenty plus horse-mounted officers off to the side were ready to break up any riotous behavior. Another hundred plus LAPD and LA county sheriffs were gathered in riot gear. The emotion of the crowd was high, and the police were ready for action. The Santa Monica courthouse was throbbing with a violent energy.

Pro-life and pro-choice spokespersons were holding their own news conferences. Religious groups also had their camera time; preachers and reverends were telling the world their interpretation of the bible and their stance on abortion. Men and women spoke to reporters preaching their side. Brainwashed children recited well-rehearsed dialogue and biblical passages purely for the emotional effect. It was a sick display by both sides, each trying to tug at the heartstrings of the viewing audience.

* * * * *

Watching the judge walk into the courtroom in his black robe, Michael felt a lump grow in his throat, the same lump he felt every time he stood for the judge's entrance. Michael glanced and looked at his wife, who was standing as the judge took his seat. She looked so much different to him. Her face had new color, and she appeared to be lucent and alert.

As the spectators took their seats, Michael's eyes remained on Susan. She was the person he had not seen in some time, almost radiant in her white dress. Michael's heart flooded with emotion as Susan leaned over and whispered something to her attorney. Her attorney was surprised by her sudden interest in the case.

Judge Fields sat quietly and read briefly from his notes. The silence was deadly as the courtroom waited with anticipation. The judge signed a sheet of paper and handed it to the clerk, then looked up. "Before we get started this morning, I'd like to see counsel, along with Mr. and Mrs. Bishope in my chambers," Judge Fields said as he slammed down the gavel and walked away from the bench.

Michael threw a questioning look over to Nash, but he just shrugged. He had no answers for Michael.

* * * * *

Michael couldn't take his eyes off his wife. She looked so real to him, not like the altered, somewhat psychotic woman he had become used to. This was the woman he fell in love with, and he wanted to reach out and touch her, hold her, kiss her.

"Are you up to speed, Mr. Vecchio?" Judge Fields asked.

"I've read the transcripts, but again I'd like to ask for a continuance. I have had little or no interaction with my client," Vecchio replied. "She spoke to me for the first time just ten minutes ago."

"We're not going to keep going over this, Mr. Vecchio. You knew coming in here that we're restricted on time," Judge Fields said. Vecchio nodded.

Judge Fields turned and addressed both attorneys. "I called you into chambers because I'd like to have a word with your clients. I want to see if we can somehow resolve this matter. As you may have witnessed, this case is creating madness that I don't want associated with my court. I wasn't particularly pleased with the bomb threat," Judge Fields said. "I want to see if we can find some middle ground before things get way out of hand."

Judge Fields turned to Michael. "Mr. Bishope, why does this mean so much to you?" Judge Fields asked. "You have obviously shown that you're willing to go all the way, but why? Is it worth losing your marriage over this?"

"Let me just say that I love my wife deeply. That's not going to change. My wish is that we can somehow resolve our differences no matter which way this case comes out," Michael said and lowered his head in a moment of reflection. "I mean no disrespect, Your Honor, but how can you ask such a question? That's my baby she's carrying. It's my blood. How could any potential father stand idly by and watch somebody kill something that is physically part of him? I'd rather you kill me, Judge," Michael said. He paused a moment as he and the judge exchanged looks.

Michael continued, "My parents died when I was very young, and I never had the chance to do all the things with my dad that I wanted to. I was jealous of other kids when they went on outings with their fathers, when they went to ball games or tossed the ball in the front yard. It was a bond that a father has with his child that I never experienced. Since my parents died, I knew I would never have that feeling with my dad. And I knew if I were ever going to experience that feeling, it would be as a father myself. I know this is going to sound a bit silly, but I have dreamed of being a father. I have dreamed of taking my son on fishing trips, tossing the ball in the yard, all the things my father couldn't do with me." Michael paused for a long moment as the judge waited.

Judge Fields smiled. "You sound so sure it's going to be a boy, Mr. Bishope."

"Just hoping, sir."

Judge Fields held his smile as he jotted down another note.

Michael continued, "Your Honor, how many times in life do you get a second chance?"

"Not very often, Mr. Bishope," Judge Fields replied.

"Exactly," Michael said. "I want a baby more than anything, sir, and who's to say that if my baby is aborted now, I will ever have another chance to be a father? I've always wanted this baby, even before Susan told me she was pregnant. It might be my only chance, Your Honor," Michael said with pleading eyes.

Judge Fields jotted down a few quick notes then turned toward Susan. "So, Mrs. Bishope, why do you want to have an abortion?" Judge Fields asked her directly. "Why are you going to such extremes?"

His sudden question and bluntness took her by surprise. Susan hesitated and froze in a state of suspended fear. Her throat dried up as she sank deeper into the leather chair.

"Mrs. Bishope?" Judge Fields asked. He was hit with further silence. "I can understand that you're a little nervous, but I need you to answer the question."

Susan sat motionless and was silent. Her attorney patted her on the back for support, but still she sat alone in the room full of strangers. Faces started to blur and fade as she began tuning them out, and she was left alone. Her eyes began darting in all directions, moving wildly about the room, anything to avoid eye contact with anybody, especially the judge.

"Mrs. Bishope?" Judge Fields said with a firm voice.

Susan's eyes latched onto his stare. He was now the enemy. "I just can't have this baby!" she said with heated breath. "You would never understand my reasons."

"I understand a lot of things, Mrs. Bishope. I've been around a long time and have seen things that are very hard to understand," Judge Fields said. "Yet somehow they all seem to make perfect sense to me. If they don't, I usually try my best to find the answers and understand them."

"You wanted an answer, I gave you an answer. I am not going to have this baby!"

"That's it then?"

"That's it!" she abruptly replied.

"Thank you for your cooperation, Mrs. Bishope," Judge Fields said through narrowed eyes.

* * * * *

The courtroom went silent when Judge Fields took his seat. Renee said a final word to Susan, a word of encouragement, no doubt. Nick was sitting next to both of his parents at his usual place, directly behind Michael.

Glancing around the quiet courtroom, Michael took a mental note of the gathering. He locked eyes with Frank Chandler for a moment. Chandler was wearing his best menacing smile. Michel knew right then what he was going to do. There was no sense in prolonging the inevitable. He knew Chandler wasn't going to do the right thing, so Michael was going to have to take matters into his own hands. He shot Chandler with a look of pity and then returned his eyes to the judge.

"Let it show for the record, an unsuccessful attempt in chambers had been made to intervene in this matter," Judge Fields said. "Both parties wish to continue with the proceedings." Judge Fields handed a sheet of paper to his clerk and then looked back at the courtroom.

Judge Fields went over the ramifications of his decision. Whatever the decision, he was bound to upset a lot of people. This was the only case he long feared—no winners, only losers, including him. He quickly pondered retirement. He finally nodded to counsel. "Mister Vecchio," Judge Fields said, giving him the floor.

Vecchio stood up and walked over to the podium in the center of the room. "Your Honor, my client, Susan Bishope, is faced with a difficult decision. On one hand, she loves her husband and wants to spend a long, happy life with him. She has dreams and wants to share those dreams, live those dreams, with her husband." Vecchio paused a moment. He too began thinking about his own career and where these proceedings might take him. This was an epic case he was thrown into, and he wished he had more time to prepare, more time to talk to Susan.

"Our justice system is based on the people, for the people. We have the right to free speech, the right to bear arms, and the right to choose life. And since 1973, we have had the right to abortion, which is exactly what Susan Bishope is being told that she cannot do. It is her constitutional right to choose whether or not to have this child. Right or wrong, she has made her choice. It is her body, and it is her right to have an abortion. No disrespect, Your Honor, but it is ridiculous that she is even here at this juncture," he said and paused. Judge Fields continued his firm glare. "Your Honor, if you take away the mothers right to choose, doesn't that nullify our system? Does that not place our country under government control and jeopardize our constitution? A single word could be the first strike against the constitution and ultimately lead to its downfall. With that, anarchy would reign."

"Very colorful, Mr. Vecchio. I don't think we have to go that far. Though I do understand the embellishment," Judge Fields said.

"Win or lose, we all lose!" Vecchio almost shouted. He pointed. "Because that massive crowd outside your courtroom has been waiting since 1973 to jump onto something this large. Their fuse is burning, and God help us when that fuse reaches its end. I don't want to be around for that explosion. Do you?"

Judge Fields shot him with a contemptuous glare.

Nash smiled.

Vecchio lowered his head a moment and took a deep breath. "The riot that follows this case, Your Honor, will not be limited to Los Angeles, especially if the constitution is breached. The riot that follows this case will be a national crisis." Again he paused and read over his few notes. "I don't think I have to state any case law as I'm sure you're aware of standing," Vecchio said as he searched the judge's face for reaction. "At any given moment, people are bound and subject to the laws that are in force at the moment. This is a fundamental legal principle, and the constitution prohibits Congress from enacting ex-post facto laws. This includes pregnancy. The First, Fourth, Fifth, Eleventh, Fourteenth, and Fifteenth Amendments as cited in *Roe v. Wade* rendered a five to two vote by the Supreme Court justices—a decision that today has remained unchanged. Therefore, the subject as to whether or not Mrs. Bishope has the right to terminate her pregnancy is a question not for the state but for Mrs. Bishope alone. It would be a grave miscarriage of our justice system to render a decision to the contrary." Vecchio nodded and returned to his seat next to Susan.

Judge Fields didn't appear very happy with Vecchio. He wanted to lash out at him and give him a piece of his mind, but the massive gathering intimidated him.

Susan didn't need to turn and see the door opening in the courtroom. She knew who was entering, but she turned anyway as the door squeaked slightly. The reporters and people sitting in the gallery came to life as she turned and faced them head-on. Susan's lawyer tried to stop her from turning and disrupting the court. He didn't want anything to appear out of place in front of Judge Fields—and especially in front of the media's watchful eyes.

But Susan turned anyway and watched as Macy entered the courtroom and walked slowly toward the front of the room. The posted guards let her by without any questions.

Susan locked eyes with Macy in a long time lapse. Macy floated across the room as if she were in slow motion. Susan's head swam in a violent sea of conflicting emotions. She knew that this was probably not the right time for an appearance by Macy, but she had no control over her. She had no control over anything, not at this late junction.

Macy passed through the small gates as the spectators looked on. Macy looked up at the judge and turned toward Susan. She was wearing the same Gingham sundress, with tiny orange sunflowers splashed intermittently throughout the material. Susan found it a little strange that she was wearing the exact same thing she wore when she first came over before the wedding. She had the same hair and same yellow bow. Now that she thought about it, Susan realized that she used to wear the same clothes when they were children. They were the exact same clothes. She couldn't remember her in anything else. Ever.

Macy leaned on the table and hovered above Susan like the executioner in a hooded cloak, waiting for the beheading.

Nash was smooth as he glided over to the podium in front of the judge's bench. He cleared his throat and briefly read from his notes. He smiled for the KNRQ camera that was trained on him.

Judge Fields's attentions were elsewhere. His eyes were on Vecchio, Susan, and Macy. He was almost livid with the events that were taking place in his courtroom and held Vecchio in his sights. He began twirling the silver pen between his fingers. A sketch artist in the audience tried to render his distinguished image on paper. He caught his vivid scowl perfectly.

"He's going to throw you in jail, Susan. Is that where you want to be?" Macy asked.

"Jail is better than the alternative," Susan said aloud.

The crowd let out a collective groan as heads maneuvered for a better viewing position. Her abrupt comment was drastically out of the ordinary, and everybody noticed, even Judge Fields who looked across at Mrs. Bishope. The KNRQ camera quickly pulled focus onto Susan after her curious outburst.

Tyson Nash turned with curiosity. Had he really heard what he thought he just heard? His pasty face was creased with a smile. Michael's mouth was agape as he looked on the disturbing scene.

"She's lost her mind," someone in the audience said.

Judge Fields looked at her with a strain in his eyes. "Mrs. Bishope, I do have to warn you that you are not immune to a contempt-of-court citation."

Susan did not acknowledge the man in the black dress. She did not see him or anyone else in the room. Everybody in the room was tuned out, leaving her alone in the room with Macy in a surreal, hazy setting.

"See, what did I tell you?" Macy said as she walked in front of the judge's bench and leaned on the empty jury box. "You need to stand up right now and tell Michael that you are going to have his child. It the right thing to do, Susan," Macy said as she again approached Susan at the table.

"I am not going to have his baby!" Susan replied aloud, almost shouting.

Michael felt the intensity of her voice cut him right down to his bones.

The crowd gasped as a buzz filled the room with wild abandon. This historic story was quickly becoming one of twisted events, a reporter's wet dream.

Michael and Nash were in a death stare, with their mouths parted, both confused as they watched. Nash was a little more willing to let this rant play out. She was doing his job for him. Michael was terror-filled. Never again did he want to see this side of his wife, especially not in front of the world's eyes.

"Mrs. Bishope!" Judge Fields shouted.

Susan didn't hear the judge's plea. She had a single vision, a single request before her, one only she could see and hear.

"What happened in the past is long behind you, Susan. You have to move on now," Macy said with pleading eyes.

"I have moved on, and look where it's gotten me!" Susan shouted. "It's too late for me now. He will kill me, and you know it!" Susan shouted.

Everybody in the courtroom, including Judge Fields, looked directly at Michael. All of a sudden, Michael was guilty by suspicion. A rush of guilt washed over him. The reporters took notice and made their secret notes; some spoke quietly into the microrecorders.

"Who is going to kill you, Mrs. Bishope? Better yet, whom are you talking to?" Judge Fields asked with a raised voice.

"Do you really want to go through this, Susan? Look around you. You're at the center of a freak show. The whole world knows about this," Macy said quietly.

"This is what I have to do," Susan replied.

Her lawyer tried to calm her, but his words went unheard; he wasn't even a blip on her radar screen. He quickly turned toward the judge and demanded a recess, but Judge Fields was so shocked by Susan's actions he had not heard the attorney's plea.

More shock murmurs resonated throughout the crowd. It was so loud and the judge was so beside himself that he took no notice of the volume in his courtroom. As the excitement grew into an uproar, Judge Fields slammed the gavel down and looked at his clerk, who was frozen in time. Her stare was on Susan. She too had never been witness to such a breakdown in mental stability.

Michael's eyes began filling with tears. It tore him apart to see his wife dance through the dark as she was now, alone and naked before the whole country, the whole world. "Susan, stop!" Michael shouted across to her.

Nash quickly grabbed his arm. He knew Susan was hanging herself. He wasn't about to let Michael or anyone else halt her bout with insanity and Nash's date with fame and fortune.

Renee began crying in the seat behind Susan. She tried to stop her, tried to reach out, but her attempts went unnoticed.

Nick couldn't take his eyes off Renee. He felt so bad for her, so bad for Susan. But it was the sight of Renee crying that was tugging at his heartstrings.

"Mrs. Bishope!" Judge Fields shouted. "I order you to cease this nonsense immediately!"

"God, Macy, why'd you have to come here today? Why now?"

Judge Fields, along with everybody else present, was beside himself with confusion. Susan was talking to the air, a vision floating on room dust, looking around the room as if she held eye contact with a person that just wasn't there. Reporters, against the judge's orders, were snapping still photos of Susan. Sketch artists quickly rendered their version of her breakdown.

"Because you wouldn't quit. You insisted on having an abortion, which is the wrong choice altogether. For the first time in your life, you have something special. It's time that you realize where you are!"

Susan shook her head and closed her eyes, trying to fend off the attack. Perhaps if she ignored Macy long enough, she would just go away. Macy smiled and moved around to the end of the table. "Where do you think I came from, Susan?" Macy asked.

Susan held her eyes tightly closed. Her head rocked vigorously back and forth like an angered child trying to break free of this torment.

The bailiffs began moving toward her, but they too were confused as to what to do. They usually waited orders from the judge, but he was too enraged to direct them.

"Where did we first meet? What were my parents' names? What did they look like? Did I have any brothers or sisters?" Macy asked.

Susan continued shaking her head like a deranged psychopath, faster and harder. The judge slammed the gavel and yelled at her. His face was red with anger. The courtroom took notice of his wrath and came to an abrupt, silent halt. His voice remained in the room, hot and loud, repeating his orders over and over again.

Susan's eyes jerked open and locked onto Macy's stare. "You lived next door to me," Susan replied with conviction.

"I never lived next door to you."

"That's impossible!" Susan shouted. "You were there every day. Whenever I needed you."

"Yes, Susan, when you needed me. I was there, with you, at your house." Macy moaned softly.

Susan shook her head and looked morbidly confused. A thousand thoughts and images flashed through her mind. She was trying somehow to pull up the image of Macy's house, of her family, but nothing was there.

Macy smiled and moved closer to Susan. She lifted her hand and swept it across Susan's face, gently touching her soft skin. "I am not real, Susan. I don't live in your world. I never have."

"No…no. No."

"I live in your mind."

"No!" Susan screamed. "I don't believe you! You are real. You've always been real. I am not crazy."

Crazy or not, the reporters caught that little exchange of fantasy-driven dialogue, and they were going to report it how they saw it. The general public would form their own opinion.

"Susan, you created me when you were very young, when all those bad things happened to you. I was your outlet. You needed me, and I needed you to live. You're my mother, Susan."

"I am not your mother!" Susan shouted.

Another groan wavered over the seated spectators.

"If it wasn't for you, I would have never been born into your mind. I would have never seen the world of lightness and reality you have shown me. I would have remained in the darkness forever. There's nobody to talk to in the darkness, Susan," Macy said quietly. She knew Susan was at her breaking point. "You know about the darkness, don't you, Susan? That's why you created me in darkness. You kept me in the dark for weeks, months even. You weren't the only one who was scared."

"No!"

"I have many functions, Susan. I am your conscience."

"No, you're not!" Susan shouted.

Judge Fields shouted. His face was beet red.

"Oh yes, I am. I have been ever since you gave birth to me. I am also your punisher. You were just never aware of what I have done."

Judge Fields was screaming, slamming the gavel.

"I've been your teacher, and I have answered your questions. I am what we shall be."

Susan continued shaking her head violently, wholeheartedly disagreeing with Macy as she went on. She didn't want to hear the truth, but it was coming from all directions.

Judge Fields was livid. He didn't realize that he was repeatedly slamming the gavel.

"I will always be here. If I am gone, you are just a body, nothing else," Macy said. She tried to hold Susan's hand, but she ripped away from her touch. "Susan, I have been sorting out your problems for years. Why do you think I'm here now? I am here to fix another problem you have created."

"If you only exist in my mind, then how can I see you? How am I looking at you right now?" Susan shouted with rapid hand gestures. "How have I touched you? How have I felt your tears?"

"They were your tears, Susan."

"No!"

Judge Field's continued shouting and slamming the gavel.

The reporters were completely shocked. This was going to make a great story.

Macy looked around the courtroom and found Michael shouting at Susan to be quiet. The judge was shouting at her. Her lawyer pulled at her arms. The reporters in the gallery held up their recorders and cameras.

"Look around you. You're the only one who can see me, Susan. Nobody else sees me. As far as they know, you're talking to yourself right now. How do you think that looks?" Macy finished.

Susan refused to look at anything. "I don't believe you," Susan said quietly in case Macy was right.

"Look at what I'm wearing, Susan. This is what you put me in when you created me. I have been wearing it since you created me. You created me in the image you always wanted to be. Why do you think we look so much alike?"

Susan continued shaking her head until she finally, with all her might, pounded her fist onto the table. Judge Fields stopped yelling. Michael stopped yelling. The courtroom fell silent as Susan flared her eyes into Macy's stare.

"I'm now God, and I can create people out of thin air?" Susan asked with a bitter look on her face. It was a question for Macy, but the reporters, the judge, and Michael took it as a statement. She was convicted and sentenced to death row on the spot by the court of public appeal.

Nash loved it.

Macy shook her head. "Yes, Susan, that's exactly what you did." She paused for a moment as she tried to remember some of the old tricks she used to use on Susan to make her see things her way. But Susan was a different foe than she remembered. She was so much stronger of mind and will. She was much more stubborn than before. "You need to do the right thing, Susan."

"You know I can't have this baby!" Susan shouted.

The judge was pissed. He was yelling at Susan, yelling at her lawyer, yelling at the bailiffs, yelling at the crowd in the gallery, all while slamming the gavel onto the bench. Everyone was in stunned shock, even Chandler, whose face actually showed concern.

"Having this baby will set you free, Susan," Macy said. "It will eliminate your entire past and allow you to live a normal life. Look at Michael," Macy said. "Go on, look at him," she said as she moved over in front of Michael. His eyes remained full of tears and focused on Susan. "He doesn't see me." Susan glanced over at her husband but could only see a wall of haze, blurred faces in the dense fog.

Michael roughly grabbed Nash by the arm and pulled him close. He told him that he wanted to drop the case immediately. Nash nodded, but he didn't hear a word Michael said. His eyes and ears were focused on Susan and her complete descent into lunacy.

"That's your husband, Susan, and he's hurting because of you, because of what you're doing to yourself right now. He loves you! Do you think he's going to let anything happen to you? Do you?"

"I will never be free!" Susan shouted to her imaginary foe. "My fate was sealed long ago, just like it was promised. Don't you see?" Susan asked. She followed Macy with her eyes, and Macy moved back and forth. "I will not live to see this baby grow up."

"Yes, you will," Macy responded.

"Mrs. Bishope! You are in contempt of court!" Judge Fields shouted.

"No, I won't!" Susan shouted to the silent room of stunned faces. "I don't care what you say to me!" Susan had fire in her eyes and an angry face.

Macy stopped in her tracks. When she reined in, she was standing directly in front of the judge. Susan appeared to be looking straight at Judge Fields, who was already livid and wasn't pleased with her statement, but she wasn't talking to him.

Susan was still eye-to-eye with Macy and the judge. "I had to deal with what happened to me! You were only there to clean up the mess and put me back together. It was me who lived with the ugliness!" Susan shouted. Tears were pouring down her face.

Michael broke down on the table with his face in his hands, crying like a child. Nick reached over the railing and placed a comforting hand on his friend's shoulder. Nick began to feel choked up himself, but there was nothing he could do. There was nothing anybody could do.

"Susan, shut up!" Renee shouted from the gallery. She too was in tears.

The courtroom was in mayhem. Vecchio was right about the riot, but he had no idea that the riot would be held within the sanctity of the courtroom.

Susan continued through the chaos and shouts as if she and Macy were the only people in the courtroom. "This is my life, and I want to live. Don't you understand, Macy? That's the reason I ran away! I ran so far away from there I thought I left it all behind me. But I was wrong. It followed me. It's just something that I will never get away from."

"Bailiffs, take her into custody!"

"No!" Michael shouted to the judge.

The bailiffs were too stunned by the action to move.

"Don't you see that me being here is a sign of help?" Macy asked. "Susan, this thing is going to stay here until you face it. You will always run and hide, but it will always find you. Having this baby is your weapon against the past, Susan. If you want to live, then stand up now and do the right thing. Look at your husband," she said, pointing. "He's falling apart because of you."

Susan began crying aloud. Sobbing spasms began ravaging her body. Silence fell upon the courtroom as they watched Susan fighting with herself.

The slamming of the gavel continued. It never actually stopped. Judge Fields unknowingly had been repeatedly slamming the gavel in anger over and over again.

Susan looked up. Her face was wet with salty tears. "I can't have this baby," she said.

"I love you, Susan," Macy said.

"I love you too," Susan replied and began crying harder, louder.

"This is the end, you know?"

"I know," she barely replied through her sobbing.

"Goodbye, Susan," Macy said as she started walking toward the door and vanished before her eyes.

"Goodbye…goodbye, Macy. I love you," she called after her. Susan laid her head on the table, crying uncontrollably.

The burly bailiffs cautiously made their way across the room and grabbed Susan by the arms. Susan was startled and jumped. She forced eye contact with the bailiff and then scanned the room. "Where am I?" she asked aloud.

The KNRQ camera held a tight focus on Susan's face.

"Mrs. Bishope, that was an outrage! That was a display such as I have never seen before, and frankly, I am concerned," Judge Fields said. His voice still raised with anger. His face still red, but he tried to calm himself down. "Do you know where you are, Mrs. Bishope?"

Michael looked over and wiped his eyes.

"I'm in court," she replied softly.

"Whom were you talking to?" Judge Fields asked.

"I was just talking to—" Susan stopped herself before she could do any further damage.

"Mrs. Bishope, I am inclined to believe that you are in serious need of psychological counseling. I have never witnessed such a breakdown in sanity before in my entire life," Judge Fields said and paused. He fought against his better judgment. He shook his head. "I'm afraid I have no choice. I am ordering you held for a 730 psychological evaluation effective immediately," Judge Fields said. "The evaluation will take place in the hospital ward of the Los Angeles county jail for a period of thirty days."

"I object, Your Honor!" Vecchio shouted, but his voice was drowned out as the courtroom erupted in pandemonium. A few reporters ran from the room to get a head start on their stories. Others ran to the crowd outside the courthouse to share the news.

"I object, Your Honor," Vecchio said again.

"Object all you want, Mr. Vecchio."

"There are no grounds for a custody order."

"Look around you, Mr. Vecchio. We're setting new precedence every day," Judge Fields roared back and slammed his gavel. "Objection overruled."

Nash smiled. He had just become the most famous lawyer in Los Angeles, if not the whole country. Michael looked on with confusion, his eyes still wet with tears.

Renee was crying and on the verge of hysterics as she tried to grab Susan. She fell back in her chair and held her face in her hands. Nick wanted to go to her and comfort her. Her sadness hurt him deeply. Nick still loved her and hated to see her in such pain.

"Bailiffs, remove Mrs. Bishope from the courtroom," Judge Fields ordered.

The bailiffs began walking Susan toward the side door.

"I order all parties back here thirty days from today's date. At which time, this will be a closed courtroom. No more circus and no more cameras!" Judge Fields said sternly. His nerves were so rattled by the audacity of Susan's behavior that he was looking forward to that twenty-five-year-old bottle of bourbon in his chambers. He slammed the gavel to the bench. "Court dismissed," Judge Fields said. He got up and stormed out of the courtroom. He passed right by the two bailiffs leading Susan from the room.

On the way out of the courtroom, Susan fainted and fell into the arms of one of the bailiffs. Michael yelled after her as the large bailiff with blond hair whisked her up in his arms and carried her through the side door.

Reporters swarmed Michael and Nash when the judge left the room. Michael was in no mood for reporters. He wanted to bust each and every one of them in the chops, starting with Chandler.

But they came—reporters and questions, one after the other, hordes of flashbulbs bursting in their faces. Nash played it cool; he knew he was going to be all over the news again tonight. He knew he was going to be on the news every night for weeks and months to come. He was walking on air, but again he played it cool. Michael still wanted to know what had happened and what was going to happen. Michael tried to pull Nash aside, but the reporters would not let this go. They continued with their barrage of questions as they surged upon them.

Nick leaned over to speak to his distraught mother, who was in tears; and out of the corner of his eye, he saw Renee, who was the only person who remained sitting in the courtroom. Her face was buried in her hands, and she was clearly crying. That pulled at Nick's heartstrings. He made his way through the wild crowd and over to Renee.

Renee was startled when Nick placed his hand on her shoulder. She looked up with tear-filled eyes. Her despair diminished slightly when her eyes met his loving gaze. She immediately jumped into his arms and wrapped her arms tightly around him. "Oh, Nicky, I'm so sorry," she started, trying to quell the choke in her throat. "I am so sorry I didn't see what you were trying to tell me. You were right. Michael had every right to try to save his baby." Her tears came slower now, and she was able to look at him. "But what do I do now? I've lost her. I've lost Susan."

"It's all right," Nick said as she buried her head into his massive shoulder. "You still have me."

Renee looked back up into his eyes. At that moment, she felt closer to Nick than she had ever felt to anyone. "Will you drive me home, Nicky?"

Nick looked into her misty eyes and felt a lump in his stomach. He wanted this so much. "To our home?"

"Yes," she said softly, "to our home."

*****

The massive crowd outside was a melting pot of nuclear weapons, and the timer was counting down nearing its conclusion. The bomb unit parked on the street in front of the courthouse would prove to be of no assistance if this time bomb went off.

The pro-life camp was delighted with the news from inside the courtroom. It was a victory they had long waited for. Some could see a permanent end to abortion on the horizon. They were thrilled and cheered the judge's decision and began chanting a pro-life slogan. Some were taunting the pro-choice side, who was already livid with the court's decision. The paroxysms of rage had begun with a trigger effect on the horizon.

News cameras rolled continually as the mayhem began its snowball roll down that mountain of promised violence. Pro-choice fanatics began hurling insults across the way. Signs began flying through the air into the pro-life group, hitting people—men, women, and children—in the face and head. The yelling escalated into a rage on both sides. More signs from both sides began flying into the massive crowd. Bottles and rocks and shoes and trash cans were thrown, hitting women and children.

As the riot police began their surge into the crowd, they let out a loud, high-pitched whistle, like something exploding at a Fourth of July celebration, but that further incensed the crowd. They began a physical attack on one another—fists flying, feet kicking, as an all-out war began on the battlefield. Men and women engaged in hand-to-hand combat. Most ran to get away from the violence. But the hard-liners stayed and fought. People were caught in the stampede and were bleeding and bruised. Men fighting men, women fighting women. Bottles, rocks, signs, anything that could be thrown was hurled in the direction of the other side.

Lost children were crying in the faceless crowd. They were looking for their parents, who abandoned them in search of a proper war of words or other means. People ran everywhere with no particular place to go, stepping and trampling on one another. People were frantic as they ran for their lives, trying to flee the hostile grounds. Helicopters continued circling above the frenzied battlefield. Main Street was filling with people moving fast in all directions. Some ran down to the Santa Monica Pier.

Reporters and cameras captured every moment of the chaos. It was like a war zone. Cameras caught three men beating a teenage boy. A reverend came to the boy's rescue. The men moved on to their next victim. A man and a woman almost twice his size were throwing blows at each another. Others were beating one another with signs and sticks, using them as swords.

A reporter was thrown to the ground and beaten. His cameraman caught the whole incident on tape, but he too was severely beaten and left for dead. His camera was stolen and later found smashed through a storefront window over two miles away. Cars in parking lots were destroyed, windows smashed, some burning. The eye of the storm was here as promised, and tainted memories of the LA riots came rushing back.

Smoke started rising from within the crowd. People started choking and gasping for air as the tear gas became too much. Most of the crowd began running for cover as the riot police stormed the crowd. As the grounds in front of the courthouse began to clear, injured bodies remained lying on the grass. People were crawling and crying; some were convulsing. Others threw up from the strong tear gas.

Pro-life and pro-choice continued their fight into the streets in front of the police barricade, smashing windows of police cars and storefront windows in Venice a mile away. Violence was spreading everywhere: on the Santa Monica Pier, the Third Street Promenade, nothing was safe. Glass was shattered all over the place. Tourists snapped pictures of the thousands of people running through the upscale shopping street. Crazed people tore through businesses and loitered racks of goods.

From an underground parking lot nearby came thick black smoke rising up into the pristine blue sky. More smoke came from another parking structure on Fourth Street.

The looting had started, and this time, it wasn't in "the hood." The center of this riot was in the affluent upper-class community of Santa Monica, California.

Inside the mall at the Santa Monica Place was sheer terror and pandemonium on all three levels as people ran in and out of stores, breaking windows, throwing things, clothes, tables, carts, food, and trash from the second and third floors of the mall. A hot-dog vendor lost his cart of goods as a group of enraged teens knocked the man to the ground and hurled his cart from the second floor of the mall. They watched and laughed as the cart smashed into the water of the fountain below.

It wasn't long before others joined in the looting. People were running out of stores with arms full of stolen goods, clothes, sunglasses, lingerie, shoes, and televisions. Stark, raving mad people carried everything that could be carried away.

Fires were blazing in trash cans on the street. More people were running. Some were running away from the violence; others were running toward the violence, throwing things as they moved. It was a free-for-all. They were hitting people, knocking them to the ground, some throwing wild sucker punches, devastating people they connected with.

A blaze of fire came from a high-end store at the end of the Third Street Promenade; flames were licking toward the sky. Black smoke was choking the air. Tourists were screaming in fear. The rioters were screaming, letting the pent-up anger lose in the sea air on a warm Southern California day. This was the place where dreams come true, and if they could not get it one way, they were going to take it another.

23

Shadows filled the parking lot as dusk strained against the horizon in the Western sky. Michael pulled his car to a stop in the slot with his name painted on the curb. He turned the key, killing the engine, and studied the building with a long, lingering gaze. There were a lot of sleepless nights in there, he thought. Stepping out of the car, he glanced around the lot and was surprised by the number of cars in the parking lot at this hour.

Michael felt somewhat nostalgic as he approached the entrance of the KNRQ studios. Memories came rushing back to him, most of them were happy memories of long hours and great stories and even greater friends. But he was dirtied by the business and the politics and tainted with its recent direction, especially after witnessing firsthand the direction it was going. He was sick of the car chases and tabloid television Chandler thought was so important. It was all about ratings to him. Glorifying a person's misery wasn't what Michael had in mind when he signed on. The industry had integrity when he first started, and Michael wanted to hold on to what little he had left.

Michael could hear the electrically charged emotion of the newsroom beyond the glass doors just ahead of him as he approached. Though he had passed through the doors a thousand times before, his heart began to race as it did his first day on the job. It was a rush he relished then but now loathed. He stopped next to the heavy glass doors and placed his hand on its cold surface. He could feel the energy through the glass. He waited.

Michael took a deep breath and pushed through the glass doors and entered the noisy office. He was surprised when his eyes caught the sight of all the people in the office. My God! He did not want to see so many faces here!

He had planned to lower his head and walk directly to his office, close the door, and not talk to anyone. But upon entering, silence fell upon the room, and all eyes focused on him. He froze in his tracks. He stood silent by the front doors, contemplating his next move. He wasn't ready for all these people, not at this hour of the day. Even though most of them were his people, friends, coworkers, his hires, he wanted to turn and run. Chandler had dragged Michael through the mud, stabbed him in the back, and gave him a bad name around the office. Even worse, Chandler made sure that Michael's story went worldwide just to make sure that when Michael fell, he would fall hard and shatter into unfixable pieces.

A young assistant field producer, Rachelle Webster, one of the last people Michael hired straight off the UCLA campus, walked right up to Michael and embraced him. "You're doing a very brave thing, Michael. I hope you get to keep your baby," she said softly.

"Thank you," he replied.

People in the background returned to their work, but they kept eyeing Michael. The white noise once again filled the room, but the volume was dimmed down low.

"Can I tell you something?" she asked.

"Of course, Rachelle."

She led Michael off into a darkened corner away from earshot. "Like I said, you're doing the right thing," she started and paused. Tears began pooling in her blue eyes.

"Are you all right?" Michael asked.

Rachelle smiled. "You're a gem, you know that? Here you are, going through complete hell, and you're concerned because I'm about to cry like a baby. It's no wonder why everybody around here loves you so much," she said and kissed him on the cheek. "Michael, I wanted to tell you that during my freshman year in college, I became pregnant, and I had an abortion," she whispered softly. "And I've regretted my decision every day since. I wish I hadn't done it. That might have been my only chance to have a child, and I only thought about my future, about my career. I was too young, Michael, and so selfish," she said pleadingly. Tears began pouring from her eyes. "Michael, you have no idea how many times I wanted to kill myself over what I did to my baby. It is so hard to live with the choice I made. I think about it every day."

"Rachelle, I would never hold that against you, or anyone else. That was something you had to do," Michael started. His eyes showed compassion and understanding. He felt for her and wanted to ease her pain. "You were too young to have a baby, and you had too much to look forward to. Just think if you would have had the baby. You might not have finished your education." Michael paused a moment to let Rachelle gather herself. "You can't dwell on the decisions you've made in the past because there is nothing you can do about it. You made your choice, and you had to move on, which you did. You're here now. And this is where you were meant to be. You will have a baby someday, Rachelle. When you're ready—and you'll know when you're ready—you will have a baby."

Rachelle wiped her eyes. People in the background looked on now and then. Michael was the circus sideshow freak, and the plebeians would forever remain curious.

"I am not against abortion. Please don't think that because I am fighting for my child's life, that I'm against it, because I'm not. This is just something that I have to do. It's the right thing for me. And what you did was the right thing for you to do," he said.

"I know," she replied. "I just wanted to share my feelings of regret with you so you could see that you are doing the right thing. I wouldn't want you to go through what I went through, always looking back and wondering what if," she said. Tears continued pooling in her soft eyes. "I'm tired of living in that moment, Michael, and because you're going through this, it has helped me come to grips with what I did. I feel much better about myself and the choice I made. I have felt less suicidal, and I now feel like I can move on with my life." She stared into his eyes in a long, silent moment. She smiled. "I just wanted to say thanks, Michael. And I love you," she said and again hugged him.

"Thank you for sharing that with me, Rachelle. I know that wasn't an easy thing to say," he whispered. "Please stay in touch."

"God bless you, Michael. I hope your get to keep your baby. You're going to make a wonderful father," she whispered.

Breaking from the embrace, Michael started moving across the room toward his office. Rachelle didn't catch on when he said it, but she quickly realized he had come here to clear out his office. A look of concern swept across her face.

A few people approached Michael and stopped him. They shook his hand; others hugged him, wished him luck. Most told him that they were behind him. One lady gave Michael a bouquet of flowers and a "wish you luck" balloon. Michael hugged and thanked her, then moved toward his office.

As he approached his office, David stood up from his chair. He stared at Michael a long, awkward moment. Michael could see the stress and concern on his face as he searched for the right words.

"It's all right, David," Michael said with a smile and patted him on the shoulder.

David blew a sigh of relief then opened the office door for him. He watched as Michael closed the door behind him. There was so much he wanted to say to his mentor, his boss, his friend; but when he was finally face-to-face with him, he was tongue-tied and lost his focus and nerve. He slouched over in his chair and laid his head on the desk.

Crossing the floor, Michael walked pensively toward his desk, where he stood a long moment glancing around the room. There were so many great and hectic moments spent in this office, he thought. Michael took a last look out the picture window at the city, sprawling out in the distance.

The word was spreading rapidly throughout the office that Michael was leaving the station. Concerned assistants and coworkers approached David wanting answers and to see Michael before he left. David was shocked to learn that he was leaving, but still he would not allow anyone into Michael's office.

It didn't take Michael long to box up his things in the office. He packed only the more personal things: pictures, signed baseballs, knickknacks, and the three stones he chipped from the Berlin Wall. That was the most important thing to him. They had always kept him grounded, made him think about the inhumanity man has had to endure through the ages.

With a box tucked under his arm, Michael crossed the floor for the last time as he moved toward the door. He turned for one final look. He smiled and walked out.

"David, can you make sure I get the rest of my things? Have them sent to me, will you?" he asked.

"Sure," David replied and stood up from his chair. "Hey, listen, Mike. I just wanted to say how much I loved working for you, and I wish that none of this were happening. You're the greatest guy, Mike. You're the best boss I could have ever had. You have taught me so much, and I just wanted to say thank you."

Michael smiled and placed a hand on his shoulder.

"Well, well, if it isn't the man of the hour," Chandler said with an evil smile. "Told you I'd make you famous."

"You know, Frank, you're an asshole. Everything about you stinks. I feel sorry for you, you pathetic little dweeb," Michael said with spite. Dweeb? Michael couldn't believe he said that. He hadn't heard that since high school. He had no idea where the word came from, but for a moment, it threw him for a loop.

The newsroom became quiet as everybody stopped and listened to the private conversation Chandler made public.

"You've lost touch with reality and lost sight of what this business is all about," Michael continued. "It's not about glamorizing another person's misery. It's not about kicking a person when he's down. That's supermarket-tabloid shit, not the news! And everybody knows you're pulling all the strings, you motherfucker!"

"You're right, I am. And you're the one who has to take his wife to court just to have a kid," Chandler said with a smile. "How's it feel to have a nutjob for a wife?"

Michael dropped the box and stepped toward him in anger. He wanted to pummel him into the floor, but David grabbed his arm before Michael could cave in Chandler's face. Chandler retreated in fear.

"You will always be an asshole!" Michael said and then started walking toward the door.

"You'll—"

"SHUT UP!" David shouted. "Enough is enough, Frank!"

Chandler shot him with a blistering glare. He wanted to fire him on the spot, but there were too many eyes on him and he froze. He made a note, though, and added David to his Christmas fire list.

David picked up the box and started after Michael.

As Michael walked through the newsroom for the last time, a woman stood up and started clapping. Others stood and followed her lead. Soon after, everybody in the newsroom showered Michael with applause as he left the room. They wanted Michael to feel their love and support and to show Chandler their disapproval with him and his tactics. Chandler was livid and shouted at them to shut up, but they continued even after Michael had left the newsroom. Chandler screamed louder and louder, but they continued cheering for Michael. Chandler stormed across the room, past his secretary, and slammed the door to his office as he entered.

* * * * *

Frank Chandler maneuvered his way through a maze of cameras being pushed to their locations by camera assistants as he walked across the stage and over to the news desk.

Makeup artists did their final touches on the talent as the two news anchors sat for their eleven o'clock broadcast. Dawn August wiped lipstick from her mouth. She glared through the bright lights and rolled her eyes. "Here comes trouble," she said.

David Weathers looked on and caught the sight of Chandler approaching the news desk. Weathers lowered his head.

Chandler stepped into the scene and handed them each a sheet of paper in which to read from. Weathers looked up from the sheet. "I'm not going to read this," he said to Chandler.

"Yes, you are!" Chandler shot back.

"No, I most certainly will not. This is garbage, Frank," he stated. "And frankly, you have been making this a personal assault on Michael for weeks, and I think it's in bad taste." For years, David Weathers had been a local icon of sorts in the media. Most people in and around the Los Angeles area recognized him. In his late fifties, Weathers's snow-white hair and dashing face made him a very recognizable figure around town.

"I agree," Dawn, said.

"You stay out of this," Chandler said.

"One minute," shouted a stagehand. "We're on in one minute," he repeated.

"I will not stay out of this," she replied. Chandler could sense the fire building within her. She was a firecracker who always questioned everything, and that angered Chandler. He thought she was a spoiled brat. She was just a pretty face that couldn't make it as an actor. "I am not going to read this crap either. If you want us to cover the trial, that's one thing, but when you make this a personal attack on a good person, somebody we all know and love, that is out-and-out bullshit! I won't do it!"

"What are you going to do, Frank?" Weathers asked. "We're on in thirty seconds." He knew he had him by the short hairs. And he could almost see smoke billowing from Chandler's ears.

"You guys are a dime a dozen!" he said with violent displeasure written all over his bitter face. "We have people waiting for your seats, and if you don't report the news like it was given to you, neither one of you will ever work in this town again!" Chandler shouted.

Weathers smiled. This little pipsqueak would not test his resolve.

"Now do your jobs and read the fucking news!"

"We're on in five…four…"

"Read the fucking copy!"

"Three…two…," said the assistant cameraman, who finished counting with his fingers, *One*. Chandler quickly backed into the shadows out of camera shot and stood next to the news director. He couldn't wait for his propaganda to be broadcast over the airwaves.

"Good evening, California. I'm David Weathers."

"And I'm Dawn August. Welcome, Los Angeles."

The camera focused on Weathers, who hesitated a moment before speaking. He briefly read from the sheet of paper Chandler handed him. He smiled and paused in silence. He was shaking his head slightly. He chuckled lightly and smiled.

Chandler and the news director were frantic over the dead air being broadcast.

"From time to time," Weathers started, "we as humans are faced with certain dilemmas. It is a quagmire of moral issues. Sometimes we are faced with having to choose between right and wrong."

"That's not the fucking script!" Chandler said under his breath. He was seething with anger as he looked on from behind the camera. "Cut him off!" he said to the director. "Cut that motherfucker off! Go to commercial!"

"I can't do that from here," the director whispered back. "It can only be done from the control room." He could have cut him off, but he wanted to let this play out. He knew Chandler was going to storm off like a little girl. And that's exactly what he did. The director didn't want him on the stage anyway.

Chandler stormed toward the control room as Weathers continued. The news director whispered into his headset. "Gabe. Chandler's on his way to see you. Stall him," said the director.

"It's a difficult decision, especially when the consequences are career-threatening, as is the case tonight," David said as he pulled the mic from his jacket and held it in front of his mouth. "Management here at KNRQ feels that tabloid television is more appropriate than reporting the news how it truly is. This station, for as long as I've been here, has never been about hurting people or maligning their character as the management here is now attempting to do for personal and vindictive reasons," Weathers said and stood up from his seat.

The camera followed him. "For thirteen years now, I have been proud of bringing you the news and being a part of your lives on a nightly basis. But tonight, with a heavy heart, I must say to you, the viewers, my friends, that effective immediately, I am no longer a part of the KNRQ family. I am at a crossroads and am myself faced with my own moral dilemma, and I have chosen. I believe in my heart that my choice is the morally correct choice. It is the right thing for me to do." He paused a moment as tears welled in his eyes. "So it is with a sad heart, I say good night, Los Angeles. Good night, my friends, and thank you for supporting me for over a decade," he said and placed the mic on the desk in front of him and walked off the set.

Dawn was utterly shocked and unaware that the camera was now trained on her. But as she was about to speak, the red tally light on the camera went off.

"We're at commercial," the director said. Dawn and the film crew could hear Chandler cursing as he approached the set.

Dawn pushed her chair back and pulled the mic from her blouse and started walking off the set.

"Where the fuck do you think you're going?" Chandler shouted across the room.

"I told you, I'm not reading that crap either! I quit! Read it yourself, asshole!" she said as she stormed off the set.

Most of the stagehands were in shock; a few began laughing but stopped as soon as Chandler swung his head around.

* * * * *

The following morning, Larry Moranville walked into the newsroom and took everybody by surprise. He flew out from the corporate headquarters in New York, and his appearance usually meant that changes were coming. He was Chandler's boss and the person who was grooming Michael Bishope to take over Chandler's job and run the stations. He liked Michael a lot and hated seeing him being dragged through the press as he had been.

Unable to take the corporate jet, Larry had to take a commercial flight, which already put him in a rotten mood. But taking the commercial flight allowed him to overhear people talking about the case on the plane the whole six-hour flight from New York, and he was sick of it—sick of seeing a friend being browbeaten, especially by his own station, the people who should have supported him. Larry felt guilty for his station turning its back on Michael.

Larry casually walked over to David sitting in front of Michael's office.

"Mr. Moranville, how are you today, sir?" he stammered as he awkwardly got up from the chair. He wasn't used to being face-to-face with the bigwigs from corporate.

"Fine. Long flight. Is he in?" Moranville asked, nodding.

"Uh, sir, uh, Michael quit yesterday."

"What!"

David was tongue-tied for a moment. "Uh, he just came in and packed up his office. He asked me to send the rest of his things," David said.

"Jesus Christ," Moranville said and shook his head. "This has gone way too far," he said under his breath. "I should have moved on this sooner."

"Excuse me?" David said.

"Nothing," Moranville said. "Point me to Weathers's office."

David showed him the way to the corner office overlooking the newsroom.

* * * * *

David Weathers was wearing jeans and a T-shirt as he too was boxing his own things when Moranville walked in.

"Where do you think you're going?" Moranville asked.

Weathers looked up and brushed the sweat from his face. "Well, hi, Larry. How've you been?" he asked.

"Don't give me that, David," Moranville said.

Weathers walked over to the door where Moranville stood, bracing himself against the doorway, and shook his hand. "I can't be a part of this anymore, Larry," he said and paused. "I'm sure you heard all about last night's broadcast. It was my last at this network."

"Bullshit! I'm not letting you go," Moranville said, pointing. "You're too valuable to this network, and so is August," he finished.

"With all due respect, Larry, Michael quit yesterday, and I quit last night. I will not work for that clown you have running things about here. I just can't do it."

"I'm here to rectify that," Moranville started. "You're staying, David. You stay, and I'll take care of you."

"Larry..."

"You salary is doubled, no questions. Stocks, whatever it takes. That goes for August as well. If Chandler was the problem, he won't be a problem anymore. You have my word."

"What he did to Michael was uncalled for."

"Either way, he would have been gone at the end of the month. I was going to put Michael Bishope in charge of the station. I always planned on that."

David peered over Larry's shoulder with beady eyes. Larry turned and followed his gaze. His eyes fell upon Frank Chandler walking into the newsroom. Larry turned back to David. "You want reassurance?"

Larry turned and stepped into the newsroom. David followed him into the large room.

"Chandler!" Moranville shouted across the noisy room.

Chandler turned quickly. A hush fell over the newsroom.

"Oh, hey, Larry," Chandler said as he started walking toward him.

Larry held up his hand. "Stay there," he said. "I want to make this as public as you made the Bishope case."

Chandler stopped in his tracks. Confusion swept over his face. "Excuse me?"

"You're fired!"

A moan wavered over the employees in the newsroom. Most smiled.

"What?"

"You heard me, you self-righteous prick!" Moranville shouted.

"You can't talk to me that way. And you can't fire me. I have a contract," he protested.

"I will talk to you any damn way I please, and your contract isn't worth a damn, just like you! Our lawyers already went through your contract and brought it to the point where you won't even get one day of severance pay," Larry said, pointing.

Chandler looked pissed, and he wasn't about stand for any of this, especially not in front all these people. "I'm going to sue this station for slander!" Chandler said, trying to save face.

"Slander? I don't think so. You're a prick, and that's just a fact of life!"

"I've got witnesses—all these people heard what you said!" Chandler shouted.

Chandler's secretary stood up. "I didn't hear anything," she said loudly. Chandler turned and shot her with a hate-filled glare. She cracked a slight smile. She knew there was nothing more he could do to her. No more threats, no more working excessive hours, no more asshole for a boss. She would now have more time for her children and her marriage, which was already on the rocks from her working far too many hours.

Michael's assistant, David, stood up. "I didn't hear anything either," he shouted from across the room.

He was followed by most of the people in the room, standing and proclaiming their mute defiance. They all shared an intense dislike for Chandler and were going to do anything they could to gain peace and harmony at their place of employment.

"Got anymore witnesses?" Moranville asked with sarcasm. "If anybody should sue, it should be Bishope. He should sue this station, and he should sue you for slander. You had no right dragging him through the mud like that. Not one station across the country slammed him like you did!" Moranville shouted, jabbing him with his finger from across the room.

"He deserved it!"

"Why? Because I was giving him your job at the end of the month?"

Chandler narrowed his eyes and burned him with a contemptuous glare. He quickly looked around the room as all the nameless faces were staring back at him. Most were delirious with joy. He felt their eyes on him, mocking him. He felt as though everybody hated him; he could feel it.

"You have one hour to gather your things and get the fuck out of my newsrooms!" Moranville shouted.

Chandler continued looking at the faces staring back at him. They all sat in silence, but his mind twisted reality. He saw them all laughing at him, teasing him and calling him names. They were the schoolyard bullies that always picked on him as a child. He finally looked back at Moranville, who lifted his hand and gestured to his watch.

Chandler stormed into his office and slammed the door for the very last time.

Larry turned to Dave Weathers, who nodded and extended his hand. "I'll stay," David said. Larry shook his hand. "What are you going to do about Michael?"

"I'm going to see if I can tempt him back with Chandler's job," Moranville replied. "That and a big raise."

"This trial has devastated him," David said softly.

"Yeah, I know. I've seen him sink deeper into despair every night on the news," Moranville started and sighed. "You know, this story is the white elephant everybody wants. I just wish it wasn't in our own family."

"I'd rather not cover it at all," David replied.

24

Twenty weeks

CRIMSON-COLORED FEAR melted from the walls and lingered in the haze of emotion clouding the long, narrowed corridors. The penetrating stench was acid to the senses. It mixed with the haze that held heavy with so many voices of hate, fear, pain, and violence that had amassed over the years. It was a smell that entered a person's essence and never left their mind; it stained their skin for the rest of their natural life. A constant reminder of a place that few people have ventured into; those who have will never forget the odor or feeling of desperation.

Having viewed Susan Bishope's courtroom breakdown several times on tape, Dr. Lauren Tinker glanced through a forensic psychiatry book the size of a large metropolitan phone book.

Dr. Tinker was in her forties. Her teal blue eyes stood out in striking contrast to her long mahogany hair and natural curls, though she wears it pinned tight to her head most of the time. She was old-fashioned in all regards with graceful movements and a body not befitting a doctor of forensic psychiatry. Her voice was faint, medium, high-pitched. Her soft manner made her very approachable to her patients. She was deliberate with them and enunciated herself softly and clearly for their behalf.

Dr. Tinker pulled the file on Susan Bishope and made a few notes of her own. She placed a microrecorder on the desk in front of her. She shook her head as she thought about the sheer magnitude of this case. She couldn't imagine what was going through Susan's mind, but she had her suspicions. Everybody did after repeatedly watching her courtroom breakdown on the evening news, on every channel, every night.

After a swift rap on the heavy door, a uniformed guard led Susan by the arm into the office and sat her in the chair across from Dr. Tinker.

Dr. Tinker nodded to the guard, and he left the room. Susan followed him out with her eyes, anything to avoid the inevitable. She knew why she was here and what this doctor was looking for. But she was not about to impart any answers to a stranger. Outsider interference was never an option and would only worsen the situation in her mind.

"Hello, Susan. I am Dr. Lauren Tinker," she said, as if talking to a child. "I am a forensic psychiatrist appointed by the court."

Susan did her best not to look toward her voice. She wanted to avoid eye contact. Susan had heard about these shrinks and how sly they were. She knew if the doctor had the slightest chance, she would easily see what Susan had been trying to hide all along. That can never be an option.

"Now, before we get started, there is something you should know," Dr. Tinker said softly. She could sense how fragile Susan was and approached her very carefully. "In an ordinary case, I would not be allowed to speak of our meeting. Since you were ordered here by the court, I have to report what happens in our meetings directly to the court."

Susan avoided the doctor altogether and let her eyes roam around the room to familiarize herself with the surroundings. Susan stopped and held her stare on one of the two diplomas hanging on the wall: the first from Harvard; then she fixed her stare on the second from Stanford University.

"Now how can I help you, Susan?" Dr. Tinker asked.

Susan said nothing and sat quietly in the chair. She was a prisoner, confined by these walls, interrogated by this stranger sitting across from her. She learned long ago never talk to strangers; it was strictly forbidden! *Never tell them anything they don't need to know. Family business is family business.*

"Do you know why you are here?"

Sure, I know why I'm here, because you're a nosey bitch! Because that stupid man in the black dress is an asshole. He just can't stay out of other people's family business. Just like you, you want to know my business. You're a stranger, and you have no right to know my family business. It's a secret from the outside world, just as it should be!

Dr. Tinker could sense that Susan did not want to look at her, so she instinctively glanced at her notes on the table, avoiding Susan altogether. Dr. Tinker learned early in her career that she had to learn each patient, their habits, what they want, and how to approach them. "I can understand you not wanting to talk to me, Susan. I can understand that you do not want to be here. I want to assure you that I will not harm you in any way. I am here to help you if you will allow me," Dr. Tinker said softly.

Susan heard nothing the doctor said. Her ears were deaf to the prying outsider. Other voices in her head yammered loudly and guided her eyes quickly around the room like a caged animal searching for an escape. They wanted to look around their new surroundings as well. Susan began rocking and craning her head quickly from side to side. Dr. Tinker sensed a panic building within Susan.

"Close your eyes, Susan," Dr. Tinker said in a soft, calming voice. She saw that Susan was losing her grip. Her strange body movements were a classic example. "Close your eyes, Susan," Dr. Tinker repeated.

Susan continued rocking. Her eyes darted from one side of the room to the other. Faster and faster, her head was like a spinning top.

"Close your eyes," Dr. Tinker said once more, this time with a more comforting voice. Susan continued and escalated her gestures to the point she almost lifted herself out of the chair.

"One…two…three," Dr. Tinker said, then snapped her fingers.

The snapping of fingers was a trigger effect for the subconscious. Now there was a light. Susan stopped completely and actually appeared satisfied. She looked at the doctor a brief moment before her head fell limp onto her chest. Her breathing still came rapid.

Dr. Tinker shifted in her seat. "Susan?"

Susan moaned slightly, letting the doctor know she was still kicking. Again Dr. Tinker called her name, but received no response.

She noted down each gesture and pattern Susan produced. As she was about to call Susan's name, Susan spoke in a very slow and sketchy voice, one very different from the one the doctor heard on the courtroom tape.

"I don't wanna talk today," Susan said, her head still pinned to her chest.

Dr. Tinker found that rather odd but showed no emotion whatsoever. She made her notes. "You do realize that us talking is very important—"

"She said she doesn't want to talk!" an evil voice screamed out. The pitch of the voice was clearly different than it was only a moment before. Susan's head lifted slightly as if controlled by another entity altogether, but only far enough for her to glimpse the doctor through malicious eyes. The eyes were trying to mentally scorn the doctor, who still held in her gaze.

Dr. Tinker moved out of her line of vision and made another note. She was the master of avoiding eye contact and uncomfortable situations. She was not about to let Susan gain the upper hand. "Okay," Dr. Tinker said, her head still down and her eyes averted as she spoke. "But before I let her go, can you tell me who you are?"

"Fuck off!" a deep, almost manly voice shot back.

Another one! The doctor made her appropriate notes and gave this one a name: "Number 3."

"Okay. I can see Susan later today," Dr. Tinker said finally. She pushed a button on the edge of her desk and wrote another note in Susan's file.

Susan let her chin fall back down on her chest.

The door to the office opened, and the burly guard walked in and over to Susan. He gently grabbed Susan by the arm and led her across the floor and out of the office.

* * * * *

Turning the corner onto Pacific Avenue, Michael stopped his car when he caught the sight of a large crowd on the street ahead. He knew the crowd was gathered at Nash's house. As he approached,

Michael counted two satellite trucks but was sure there were a few more in the alley.

Before he reached the reporters, Michael swung a hard right into an alley and made his way toward Speedway and came to a quick stop. He reached over and opened his passenger door and waited. He heard fast-approaching footsteps echoing in the darkened parking structure. His heart began to race; was it friend or foe? He peered into the darkness and saw Nash quickly approaching. He jumped into the passenger seat, and Michael took off.

"What's so important that we need to meet under these bullshit cloak-and-dagger circumstances?" Nash asked. He slouched down in the passenger seat.

"I'm sick and tired of all this shit!" Michael started. He was almost enraged. His face showed the stress he had been under. It showed in his driving as well as he quickly turned onto Washington and sped through the red light. "They're at my house twenty-four hours a day. They're knocking on my door at three in the fucking morning! It never fucking stops!" Michael's voice continued growing louder. "My neighbors are all pissed off at me. They're going to run me out of town."

"I told you things were going to get ugly. You knew reporters were going to hound you and your life was never going to be the same again," Nash roared back.

"This isn't a fucking game, it's my life!" Michael shouted. He looked over at Nash, then back at the road. Then back at Nash. He clenched his teeth and pulled the car to a screeching halt on the side of the road. Nash slammed against the passenger door.

"What the hell!" Nash shouted.

"Is that all this is to you, a game?" Michael shouted. His voice was peppered with anger.

"No! It's a case for me—just like any other case! That's all it is," Nash said. "I can't favor one case over the other just because of who I know or what the circumstances are. That would betray my own set of ethics!" Nash said. His voice still raised. Michael really stirred his vigor, and now Nash was almost at his boiling point. "Yeah, your circumstances are a little more crucial than the scumbag drug dealers

I defend, but in either case, I have to keep my emotions on an even keel. Sometimes my clients don't like it, but that's the way it has to be!" Nash finished, his face red with anger, but he cooled himself off in the long stare he held across at Michael, who remained silent. "Now what did you really want to see me about?"

Michael looked at him another moment. Tension held in the thick air of the car. Michael sighed to regain his composure. "I just want to see my wife." He followed with another sigh. "I tried to visit her, but they said she wasn't allowed any visitors."

"Sorry, Mike, but until this 730 order is satisfied, you will not be allowed to see her."

"For a month?"

"Yes, if not longer," Nash said.

"What do you mean longer?" Michael asked.

"Various things could happen in treatment. One, she could come clean and resolve her issues, go to court, and kick your ass. Two, she could fall deeper into her depression. Three, the doctor could petition the court for her to be held for additional treatment."

"I don't want her to be in there one second longer that she has to be. It's bullshit that she's in there in the first place! She's not a criminal!" Michael shouted.

"Take it easy."

"You take it easy!" Michael shot back. "It's my life that is all fucked up at the moment, not yours!"

"I'm sorry that she's there," Nash said in a brief moment of compassion. "But right now there's nothing we can do other than wait and see."

There was a long silence between them.

"What if I drop the case? Will they let her out?" Michael asked.

"There's no turning back, Mike. The downward spiral has already started, and the wheels are in motion. It has to play itself out now," Nash started, lowering his voice. "This was ordered by a sitting judge, and she has to satisfy his order. I'm sorry," Nash said softly.

Michael lowered his head onto his chest. Tears welled in his eyes. He fought back a choke building in his throat. This was so overwhelming to him. Again he wanted to run, take the first taxi off this planet, and never look back.

"Why don't you take some time and get the hell out of town? Get away from the reporters," Nash started. "I mean, you can't see your wife for a month anyway, and there's really nothing for you to do other than sit at home and feel sorry for yourself."

All at once, reporters swarmed the car in an instant. Cameras flashed into the car. Michael yelled an obscenity at the reporters and kicked the car into gear. He revved the engine to shake the press, and he sped away and out of sight. What he really wanted to do was turn back and run them all over for ruining his life.

*****

Susan sat across the desk from Dr. Tinker in silence. She was pale, ghostly white, and thinner than ever. Her hair was stringy and dirty, as if it hadn't seen a brush in weeks. Her mouth felt filthy, like a trash can, she thought.

Susan had a lot of time to think in her small cell, and she came to the conclusion that she wasn't going to say a word to the doctor no matter what happened. Sooner or later, they would let her out, and she would carry out with her plan, have the abortion, and somehow try to move on with her life. She figured Michael was long gone and thought about a life without him. But she needed to get out of here first, and she figured silence couldn't hurt.

"Susan," Dr. Tinker started in a friendly voice. She was cognizant of the dialogue that may be taking place inside a patient's mind. She always approached things very deliberately. "I will never hurt or betray you, Susan. I will never break your trust—"

"Hurt betray! Hurt betray!" blurted a voice from Susan's mouth and repeated quickly, mocking the doctor's words. So much for Susan's grand plan of silence.

It was another voice that the doctor had not heard yet. She made her notes and named this with another number. Dr. Tinker held her eyes down on her notes. She wanted to give the impression that she was uninterested in the new voice.

"Trust? Trust? There is no trust! There's no trust! That's a lie! Trust is a lie!" This was another voice altogether. The voice was deeper than Susan's. It was strong, crisp, and loud. It was heavily laced with a strange accent, not European, but from where? the doctor thought.

Dr. Tinker was taken by surprise when this new voice came to light. She double-checked the recorder, hoping there would be more to come. She didn't have to wait long.

"Don't talk to her!"

"Shhh…"

"I'm not going to talk to her! Why don't you shut up!"

Three separate voices danced on a single breath. They were holding their own conversation using Susan's mouth. Susan's eyes were glazed over, rolling back in her head, a lot of white showing.

"Shut up, she'll hear you!"

"She can't hear us, she can't hear us, she only hears Susan, hears Susan, and she's so stupid she won't say anything. Did you hear her? Did you hear her sitting all alone in the cell feeling sorry for herself? She said, 'I'm not going to talk. I'm not going to say anything to that stupid doctor!' She said she is not going to talk to anyone! She thinks she's going to walk right out of here and kill the baby. That's what she kept saying!"

This voice was rapid and repetitive. It reminded the doctor of an uneducated teenager who had been drinking.

Dr. Tinker was taken aback by the sudden outburst. She tried to keep track of the different voices coming from Susan's mouth. It was so fragile and yet so dangerous. A war was raging within Susan's mind, and if Dr. Tinker didn't come with the cavalry soon, there might be no turning back for Susan.

"Sussy is not stupid! She just doesn't like you! You're stupid."

"What do you know? What do you know? You're the dumb one. You're dumb!"

"Why don't you just shut up? All you can do is hurt people. Boy, oh boy, I sure miss Macy. She didn't let you talk that way."

"She was an idiot. She was an idiot too!"

"You're mean."

"And you're ugly! And you're stupid too! Stupid, stupid!"

All of a sudden, Susan began crying hysterically, almost childlike.

Dr. Tinker leaned forward, but then stopped herself short of showing sympathy. She slid a box of Kleenex across the desk; Susan didn't notice.

Dr. Tinker waited for Susan to compose herself before she spoke, "Are you all right, Susan?"

Susan didn't say a word, but her head nodded slightly, giving the good doctor incentive to push on.

"Who is in there with you, Susan?" Dr. Tinker asked. "Who was talking for you?" Dr. Tinker waited patiently, hoping for a response, but none was forthcoming. Dr. Tinker looked on. She nodded her head and made more notes, hoping her indirect attention would weigh on Susan and tempt her out of this shell. The doctor leaned back in the chair and said nothing. Silence wrapped around them both. Susan continued crying softly. And Dr. Tinker waited. Her eyes veered away from Susan so as to not make her feel even more uncomfortable.

Fifteen minutes later, Susan remained silent. When Dr. Tinker finally glanced in her direction, she found Susan with her head down and her eyes on the floor. She was almost catatonic. The doctor made a few more notes and then leaned forward on the desk. "Susan, I would like to talk with you now," Dr. Tinker said and waited. And waited. "Susan?" She further waited.

Nothing.

No response. No movement. Silence. "Susan, I know you can hear me," Dr. Tinker said. "I need you to talk with me. I can help you, but you need to open up and let me in. We have to start a dialogue," Dr. Tinker finished.

Nothing. No movement. Not a flinch. Susan remained frozen in the chair. She hoped against hope that the doctor did not hear any of her rambling. She thought perhaps Dr. Tinker didn't, and maybe things would be all right after all. She wanted to sit there and say nothing until the doctor escorted her back to her cell. She just wanted the doctor to shut up and not speak another word to her.

"We really don't have much time, Susan, and I fear that your problem is far more serious than anybody would have imagined. We really need to get started, for your sake," Dr. Tinker said softly.

Susan continued staring into another world, searching for an escape. She could hear the voices yammering inside, fighting their way back to the surface. She appeared uncomfortable. Her facial expression looked damaged.

As the voices came closer, Susan adjusted herself in the seat. She began tilting her head back and forth, as if someone was banging her skull with a hammer from within.

"Susan, we really need to talk, honey."

Susan said nothing still. She looked frightened, ready to explode into tears once more. A panic began to build from within. She started rocking like a scared child.

Not wanting to startle her in any way, Dr. Tinker waited. She felt frustrated. This was their fifth session, and until this session, the real Susan had not uttered a single word. Sure, it was a breakthrough, but of what sorts? How many twisted layers did her psychosis hold? One thing Dr. Tinker knew for sure: time was running out for Susan. She needed to do something fast.

"Susan?" The doctor watched and waited for her response.

Nothing.

Dr. Tinker's frustration doubled, but she didn't let it show. She instead looked for another approach. "Okay, Susan," Dr. Tinker started, "this is going to get done one way or another." She waited and watched for some sign of life from Susan.

Nothing. No response whatsoever.

"We can do this the easy way, which is the approach we have been taking—or we can do it the hard way. How we take it from here is entirely up to you, Susan," Dr. Tinker said and waited, hoping that what she said would spark a response from her patient.

Susan appeared even more agitated, rocking faster. Her eyes shifted back and forth. Then she stopped all at once. Susan looked up at the doctor with dark empty eyes. "We are never going to talk to you, bitch!" a voice said from Susan's sullen face. This was another voice entirely. It came as a deep and evil voice. Susan's eyes remained calm and gentle. Dr. Tinker focused on her eyes; they were honest and open for the first time, as if they were crying for help. They showed that a real person was still alive inside and was in dire need of radical assistance.

The look Susan gave her sent shivers through the doctor's core. "I see," Dr. Tinker said and averted eye contact a moment. "You feel threatened. Is that why someone else is talking for you, Susan? Who is talking to me now? What is your name?"

With that, Susan's eyes narrowed, and what little hope she had was now lost. An evil glare scorned the doctor as she waited. Susan didn't answer. She stared straight ahead, trying to intimidate the doctor, giving her the old stink eye.

Dr. Tinker carefully pulled away from Susan's stare.

Susan lost interest after she no longer had the doctor's attention and returned her stare to the floor.

The doctor waited. No response. Five minutes. Nothing. Ten minutes, nothing.

"Susan?"

Nothing…

Frustration.

"Susan?" Dr. Tinker said softly.

Another voice told her to fuck off. Susan remained completely unresponsive to the doctor's attempts. Dr. Tinker shook her head slightly as Susan's other side once again showed itself. The doctor reached for the microrecorder on the edge of the desk. She lifted the mic. "Mrs. Bishope wishes to do this the hard way," Dr. Tinker said into the microphone.

Snap!

That got a reaction from Susan. She locked her eyes onto the doctor, not knowing what she meant. Susan looked concerned, but still wasn't about to impart any information to an outsider. Susan wanted to know what the hard way was, but she wasn't about to ask. She would play it out, wait for the end game. She would hold fast and wait for the sweet taste of fresh air, the sun on her face, and the stars at night.

The door to the office opened, and it was a little too early for Susan, not with that last comment dangling in the air. The burly guard entered the office and walked directly to Susan and clutched her arm.

Dr. Tinker handed him a slip of paper, which he read, and led Susan toward the door. By the door, Susan turned and gave a curious parting glance back at the doctor. Dr. Tinker lifted the microphone to her mouth.

The guard opened the office door. Susan hesitated a moment as the doctor started talking into the little machine.

"What happened to you, Susan? Who hurt you at such a young age? This had to have started when you were young. That's why there are so many children's voices. You needed them…but why? Why did you need them, Susan?"

Susan continued looking on, but the guard was becoming impatient.

The doctor looked on for what felt like an eternity. Then, "How do I reach you?" Dr. Tinker said with a hint of frustration. "How do I take you out of this darkness?" Dr. Tinker switched off the recorder and looked back across toward Susan.

Flash!

25

Melissa's Spark

"Where are you?"
"I'm nine…"
"Where's the light?"
"Doesn't come anymore…"
"What comes?"
"Nothing…there is nothing…"
"Yes, there is."
"No…"
"There is something. There is me. I kame."
"I don't know who you are…"
"Yes, you doo."
"I'm not apposed to talk to people when I don't know who they are…"
"Well, you kan talk to me because I kan keep a seekret."
"A seekret?"
"Yes. No-won will ever know you and me talked. You think that wood be all right?"
"Well, if no one will know—"
"No-won will never ever know."
"Okay… I'm really eight and a half. I will be nine on my next birthday, you know…"
"I know. You're silly. I'm going to turn on a light—"
"No!"

Brilliant white lightning shot hot and exploded over the swift water of the great river as it wove its way through the city of spirits. And for a moment, night morphed into bright daylight.

At first, they frightened her, both the lightning and the river, but she became used to the violence of both and now called them friend. She was used to their sound, knew their voices; she expected nothing and anticipated everything. It was just another part of her life, one she regarded as normalcy like the coming of a new dawn through the fog of the marsh and the stars in the night sky. Violence, for as long as she had known, had always been a part of her life. It came to be expected, like breathing. But for her, it came in many forms and with just as many faces.

She had often dreamed about stealing away on the back of the great river, moving down the water like Tom and Huck, past the riverboats, barges, and giant ships and into the Gulf of Mexico. She wanted to be swept out to sea like a piece of driftwood set on a course to nowhere, where her chance at the violent sea was better than what she had now. Violence she was used to, and the sea seemed tame by comparison.

The wrought iron gates outside her window reminded her all too well of a dark gothic prison, one surely meant to hold her prisoner. The sweet smell of jasmine growing wild in the yard came through the lone window and betrayed her solitude, betrayed the gothic mindset she cast upon herself. She was in solitary confinement with no chance of parole.

Oh, how her imagination kept her going—kept her traveling a safe distance away from all the violence she had names for. There were so many names and so much violence. She traveled there often, down the river and out to sea, landing in exotic ports of call and starting life all over again. She could journey through the deserts of Africa she had heard about in school, when she went to school. She could climb the highest mountains and breathe the rocky mountain air. She could trudge through the snow in some far off-land she had never heard of. All was possible within her mind. Most of all, everything was safe there. There was no pain in her dreams. No dark thoughts, just happiness and freedom and escape.

The lightning strike near the gulf lit the room with bright hot-white light. It reminded her of a camera flash, a photo her mother once took of her. It was the only photo her mother ever took of her. Another quick flash of brilliant light, and this was her hell; she was used to it. Used to the blazing flashes of light. Used to the violent cracking thunder, the way it roared in her stomach. That was nothing to her anymore. In fact, it was almost comforting in a way. She was a seasoned veteran of Mother Nature's rapture. She learned quickly that Mother Nature was not the one to fear. It was another evil altogether. It was…

"I kan't see!"
"You'll get used to it… "
"It's getting darker!"
"It always does… "
"I'm skared!"
"Meee toooo… "

The young girl was emaciated, painfully thin, skin over bones, and had bruises on both arms. The dark circles under her eyes were not due to lack of sleep. She fell down; that's what she would tell outsiders and strangers, teachers. But they knew better; she was an awful liar at this age. It wasn't until much later in life that she earned her degree in the art of lies, half-truths, and misdirection.

A bruised handprint—all five fingers were marked in dark purple and green on her neck. How close was she to death on that occasion? How close was she all the other times? It was a question she stopped trying to answer long ago. She learned one thing about herself back then: she was a survivor. No matter what it took, no matter what pain she had to endure, she was going to survive and get past all this evil.

There has to be a better life out there for me. Someday I'll find it. I'll find happiness and peace.

Her teeth chattered slightly, but not from the bitter cold in her room, not from the storm that was raging outside her broken bedroom window. Storms come in many variations; she knew that and experienced a great many of them. This storm was—

> *"Things happen."*
> *"I know why they happen."*
> *"No, because you is a outsider. You kan't know. Outsiders don't know none of our family stuff. It's a seekret…"*
> *"I am not as outsider anymore. And besides, I kan keep a seekret. Like I told you, we kan be friends now."*
> *"Are you real?"*
> *"Are you real?"*
> *"Do you want to play?"*
> *"I don't know how…"*
> *"But you don't know what I was going to ask you to play."*
> *"So?"*
> *"So then you don't know if you know how to play it or not."*
> *"Au-huh. Because I have never played anything before…"*
> *"I like you. You're silly."*
> *"Really?"*
> *"Yeah."*

Absent were the pretty yellow ribbons that were supposed to be in a young girl's hair. So too were the pigment in her face and the hope in her eyes. There was no more lovely luster in her eyes; they were barren, almost toxic, and always crying. What made it harder for her was, nobody was there to hear her cries. Nobody to hold her, care for her, and stop her tears from stinging. She knew from a young age that she was on a solitary journey in the illusion of life.

"There is evil all around you, girl! You got the juju," she remembered old Mabel once saying but couldn't, for the life of her, understand what she meant by that statement. It haunted and echoed in her mind in times like these.

She lay clutching herself in the fetal position on the dirty water—and urine-stained sheetless mattress that sat on the filthy floor. The floor was rotting planks of wood, stripped bare from the sea air, and barely held the mattress from falling into the basement. Wide hollow slats between the wood allowed cold air to pour into the room from the basement. She hated her room, hated being in her room. But she hated the basement even more. She feared its uncertain darkness. And since her mother died, she would only venture down there when it was absolutely, positively necessary.

She was cold almost every night. She shivered in silence. But that was good; it helped her stay awake for long periods of time. Remaining awake and alert was lifesaving. She didn't dare speak of an extra blanket or heat in the room. Nobody would listen anyway. In fact, she didn't dare to speak at all most of the time. She avoided talking altogether; she feared the consequences. *Kan't be too loud. Kan't make any noise. Kan't be seen—stay out of sight!*

She always listened for any approaching sound or threat. Everything was a threat, and everything brought possible danger. But she only heard the katydids singing their chorus from the trees outside her broken bedroom window. She wanted them to shut up. She needed to listen for any impending danger. A streetcar passed in the distance; its steel wheels grinded with electricity, screeching into the scented dusk. *Shut up! Just shut up! You don't understand! Be quiet!* She knew one thing: night was coming! That was the worst time for her. The deep night was when the darkness was at its most deadly stage of reality. That's when the evil really came to life and showed its ugly head of absolution.

* * * * *

It wasn't far to Saint Mary's Church. She had held up there on a few occasions, spent the night there once. The young priest said nothing to her and covered her with a blanket when she fell asleep. It was the warmest, most comfortable sleep she had ever known. The priest knew there was trouble in her heart and hated to see a child of God so saddened. He asked her to come back and talk, but she never did. He was just another stranger, an outsider. He had no business knowing family business! She would not return to talk to him or anyone else.

She could run, she thought, but could she chance it? Could she chance giving up this perfect hiding place? Would she make it all the way to the church without—

Would the priest cover her in the warmth of a peaceful blanket again?

Would she sleep safe, like an angel sleeping on a cotton-like, puffy cloud under the watchful eyes of God?

Would she make it past—

I miss my mommy!

The front door ripped open with a loud jolt. She felt the vibrations rattle through her room. She heard heavy footsteps on the old wooden porch. The person outside, the person she feared most, hawked a loogie from deep in his throat and spat somewhere outside. She cringed. She always felt sick to her stomach whenever he did that. It was gross. Her shoulders dropped in relief, but she held on to the fear. She could never let go of the fear. She needed it to stay alert and keep her senses sharp. For now the weight of the world was gone; the bad man was outside.

She crept over to the window when she heard the old truck's ignition sputter and spit before roaring to life. The old truck sputtered, then clanked, coughing up a lung as it rolled onto the stone street with its squeaky wheel squealing all the way until the truck was gone from view.

"I don't like the dark."
"Neither do I…"
"What color is my hair?"
"Hummm…"
"I can't see it in the dark."
"You have long blonde hair, kind of like mine…"
"Really?"
"But you have a pretty yellow bow…"

"Really?"
"Yeah, and I don't have one…"
"I'll give you mine."
"You have green eyes just like mine…"
"Really? Like sisters, huh?"
"Yeah, 'cept for your teeth are pretty—and straight and shinny and white…and…"

*****

Melissa watched through her window and made sure the coast was clear. She could never rest as long as the bad man was there. She didn't dare let herself fall asleep, not if she wanted to remain unharmed. That's when she was most vulnerable. That's when the demons came and the bad things happened. At least in her waking hours, she had a chance: a chance to run, a chance to hide, a chance to get away. It was when she was sleeping a child's sleep, deep and long, that the demons took her at will. They usually woke her up out of a deep slumber. That's how they usually got her, when she could not fight back. And at the tender age of eight, it was sometimes hard to fight off the sandman. But she tried. Oh, how she tried.

*****

"…wait! Susan," Dr. Tinker called out before the guard could lead her out of the room.

Susan snapped back to the here and now.

"I gave you the option of how we're going to proceed in our sessions. Time is of the essence, Susan. It's crucial that you talk with me," Dr. Tinker said softly so as not to alarm her. She waited for a response but gave up hope quickly. She knew there was no chance of any response from Susan, not in her catatonic state of emotional nothingness.

"We have tried it the easy way. But I'm afraid, Susan, that we're now going to have to take a different approach. One I don't particularly want to do. You have left me with no choice."

Susan just stared at the doctor. Her facial expression never changed, never quivered; she was as lifeless as ever. Even that slight threat didn't get to her.

Inside, Dr. Tinker was raging, and she knew Susan was as well. That was the cause for the doctor's rage: her inability to reach her patient with less-than-extreme methods.

Dr. Tinker nodded to the guard. She looked more frustrated than ever as Susan was escorted from her office. The mention of alternative methods was more of a backhanded threat. Dr. Tinker hated the inference—it just wasn't her style—but she felt she had no choice. Besides, she wanted to see how Susan would respond to such a statement. It was the last remaining option, and there was no progress whatsoever up to this point. She feared time was running out. Susan did not heed her warnings. She remained defiant, even more standoffish than ever.

There has to be a way inside her head, Dr. Tinker thought. She lifted the microrecorder and hit record. "You need to think outside the box, Lauren," Dr. Tinker said into the machine.

* * * * *

Michael didn't pay much attention to the bevy of reporters still gathered out front. They were a permanent fixture like the landscape growing wildly out of control in front of his house. Unlike the natural landscape, this one added certain ugliness to the entire neighborhood. Michael's neighbors were not happy about it either they were furious. Michael had not been out of the house in three days, and the reporters were growing antsy. Yet they waited.

Nick had been calling day and night, but Michael never answered. He was too busy indulging in self-pity and regret to even answer the door. Michael wanted nothing to do with anybody, friend or foe.

For an instant, he wished he had never started this whole thing. He wanted to go back to the day Susan told him she was pregnant and say, "It's your body, honey. I don't agree with you. I want the baby, you know that. But it's your body, and if you want to have an abortion, then I will stand behind you." He longed for his muse, longed to hold her in his arms again. He longed for the courage to be a better person, especially for her.

Michael sat silent a moment, listening to the gentle rumble of the reporters on the street. They were relentless. He waited for the inevitable, another knock. It didn't take long for one of the news monkeys to announce him or herself with an ill-tempered thumping on the door.

Once it seemed they had gone back to the gaggle of misfits on the street, Michael got up from the couch and slowly headed up to the bedroom to try sleep. He had not slept more than a few hours in the past three days, and he was tired. And from the deep heaviness weighing down his soul, he wouldn't get much sleep on this night either.

26

At the ripe age of eight, trust and love is something that comes with the love of caring parents. But not to Melissa. Those emotions were burnt from her core. Especially trust. She doesn't trust anybody anymore, not that she ever did, not since her mother died. Her life from that tragic event on had been a living nightmare.

Her father told her it was a terrible car accident, but Melissa had her suspicions. She heard them fighting the night she died. They were yelling and screaming and arguing. They always fought; Melissa was used to it. It was as common as breathing to her.

As common as it was, she hated to see or hear them fighting; it tore her apart. They were supposed to love each other; that's how mommies and daddies are supposed to be. But not between her mommy and daddy. They always fought when her father was drinking, which was every night. Melissa hated when he drank. His breath was yucky, and he was meaner than an old 'gator in the swamp who hadn't eaten in a week.

They began fighting and hitting each other, like she had seen other kids do at school a few times. Melissa ran into the bedroom and hid in the closet where it was safe. She could still hear them arguing; then she heard the sudden sharp smack of a vicious slap, most likely her mommy's face. Her mommy yelled with spiteful anger and said bad, dirty words that only adults say.

Another vicious slap, or was it a punch? Somebody lost their air; Melissa never could figure it out. Mommy? But that sound, that one sound, would come to stay with Melissa for the rest of her life. The sound was brutally violent, and the sheer force was indescribable to her. It sounded like something broke inside of her mommy. Then came a gurgling sound, like someone choking on water. What was that sound? Melissa wasn't sure where it came from or what the sound was or what caused it, but it troubled her deeply. Melissa vividly remembered that sound because it was the last sound her mommy ever made.

Then there was silence.

A long, deep, spooky silence. She became aware of the sound of her own breathing in the darkened closet. She tried to stop it altogether so nobody would hear her. She continued peering through the slats of the closet door and barely saw her daddy's legs. He was sitting on the couch where he remained for well over an hour. She couldn't tell how long he was there because she fell asleep and woke up the next morning in the closet.

The house was too quiet when she came out and saw her daddy sitting on the couch alone. Mommy was nowhere to be found. Then he spoke to her for the first time in a month. And the way he told her really terrified her. Not that the fact her mommy was dead but the emotionless plane of his voice, like she never mattered, like she never existed, frightened Melissa terribly.

"Your mother ain't coming back no more. She dead!" He was so blunt and so direct. It was heartless and without feeling. Melissa's heart imploded, and the tears started flowing down her cheeks. Her daddy blew a huff and grunted before he stormed out of the room.

They never let Melissa go to her mommy's funeral. She didn't know it at the time, but her father didn't even go to the funeral. He was out getting drunk while Melissa was home crying. Her daddy said a funeral was no place for a kid. That's what her father told her. He was so cold.

"An' it's all yer fault that she's dead!"

Even at that age, she still had her suspicions.

Melissa knew that family members should be at the funeral when someone died. *It was strange that Daddy didn't let me go. Mama didn't have no family 'cept for us, so nobody would have come anyway. And nobody would be callin' for her, nobody would miss her, 'cept for me. I miss her every day. I miss her every night, especially now that the evil comes*. It just seemed to her that there was something not quite right about the whole thing. Her daddy wasn't telling her the truth; he never did. Again she felt that something horrible had happened to her mother, and nobody would ever really know. There were a lot of places to hide a body in these parts; even she knew that. Her father didn't have to remind her like he always did.

"Ya ain't nothin' but a rotten, no-good-fer-nothin' baby-makin' machine!" Right then, he was struck by an epiphany, and a light sparked in his eyes. He stared at her for a long time. She felt uncomfortable about the strange way he was looking at her. His stare went right through her, and his eyes glazed over as taboo images flooded his wretched mind. At that very moment, she wondered what he was thinking, but she wasn't about to speak and risk another beating. She already had enough bruises.

From then on, Melissa tried to toe the line and walk on eggshells around her father. She still went to school back then because she had nothing to hide, except for her bruises. But she learned to explain them away. She was good at it. Good or bad, her father was family, and he was all she had left in this world. And her father by no means was up for the father-of-the-year award. Melissa went to bed hungry many nights, but her father made sure he had plenty of alcohol, beer, whiskey, and rum. What he drank really didn't matter to him as long he could drink his responsibility away.

He resented this kid living with him, resented her every time he looked at her, and he made sure she knew it. On many occasions, he blamed her for her mother's death. He repeated it over and over so much Melissa started to believe it herself, and she became tormented with guilt. The guilt of her being responsible for her mother's death has never left her.

Melissa's Blaze

"Why is it dark all the time?"
"It's safer that way..."
"But I kan't see anything."
"You're not apposed to..."

Old Mabel Toullier was the crazy woman who lived in the rickety old shack next door and slightly behind the house where Melissa grew up. Her father had a more colorful name for her: "crazy old coon-ass nigger bitch," but Melissa didn't like it when he said that. She hated when he spoke bad of other people, which was all the time. Her father said that the crazy old lady was into voodoo and witchcraft and warned Melissa to stay away from her, or she would get a beating. Her father was simpleminded, and his suspicions were all that mattered to him.

The only time he caught old Mabel talking to his daughter, he threatened to kill her if he ever caught her talking to his kid again. He meant every word of it. He beat the hell out of Melissa for the chat she had with the old lady.

Old Mabel mostly stayed out of his way. She was smart. Melissa wished she too could stay out of his way, so far out of his way that she would never see him again, that she would just disappear like dust in the wind.

"What's your name?"
"What's yours?"
"I asked you first."
"So this is my house..."
"So? And you're my friend."
"Really? Am I really?"
"Of course. You are silly."
"Humm...okay. Your name is Macy, isn't it?"
"Yes! How did you know?"
"Just because..."

"Wow! It's like you kan read what I'm thinking or something."
"I just had a feeling. You sound like a Macy..."
"What does a Macy sound like?"
"I don't know. Well, like you, I guess..."
"You're funny."
"I saw your name once..."
"Really?"
"Yes. It was on the side of a really, really big building..."
"Really? How big?"
"I don't know. Really, really big..."
"Wow."
"It was a real pretty name, and it was sparkly..."
"Really? Wow!"
"Yeah..."
"What's your name?"
"My name is Meelissssa..."
"Macy and Melissa, friends for tea—"
"Macy and Melissa, been friends since three..."
"You're so silly."
"You have such a pretty sundress..."
"I do?"
"Yes. It has pretty little orange sunflowers all over it..."
"Really? Like summer all the time, huh?"
"Yes. And it's beautiful. And it's warm. And it's... safe..."
"It's getting darker now."
"I know..."
"I kan't see anything."
"...you don't want to—"

"Run, child!"

She smelled him first, smelled alcohol around the corner, lurking like a shadow creeping up the face of time. She always knew it was him from that awful smell. Melissa knew she was the kindling for his rage, and it was her that was going to burn like fire when he caught her.

Footsteps came fast, strong and heavy. She bolted and was out the front door, running faster than she had ever run before. He wasn't far behind, but his heavy boot crashed through the old wood on the front porch near the door, leaving a gaping hole. He yelled a bad, bad curse word and kept coming.

She kept running.

She stopped suddenly as a blast of white hot lightning crashed across the sky, tearing into its blackness. She looked back and saw him clearly. He was illuminated for a moment by the bright flash from the sky. He was leaving the front of the house and moving fast. His eyes were dead, like a walking corpse. He was still coming and moving faster. He wouldn't stop.

Melissa continued running toward the street. As she ran past the wrought iron gates and the pecan tree, old Mabel suddenly appeared from behind the fig tree near the street.

"Run, child! He gonna hurt'cha bad this time!"

Melissa froze in her tracks. She was terrified and stared into her eyes. The old lady didn't have any eyes. They were pure white and evil-looking. There was no colored pupils, just white glowing eyes. Melissa couldn't move, not even when she heard him coming closer.

"Fuckin' crazy bitch! Ya go on an' stay the hell away from my damn kid!" She heard him shouting, and she instinctively flinched and looked back at him. Then she turned back and became even more frightened as she was face-to-face with old Mabel.

"Run, child!"

Then she ran! Faster and faster.

She found it strange that she wasn't breathing hard and didn't blink once. She saw everything more clearly than ever before as she ran. The darkness of night was clearer and more vivid than in the bright shine of daylight, and the contrasting colors were like nothing she had ever seen. Her eyes were strangely happy as she took in all this marvelous scenery. She continued running with more energy than she ever had before. She felt as if she could run forever, which was a thought that quickly crossed her mind. *I'll keep running, and he'll never find me! I'll run all the way to Kalifornia! All the way to the ocean and just swim until I find land and hide forever in the trees!*

The aromatic smells of the great city came to her, but they were all wrong, strangely twisted and confusing. But she didn't have time to sort out the contradictions. She came quickly to the corner and stopped, not knowing which way to run. She held still a moment and waited for the streetcar to pass in front of her. As it passed, Melissa saw him standing across the street yelling. "You stay the fuck away from my damn kid!"

Melissa turned quickly and ran into—

—Mabel.

"You go on that away, child! Hurry yerself," old Mabel said, pointing.

Melissa was paralyzed with fear. She knew old Mabel was there to help her, though for the life of her, she couldn't figure out why. She was an outsider; they don't have no right knowing family business! Melissa remained standing on the dark street corner, frozen, focused on old Mabel's blank white eyes. *How can she see me? She doesn't have any eyes!* Melissa thought.

"Go, child!" urged old Mabel.

Melissa ran.

When she ran past the pretty pink oleanders planted in a yard, she smelled the scent of morning glory that was nowhere to be found. Perhaps it was growing nearby, she thought. The low roar of the mighty river flooded her senses. She didn't have time to analyze her thoughts and twisted sense of smell. She ran.

That's it! Saint Mary's. I'll be safe there! She darted across the street to the riverfront, over the railroad tracks and past the wharf. Her head turned toward the curious river as she ran. There was no more sound. The mighty river lost its voice and appeared to be frozen. It just wasn't moving.

Melissa continued running. Faster.

Another blast of lightning flashed over the broad expanse of water as it flowed swiftly toward the sea. The water was moving once again. But now the sound of thunder came from the river itself. That wasn't right, she thought and continued running for her life. She smelled the sweet scent of jasmine. Oh, how she loved jasmine, but that smell shouldn't be here, not coming off the water, she thought. The river was its own smell. Strange!

Then the burn of the lightning came and wiped out the alluring smell of jasmine. The burn smelled like charred human flesh. Was it hers? She feared the worst and ran more fluidly down the street. She quickly checked over her shoulder. He was still there, still coming.

"You mind yer own business, ya crazy old lady!" he shouted.

Melissa ran right into—-

—-Mabel.

"Ya go on ta Saint Mary's, child. It's the safest place fo' ya! Run child, run!"

She ran!

"You gonna die, old woman!" Melissa heard him scream. Strangely, he wasn't getting any closer, but she felt him just the same; he was all around her. Everywhere she ran, he was there like a spooky thought that wouldn't leave her mind.

She darted back across the street, past the purple althea, and smelled white magnolias. She didn't have time to think; she just ran. Her mind was tripping her with misdirection. She ran past old Mabel again. She was sure it was old Mabel, and she was chanting something in a strange language. Melissa rounded the corner in a dead sprint.

As she turned the corner, she saw the lofty arches and wooden statues of the saints in front of Saint Mary's. The grounds were spooky, especially to a kid. The statues used to scare her, even more so in the darkness when they appeared to come to life in the shadows of the mind's eyes. The statues were no longer the root of her fear; that was still behind her, and coming fast.

She ran up the concrete steps and into the church. All was quiet; even the church mice lay still after their late-night meal. Melissa stopped and peered through the dim light. She wasn't breathing any harder than normal. She found it strange after the marathon she had just run. Her eyes found the young priest standing near the rectory with his back toward her. His black flowing gown was a haven of safety for her.

She ran to him.

As she ran down the aisle toward the priest, the room stretched, and he was getting farther and farther away from her as she ran. It was a surreal experience to her little eyes, so close and yet so very far way, and ever so frightening. She continued with more determination. She finally lunged and latched onto the priest's leg and held on tight.

The priest was startled by the sudden attack and jumped slightly. He realized quickly that it was a small child who looked terrified. He patted her on the head as she continued squeezing his leg with all her might. She rambled incoherently about a story of somebody chasing her. The priest couldn't quite make out what she was saying; her words were so frantic and jumbled. But it sounded like her father was chasing her, but that made no sense to him.

After a few whispers of solace from the priest, Melissa loosened her grip on his leg and looked up. She screamed bloody murder when she saw that she was holding on to her father's leg. She screamed even louder and—

—she woke up from her terror-induced dream.

A bittersweet smile crossed her face when she came to the realization that it was only a dream. It was a bad dream, the absolute worst. She sat upright on the bare mattress and waited as her eyes adjusted to the darkness. There was something very fragile in her expression.

Then there was a certain smell in the room. Her vision cleared. Then…

SMACK!

She was leveled by her father's open hand that smashed across her face. He had been standing over her the whole time, watching her run through her nightmare. Melissa smelled the whiskey on his breath before she fell onto the cold floor with a jarring thud. She became dazed from hitting her head on the floor. "You no-good-fo'-nothin', worthless piece of shit! Ya don't do a'nothin' 'cept fer sittin' an' runnin' off at the mouth!" he shouted.

"I'll be good! I'll be good! I'll be good, Daddy," she repeated quickly in fear. "I'll behave."

He came around the bed and circled around her, looking at her on the floor through narrowed angry eyes. His fists were clenched, ready to strike. She pushed with her feet away from him, backing toward the wall that abruptly stopped her progress. She was trapped. She held up her hands in front of her face. She knew there was more coming; there was always more coming. He yanked her up by the arms so hard that her shoulder popped. She thought it was broken, but she was too afraid to think about the pain. She cried as he began shaking her violently. Her head rocked back and forth like a bobble-head doll, and she couldn't catch her breath.

She felt like a stuffed animal, one she used to have when her mother was alive. A brown bear named Mr. Goo Goo, who was missing one of his button eyes. Melissa and her mother looked all over the house for that button but never found it. The day after her mother died, her father threw the teddy bear away. He said she was too old for childish things.

"Ya done took my money!" he shouted. He didn't realize that he drank it all that night at the local juke joint. That's why his breath was so flammable. Melissa wished she had a match; maybe then she could light the toxic air coming from his mouth long enough for her to get away. Melissa could not hear the awful things he was screaming at her; she only saw his wretched mouth moving fast.

It was another dream, wasn't it?

But dreams never felt like this; they never hurt as bad as she was hurting now. They never had sharpshooting pain zapping her arms and limbs. They never had the jolting, head-pounding vibrations shooting through her head. She smelled the whiskey, hot on his breath. Strangely, that's all she focused on, that God-awful smell coming from his disgusting mouth. She thought it was going to make her throw up, but that would have only enraged him even more.

He continued shaking her and screaming appalling things she could not hear; he was spraying his hot, nasty breath and spittle in her face. She collapsed, and her body went limp. She passed out in his hands. Her head hung limp and fell down to her chest. He stopped shaking her and looked at her a moment through blurry eyes. It was hard for him to focus in the dark room. He held her closer for a better look.

Nothing. She didn't move.

He tossed her onto the mattress like the morning trash and left the room. He farted on his way out and slammed the door.

27

THE HEAVY METAL door to Susan's cell opened abruptly. It startled her. They never came like this, not this fast. Usually when they came for her, she could hear them approaching. She could hear their keys hit the tumbler, and she was able to prepare herself. But not this time. They were stealthy for some reason and on her quick.

Three guards rushed into her cell and overtook Susan, who held up her hands in self-defense and crossed her arms in fear. It was a reflex she knew all too well.

Two burly guards in their brown uniforms quickly clutched her arms and pulled her to her feet against her shouts of protest. The third guard was holding a white cloth-looking jacket. He held it out, and the guards forced her arms through the straitjacket. Susan screamed in fear as they wrapped it around her back and cinched it tight. She lost her breath and gasped for air.

Susan screamed like she had never screamed before. She couldn't control herself; she screamed even louder in a nonstop panic, pausing only to catch the next breath before screaming again.

The guards spoke to each other. Susan saw their mouths moving, but she heard no sound, just the sound of her wails echoing in the small cell. Just then, another guard came quickly into the cell and straight toward Susan. He lifted a strap to Susan's face and smothered her fearful screams with an archaic-looking muzzle that he strapped around her head. The leather strap with what appeared to be a rolled-up sock went into her mouth. "She's ready for transport," one guard said. He sounded like a beast and appeared to be the one in charge.

The guards pulled her from her cell, yanking her bound arms as if she were a nonliving thing. They were heartless and cold. Susan continued screaming behind the rolled-up sock. Her sounds were muffled, but still loud enough through the narrow puke-green corridor to invoke fear in other inmates.

They turned a corner and walked to a door another guard was holding open. The halls were empty, except for the guards leading Susan into her new holding cell. The guards threw Susan into the new cell and slammed the heavy metal door behind her.

Susan landed hard on her side, which knocked the wind out of her. She gasped, but was choked by the old stinky sock in her mouth. When she landed, she landed onto soft padding, very soft, like a bed, she thought. The whole floor was padded. The whole room was padded—walls, floor, and ceiling. The cell was half the size of her old cell, which was already pretty small. She immediately felt the narrow confinement, which quickly added to her raging fears.

Her eyes were ready to explode; they showed the fear in her mind. The core was nearing, and a full-out nuclear blast was imminent. Again she tried to scream, but the rag on the headgear muffled her sound. Susan began rocking and shaking violently. She was looking around the room like a rabid caged animal. Her eyes diced the room, looking for a quick escape—

*****

Smash! Crack!

Melissa's head rocked back in a violent gesture as the closed fist connected hard with her face in the darkness. Her eyes watered, and blood came from her nose, slow at first, but then it really started flowing. Black metallic streaming from her nose in the darkened room. She began weeping.

Thud!

She was rocked again with another striking blow from the presence in the shadows. It was coming from nowhere; it was coming from everywhere. She couldn't see anything; it was so dark. *Why doesn't he stop? Go away!* Her eyes watered with pools of tears. She wanted to tear her eyes from her head and not see any of this madness and just make it all go away.

Run! Run! echoed through her mind.

I *can't! My legs won't move! My arms are stuck!*

Another nightmare? It was all too real—the feel, the scent in the air, the taste of the darkness was all too real to be a bad dream. This was reality, and like it or not, it was her reality.

Melissa struggled and tried to hold her hands in front of her face for protection against another blow from the darkness. She quickly realized that her hands and feet were tightly bound to the chair she was sitting in. Her mouth was also gagged with what smelled like an old rag. Sudden terror tore through her mind. She screamed in panic, but only muffled murmurs of protest came through. She was helpless and at the mercy of her tormenter.

If I could only see, then I might have a chance. A chance to do what? she asked herself mockingly. Then the voices came which brought her the comfort of knowing that she was not walking the crooked mile all alone.

There's nothing you can do except to sit here unless he unties you.

You know it's him, don't you?

Yes, I do! I can smell him. His rotten mouth smells like booze.

CRACK!

Melissa was hit with yet another vicious punch to the face. It jarred her head so hard it felt like her brains were scrambled.

Make him stop!

A child—no, there was more than just one—began crying as if they too were hurt by the blow that Melissa took to the face. The sounds of children crying startled Melissa more than the blow to her face. She was already numb from the repeated blows, so another punch didn't really hurt that much. She was numb to the point of feeling nothing, no physical pain whatsoever. But she was confused now. She had never heard the voices before, never knew they existed. She wanted to see them, but she knew if they showed themselves, they too would get a beating, and she didn't want that, not to her new friends.

Shhhhh, another voice called out, trying to stop the crying children. *You're not supposed to be here.*

Melissa heard that loud and clear, but she couldn't place the voice or where it came from. Where in the world were these voices coming from?

What was that? She heard somebody else. *Who's there?* Melissa called out into the labyrinth of her mind. Her sound echoed through the confined walls and returned to her. *Hello?* No answer. *Hello? Are you still there? Mommy? Hello? Mommy!* she shouted loud so the sound would carry through the old rag. *Mommmyyyy!*

* * * * *

When Susan pulled her eyes into focus, she found Dr. Tinker looming above her. She saw the doctor's mouth moving, but she heard nothing except the memory of crying children still floating in the back of her mind. Susan shook her head, trying to clear out the strange sounds.

Dr. Tinker could see that Susan was terrified, more frightened than the doctor had ever seen before. Her eyes were wide with fear, and that got under the doctor's skin. She hated putting her in the jacket. She knew it could be devastating to her; she knew that Susan could go into a catatonic state and never come out. But she went with her hunch.

Susan shook her head again. Fear held strong in her tear-filled eyes. "This is the hard way, Susan. The alternative method I spoke to you about in our last session," Dr. Tinker said softly.

Susan's eyes widened.

"Now, we can either continue with this treatment—"

Susan shook her head. She wanted this to end immediately!

"—and see how we proceed. Or we can resume our sessions as scheduled in my office."

Susan nodded vigorously. She would do anything to break free.

"But I will need your full cooperation," Dr. Tinker finished.

Susan nodded. She hadn't stopped, not since she saw a way out.

"That means you come in and talk with me. Will you do that, Susan?"

Susan nodded and tried to speak but couldn't.

Dr. Tinker bent over and reached around Susan's head and unshackled the headgear. "I'm here to help you, Susan, nothing else. I want to see you get better, that's all," Dr. Tinker said as the headgear fell to the floor.

"I'll be good!" Susan said quickly. "I'll be good. I'll behave!" she repeated. She sounded like a young child begging for forgiveness from a strict parent. Dr. Tinker briefly wondered if this was Susan talking or another person she carried with her. She came to the conclusion that it was Susan controlling the speech. It was Susan's thoughts and feeling that came clear. They were the ones Dr. Tinker was worried about.

* * * * *

WALKING INTO Dr. Tinker's office felt a little strange to Susan. She had been there before; she knew she had. There were too many sets of memories for her to choose from to be sure. It was as if she forever had to choose between fact and fiction, a game she was seriously getting tired of playing.

This time, she felt bare, as if the good doctor had somehow seen inside her head and understood the ramifications of what was going on in there. But she couldn't have, could she? Susan wasn't sure. She was not sure how to approach the doctor; she didn't even remember her name. Whatever her name was, she was sitting across the desk, waiting for Susan to make herself comfortable.

She looked at the doctor, who motioned for her to have a seat. Susan approached cautiously and rubbed the palm of her hand across the soft leather chair. It reminded her of something that she couldn't place. It was as though she were seeing a chair for the first time in her life and examining it with curiosity before she dared to sit in it.

"Are you okay, Susan?" Dr. Tinker asked.

Susan nodded. She was still upset with the doctor for the padded room but wasn't about to show any signs of anger for fear of returning to that awful room and white jacket.

"Susan, when I came to see you in the quiet room—"

"I don't want to go back there again. Please don't make me go back in there again! Please! I'll be good, I'll behave," Susan said quickly with pitiful desperation ringing in her voice.

Dr. Tinker found her statement peculiar. She used the exact same words, phrased it exactly as she did in the quiet room. What was triggered inside her to cause her to react as she did? This has to be the starting point. Straight faced and casual, Dr. Tinker nodded and wrote down another notation. She could have been writing down directions to her favorite restaurant for all Susan knew or cared. "I don't think it will be necessary for us to go back there, Susan."

Us? I don't remember you being tied up and gagged in the room!

"I'll be good. I'll behave, I promise," Susan said softly.

"Okay, Susan. You don't need to worry," Dr. Tinker said with a reassuring smile. She tried to approach Susan as her friend during every session to gain her trust. "When you were in the quiet room, it sounded as if you were calling your mother," Dr. Tinker said. "Can you tell me about your mother? And about the relationship you had with her?"

"I never had a relationship with her. She died when I was a kid," Susan replied bluntly, but doing so only because she feared the consequences of the room. "Maybe if I did have a relationship with her, my life wouldn't be so messed up. Maybe I wouldn't be here now. But you're the expert, so you tell me."

"Well, some things are just not that easy, Susan," Dr. Tinker said with a slight movement of her hand. "There's a lot more to a person's mind that one can imagine."

"I can imagine a lot," Susan replied through piercing eyes.

"You want to tell me about what you can imagine?" Dr. Tinker asked.

"I'd rather not talk about my mother, if that's all right with you," Susan said. "Anything else, but not my mother, okay?" She wasn't about to talk to the doctor about anything, really. She was just going to lead her in circles until her time was up.

"Okay then. Let's talk about your father—"

Susan's eyes latched onto the doctor. She didn't see that one coming. Dr. Tinker felt the burning glare and knew it had a significant meaning. She made her note to revisit later.

"Well, like I said, my mother is dead."

"You don't want to talk about your father?"

"No… I don't. I'll talk about my mother."

"Okay, Susan." Dr. Tinker already had her suspicions as to where the problem came from, but she was going to be extremely thorough. She was pleased that Susan was finally starting to peel away the most sensitive first layer. But she also knew there were many more layers to this jungle of twisted emotions Susan had growing wild in her head. "How old were you when she died?"

"Oh God," Susan started and paused for a long moment as her mind wandered off for the answer. "Six…seven, eight. I think I was eight years old," she said finally with a quizzical expression. Her expression also struck the doctor as odd. "I don't really remember much from back then."

"Why not?"

Susan shrugged her shoulders. "It's just not there…kind of hazy, I guess. Maybe it just isn't worth remembering. It's over anyway. I'm an adult now. No sense in going back there." It was a feeble attempt at changing the subject, but the doctor wasn't having any of it. She was far too clever.

"Suppressed memories," Dr. Tinker wrote down in her notes and circled it. "How did your mother die?"

"Next question please," Susan said coldly.

"You don't want to talk about that?"

"Not especially," Susan replied with a deep scowl.

"You were more interested in talking about your mother than your father. Why?"

Susan thought about which way to answer her question. This lady really knew how to get right at it, Susan thought. It appeared to her that it was going to be much harder to avoid certain questions, the type of questions she had been avoiding much of her adult life. She brushed the locks of tangled hair out of her eyes and tucked her hair behind her ears. "Because she was more interesting, I guess."

"So how did she die? It is very important to our progress, Susan. Surely you know how she died. Was it unexpected?" Dr. Tinker asked.

"You can say that," Susan replied.

"That's good. You're doing very well, Susan," Dr. Tinker said with encouragement. "An unexpected death of a parent can have a tremendous effect on a young child."

"More than you will ever know, lady."

Dr. Tinker didn't really know how to take her last statement. She made her notes for further examination. Surely at the core of it, there had to be a gold mine of information. "Susan, I am here to help you, nothing more," Dr. Tinker started carefully. She could not give Susan the guarantee that it would not hurt. She knew that the discoveries made during their sessions could be every bit as painful and traumatic as the actual events themselves. "I can only say that the more you talk to me, the more I will be able to help you sort out whatever it is you are going through."

"You can't even begin to understand what I am going through! I don't care how smart you are or how long you went to school. You'll just never understand," Susan said.

"How do you know if you—"

"Because I don't understand it, and I've been living with it all my life!" Susan shouted. "And if I don't understand it, how the hell is anyone else supposed to?" Her voice was hot and laced with venom.

Dr. Tinker released eye contact halfway through Susan's rant. She didn't want to further upset her. When she was done, the doctor scratched another note in Susan's file. "With both of us working on this together, talking about it, perhaps we can somehow understand what has been happening. If we work as a team, we can solve this puzzle," Dr. Tinker said.

Silence.

"Susan?"

More silence.

"Susan?"

Susan sat there staring at the floor for what seemed like an entire hour. She heard the doctor calling her name and still said nothing.

"Susan?" Dr. Tinker said again. She appeared to become frustrated. So much progress and then to hit a wall of silence was troubling to the doctor. This was a tremendous setback in her mind. She began searching for a different approach.

Dr. Tinker hadn't thought much about her chosen profession in those fleeting moments of silence. If she would have, she would have realized that each of her patients were ideally unique. And for a brief moment, she let herself get flustered by a patient's silence. It was becoming a frequent occurrence with this particular patient. All of a sudden, she realized that the quiet room probably was not such a good idea. She hated herself for even entertaining the thought.

"My mother died in a car accident. At least that's what they told me," Susan said abruptly.

Dr. Tinker was relieved when Susan finally broke her silence. She thought that she had lost her. Something in Susan's face told the doctor that she didn't believe the story of her mother's death. Maybe it was the way she said it. "You think something else happened to her, don't you, Susan?" the doctor asked.

Susan focused on the doctor. This time, the eye contact came with a look of relief. It was as though somebody other than herself finally understood what she had kept a secret all these years. Susan's eyes softened, and the doctor noticed. So did Susan, and she smiled for the first time in months.

"What do you think happened to your mother, Susan?"

Susan said nothing and sat there staring with a blank face. For a moment, the doctor felt uneasy. There was something peculiar in the way she was looking at her that set her mind whirling into abnormal thought patterns.

"Susan, this is a very big step for us," Dr. Tinker started. "It is important you feel that you can trust me and be able to share your thoughts and feelings with me."

Susan remained silent and continued staring at the doctor.

"What do you think happened to your mother, Susan?"

Nothing.

"You still don't want to answer that question, Susan?"

Nothing. *Pure white silence.*

"Would you like to talk about something else?"

Dead air.

Dr. Tinker checked her notes and made another notation in Susan's file. "Would you like to talk about Macy?"

Susan looked shocked and dropped her chin. That was a name nobody knew about, absolutely nobody! It was a secret known only to her. Michael didn't even know about Macy. "How do you know about Macy?" she asked with sparked curiosity.

"I have the video tape from the courtroom," Dr. Tinker replied cautiously and softly.

"The courtroom? So?" Susan said with a perplexed look on her face. "What does that have to do with anything?"

"You…don't remember anything that happened in the courtroom?" Dr. Tinker asked.

"I know exactly what happened. I was arrested and thrown into this place!" Susan shot back with daggers of spite. "I want to know how you know about Macy!" Susan was becoming more upset.

"Susan, Macy came to court with you," Dr. Tinker started. "You had an episode in the courtroom, and you spoke to her for several minutes. Everybody witnessed you talking to her. It was on the national news."

"Shit," Susan said. She was totally deflated.

Susan's face went blank as she searched her mind for misdirection, a lie she could throw at the doctor, but nothing was coming to her. All her lies and half-truths were fading fast. "Well, Doc, you're the expert, so you tell me who Macy is. You answer that, and I'll give you something," Susan said.

"What will you give me, Susan?"

So confident the doctor couldn't place Macy, couldn't possibly imagine where or who she is, Susan became bold. "I'll tell you about my mother. How I think she died." Her face was now more alive. She wanted to know if this outsider knew about her best friend. "So what do you know about Macy, Doc?"

"What I know may surprise you, Susan."

"So surprise me," Susan said, brimming with confidence.

"Okay. Are you sure about this?"

"Absolutely," Susan responded with a cocky smirk.

"Macy first came to you when you were a young child, probably before you were ten years old," Dr. Tinker started.

Susan's face went cold, as did her posture. She slouched in the chair. Dr. Tinker noticed. It was her job to notice the little things, read the patient's body language. The good doctor was right, but Susan tried not letting it show. She tried to remain calm and stone-faced.

Mr. Piggy, will you please let me in?

"You probably didn't have a name for her back then. She was just a voice at first," Dr. Tinker said. She was sure of the direction she was going. "Then she started coming to you more often, so you had to give her a name. You had to call her something. You gave her a name, and you had to give her a face. You painted her hair, you colored her eyes."

Susan felt her stomach tighten. The good doctor appeared to know more than Susan would have liked. She just couldn't figure out how she knew. Susan had never talked about Macy in any of these sessions.

Not by the hair on my chinny chin chin!

"Macy was inquisitive. She wanted to know everything. She probably talked to you all the time. She kept you awake at night," Dr. Tinker said with perfect pitch. "The more you answered her questions, the more she learned about the outside world, and the more she grew. And because she grew, it made it much harder for her to return to her world of your subconscious. She most likely wanted to be the one in control. She wanted to take over completely. She wanted to see the outside world as you do."

Susan couldn't sit there in silence any longer. She had been caught, and she knew it. She had to cut in before the doctor cut any deeper. "Take over what?"

Dr. Tinker looked at her for a long moment. Susan's eyes hungered for the truth. Deep down, she wanted somebody to know the truth, but she would never tell. That had been brutally instilled in her: *Never tell nobody nothin'! Outsiders is what they is! If they ain't with us, they is against us!* Dr. Tinker was an outsider by all accounts, but there was no doubt Susan wanted the good doctor to know her secrets. But even still, she was going to have to work for them. Susan was not about to help dig her own grave.

Then I'll huff, and I'll puff—and I'll blooow your house down!

"You," Dr. Tinker said bluntly. That one word hung in the air and worried Susan. She felt a numbing silence fall around her. It echoed throughout the walls of her convoluted mind. She was ready to impart absolutely nothing.

You can huff...and you can puff...

"That doesn't make any sense! How can she take over me? I think you're way off track, Doctor," Susan said with a wan smile.

Dr. Tinker leaned forward over the desk. "Susan, Macy is not real. She lives in your mind."

BOOM!

There was an explosion of bright light. Alarm bells sounded. Sirens screamed and flares went off all within the confines of Susan's mind. Susan was astounded by the doctor's observations. She was beside herself. How could an outsider know her secrets?

"I am pretty sure Macy is not the only one you have in there. There are others, aren't there, Susan?"

You huffed and you puffed, and you just blew my house over!

Susan knew the doctor had been right about everything she had said. She just couldn't figure out how she knew so much. She couldn't for the life of her remember talking about the "other people," or did she?

"I just...how do...," Susan hesitated. "How did you know about Macy?"

"Susan," Dr. Tinker started, "you still don't remember what happened in court, do you?"

Susan shrugged her shoulders. She held a blank, expressionless look on her face.

"When you were in court, you had a conversation with Macy, a very detailed conversation. You did it in front of the judge. In front of your husband and in front of the news cameras. I first saw it that night on the evening news at home, Susan." The doctor paused a moment as Susan searched her memory. "I have the tape from the courtroom. You were talking to somebody who just wasn't there. You were the only person who saw her, and you said her name. You called her Macy, your friend." Dr. Tinker stopped. She could see that Susan was becoming flustered. Susan raised a hand to her chest. She thought her heart was going to stop.

"You know..." Susan rejoiced softly, "somebody knows," realizing a long kept secret was finally known. The weight of the world was finally off her shoulders. But with somebody knowing, the repercussions would surely follow. Susan knew that all too well, and she knew it was just a matter of time before—

"Yes, Susan. I know. But now that we know what we are dealing with, we can treat it. We can take steps to stop it."

Susan began crying softly. The burden was finally lifted. Dr. Tinker didn't identify it as a hurtful cry but a cry of happiness. But what happiness could she really be experiencing? Her mind was littered with maddening voices and birds' nests of tangled and twisted memories. Yet now she sat in front of the good doctor crying tears of joy.

Then it came from nowhere. Words Dr. Tinker never thought she would hear. "They told me my mother was killed in a car accident," Susan said softly.

Dr. Tinker was a little startled to hear them from Susan. She double-checked the micro-cassette recorder to make sure the tape was not running low. It wasn't.

"But I don't think that was true." Susan stopped herself abruptly. She wasn't sure how to continue. The thoughts and images were buried so deep and so hard to recall. She fought through twisted images in her mind just to form a coherent thought. Her mother's death was such a long time ago. "I think..." She stopped again. "This is so hard," she said.

"Take your time, Susan. I am here with you. We can do this together," Dr. Tinker said softly.

Susan continued staring at the doctor. As she did, Dr. Tinker could see the wheels turning in her head. Susan was searching through the years, trying to catch the date—catch the feelings and emotions surrounding her mother's death.

"I think maybe somebody else had something to do with my mother's disappearance."

"You mean death? Because you said disappearance, Susan."

"No, I didn't, did I?"

"Yes, Susan, you said disappearance."

Again Susan searched her cluttered mind looking for the truth.

Dr. Tinker could see that she was having trouble with this entire situation. It looked as though a war was raging inside her head. Susan's face looked troubled as she flipped through the years of memories. "Take your time, Susan. Close your eyes and go back to the day when you found out about your mother."

Susan closed her eyes, but the troubled look remained on her face.

"Take me back, Susan. Take me back to the day you found out about your mother's death."

Susan shook her head with three quick jolts. It was an odd gesture. Then she began in a strange voice. "Melissa, you run and hide. That's what Mommy said to me," Susan said in her eight-year-old voice.

A curveball! Dr. Tinker wrote down the name MELISSA on her notepad.

Susan continued.

"They were fighting. Mommy and Daddy were fighting," Susan said in her child's voice.

Dr. Tinker felt an icicle run up her spine. That voice really got to the doctor. It was clearly the voice of an innocent child, and it was unlike anything the doctor had ever heard before. This grown woman in front of her was a child. She was a fully grown, living child. She was living in a day some twenty years removed, and it was a bit spooky to the doctor. The goose bumps remained on her arms.

"He yelled at Mommy and said a bad, bad word that I'm not apposed to say. An'…an'…and then he hit her. He hit her on the face. It went *smack!* He smelled. He always smelled, and it was bad when he'd been drinking. He smelled like drinking. I didn't like it when he was drunk," Susan said, still in her realistic child's voice. Her eyes remained closed, and a look of horror was etched on her face.

The goose bumps were never ending to the doctor. She herself was feeling a bit uneasy. She thought about stopping this, but she cautiously let her continue. She might not get another chance to delve so deep into Susan's hidden past again, so she ran with it.

"Mommy was crying and yelling at him."

That voice was so chilling to the doctor. It was a time capsule from the past, and so perfectly preserved. She had no doubts that Susan sounded identical to this voice when she was a child. That was the spooky part for the doctor. Susan was there *now*. She had actually taken herself back to that exact time and place.

"I ran into the bedroom an' went into the closet. It was dark in the closet and hard to see. But I looked out through the cracks. An' I saw him hit her so many times. I saw him hit Mommy. They were fighting. 'Stop it! Stop it,' I yelled, but he hit her again," Susan stopped a moment. Her pause gave the doctor time to catch up with her handwritten notes. There was no telling how deep this maze was and how many layers it possessed.

"Then there was that awful sound, awful sound, like someone dropping a big rock on the sidewalk. Mommy stopped crying. She stopped everything, even talking and yelling. She didn't make no more sound. It all stopped," Susan said. She was frightened and clearly distressed. Her face continued twitching. Sweat beads were forming on her brow. She was there, watching her life crash in front of her innocent eyes for the second time. Where she was, she did not have the protective hand of the doctor ready to snap her fingers and whisk her away from danger.

"I kan't hear anything. They're not talking. Mommy is on the floor, but she doesn't look right." Her words were coming painfully as she pushed forward. "He's sitting on the couch, and he has a beer, but Mommy is still on the floor…my heart is beating so fast. It's so very loud and fast. I hope he doesn't hear me. I hope he doesn't hear my heart beating so loud. It's so loud! Why doesn't it stop?" Susan said in her child's voice. It was a perfect rendition of herself twenty years ago.

Dr. Tinker was still a little miffed at the perfect recognition, the perfect dialect of a child. The goose bumps were coming fast.

"Uh-oh! I kan't let him know I pe-peed my pants. I just couldn't hold it no more. Don't tell, please don't tell," Susan said as Melissa. Even sitting there, in front of the doctor some twenty years later, Susan squirmed with embarrassment, and she was clearly terrified. Her eyes remained shut, locked tight in a flashback of a tainted memory of vital importance.

"He helped mommy up off the floor. He picked her up, but she didn't look right. She didn't look right. She wasn't okay. I couldn't see where he took her. I was too ascared to come out of the closet. And he left the house with her. It was hours and hours before he kame back, but Mommy wasn't with him. She was gone," Susan said. Her eyes remained shut, and the look on her face continued to bring shivers to the doctor. "He was so mean about it, so mean about it. When he kame back, he told me that Mommy was dead from a car accident. So mean, like he didn't kare at all. I didn't like that because he was apposed to kare. He was my daddy. He was apposed to kare about my mommy." Susan's face became squeamish.

"But...but...but that wasn't right. He smelled like the swamp. He was all wet and muddy and stinky like the swamp." Susan began crying like an eight-year-old. "I...he...he...he hurt her! He hurt my mommy. She's in the swamp," she said through a sobbing cry. "She's in the swamp...she's in the swamp, not in the car. Not in the car. She's in the swamp."

Her panicked eyes flashed open and danced wildly around the room. They finally settled, focusing harshly on the doctor. She was back to the here and now, to the surrealism of the good doctor gaping at her every word. Susan tried to gather her bearings. She looked around the room for an escape route, a place to hide in case he followed her through the porthole of time.

Hiding and keeping her eye on his whereabouts was an instinct. It was an act of self-preservation. She was there a moment ago, watching him. It was all too real, and now she was back here and worried. Could he be right behind her? Her mind had to pick which reality she was occupying and act accordingly. Scenarios such as her current revelation had put a lot of stress on her mind over the years. It was something she could never get used to.

She had put a stop to it once, but it was here now, again, and it was most likely here to stay. Susan clearly remembered having long detailed conversations with her voices, her friends and protectors. They were not just an illusion! Were they? What had the doctor said about them? About Macy? What was the doctor's name? *I just kan't remember,* Susan thought as she tried to make sense of the lingering thoughts and feelings.

She focused and redoubled her attention, and Dr. Tinker's face came into clear view, as if suddenly appearing out of a fog. Susan jumped slightly as she laid into her direct eye contact. She felt as though she had lost control of herself for a moment. She couldn't remember what she said or did. She paused and scanned the surface of her brain, trying to put the pieces together. The jigsaw puzzle was incomplete. Vertigo strapped her mind, and she felt disconnected. *Where am I, here or there?*

"What did I say?" Susan asked in a single soft breath. Her normal adult voice had returned.

Dr. Tinker had written volumes of notes on this one session alone. It would take some time for her assistant to decipher them all, she thought.

"You told me about what you think happened to your mother, Susan."

"All of it?"

"Yes, Susan. You told me everything."

Susan looked a bit worried. Deep down, she wanted somebody to know. The emotions and laboring thoughts ran deep. They ran a lot deeper than she could have imagined.

"How does that make you feel, Susan?"

"Scared," Susan said softly. She had done something she hadn't done since she started these sessions: she answered without thought. She was no longer standoffish. Dr. Tinker was concerned about some of her other questions. Questions that would dig deep and tear at the fragile shell that protected Susan's inner soul.

Dr. Tinker made her notes and checked the recorder. It was still running and had plenty of tape. "Okay, Susan. This is where we will end our session this morning. We have made wonderful progress, and I think you need to rest," Dr. Tinker said with a smile. "I would like to see you again this afternoon. Would you be okay with talking with me then?"

Susan didn't have to think much about that question. As much as she hated talking to the doctor, she disliked being caged up like an animal even worse. "I don't mind. Anything to get me out of that room," Susan replied with a halfhearted smile.

28

It was the first time since she started her sessions with Susan that Dr. Tinker had seen Susan's hair combed and her reckless appearance somewhat neat when she entered her office. Susan appeared to be a different version of herself as she approached the seat across from the doctor. It was just another face she learned to put on for the prying eyes of the outside world, another Jekyll and Hyde, presto chanjo. Susan slid back the chair and quietly sat. Something weighed heavy on her mind, but she waited patiently.

Dr. Tinker noticed right away. She looked concerned. "What is it, Susan? You look as though you want to tell me something.

"Well...," Susan started timidly, like a kid who was too afraid to ask Santa the big question: Have I been naughty or nice? "Um, well... I was wondering...if you had some lip gloss or Chapstick? My lips are so dry, and they won't let me have anything, so—"

"Oh goodness, yes, Susan," Dr. Tinker replied as she pulled out her desk drawer. She located a tube of lightly tinted lip moisturizer. She handed it to Susan.

"Thank you, Dr."—Susan looked down at the gold-plated name plaque on the desk and finished her name—"Tinker." Susan couldn't figure out why she hadn't known her name by now. Susan rubbed the soft lip balm on her lips. She felt her dry lips soak in the moisture like a sponge to water. "Thank you so much. Oh wow, this feels so wonderful."

"You're welcome, Susan," Dr. Tinker replied. She thought a moment as she watched Susan relax in the chair. For the first time, Susan appeared comfortable in her surroundings. "How are you feeling, Susan? Because you look very pretty today. You look refreshed and, well, happier than I have seen you since we started," Dr. Tinker said with a gleam in her eyes.

"I've been better, but given the circumstances," Susan said with a shrug. Her hand gestured to her surroundings.

Dr. Tinker nodded. "You look lovely, Susan."

"Thank you."

"Today I would like to talk about Melissa."

Susan shifted in her seat and slowly reached up to her hair and absentmindedly pulled strands loose and began twirling it between her fingers. The name *Melissa* made her fidget and become uncomfortable. Dr. Tinker noticed, but she pressed on.

"I would also like to talk about the other voices, the other friends you have."

How do you know about the others? Susan became flushed and was becoming warm. *Is the heat on in here?* Then buzzing started. She could hear them coming. It was like a phone ringing, and all the kids were running to answer it. Footsteps exploded on the floor of her mind. They wanted to come out and play. They were excited. Nobody had ever wanted to talk to them before, just boring old Melissa, and they had had enough of her.

Susan didn't want that, not in front of the doctor. *How much does this lady really know? How could she know?* Susan had kept the gates locked and guarded them so closely. It was something she didn't want to talk to the doctor about.

Susan continued to fidget in her seat.

The doctor sensed something was about to give.

Susan began shaking her head from side to side, trying to stave off the oncoming voices. It was too late, and she knew it. Perhaps, deep down inside, Susan had hoped for this, a chance for the ultimate taboo, a chance for an outsider to see the truth.

Susan pulled her legs up and folded them under her neatly. She clutched onto her knees and began rocking slowly. Her eyes felt numb, dull, and lifeless. Her vision and movements slowed. Everything appeared to be in slow motion just before the transition of form and entity. She became lost within her tormented thoughts as the others pushed her aside and held her down. They wanted their turn.

"I know this is uncomfortable for you, Susan. But it's very important that we get this out in the open so that we can deal with it and treat it," Dr. Tinker said calmly.

"Do you have a cigarette?" a new voice asked. This voice was seductive, almost inviting to a member of any sex. "I always like to have a cigarette after I've been fucked." She took a deep breath, an inward sigh. "Mmmmm." Susan let loose of a beguiling moan that hung in the air.

The air in the room suddenly became think and heavy.

"No, I'm sorry, I don't," Dr. Tinker said calmly and made another note on the yellow legal pad. "I am Dr. Lauren Tinker—"

"I know who you are. We all do," said the voice. It was nothing at all like Susan's voice or the other voices the doctor had heard. This was a smoky bedroom voice, far more seductive than Susan's normal sound and much older than the others.

"What is your name?" Dr. Tinker asked as if talking to a child.

"Tammy!" she said abruptly. "You don't have to be so damn condescending. I'm so much stronger and far more experienced than the others you've been talking to." Susan blew a sigh and relaxed in the chair as the doctor looked on. "We would have met before, but you're not exactly what I'm looking for."

"What is it you're looking for, Tammy?" She was still quite cautious in her approach with the new voice.

She turned her head, looking past the thick wooden door. "Mmmm, that guard out there. He'll do just fine. Boy, what I can do with him," she said as she adjusted herself in the chair. "I bet he's hung like a bull," she finished with a longing smile.

Susan unfolded her legs and spread them slightly. She was looking at Dr. Tinker with her fuck-me green eyes in a seductive stare. She hiked up her dull-blue LA County—issue gown past her knees and began rubbing her pale thigh softly. She could sense the doctor was becoming uncomfortable.

She smiled at the doctor's awkwardness. "Don't you just love cock straight inside your cunt? I mean hot and hard, mmmm," she said with a groan. "It makes you feel so delicious, so used." She began touching herself in a more provocative way. She looked on, waiting for some kind of response from the doctor. It never came.

Dr. Tinker was beginning to feel a little embarrassed for Susan. She certainly did not want this to continue, but on the other hand, she didn't want to lose this link to the new voice. She wanted to keep it playing as long as possible and see where it leads.

"Do you sleep with a lot of men, Tammy?"

"*Fuck* them would be the more correct word. And I fuck as many as I can, yes."

"You do that when Susan is not around?"

"Hell, yes! I have to!" she said abruptly. "And for your information, her name is Melissa." Susan shot her with a blistering glare. "Damn, I thought you were supposed to be smart." Susan gave her a sinister smirk. "That plain-ass bitch won't let me do anything. She's a bore and such a prude: strictly missionary position. She won't do any of the fun stuff. Yawn, yawn, and yawn. And I don't get it either, especially after all that stuff w—"

"Don't you dare say anything about that!" another voice shouted from Susan's mouth. It was a teenager's voice. It was firm and strong and clearly upset. Perhaps she was the leader of the group. Dr. Tinker wondered just how many that group consisted of. "That is none of her business. She's trying to help Melissa, so you just shut up and leave her alone!" the voice finished. "You're just a slut, and we never liked the things you have done to Melissa! So just go away!"

Dr. Tinker's eyes widened. This was certainly a once-in-a-lifetime case study. More thoughts of publication rushed to her mind. She had to fight them off, but they called to her and lingered somewhere around her thought process.

"You are too. You won't do anything fun, just like her! You're still a virgin," Tammy said with anger.

"You're right, I am still a virgin, and I will die that way! At least I'm not a slut who will sleep with anybody who has a thingy."

Tammy laughed. "You can't even say it. It's a cock!"

"Shut up!"

"A cock!"

"Stop it! Shut up!"

"A rod, a hose, a fuck tool!" Tammy started laughing.

The sudden voice change with every exchange fascinated the doctor.

"Shut up, you nasty slut! Just go away. Nobody wants you here! You're gross," the teen voice said. "As long as you're here, I'm staying! I won't let you do anything to Melissa."

Susan screamed in Tammy's voice. It was a bloodcurdling yell that caused the doctor to flinch. "I hate you, you fucking bitch! You're a goody-goody! You're good for nothing is what you are!" Susan was shaking. Her face was beading with sweat. "I hate you!" Tammy screamed again. That was it.

Susan's face held still a moment. No movement whatsoever. Her unblinking eyes stared straight forward. It was as if Susan's body was completely unoccupied, waiting for the next guest to take over.

Dr. Tinker leaned forward and was visibly concerned.

Then out of the blue, she spoke. "She's gone," the teen voice said to the doctor. Her new voice came softly and cautiously. Susan's posture quickly changed. She closed her legs and pulled the gown down past her knees. She folded one over the other and sat like a proper young lady.

"What's your name?" Dr. Tinker asked.

"My name is Robin, and I really don't want to talk to you," she said without any hesitation, though she was very polite with her tone.

"Why don't you want to talk to me, Robin?"

"Because I am afraid of you."

"Why are you afraid of me, Robin?"

"Because you're an adult, and adults just don't make any sense. They do things that they just shouldn't do."

"What kind of things, Robin?"

"Why do you keep saying my name?" she asked. Susan again shifted in the chair. Her appearance became a little more discomforting.

"Because that's your name."

"Well, I don't like it."

"Okay. Well then, what should I call you?"

"Don't call me anything. I'm not going to be here very long anyway," she said.

"Why don't you want to talk to me?"

"Because you're an adult, and we just don't trust you. The things adults do are just not right."

"I am an adult, but that doesn't mean that I am going to hurt you or Susan."

"Her name is Melissa. That's what she wants to be called."

"Okay, Melissa it is," Dr. Tinker said and noted it on her pad: MELISSA! She circled it. "You said you're not going to be here that long. Do you want to explain that statement? Are you going somewhere?"

Susan sat pensive and quiet for a moment as Robin weighed out the ramifications of such an answer. She shrugged her shoulders. "Because I am going to be dead soon."

That sent alarm bells off in the doctor's head. She became quite concerned. Talk of death is something she took very seriously. Having lost three patients over the last five years after talk of death, Dr. Tinker was very concerned even though the threat came from an inner self helper. She was going to have to rethink her whole approach with Melissa. "What you just said, about being dead soon, is very serious, Robin."

Susan lowered her head and thought a moment. She looked back up at the lady sitting across from her and shrugged. "Can't really get more serious than death."

"Do you know something the rest of them don't know?"

"Yes." There was nothing more.

"Does Melissa know?"

"Not yet, but she will…very soon…"

"Robin, what makes you think that you are going to be dead soon?" This was a five alarm fire raging in the doctor's mind. She had seen it before. Oh, the signs, why the hell hadn't she seen it earlier? The children's voices—that's what threw her off. They were innocent children incapable of such thoughts of resolution.

"Because I can see it coming. I can see the line, and it's getting close." That sent shivers deep into the doctor's soul. "Soon Melissa will see it too. So will all the others. The children will see it last, but when they do, that's it. It's all over."

Dr. Tinker couldn't let it go; she wouldn't let it go. "Robin, what is the line? What is going to happen when Melissa sees the line?"

Susan suddenly arched her body as if she were shot in the small of her back. She inhaled a massive amount of air into her lungs. Her gesture was so violent and out of the blue the good doctor really didn't know what to think. Then Susan began shaking in the chair as if another entity had taken hold of her.

Susan's eyes rolled back in her head just before she closed them to the world. Dr. Tinker stood up for a moment as if to offer assistance. Susan stopped before the doctor could say anything. This was something she had done before.

Susan opened her eyes as the doctor was reaching out to her. Susan was again left with vertigo and remained nowhere. The thick haze was clearing quickly. She swiftly scanned the room to gather herself but returned to the familiar face of Dr. Lauren Tinker, who was sitting back down in her chair. Susan's eyes settled as she realized where she was and who she was and why she was here. Susan sighed inwardly.

"They came again, didn't they?" Susan asked quietly.

"Yes, Susan, they did," Dr. Tinker said.

"I figured they would," she replied.

"They said you would rather be called by your given name, Melissa. Is that true?"

Susan shrugged her shoulders. "I guess it doesn't matter anymore," she replied and thought a moment. "Yes. I think I would like that… It's been a long time. It's been a very long time," she said, reflecting.

"You changed your name when you left home, didn't you, Melissa?"

"Yes."

"You wanted to leave your past behind and start fresh and become somebody new from who you were," Dr. Tinker said. "Just leave it all behind."

"Yes."

"But it caught up with you, didn't it, Melissa?"

Melissa drew a quick focus onto the doctor's soft gaze. Dr. Tinker didn't need to hear the answer; her fearful look said it all. She made her notes.

Of all the patients Dr. Tinker had, more than thirty in all, Melissa's was by far her most interesting case. The doctor was going to devote most of her time to Melissa from now on. She was frightened by the talk of death and wanted to make sure that it was just talk by a disillusioned patient.

"Robin, one of your inner self helpers—we call them ISH for short—said something rather disturbing when she came out to me."

"That means that Tammy also came out, didn't she?"

"Yes."

"She doesn't like Tammy very much. She hates her, in fact." Her voice trailed off. Then, "She wants to kill her, but...she doesn't know how." She paused. "She hates what she does to me. Robin only comes out to protect me from her. She's a good kid," Melissa said in a cold withdrawn voice. She took herself away from the scene. She was not only absent form herself but also from the room. She was soaring in another solar system altogether in her mind.

"Robin said that she is going to die soon." Dr. Tinker gave Melissa a stern look. "Frankly, Melissa, that concerns me deeply. I am very troubled by what she said."

Melissa pulled herself back to the here and now and stared through the doctor. The doctor couldn't imagine what was going through Melissa's mind.

"We're all going to die," she spoke in a tone that was cold and completely devoid of any emotion. "It's part of life, you know. You live...you die. People get over it," she said with a shrug. There was no soul in her voice. No emotion, just a monotone sound. For a brief moment, the doctor bought into Melissa's gothic creation of darkness. Shivers came all too quickly to the doctor.

"Yes, Melissa, that is part of life, but we don't have to help it. We must let that happen naturally," Dr. Tinker said sympathetically.

Melissa held her stare. She was utterly disconnected with reality. It was spooky to the doctor. "Yeah, well, some of us will never get a chance to die naturally," Melissa said with no emotion. They were heartless, shallow words from an abandoned soul. It was as if she knew where her fate lay and was determined to do absolutely nothing about the inevitable.

"Why do you feel that way, Melissa?"

Melissa continued holding her blinkless stare. "I don't feel. I don't feel anything," she responded. Her tone held a vast wasteland of anger behind the soft tone.

Dr. Tinker nodded and jotted down another note: "Get back to that later."

"Robin said something about a line—"

That got Melissa's attention. She pulled focus and studied the doctor's face. Her eyes became alert with curiosity.

"Does that mean something to you, Melissa?"

Melissa continued holding on to the doctor's concerned face, but the life ran out of her eyes. "Not anymore, it doesn't." Melissa was done. She was done for the day, done for the week, and done for the year. She was done for her life. She had no more in her. She couldn't do anything more but return to her cell.

Melissa's Storm

"I've got a seekret to tell you…"
"Oh, goody! I like seekrets, an' I kan keep 'em to."
"It's my birthday today…"
"Kan we have cake?"
"No… I don't think so…"
"Well, happy birthday."
"Thank you…"
"Kan we come out of the dark now?"
"No, not now. Maybe next year…"
"Yeah, maybe."
"What do you want to be when you grow up?"
"Alive…"
"Okay, so what do you want to do?"

"Dream..."
"You have all this time now to dream. We're still kids."
"I'm too busy trying to survive to waste time dreaming..."
"Dreaming is never a waste of time."
"For me it is..."
"No, it's not."
"Yes, it is..."
"No, it's not."
"You'll never understand..."
"I already do, Melissa."

Through the thin walls of the old run-down house came the sound of heavy footsteps in the kitchen. Melissa recognized them right away and came alert and responsive. Her survival instincts taught her to quickly recognize the sound of danger. A cloak of silence quickly fell over her.

As the heavy step drew closer, the vibrations in the walls and floor shook beneath her weight. Melissa held her breath for fear he would hear the slight exhale of air releasing from her lungs. The footsteps moved past the door to her room and moved deeper into the house. She let her breath out very quietly and ever so carefully.

A sudden thought entered her mind, and she decided to go with it and move to the closet for cover. That was always the safest place. As she stealthily moved across the floor, the door to her room opened quickly. "Melissa!" her father said roughly. His voice was groggy and loaded with phlegm.

Melissa froze in her tracks. She was too frightened to move or even look in his general direction. What had she done now? What were the consequences going to be this time—another bruise, another black eye, a fat lip, and a scar? She hoped there would be no blood this time. She hated the sight of her own blood, especially when it came from her mouth. She hated the taste of it on her tongue, hated the smell.

"I want you should come on out'cher fer a minute. Got somethin' I wanna talk ta ya 'bout." With that, the door closed behind him. Melissa remained in the dark room, frozen like a statue in the park. She stood morbidly confused by this confrontation, or lack thereof. Not once since her mother died had their encounters been this civil.

As the heavy footsteps faded away as he entered the small living room, Melissa's mind was racing with fear. Her pulse was steadily increasing. She was terrified and wondered what she had done wrong this time; she wondered how severe her beating was going to be.

Melissa poked her head out and peered into the dirty kitchen. All clear. Maybe it was all a dream, a bad dream, and he wasn't here at all. But as she looked, she could see him sitting on the couch watching television. The flickering screen was the only light in the dark living room. It was always dark in there; it was always dark in the entire house. He liked it dark and gloomy. Melissa inched her way across the cold kitchen floor.

Since her mother died, she had never been out there in the open while he was home. That was always too dangerous for her. Something bad was going to happen; she could feel it in her bones. Melissa stood up straight and lingered in the doorway leading to the living room. She was careful not to step on the floorboard near the refrigerator; it squeaked. She had to know all the noisy parts of the house.

Her heart skipped a beat when he turned and saw her standing there. "Well, come on in here, girl," he said above the roar of the television.

Melissa hesitated and began to move pensively toward him. She wanted so much to believe that there was still something good in him. After all, he was her father. She hoped so much that this was the start of a new beginning. But having grown up fast and always walking on the cutting edge of the blade, she was very careful of his offerings. They had proved in the past to be very hazardous to her health. He turned again and saw that she was moving very slowly.

"Well, come on in here. I ain't gonna bite ya. 'Less ya want me to," he said and broke out in roaring laughter. He laughed so hard he began coughing, almost choking.

This was a different person altogether, she thought. Melissa had never seen him smile, let alone laugh. She wasn't sure if she should smile, so she held it back just in case. Cautiously, she moved forward. She stopped and stood next to him by the couch. She stiffened, waiting for the knockout blow.

"Bet ya thought I forgot, huh?"

Melissa was utterly confused as he handed her an unwrapped plain brown box. She wasn't sure if she should take it from him. Was it safe? She studied the box for a minute. She wasn't sure of what to do next.

"Go on," he encouraged. "It's your birthday. Ya thought I forgot, didn't ya?"

Forgot? I didn't even think you remembered my name, let alone my birthday! Then a thought occurred to her: it was her birthday! Her mother always told her when her birthday was coming. Melissa couldn't remember the exact date, but she knew it was close, and hey, wow, it is today! But then lately, the thought of her birthday was the last thing on her mind.

A smile slowly crept across her face. Her recent bruises had faded, and she looked good, but the memories were still there. They would always be there. But right now none of the bad memories could wipe away the brilliant smile that swept across her face. She felt overjoyed with a rush of emotion, but she was not about to show it in front of him.

Melissa didn't wait; she reached into the box. She was expecting to be held up in her room until he ran off to the bar, his usual nightly routine. Letting the box fall to the floor, she held up a white dress. It was a little shorter than she thought it should be, but a pretty dress just the same. The genuine smile remained on her face. She was shocked, not only that her daddy remembered her birthday but he was also being very nice to her. It was something he had not done since her mommy died. Melissa held the dress up to her chest.

"Go on with yerself an' try it on," he said with encouragement. Then he lifted the brown bottle up to his mouth and took a long drink of whiskey. This was not like other nights, and Melissa wasn't concerned about him drinking tonight. This was her birthday.

Maybe he had changed after all. *This is one of my most special nights I can remember*, she thought as she ran back into her room to try on her new dress.

A few minutes later, Melissa came back out wearing her new white dress. She was happy, but she looked very uncomfortable. The dress showed a lot of legs and barely covered her bottom. She tried pulling it down to her knees, but it wouldn't stretch. She stood in the doorway and waited for him to notice.

He did. "Boy, howdy. Don't ya look purtty!" he said as he got up from the couch. "Turn aroun', let me kook at ya."

Melissa quickly turned a full circle. The smile never left her face. She couldn't remember being this happy. She hardly knew what happiness was anymore, but this felt good. Things were going to change. They were going to be a family after all; she just knew they were.

"Let me see ya turn again," he said. "Do it quick."

Melissa spun quickly and showed off her new dress. Her daddy looked on with a broad smile. "Yeah," he said under his breath. "I like that."

Melissa didn't notice how he was rubbing his belly. It didn't mean much to her, nor did she think about the way he was looking at her.

"I like my new dress. Thank you," she said. She didn't want to say too much, not yet at least. The night was still young, and there was no telling how it would all turn out. If this was her new daddy, she was going to play it careful until she knew for sure. So far, she liked what she was seeing.

"There's somethin' else I'd like to give ya," he said.

More presents? Wow! This is just turning out so wonderful, she thought. She didn't dare show any emotion other than a faint smile. There's no telling how he would react to excitement. So she played it cool; she had to.

He walked past her and into the kitchen. "It's down here in the basement," he said and motioned for her to follow. "Ya leave the dress on an' come on down. I's gonna teach ya somethin'. An' it's gonna make Daddy real happy too…"

That was always a good thing: for him to be happy. Maybe then he wouldn't beat her as much as he did. She was like a lamb to the slaughter and happily followed him. She was eager, hoping against hope that things were going to change.

He opened the door and turned on the light at the top of the stairs. The dull exposed bulb came on and dimly lit the top of the stairs. The basement was still painted in darkness.

"Go on with ya."

Wide-eyed, Melissa moved past him and paused a moment before she started down the stairs. She always feared the basement, but her brave daddy was going down there with her, so she guessed it would be safe.

Good old daddy watched her walk down the wooden stairs. He watched as the short dress showed off her legs. "Yeah, boy," he said under his breath. "You just might be real useful 'round here after all," he mumbled and started down the stairs after her.

"I exist now."
"Yes…"
"You gave me life."
"Yes…"
"You painted me with golden hair."
"Yes…"
"And green eyes."
"Yes…"
"Now look at me."
"Okay…"
"Not in the darkness. Look at me in the light."
"Yes. It is time…"

29

Twenty-four weeks

WORLD WAR III was the feeling as the masses gathered in front of the Santa Monica courthouse. Well over six thousand people surged upon the grounds for this bittersweet conclusion. All the major groups were there in force. The sheer numbers were overwhelming and growing by the minute as more people arrived to join the mêlée. Most just wanted a chance to be on the local news.

There were another ten thousand people gathered down at the Santa Monica pier and on the beach. And thousands more right down the street at the Santa Monica shopping mall and Third Street Promenade. They were also gathered and clumped together down Main Street and into Venice.

It was one of those days, eighty-five degrees at eight in the morning. But as the ten o'clock hour rapidly approached, temps were hovering around the century mark. The day was early, hot, and sunny. It was a perfect oven for the furnace of anger that was clearly waiting for the hammer to drop.

The courthouse was a magnet for human curiosity; they came from everywhere. News crews were gathered from all over the world. Satellite trucks were parked around the block and down side streets, and twenty more were parked at the Santa Monica Pier. Film crews shot live remotes, broadcasting the disorderly quagmire around the world in real time. A small group of reporters were covering the speaker on the courthouse steps. Others covered the growing tension between the pro-life and pro-choice camps. Two strong lines of uniformed police in riot gear separated each side. Religious groups mingled through both sides preaching their word of God.

LAPD and LA County sheriffs were gathered, working together in massive, overwhelming numbers of uniformed lawmen ready for anything. Their great numbers didn't come close to the massive amount of incorrigible civilians that were growing by the minute. The police were clearly outnumbered.

People were holding signs of all kinds, pro this, anti that. "Peace," "Love," "No war," etc., etc.—the signs were on and on. Self-appointed speakers broadcast their personal word over bullhorns and portable microphones; small groups of people gathered nearest to them cheered with reverence.

*****

Michael Bishope entered the courthouse from the rear entrance under tight security. He knew how many people were gathered in front of the courthouse, and he was greatly disturbed by the sheer numbers of people who had latched onto this event.

Michael knew how the reporters could fuel the fire and fan the flames around the world. He knew they would incite riotous behavior from a crowd. People would summon courage they never knew they had and unleash it in violent rages just to be seen on the news.

To Michael, the news had stopped being news long ago. It was now a form of entertainment, with its tabloid treatment of stories and car chases. That was one of the reasons he left his job. He didn't care what he did from this point on; at least he would be clean. Michael stopped in the corridor as the crowd in front of the building roared.

*****

The crowd was very anxious and ready to explode into conscious upheaval. Their fever pitch was toxic and spreading like wildfire. The heat of the day was growing, and so was the number of people as thousands more plebeians descended on the grounds.

On the courthouse steps, another speaker set up his podium and began spewing his spiel to the pro-choice side. They roared when their famous speaker came to life over the squawk box and cheered his every word.

Nick Vach moved his way through the crowd and made his way close to the front steps. The two sparring loud speakers greeted him. Nick was now where he didn't want to be, in direct line of the news cameras. He waited and listened to the nonsensical remarks from the speakers. He tried to tune out the crowd, but there were too many of them spewing crap all at once. He just wanted this whole thing over. He wanted to receive word from the court and go home.

* * * * *

Moving down the hallway, Michael was alone in silence. It reminded him of walking in the empty corridor at the KNRQ studios just before he passed through the glass doors. This silence was something of a misnomer; he had not seen the hallway this silent since this thing started. He did notice the two guards positioned in front of the courtroom who eyed him as he approached. As he came closer, he heard the noise coming from the front grounds.

His heart pounded with anticipation as he approached the door. He didn't want to speak to the guards as he entered. As he reached for the door handle, Michael stopped as a loud roar came from the massive crowd and bounced off the walls and echoed through the corridor. "The natives are restless," said one of the guards with a smile. Michael nodded and forced a smile before he entered the courtroom.

Michael stopped as the large wooden doors shut behind him. The room was empty. For a moment, he thought he was in the wrong courtroom. That was until he saw Tyson Nash sitting at the table in front of him. Then it dawned on him: the judge ordered a closed court. Not even the KNRQ camera was present. Michael smiled. He liked this situation. This is how he initially wanted to handle it, privately and quietly. He couldn't figure out how this became such a media explosion in the first place.

Nash greeted Michael with small talk as he sat at the table. Michael was barely aware of Nash's gesture as he sat. His mind had one sole focus and thought: he wanted to see his wife.

Warren Vecchio entered the courtroom and sat at the table across from them. Vecchio made his polite greeting across to Nash, who returned in kind. He opened his briefcase and fumbled with some papers, which he placed neatly on the table in front of him.

During Susan's incarceration, Warren Vecchio was the only person permitted to visit her, which he did three times. None of his visits bore any fruit as Susan remained mute his entire stay. But that was her modus operandi each time he tried to pry into her head. She wanted nothing to do with this guy.

It wasn't long before the side door opened. A uniformed guard entered and walked over to the clerk, who was busy with some last-minute paperwork. He leaned over and whispered to the clerk.

Michael looked on with anticipation, hoping Susan would soon appear. He looked deflated when the second guard entered the room alone. But his spirits soared when Susan walked in a short time after him. She was escorted by a female guard. Michael's heart began racing, pounding in his chest.

She was very pale, and her hair didn't look like her hair. It was as though she was wearing a wig bought at a secondhand store, ratty and uncombed. Susan was wearing the exact same white dress she was wearing at the last court appearance a month ago. Michael wondered if he should have dropped off some clothes for her. It was too late for anything but regrets.

Michael stood up as his wife approached. He moved toward her. "Susan," he called after his wife. The guard led her straight to the table where she sat. Michael felt his heart beating a little harder. He wanted to rush to her, sweep her into his arms, and kiss her long and deep. He wanted to hold her in his arms until the storm passed and keep her safe from the fallout.

Michael's eyes latched on to something only he would notice. Though her face looked frail, her stomach was a little larger than it had ever been. She was starting to show! His mind was littered with joy as he looked upon his wife from across the room. He wanted so much to walk over and place his hand on her belly and see if there was any movement from the baby.

Michael leaned over and whispered something to Nash, who then looked over toward Susan. She was definitely starting to show. Michael felt as though he had done the right thing by coming to court and fighting for his baby. All this hardship was well worth it as he continued looking over at his wife.

The bailiff called the court to order. After the judge entered the courtroom and sat, Michael and Nash returned to their seats.

Nash waited for the judge to gather himself and address the court. His hunch told him that he was going to be a hero by the day's end or at least a celebrated member of his profession.

Michael, however, waited for the slightest acknowledgement from Susan. He was watching intently and waited for the faintest glimpse. He didn't hear the judge start to address the court. Nash nudged him in the ribs to get his attention.

"... I know this has not been easy on both parties, and the media circus out there has not made it any easier. So we'll try and make this brief," Judge Fields started. "The court is first going to hear from Dr. Lauren Tinker." Judge Fields looked over a piece of paper before he went on. "There is another matter before this court, for which I will accept petitions on later," he finished.

Nash smiled. His ducks were all in order.

The bailiff positioned at the public entrance opened the door. Michael and Nash turned and watched Dr. Tinker walk gracefully down the aisle. Susan never looked at her.

After taking the oath, she handed the bailiff a folder. The bailiff placed it on the judge's bench. Dr. Tinker then waited quietly as the bailiff took his position by the judge's entrance. Judge Fields briefly read from the folder. Dr. Tinker turned toward the judge as he started to speak.

"Dr. Tinker, have you had adequate time to evaluate Mrs. Bishope?" Judge Fields asked.

"No, Your Honor, I have not," she replied simply. His look prompted another response for the doctor. "Mrs. Bishope's case is far more complex than I had anticipated. It would take far more than thirty days to complete an evaluation of this magnitude. There are extenuating circumstances in this case that reach far beyond the realm of normalcy. I think the court should be made aware of such circumstances."

"Go ahead, Dr. Tinker," Judge Fields encouraged.

"First of all, Mrs. Bishope would like to be addressed by her given name of Melissa."

The few eyes in the courtroom focused on Melissa. She felt their stare but kept her head down. Michael stared at her with another look of shock. It was a look he was sadly getting used to. This whole thing had become so disorienting to him.

"Further, I have to question whether or not it was in Melissa's best interest to hold her in custody for this evaluation," Dr. Tinker said.

"Mrs. Bishope was found in contempt of court," Judge Fields responded quickly. "She was held in custody for obvious reasons, Dr. Tinker," Judge Fields said with authority. He let her know that he was the one in charge. Melissa's outburst in his courtroom still weighed heavy on his nerves.

"Yes, Your Honor," Dr. Tinker replied apologetically.

"Is there more?"

"Yes, Your Honor." Dr. Tinker opened her notebook and briefly read from her chicken scratch. "Melissa has classic signs of having what is known as DIDS, dissociated identity disorder."

Michael never took his eyes off his wife. His mouth parted as he listened to the doctor give her opinion. He had no idea what that meant, but he didn't like the fact that she classified her problem with a name. His mind was swirling with conflicting thoughts and images.

"You're not sure if she has this disorder?" Judge Fields asked.

"No, of that I have no doubts, Your Honor. But I have not had adequate time with Melissa to determine the extent of her disorder. I would need additional time to lay such a label on a patient." Dr. Tinker finished.

"What exactly is dissociated identity disorder?" Judge Fields asked.

Strange images of his wife entered Michael's thought process and began flashing film of all the bizarre things that she had been doing in the months leading up to this point.

"It is an exaggerated form of schizophrenia. For the laymen, MPD, multiple personality disorder. When a baby is born, their body becomes separate from their mother's, and they then need their own essence and personality. The body and its neurohormones are part of a complex physical structure. The essence and personality are nonmaterial, composed of intelligent energy," Dr. Tinker said and repositioned herself in the chair. "They were bound together when they were placed into a physical body with the brain and its hormones. This happened when you, as a newborn baby, took your first breath." Dr. Tinker paused for a moment. "If a child is born into a family with a parent who is a serious abuser, that child could be subject to life-threatening trauma—which through our sessions, I have come to learn that Melissa was a child of an abusive parent."

Again all eyes were quickly focused on Melissa. The judge peered through his thin glasses, magnifying her image. Michael had no idea what her childhood was like; she had never spoken of it. Now he understood why she had been keeping it a secret all this time.

"If that child has reason to believe she is going to be hurt or killed by a parent, a survival mechanism called *dissociation* is triggered. Dissociation means splitting apart of two mental parts which were previously connected." Again Dr. Tinker paused and took a drink of water from a clear bottle.

All of a sudden, Michael found himself walking through the front door of his house, Susan greeting him at the door with a brilliant smile. He was faced with the images of what Susan had done to the house. Paint everywhere in an array of bright colors. *It wasn't her!* he thought.

"The first dissociation is the separation of the *original personality* from the *essence*. The essence takes on a sort of emergency-intervention function we call the *inner self helper* or ISH. The ISH sends the original personality, stripped of all social traits into safekeeping in the nonmaterial, in the outer space of her mind, if you will. In other words, her original personality is buried deep in her subconscious.

Then the ISH takes over all the appropriate personality traits and programs an alter personality to run the body in such a way that the abuser will not strike the child. Survival is the goal of the ISH. Once the first ISH is born into the mind, it is far more likely that others will be born as well. Hence, the many faces of Melissa." Dr. Tinker finished.

Judge Fields looked a bit perplexed. "You're 100 percent sure that Mrs. Bishope has this disorder?" Judge Fields asked.

"Not 100 percent, no, I am not. Mrs. Bishope shows advanced signs of the disorder, but again—"

"You need more time with her?"

"Yes, Your Honor, I do…she does. Melissa needs more time in therapy to get through this," Dr. Tinker started. She took another drink of water. "Melissa has many layers of suppressed memories that could flood back at any moment. She could be walking down the street, and a suppressed memory could come back to her. If that happens, well, there's no telling how she will react. Some of her alters do appear hostile, on the verge of violence. Again there's no way to determine that without further treatment," Dr. Tinker finished and held her gaze on the judge.

More vivid memories came rushing back to Michael. *That night on the bed, that wasn't her*, he thought. He now started to understand. *My God, why didn't I see it earlier?*

Nash sat quietly and listened to the doctor hang Melissa. He knew, or at least had another hunch, how this would turn out. He knew he would be standing in front of the massive news corps holding his own court as the hero attorney. He smiled inwardly.

"So you're saying Mrs. Bishope should be held in custody for more testing?" Judge Fields asked.

"Your Honor, at first I did not agree with having her incarcerated for her treatment. But as our sessions progressed and as the layers came off, I found it—and still find it absolutely necessary—for further supervised treatment."

"Why do you feel that way?"

"I believe that she is a danger to herself or possibly to others. Like I said, some of her personalities have a mind of their own. They can control what she says and does."

Michael quickly stood up. "She is not a danger to anyone! That's a lie! Can't you see she is sick?" Michael shouted. "She needs help, Your Honor, not prison!"

"Mr. Bishope!" Judge Fields shouted. "This is a court of law. We do not act like that in here. Mr. Nash, control your client."

"Yes, Your Honor," Nash replied and pulled Michael back down into his seat. He leaned over and whispered into Michael's ear.

Judge Fields turned back to the doctor. "Her condition is that serious?"

"Yes, Your Honor, it is," she started. "Melissa has a different side to her, one that cannot be controlled very easily. Within her, she has many different personalities that sometimes take over her whole being. They will act on her behalf," Dr. Tinker said. She looked at Melissa a moment as she sipped from the water bottle. "They will associate with the outside world as if they were Melissa. That is how the world would see her, as Melissa, not her alters. And they would say and do things in a way that Melissa herself would not do. In our sessions, I have learned that Melissa has lived a very rough life, one in which she watched her father kill her mother."

Michael continued staring at his wife. He was raging inside and stunned. He couldn't believe what he was hearing about his love. He wanted nothing more than to find the person responsible for his wife's mental breakdown and savagely beat him.

"Very soon after, if not before that tragic event in her life, Melissa began experiencing altered personalities—imaginary play friends, if you will. She developed a relationship with a friend who was born in her mind named Macy. I am almost certain that Macy was the first ISH born into Melissa's mind. The same Macy, in fact, that appeared before you in this courtroom, although not actually appearing. But to Melissa, Macy was here just as I am here talking with you now. And no one can tell her any differently." Dr. Tinker paused again to drink form the water bottle. She looked again at Melissa, who was looking down at the floor.

"Some of her alters are very docile and nonaggressive. Most of the ones I have seen have been children or teens because that's when the trauma first started with Melissa, when she was very young. Others, who were apparently created later in her development, can be very mischievous and could have violent tendencies."

Melissa blew a sigh that stopped the doctor from continuing. All eyes fell on Melissa, who remained with her head down. She wasn't going to be a part of this. She knew where she was going to be at the end of the day.

"This is what concerns me about Melissa. I just haven't had enough time to fully examine her alters and get to ground zero. I don't exactly know how deep they go or what they are capable of. I have seen quite a few in our sessions, even talked to them. Some were hostile and pugnacious in nature. There was even talk of death, suicide."

Again the courtroom paused to look at Melissa. Even the slight taste of freedom outside her cell for these few hours weren't enough to coax emotion or cooperation out of her. Not even her attorney could get so much as a single word from her. He wished he'd never been brought in on this case.

"In your experience, Dr. Tinker, can Mrs. Bishope recover? Will she ever be able to cope in the real world and function as a productive member of society?" Judge Fields asked.

"Yes, she is curable, and she can most definitely function in society. But again, it's going to take a lot of time and a lot of one-on-one dialogue to get to that point. And frankly, dialogue in our sessions has not been forthcoming on Melissa's part. At this point, Your Honor, I would not recommend that Melissa attempt a reintroduction into society without proper treatment," Dr. Tinker said.

"By proper treatment, you mean keep her under your care?"

"I strongly recommend that Melissa remain in my care for an indefinite duration of time. We are at a crucial stage in our progress, and any deviation from that progress, I fear, can have devastating consequences to Melissa."

Judge Fields listened to that last part with one ear as he was watching for Melissa's reaction—and there was none, absolutely nothing, no reaction whatsoever. Judge Fields found that odd. Then again, he found this whole case rather odd, and becoming more so with each turn of the page. Everything about it was something new to him, something he had never seen before.

Michael was clearly distressed by the dialogue in the courtroom between the judge and the doctor, but he was powerless to do anything about it.

"Do you feel as though Mrs. Bishope might hurt herself or somebody else?" Judge Fields asked.

No, but I sure as hell want to hurt you! Michael thought. He was pissed, at the boiling point. He was on the verge of his own contempt charge.

"Unfortunately, yes. I think she is very capable of such an act. That is my main concern, and that is the only reason I feel incarceration is vitally important for Melissa," Dr. Tinker said. She looked directly at Melissa and finished. "I feel Melissa, from what I have seen and heard from one of her alters, may have what we call a death wish. A suicide red flag, if you will. I fear that if she is released, she is quite capable of such an act on herself. And where Melissa is now, she might not even know that she's thinking about suicide. It may be one of her alters that is contemplating the act." The doctor was precise and calculated and held Melissa in her caring gaze. "I just don't want to have any regrets, Your Honor. I don't want to read about her suicide in the morning papers when it could have been prevented. Melissa is on the edge of a very dangerous cliff right now. If she does not get the immediate help she needs, she will fall. And I fear it will be a fall she may not survive," Dr. Tinker finished.

"Thank you, Doctor. You may step down," Judge Fields said.

As Dr. Tinker walked across the floor, Michael eyed her with contempt as she left the courtroom. He disliked what she had said about his wife, even though he had his own suspicions about her behavior.

Nash was beaming, almost giddy as he awaited the judge's forthcoming decision. The doctor, he felt, had just won the case for them. There was no doubt in his mind that he would soon walk away with celebrity status. That's exactly what Nash was looking for: his name up there with the big boys of the legal world.

Nash knew Vecchio was not going to put up much of a fight, he hadn't yet. The poor bastard never really had a chance in the first place. There had never been any dialogue between him and Melissa. *No, Susan—Melissa or whatever she was calling herself in her twisted psyche—doesn't stand a chance of winning this case*, Nash thought to himself. He smiled at the thought.

Tension hung in the heavy air along with deadly silence. The air felt as thick and lumpy as the gravy his grandmother used to make. Michael couldn't breathe. He pulled at the knot in his tie.

Judge Fields tapped a few keys on his computer and read the text. Light from the screen glimmered in his glasses as he peered over them.

Melissa was completely unresponsive to her attorney. Her convictions lay elsewhere along with her soul. Her court-appointed attorney wanted to crawl under a rock. This case was a major blemish on his stellar career. He never wanted it in the first place. He pleaded with the judge, but like it or not, he was stuck with the case. The hammer blow was going to be a hard one.

"Before this morning's court session, I had the chance in chambers to once again go over the videotape of Mrs. Bishope's last court performance. It troubled me then, and frankly, I still find it deeply disturbing," Judge Fields said and paused as he read from the computer.

The judge's words brought delight to Nash as he looked on.

"Mr. Vecchio, does your client have anything she wishes to say on her behalf that might sway the court in her favor?" Judge Fields asked. Hope still remained in his eyes.

Nothing! Melissa did not even look up. The floor was far more interesting to her.

Vecchio looked at Melissa and uttered a few words, but they fell on deaf ears. She feared if she spoke again in the presence of strangers, she might again invite an unwanted guest into the courtroom. *Hold your tongue! They're all outsiders!* The line was now clearly visible to her.

Melissa was screaming on the inside. She wanted the world to hear her cries. She wanted everyone to know what was going on in her head. She wanted Michael to forgive her. She wanted to tell him everything, from the cradle to the grave. Oh, how she wanted his forgiveness, his love; but for the life of her, she couldn't utter a single word on her behalf. She was a mute witness.

Warren Vecchio shook his head. He was spent.

Judge Fields nodded. "The court has no other choice. I am inclined to side with Dr. Tinker's recommendation for further supervised treatment for Mrs. Bishope," Judge Fields said halfheartedly. He didn't want it to come to this, but he was out of options.

"Your Honor," Vecchio protested as he stood up, "Mrs. Bishope had been unjustly held in custody for a month and—"

"Mr. Vecchio, might I remind you, as I pointed out to the doctor mere moments ago, Mrs. Bishope was found in contempt of this court. Upon her contempt, she displayed more than adequate cause for her to be held for a psychiatric evaluation. It's fairly common, Mr. Vecchio," Judge Fields said with a hint of anger. He was in no mood for an attorney, even one whom he held in high regard, to question his judgment.

"Yes, Your Honor," Vecchio said. "We do stipulate that further treatment is necessary for Mrs. Bishope. However, Mrs. Bishope is not a flight risk, and she will attend all court-ordered psychiatric visits as ordered. We ask that she be released on OR."

"Yes, she will attend all sessions as ordered." Judge Fields said sternly.

Vecchio knew he was not going to win this argument.

"And she will do so while in custody. Mr. Vecchio, what you are not understanding is that she is a danger to herself. There is no telling what she is capable of. That is what I surmised from the doctor's testimony. This court is not willing to bear the responsibility if Mrs. Bishope should otherwise bring harm upon herself or the baby she is carrying while unsupervised. That is a risk this court is not willing to take."

"Yes, Your Honor," Vecchio replied.

"Mrs. Bishope has clearly shown that supervised long-term treatment is necessary. Therefore, I am ordering an additional thirty-day supervised evaluation. At which time, I will again hear from Dr. Tinker, and I will make my final ruling then." Judge Fields glanced down at his notes.

"Any petitions for the court at this time?" Judge Fields looked directly at Nash.

Nash was fighting off the urge to scream for joy. He had been waiting all morning for this moment.

Michael followed Nash with his eyes as he stood. He was unaware of what was happening. Nash knew the judge had to accept their petition. He knew his day had come. He was going to walk out the doors a hero, on the cover of *Law Weekly*. "Yes, Your Honor," Nash said, trying to suppress his smile. "Your Honor, I have a petition to declare Mrs. Bishope incompetent and to declare Michael Bishope her legal and sole guardian," Nash said victoriously.

"As much as I hate to do it, Mr. Nash, I am left with no other choice. Petition granted," Judge Fields said. And with the slam of the mighty gavel, it had ended.

Vecchio abruptly stood. "I object, Your Honor," he said sharply.

"Take it up on appeal, Mr. Vecchio," Judge Fields barked.

Michael looked up at Nash as the judge removed himself from the courtroom.

"What does that mean?" Michael asked.

"It means that you're going to be a father, my friend. We won!" he said with a filmy yellow smile.

For a moment, Michael was beside himself with joy. He pictured his child growing up. Michael leaned back in his chair as he gathered himself. "But what about Susan?"

"She is going back into custody, Mike. You were granted legal custody of her, of Susan. That means you are the person who makes all her decisions. She cannot have an abortion without your permission. She can't do anything without your permission."

Michael already had regrets, but he had done what he set out to do: keep his baby. "What will this do to her?" he asked.

"It will get her the help she needs, Mike," Nash started. "Look, Mike, I'm sorry to say this to you, but she needs help. She is there for a reason. It's a reason that you or I may not understand, but it is what it is. You need to face the fact that she has a problem."

Michael remained in the chair. Nash's words hit him hard. His mind was racing over this new information, trying to piece it together. He knew for a while that there was a problem, but he didn't have the heart to admit it to himself or anyone else. Michael sat in silence as Nash gathered his papers and roughly shoved them into his briefcase. He was late for his date with destiny.

Michael sat bolt upright as the guards led Melissa toward the side entrance. He moved quickly around the table. "Wait a minute!" he shouted to the guards. They stopped. "Let me have a moment with my wife," he said.

Nash didn't care. It was over as far as he was concerned. Michael could do whatever he wanted to do. He wasn't about to stick around to watch Michael and his "wives" reunite and play kissy face. "I'll call you," Nash said and turned, moving toward the door.

Michael didn't hear a word Nash said as he moved toward Melissa. "Susan," he started. He grabbed her by the arms. The handcuffs binding her wrists alarmed him. He looked pleadingly at the guards for answers. They shrugged. *Just doing our job, dude!*

Touching her for the first time in weeks, he was overcome with a rush of warmth. It was a feeling he longed for and forgotten about since her absence. "Susan, baby, sweetie. I love you more than anything," he said. "I don't want you to go through this alone. I want to be there for you."

Melissa nodded and smiled. She brought her hands up to touch his. He grasped her hands tightly.

"Look to me to be your strength," Michael whispered.

Melissa brought her shackled hands up to touch his face. More stubble than she remembered or liked on his face but a warm feeling nonetheless. "You already are, Michael," she replied.

Michael almost lunged at her as he embraced her deeply in his arms. "God, it's so good to hear you say my name again," he whispered.

The guards intervened, and they pulled Melissa away by the arms. Michael pleaded, but the guards said they had to remove her from the courtroom.

"I'll come to you, Susan! I'll do whatever it takes to get you the help you need. I'll do whatever I can to get you out of there!" he shouted as the guards led her out of the courtroom. "I'll never let you go, Susan!" he shouted just before they shut the side door behind them

And she was gone.

Again Michael was alone. More damming thoughts would soon cascade over his darkened mind. At least he could continue with the thought that he would not lose his baby. After all, that's what he wanted all along. He wondered how things got so crazy and screwed up. Where did it all go wrong for Susan? What happened to her to make her act this way? How long had she been this way, and how did he not see it? That's when the burning questions started for Michael, questions that would not let up.

"Congratulations," Vecchio said as he patted Michael on the back. Michael hardly heard him. "For what it's worth, you did the right thing," Vecchio said.

At last, Michael turned to see Vecchio walking out of the room. A drone of emotion filled the corridor outside, no doubt coming from the grounds of the complex. He didn't want to face the crowd outside. Nash could have his fifteen minutes for all he cared. Michael would move on from here. He'd still hold his head up high. He would do what he thought was right for his wife and his child. Michael would move on, all right. And Nash would still be a yellow-bellied duplicitous lawyer driven by greed.

* * * * *

The crowd was buzzing with anxious energy. The two warring sects were on the verge of total chaos. It wasn't going to take much to set the crowd off. The day was burning, and so were the flames of violence that held so heavy in the salty sea air.

The crowd roared as Tyson Nash stepped out onto the top steps of the courthouse. Nash felt like a rock star standing on stage in a stadium full of die-hard fans. Video cameras began rolling hot. Explosions from still cameras went off like lightning flashing across the sky in a violent electric storm. News was forthcoming, and they weren't going to miss anything.

The crowd surged toward the steps. They wanted to hear the crooked mouthpiece that was about to speak. People pushed and shoved and fought for position. Some took vicious shots at the opposing side, hitting them with sticks, punching them and disappearing back into the crowd.

A makeshift podium with groups of microphones had been set up on the steps. As Tyson Nash took his place behind the podium, the crowd again roared. Nash smiled. He belonged here, he thought. He was comfortable in the spotlight.

Reporters battered him with rapid-fire questions, one after the other, meshing into one long, incoherent noise. That set in motion a landslide of more questions, cheers, and roars from the heated crowd. They wanted answers. They wanted to know their side won. With the one exception of Tyson Nash, there were no winners here. Regardless, the heated emotion from the epic crowd was swelling to a fever pitch.

Nash raised his hand to quiet the crowd. And within seconds, even the seagulls could be heard squawking as they floated on the wind overhead.

Anticipation grew. Nash played the crowd, toyed with them like puppets. He looked out over the sea of people baking in the heat of the day. Nash smiled. "The whole world's come undone," he said into all the microphones. His words echoed over the roar of the crowd. They cheered and booed and grew impatient with his tiresome act. There were far too many mouthpieces as it was, and the last thing they wanted on this scorching day was to listen to another self-righteous yak. Nash kept his smile, teasing them with the secret that only he knew. They wanted the truth, and they wanted it now.

Nash knew he couldn't keep this crowd waiting, or bullshit them in any way. "My client, Michael Bishope was awarded legal custody of his wife, Susan Bishope. What that means is, Michael Bishope won his case and will keep his baby!"

Cheers, elation swept through the pro-life army. They roared with excitement over the outcome. It was the decision they had been looking for since the debate started in the early '70s.

Outrage spread like wildfire through the pro-choice camp. Boos, hatred, and insults came hurling toward Nash. The decision infuriated them. They were almost in a feeding frenzy, screaming and yelling their displeasure of the court ruling. This was a no-lose case for them. Somebody dropped the ball, and somebody was going to pay, come hell or high water.

Water bottles, sticks, signs, pamphlets, rocks, anything that could be thrown were thrown not only at Nash but also in all directions. People began running for cover.

* * * * *

Breaking news flashed across the television screens of America. From Lovell, Maine, to Simi Valley, California, people were all tuned in to the live national station-to-station broadcast.

Cameras went off in Nash's face like fireworks on the Fourth of July. Microphones were shoved closer to capture his every word. Video cameras continued rolling, feeding their live broadcast around the world.

The police on horses moved into the crowd and tried to restore order. The screaming protests from the pro-choice side never subsided. They were louder than ever.

Nash tried to speak over the roar of the crowd, but they were relentless and overpowering. He raised his arms, trying to quiet the crowd, but to no avail. Cheering on one side, complete anarchy on the other. The ambivalence of the crowd loomed ominously with a collective subconscious that was dangerously close to exploding.

The roar finally subsided enough for Nash to continue. "My client and his wife have been through a tremendous ordeal. Michael and his wife are very private people and have asked that you respect their privacy."

Amid the growing chaos in the surging crowd, the reporters hit Nash with questions from all directions.

"Do you think you would have won the case if Mrs. Bishope would not have had a mental breakdown in court?" one reporter asked. "I mean, that must have had a great bearing on the judge's decision, right?"

Nash could barely hear the question over the noise of the crowd.

"Yes, her breakdown had a great deal to do with the judge's decision," Nash started. "Any abortion case is very difficult to win or even argue. We had a notion going in, that Mrs. Bishope might have some mental issues. Frankly, that was our only defense. It was our only shot at winning the case."

"What happened in court today?"

"We won," Nash replied with a smile.

"What will Michael do now? Our sources say that he was fired from his job at KNRQ. Does he have any other offers?"

"For the record, Michael Bishope quit his job. He was not fired."

"Why did he quit?"

Nash couldn't resist. "He wanted to keep what little of his conscience and dignity he had left." He looked directly at the reporter who asked the question. "In other words, he didn't want to be like you!" he said with a smirk. "He was sick of the direction in which he felt the media was going."

Rage was escalating in the foreground. The crowd was throbbing, more pushing and shoving; a few projectiles rocketed through the air.

"Did this case have something to do with his deciding to quit?"

"Of course, it did. He was tired of the tabloid treatment of the evening news. And since you couldn't find any evidence of collusion on the new president of the United States after chasing phantom stories for nearly two years, you leftist fucktards will just make up anything you want and call it news. Michael Bishope wanted nothing to do with it anymore."

"Mr. Nash, what happened to Susan Bishope?"

"Mrs. Bishope was remanded to custody at the hospital ward of the LA county jail."

"Was that necessary?"

"The judge seemed to think so."

"What do you think?"

"I think that's up to the judge," Nash said with a smile. He was working the crowd, but the crowd was about to explode. Nash himself might have to run for cover.

"Mr. Nash, do you think this case will have any effect on the *Roe vs. Wade* ruling?"

"No, I don't. I do, however, feel that it will affect how the abortion issue is looked at in the future. I do believe that men in general will gain more rights, or at least have more of a voice by today's ruling. That was our initial question: What rights does the father have when it comes to a woman's pregnancy?" Nash replied and moved on to another question. This was Nash day in Los Angeles. Nash would have liked for it to be a national holiday. It's Nash day, school's out, party on the beach!

Another shoving match broke out near the news conference. It was pro versus con in a prelude to war on the steps of our justice system.

Small groups in the unruly crowd began chanting barely audible slogans for their side. Others held prayer meetings. People passed out pamphlets to anyone who would take them; most ended up on the grass with all the other litter.

Other groups were hell-bent on lawlessness roughly moved through the crowd. One way or another, they were going to meet this protest with their own violent resolve.

As the press conference continued, nobody noticed as Michael slipped out of the back parking lot. He drove his car out of sight of the courthouse without a second glance from anyone.

"How long will Susan be held in custody?"

"That's up to the judge," Nash replied. Now he was being coy, playing with the news monkeys.

"Mr. Nash, will you become a spokesman for abortion rights?"

"I don't think so. This was a fluke case for me. As you may recall, I am a criminal attorney. I only took this case as a favor to a friend," Nash said.

"But you stand to reap the rewards from its notoriety."

"Absolutely!" Nash said with a smile.

"Mr. Nash, how do you feel about abortion?"

"I feel like it's a confusing issue."

"Can you elaborate?"

"Yes. It is hard to understand," he said with an enormous smile. A few reporters laughed. Nash went on, "If the woman doesn't know who the father is or was raped, then the decision as to whether or not to have an abortion should be up to her. But in a case like this, when the two people in question are married, there should absolutely be a law restricting abortion without the consent of both the husband and the wife," he finished.

"Are you pro-life, Mr. Nash?"

"I'm not pro anything! Let's get that on record right now," Nash started. "Look, I have a lot of problems with both sides of the issue. Number one, both sides are a bunch of jackasses! And you can print that! That's been proven over the years. Hell, it's been proven right here on these grounds over the last two months," he said, pointing out to the massive crowd.

"If they weren't complete idiots, they would have come to some sort of resolution to this issue by now! And the issues are going to continue to snowball out of control until people with enough sac, like Michael Bishope, stands up and fights the system. That's how *Rove v. Wade* was passed."

"So what are you going to do next?" a reporter shouted from somewhere in the crowd.

"I'm going to Disneyland!" he shouted with a smile. He had always wanted to say that into a camera, so he shot for the moon. After all, it was Nash day in Los Angeles, and he could do whatever the hell he wanted to do. Besides, that might have been his only chance to say it. A few reporters laughed it off and lobbied more questions.

Boom!

A large explosion went off somewhere in the crowd. Not large enough for a bomb but very loud nonetheless. People screamed and began running for cover, heading for the street and overpass. People were panicked; some fell and were trampled into the grass. Others skidded, bouncing on the street as they ran with the crowd.

Police tried to control the situation, but there were far too many people to corral. They ran in all directions. Others took the opportunity to inflict damage on the other party. They kicked and punched people as they ran for safety. They threw rocks and bottles at the courthouse and police; they threw anything they could at the horse-mounted officers. The situation was out of control.

LAPD began firing tear gas into the fray to disburse the crowd. White smoke from the canisters shot into the crowd. That sent waves of panic throughout the gathering, sending them out in all directions, running for their lives and gasping for air as the smoke choked their lungs and burned their eyes.

Swarms of people made it as far as the Santa Monica Pier and mixed in with the tourists. Others ran onto the beach and straight down to the water to cleanse their body of the burning tear gas. People scattered through the neighboring public streets, down alleys, over cars, entered apartment buildings. Pandemonium was at hand, and people didn't care where they ran—they just ran for their lives. Groups of people stormed through the Santa Monica Place and Third Street Promenade, in and out of stores and shops. Shop owners feared another riot.

The police were waiting in force. They were not about to have another riot in their upper-class hood. News crews were everywhere. A dozen or so helicopters buzzed overhead with their blades thumping the air. The air cameras captured the mass exodus from the Santa Monica courthouse. Smoke was everywhere as people ran, and the cameras were focused on the unfortunate victims.

The dawn's promise of the new storm was here. It was all over the country, and it was here to stay. Not even the self-indulgent, self-important, self-appointed public speakers could do anything to slow this increasing snowball from a devastating conclusion on humanity.

30

"Dr. Tinker," Melissa said with urgency as she sat across from the doctor. "I need to ask you a huge favor." She said this with an unusual sense of clarity.

"What can I do to help you, Melissa?" Dr. Tinker asked. She studied Melissa as she sat uneasy in the leather chair. Melissa's face was painted with a peculiar expression, one the doctor had never seen.

"I need to see Michael. The court won't let me have any visitors. It's very important that I speak with him at once. Will you help me? Will you allow me to talk to my husband? Please, Dr. Tinker, please help me," she begged.

The doctor nodded. "I will certainly see what I can do to help you, Melissa," Dr. Tinker started. "But why now? I mean, before you wanted nothing to do with the outside world. You hardly ever mentioned your husband, and now you want to see him. Why?"

Melissa lowered her head and paused. "I just need to see him," she said pleadingly.

Something in Melissa's eyes told the doctor that this meeting would do her a world of good. "You think seeing your husband will help with your treatment, Melissa? Do you think it will help you open up and recall your past and deal with the pain you have suffered?" Dr. Tinker asked.

Melissa sat uneasy before she answered. "Yes, I think it will help me a great deal," she replied. *Yeah, that's exactly what the doctor wanted to hear*, she thought. "It's very important that I speak with him. There are so many things I need to explain. So many answers he needs to hear from me." Melissa looked up and finally made eye contact with the doctor.

Dr. Tinker was taken in by the sincere look in Melissa's eyes. They were as honest as the doctor had ever seen.

"Okay, Melissa. This is a very important step in recovery," Dr. Tinker said. "Your husband does deserve answers. I am sure he is very confused about the whole situation, and it is wonderful that you want to reach out to him."

"I need to. It's important that I do," she replied.

Dr. Tinker nodded with a smile. She understood that she must make this reunion happen at once. She decided to call Michael herself.

* * * * *

Michael was not surprised to see the large collection of reporters when he arrived at the Los Angeles county jail. They had become part of the landscape of his everyday life. A few reporters followed him from his house. They follow him everywhere.

Michael dodged all the questions that blurred together as he moved quickly through the gauntlet of reporters and into the building where they were banned.

Michael was immediately overcome with the feeling of desperation and fear. He could not imagine having to be confined within these walls for any period of time, and he was only in the reception area. Still he could not imagine the horrors that lay behind those heavy metal doors. He feared for Melissa's safety.

Michael was separated from the other visitors and was led to the psychiatric ward of the county jail. He hated the feeling that crept across his crawling flesh. He hated the smell in the air and the eerie, echoing cries heard through the corridor. The sounds of terrified people were maddening as they cried out from behind closed doors. Michael felt sick to his stomach as the guard led him down the long, wide hallway.

The guard knocked on a large wooden door and pushed it open. He motioned for Michael to enter and pointed at the chair in front of the desk. Michael moved over to the chair as the guard left the room. As he sat in the chair, the side door opened, and Dr. Tinker stood in the doorway.

Dr. Tinker smiled at Michael and nodded. Then she stepped aside, and Melissa walked past her and into the room. "I will let you two talk," Dr. Tinker said.

Melissa hesitated at the doorway. She had a sheepish look on her face. Michael drank her in as she walked slowly toward him. Michael quickly stood and embraced his wife. Words could not describe the look on his face or the love in his eyes when they first touched.

Melissa's soul soared with the touch of her husband. She didn't want to let go of the embrace. She no longer wanted to tell him what she needed to tell him. She needed this closeness, his touch, and this embrace to last forever. Michael's love surged through her body. It was a feeling she had longed for those many nights in the cold cell. She felt the feelings and memories of their life together come rushing back, which further complicated her conflicting emotions. Melissa broke from the embrace and moved a step away from Michael.

"It's so nice to see you," she said.

"I love you, Susan," he replied. "I miss you so much."

Melissa hesitated a moment, then sat in the chair. She took his hand and led him into the seat next to her. "And I love you, Michael," she said and paused. "You were my rebirth, Michael. You were my only chance at a new life, a real life. You gave that to me, and I blew it."

"What are you talking about, Susan?"

"Please call me Melissa."

Michael stopped himself with a conflicted glance. "Whatever it is you're going through, Me…lissa"—he found it hard to throw out that name—"I want to be there to help you through it. I'm your husband."

"I know you do, Michael, but I think this is something I have to deal with myself."

"No. You don't have to do anything alone, not anymore," he protested.

"Michael," she started softly, "there are some things you need to know, that you need to hear about me."

"I know all about you, Melissa."

"About my life before you, Michael. It's very important that you listen to me. That's why I asked to see you."

"Susan—Melissa—"

"Michael, please. Listen to me. Let me say what I need to say to you," she pleaded.

Michael's posture slipped. "Okay," he said softly.

Melissa started with a sigh. "There was nothing before you, Michael, nothing. Just an empty shell. I wasn't human. I didn't think I would ever be happy. I didn't know, I mean truly know, what happiness was. Then I met you, and you changed my whole life," she said. Her eyes were full of love as she spoke. "You showed me there is love in this world after all and a person can be happy, that I could be happy and in love. You showed me a tender side of myself I never knew existed, and that allowed me to forget my past, to forget my demons. It allowed me to start all over again with you." She paused a moment.

"We can start all over again, Melissa. I love you."

"Michael"—she paused to summon her courage—"I do see people, people who aren't there," she said with her head lowered. "I have for a long time." Again she paused to reign in her racing emotions. "It all started when my mother died, when my father killed my mother."

Michael looked shocked to hear this from her. It was a glimpse at her past. Her parents were finally revealed, but he didn't like what he was hearing. He was angry with her father; he blamed him for this. He wanted to throttle the bastard. But why now? Why after all this time? *Why did I not see this coming?* he thought.

"He was a bad man, Michael."

"He's dead, right?"

"No, Michael. I lied to you. I had to, and I'm sorry that I did," she said and took his hand into hers. "I didn't want my past to ruin any chance of a future I had, but"—tears started welling in her eyes—"it looks like it did anyway." Again she paused as she searched Michael's face. "He's dead to me. I had to make him die in my mind for me to move on and away from there. Don't you see? I had to make him dead. I will never forgive him for what he did to my mother and for the things he did to me."

"I understand, honey. It's all right," he said.

"No, Michael, you don't understand. I still don't understand it myself," she started. "I may never understand it. And right now I'm not trying to understand. Right now I just have these few things I need to tell you. We can't fix my past or work on our future right now, not in here. It's going to take a lot of work." Melissa held silent for a long moment. She was fighting off the choke building in her throat and fighting through the upsetting memories racing through her mind.

Michael waited patiently. He knew she was hurting deeply.

"I just have so many things I want to say," she said with a drastic expression etched on her pale face. "Everything is just so mixed up in my mind."

Michael leaned forward and grasped her hand with his. "It's all right, honey. Take your time," Michael replied softly. He was very careful with his tone and what he said. He was afraid to say the wrong thing. He didn't know what would set her off and didn't want to risk anything.

Melissa's eyes welled with tears. Her stomach was in knots as she chocked back a cry. "Michael, I can't explain why I chose not to have the baby," she said. "You'll just have to try to forgive me for what I've done to you. You'll have to do it without an explanation because I just can't give you one. I'm sorry."

Michael wasn't happy with that, but he knew he had to accept it, at least for now. "Look, Melissa, I'm sure you have your reason for not wanting to have our baby, and that's all right. What we have to do now is deal with the past so we can start looking ahead. So we can be together again."

"What's done is done, Michael. I'm just so afraid it can't be undone," she said.

"We can move past all this. We can rebuild our future, Melissa. We can work this out, honey. I know we can. Trust your heart. Trust the love we have for each other."

"That's just it, Michael," she said as the tears began tracking down her cheeks. "I don't think I'm capable of trust."

"Sure, you are, Me…lissa." He just couldn't get used to that name.

Melissa shook her head and looked for another approach. "It was my mother that first taught me to love looking at the stars," she said. She didn't know what else to say, and he just did not understand what she was trying to say.

Michael folded his brow at the change of direction, but he went along with it. "Tell me about it, honey. Tell me about your mother."

"She used to take me out at night down near the swamps and away from the city lights. We used to listen to the voice of the swamp and watch the stars all night long. She told me many stories as we sat staring at the stars. She told me I would always find hope and answers in the stars. It fascinated me so much." She paused and wiped her eyes. Her speech was slow and deliberate. "She told me when she dies that I will always be able to find her on a star."

"You're always looking for your mother in the stars," he said more to himself. He got it and smiled. She was looking for the family she never had. Just like him. He had always been searching for that same promise of a family.

"Sadly, that's one of my only memories of my mother. She and I lying on the dirt, both of us looking up at the stars. Oh, how I loved her," she said in reflection. "We spent a lot of nights away from home, away from him." Melissa stopped.

Michael didn't know what to say. He knew why they left the house so often. A bar of silence vibrated between them. The room held still with anticipation. Echoes came from the corridors outside the office.

"I'll never see the stars again, Michael." Her head remained lowered as she wiped the tears from her eyes.

He shivered slightly. He was uncomfortable with what she said. "You're acting as if you're going to be in here forever. I won't let that happen. I am going to get you the hell out of this disgusting place as soon as possible." Michael's eyes began filling with tears of his own.

"I know what they mean to you, honey. You'll see the stars again. We'll see them together, Melissa."

She shook her head. "No, Michael," she said quietly. "It's all over now," she added in an eerie whisper. "There's no turning back now." She finished in a troubling tone that bothered Michael. The way she said it frightened him.

Michael held silent for a moment, trying to calculate the situation. He threw out a half smirk as an inner thought baffled him. The whole situation was baffling to him. There was so much he wanted to know, to ask, to say to his wife, but his thoughts were meshing together into one giant ball of confusion. He held his tongue, and they shared the foreboding silence.

"I was never who you thought I was, Michael. And for that, I am sorry. I never meant to hurt or deceive you as I did. But in the mindset I had, I felt it was my only chance," she said with a sigh. More tears welled in her eyes. "If you knew the truth, you would have never asked me out on a second date. If you only knew the circumstances behind my deception, you'd understand why I lied to you, Michael, and I am so sorry—"

"Tell me, Susan!" he almost shouted. He had had enough of the half-truths and semi-lies. He wanted it straight, the whole story. "I'm sick and tired of not knowing who you are. I mean, just when I think it's going perfectly, just when I think I have really gotten to know you, you turn into another person entirely."

Melissa didn't need to raise her head to catch his eyes; she could feel the growing heat of his glare. Michael held himself back a moment as he gathered his thoughts. He really didn't want to unleash his pent-up anger on his wife. "What else have you lied to me about, Melissa?" he asked.

"Nothing, Michael," she replied.

"Nothing?" he said sarcastically. His fuse was lit; he felt it. So did Melissa. "You lie to me about who you are. You lie to me about your past, about your parents, about your whole life basically. And now you're not lying about anything else? You expect me to believe that?" he asked. He could see that she was about to lose it, but he went on. "I mean, how the hell did you pull this off for so long? How the hell did you keep this such a secret from me?"

Melissa shook her head, trying to hold back the wall of tears about to crest the dam.

"Tell me, Melissa."

"I can't"

"Who are you?"

"I can't!" she said. "I can't, Michael," she repeated through a wailing cry. Tears tracked down her face.

Michael's love for his wife almost betrayed his anger; he wanted to reach out and stop her tears from stinging. He wanted to hold his muse in his arms and assure her that everything will work out in the end. But he was not convinced of that himself.

Everything—the baby, the court, his thoughts, visions, and unanswered questions—hit him all at once. He wanted to break through the wall and pound the crazies in the next room. He wanted to lash out at the media, beat the hell out of Frank Chandler, and then take a few swings at Tyson Nash.

Michael calmed himself and was somewhat softened by the sad look on Melissa's face. The innocent tears, the cry of a child that came from his wife, softened him. He was upset with himself that he let his anger show. "I'm sorry, Melissa. I'm so sorry for hurting you." Michael moved over and took her weeping body into his arms. He held her through her sobbing cries. "Why did you want to see me now?" he asked softly.

"It doesn't matter anymore."

"You will always matter to me, Melissa."

She held his gaze a moment and felt his love course through her body. She wanted so much to tell him her whole sordid story, but she knew he couldn't handle it. She couldn't even handle it herself. Slowly she wiped the tears from her red eyes. "I just don't want you to forget who I was."

"How can I ever do that?"

"I wanted you to remember the love we shared. I wanted to tell you what you meant to me and thank you for the love you gave to me," she said and paused. "Michael, when I said that you were my rebirth, I meant it in every way possible. No other human being could have taken me from where I was and shown me that there was a thing called love. You did that, and I will forever love you for it. I wanted to thank you for loving me like you do." Again she paused as Michael's thoughts raced through his mind. "I called you here because I didn't want you to think any of this was your fault. You didn't deserve what I brought to you."

"Yes, I did! I got what I deserved. I got you."

"That's sweet, Michael, but this is real—"

"Yes, and so are you. And so is my love for you. I will never stop fighting for you, and I'll never stop loving you," he said.

She smiled. She knew saying anything more would be pointless. Michael was unaware or unwilling to grasp the enormity of what she was trying to say. Perhaps she was unclear in her wording, she thought. Being drastically unclear with people was an old habit she couldn't break. Either way, she knew the truth: she had just crossed the line. "And I will never stop loving you."

A knock at the door interrupted their moment. Dr. Tinker opened the door and informed them their time was up. Michael nodded and looked back at Melissa. "I'll get you out of here, honey. And we'll work this out together. I will get you out of here."

Melissa smiled once more, but something about that smile bothered Michael. "Yes, Michael, you do that," she said.

Dr. Tinker watched as they embraced in each other's arms. She tried to picture them together in a normal existence, but the clear image never materialized in her mind. She knew they both had a long crooked road ahead of them. She felt for them both.

"I love you, Melissa," he whispered softly in her ear.

"You are my maker, Michael. You gave me life. You resurrected me," she whispered back. "And I love you for that. I love you for loving me. Don't ever forget about me, Michael."

"I could never forget about you, honey."

"I'm so sorry."

"It's all right, baby. You've already said it."

"Not for everything," she replied softly.

Michael pulled back from the embrace and looked into her eyes.

"Okay, kids, I have to break this up," Dr. Tinker said.

"Go, Michael. I love you, and I am sorry."

Michael hesitated a moment with curiosity still etched on his face. "I love you too. I will get you out of here."

"Do that," she said, nodding. She tried to smile, but it just wasn't there.

Michael smiled. He kissed her one last time and walked past the doctor and out of the room. Melissa watched him go.

"Remember the stars. Always remember the stars, Michael," she whispered softly to herself.

*****

Melissa was led back into her small cell of nothingness and solitude. She found the edge of the small bed and sat quietly. Her hands rested on her thighs, waiting for orders from above for her next move. The strings were still attached from the unseen puppet master. She stared through tears into the zero-dark-nothing of the room. Emptiness stared back into the black void of her soul.

In an odd gesture, Melissa raised her left hand to her mouth. She felt her lips, wiped them with the back of her hand, and outlined them with her fingertips. She began talking to herself with a curious expression on her face. Her mouth began moving, but no sound came into the small cell. She was mute to the world; even her own hearing could not capture the sound of her voice. It was gone.

Then from deep in her throat came a soft, peaceful humming. She appeared surprised at first as her facial expression changed. She knew what it was. It was the sound of the song she once knew, once heard on a cold German night. A night so long ago in her mind when she was strolling hand in hand with her new husband. The humming became stronger and more pronounced. The enchanting sound of her singing voice danced off the walls of the cell and cascaded life into a lifeless dark place. She continued, louder and louder.

Just another looney in the nuthouse spouting off, the guards thought. They were used to all sorts of strange sounds coming from within the cells.

The song, still fresh in her mind, meant something to her; she knew it did. It generated a strong, compelling emotion from deep within her. It was important! But what did it mean? She thought and continued humming right along with the singing she heard so clearly in her mind. She tried to picture the man singing the song, the strange Bohemian spirit, but his face was gone from her memory. Not even the infamous inmates running the asylum in her mind could recall his face. *Was he really there?* she wondered. *Did I even see him? I know I saw him! I was there, he was there, this happened!*

Then she sang the first line of the song in perfect German, exactly as she first heard it. "Missy, ich kann Dich rufen horen." Melissa was floored. She didn't know a single word outside the English language, yet she was singing this song in German. She repeated the first line twice more with a smile. She didn't know what she was singing, but somehow she understood exactly what the song now meant. It drove her with an emotion she had not felt in some time. Her face was serene as she sang. Her smile was genuine and absolutely breathtaking. She repeated the first line of the song again. "Missy, ich kann Dich fufen horen." Melissa smiled and finally understood why. A rush of peace washed over her.

And finally she saw.

Let go to me…

A smile warmed her heart. "I will," she said aloud in the small room.

Tell me…

Melissa understood and rose to the vision that was appearing out of the gloom like an apparition. Again she started the song in full rhythm; it was her answer to the compelling voice.

Missy, Ich kann dich rufen hören,
Missy, ich kann Dich kommen horen,
Du kommst, um mich mit Deinem Stern zu verbinden, Du kommst weit her,
Du hast das alles hinter Dir gelassen, sabald du die Grenze uberquert hast,
Lass mich Dich fuhren, damit Du Dich nie verirrst.

Und für immer hier wirst du bei mir bleiben,
meine Liebe.

Tears filled her eyes once again as the vision became clear to her. Her heart was smiling as she finally began to see for the first time. Melissa repeated the song.

Missy, I can hear you calling,
Missy, I can hear you coming,
You're coming to join me on your star; you're
coming from afar,
You'll leave it all behind once you cross the line,
Let me lead the way, and you'll never go astray,
And forever here you'll stay, with me, my love.

Melissa stopped. Her soft green eyes, still swollen and red from crying, slowly scanned the empty room. The sound of her beautiful voice no longer danced with the silence. Her lips parted as she looked on with a blank stare. Her mind was racing with thoughts and visions she had not seen or heard in years. Not even the other tenants in her head could break this train. She was focused on this one single thought. She tried to picture the face of the person who was singing that night on the Kurfürstendamm that magnificent night in Berlin.

Nothing! She searched her memory banks, but there was no face as far as she could remember.

"Mama!" she said with astounding curiosity.

"Oh my God!" she exclaimed. It was as if she finally got the joke. Finally she understood the meaning of life. She knew the song, knew what it meant, and sure as hell knew where it came from.

"Missy?" Melissa said aloud as if asking a question. She was stunned, as if she finally understood a long-forgotten secret. "Mama used to call me Missy!" The perplexed look remained on her face. Her mouth remained slightly parted. "That was her in the dark, singing. That song was for me! She was trying to talk to me, tell me something. But what?" Melissa said as she cleared her eyes with the back of her hand. She remained baffled at the suggestion that her mother came to her in the song, but in her heart she knew it was true. He was there to deliver her mother's message to her.

Yes! That's it! Of course! Her mother had been watching over her all these years, she thought. It was clear. *Now she wants me to come home.* Melissa smiled, a pure, innocent smile. It was a feeling of home, of belonging, of comfort. They were the lost emotions from Melissa's essence. These lost emotions came flooding back to her with love. Her mother was here, walking with her, protecting and watching over her.

Melissa continued smiling in her rapture as she began singing the first verse of the song.

31

THE HOT DAY BROKE somewhere out there. Even in the darkened cell, behind all the concrete and bars, Melissa knew the summer sun was blazing in the morning sky. She longed for one last look at the night stars, how they gleamed so brilliantly, like diamonds on black velvet. She wanted one last chance to utter her prayer to the stars. Wanted to hear their voice, wanted to touch her mother.

She stood up and reluctantly stepped away from the small bed and removed her county issue gown and let it fall to the ground at her feet. Halfheartedly, she leaned over and snatched up the crinkled gown. Melissa knew this was her calling; she knew it for a long time. But it was hard to take that first step. Then, hesitantly, she stepped across the line.

* * * * *

Two minutes later, when the guard, on his usual rounds, slid open the peephole, he shouted for help and tried to open the door as fast as he could, but he fumbled with the keys and dropped them on the floor. "Shit!" he yelled as he frantically went after the keys.

Melissa's legs twitched and kicked for life as they dangled in the air. Urine ran down her legs and puddled on the concrete floor below her. The rapid twitching movements in her legs abruptly stopped.

Her naked body went from pale white to ghostly gray within seconds. Her limp body dangled from the bars overhead. Her county-issue gown, twisted and fashioned into a rope, appeared to be cutting into her neck, and her neck had turned a different shade altogether, much darker and more red than the deep blue spreading over her skin.

No more sound.

No gasping.

No movement.

The door burst open, and two guards rushed into the cell. The first guard held Melissa up by the legs, trying to take the pressure off her neck. Urine ran all over the guard's arms, but he held tight as he called for more help. Eerie gasping sounds and chokes came from Melissa's limp body. The second guard jumped onto the bed, and with a knife, he quickly cut the rope. Melissa's limp body fell into the guard's arms. He carried her into the hallway and laid her on the floor and quickly checked for a pulse.

Nothing.

No breathing.

He began CPR, pumping her chest—one, two, three, four. He checked her airway as more guards rushed to their assistance. He began breathing for her, giving her mouth-to-mouth. Another guard came in carrying a mini-first aid kit with an oxygen bottle. More cries for help. "Call 911!" "Get a doctor!"

Melissa was not moving.

"She's got no pulse!" shouted the guard as his partner continued CPR.

*****

The black-and-white police cruiser screamed around the corner sideways with sirens and lights and smoke from burnt rubber from the tires. The cruiser pulled to a screeching stop at the emergency entrance of the hospital. Michael jumped out of the passenger seat and rushed toward the entrance. Michael was greeted by hordes of reporters who descended upon him, blocking his path to the doors. How the hell did they find out about this so quickly? he thought as he pushed past them with the help from the police. They weren't about to put up with any shit from the media, and they forcefully pushed and made a hole for Michael as he entered the hospital.

Michael marched briskly down the long corridor with the uniformed LAPD officer in toe. He was greeted by the doctor, who began explaining Melissa's situation. But Michael's attention was immediately drawn, with a timeless stare at the priest who was approaching him. The priest pulled up behind the doctor and held his solemn gaze on Michael. The priest's presence unnerved Michael, and it took him back to the hospital when his parents died and he was greeted by another priest. It was a memory he never forgot and never wanted to experience again.

He watched as the priest comforted Michael's brother after the doctor made him cry. He always hated that doctor for making his older brother cry. Michael never got over the sight of the priest and Michael's brother walking down the corridor. He knew after that day, Mommy and Daddy were never coming home again. And he knew now that he wanted nothing to do with the priest standing behind the doctor. He could only bring unwanted news.

"Mr. Bishope. I am sorry to say, at this point, there's really nothing more we can do for your wife. We can, however, save your baby if we act right away," said Dr. Sanji.

Michael was floored, devastated. His head swam in a sea of grief and guilt. He felt dizzy with confusion. But the vast desert of endless guilt was overwhelming to him.

"The depravation of oxygen to her brain has caused her to slip into a deep coma. She is clinically brain dead. We have kept her sustained on life support for the sake of the fetus. However, we have now come to the crossroads where you must make the ultimate decision," said the doctor. He looked at Michael with very little compassion through his dark eyes. He was all business—here and now, yes and no.

Michael hardly noticed the doctor's approach to the news; he barely heard a word he said anyway. *She's dead* echoed through his head. *She's dead!* The fact that she was pregnant didn't even register in his mind; he lost the woman he loved.

"Upon examination, it appears that your wife is approximately twenty-five to twenty-eight weeks along in her pregnancy. Now, there have been cases where babies have survived as early as twenty weeks."

Dr. Sanji folded his arms across his chest with no concern of how he looked to the grieving husband.

"You have to be aware, it is an uphill battle with no guarantees because, of course, we're not sure of the exact condition of the fetus or that it will survive the trauma your wife has caused. We can, however, continue maintaining life support, and that will treat your wife as an incubator." He paused briefly. "Keeping her alive for another week, maybe two, would give the baby more of a chance for survival outside the womb."

She's dead…

Michael's world crashed down around him as he stood in stunned silence, his mouth parted slightly. Of everything the doctor said, the only words that registered with him was, "She's dead." That echoed like a bad dream in his waking mind.

Dr. Sanji stood impatiently waiting.

"So my wife is dead?" Michael said with a questioning glare. "If she's dead, how can the baby possibly still be alive? How does that work? Why isn't the baby dead as well?"

"Your wife's heart is keeping the fetus alive. We're keeping her alive with machines."

"It's all my fault," Michael mumbled.

"Regardless of whose fault it is, we need a decision from you as to what to do with the fetus," the doctor barked. "We need your answer now, Mr. Bishope. Time is very critical."

Michael latched onto his brown eyes. In another time and other circumstances, he would have busted him in the chops for his cold-hearted rudeness.

"What do you want us to do, Mr. Bishope?"

"I want my baby to live."

* * * * *

A chill stood before Michael. It encompassed him and entered his soul as he stood quietly in the corridor. He watched through the glass as the two doctors fussed over Melissa. There were tubes and hoses coming and going from her body. Crazy-looking, futuristic machines were all around her with flashing lights and beeping sounds. His best efforts kept his body from shaking and falling to the floor. *This still can't be real! Not Susan, not Melissa! You're not dead! Wake up! Wake up and come back to me!* Tears welled in Michael's eyes as he peered through the glass. A nurse moved over and took his arm and led him to the glass doors.

*****

Gaggles of reporters descended on the hospital as the story of the year took an unexpected twist. Satellite trucks lined front to back stretched the length of the street and around the corner. Groups of people were holding a candlelight vigil off to the side of the hospital. The usual groups of protesters, pro-life and pro-choice, gathered in great numbers as the promise of the debate rang true.

"Susan Bishope has died," said the KNRQ news anchor as he came through on the television screen of John Q. Public with breaking news. Every television station in American broke into programming and carried many variations of the same newscast. "In what was an apparent suicide, Susan Bishope has taken her own life today in the medical ward of the Los Angeles county jail."

The NBC telecast: "In another strange twist to the story, the doctors at county USC hospital were able to save the baby she was carrying, although some four months premature."

CBS, ABC, CNN, and FOX had their own version. The competing telecasts would continue all day and well into the night.

Day 3

Michael still had not left the hospital. The reporters were growing anxious and weary. A few daring reporters tried breaking into the hospital for that larger-than-life scoop, but they were promptly arrested by the massive support of police gathered around the entire hospital. The once-massive crowd had dwindled slightly. At this gathering of divided opinions, people didn't stay and linger very long. They came and went in droves. Melissa Bishope's suicide hit everybody on both sides of the issue very hard, and they were mostly there to show their support.

Day 5

By now the reporters almost outnumbered the crowd, which was down to a few hundred die-hard protesters. Both pro-life and pro-choice and religious groups remained and were separated by the Los Angeles Police Department, who were still out in force. They were not about to have any unrest in front of the hospital.

Facial stubble covered Michael's face as he waited in the corridor. Nick's parents, Dale and Lisa Vach, sat and watched as Michael drove himself to madness and paced himself into oblivion. Lisa tried to comfort him as she led him over to the bench and sat with him. She and Dale spoke to him and tried to convince him that he needed to leave and try to live a normal life. He remained steadfast; he must stay and see this through.

Dr. Sanji approached them and informed Michael that nothing would happen in the next few days and that he should go home and get some rest. Dale and Lisa finally convinced Michael that he should leave and agreed that they would take him home with them. They worked in conjunction with the police to sneak Michael out of the hospital. Nick had already raided Michael's house for a change of clothes and other essentials he might need for a few days.

* * * * *

Another night and a different location yielded no sleep again for Michael as he tossed through the night. His troubled heart combed over the wrong choices he thought he had made. He blamed himself for Melissa's death. He blamed himself for this whole fiasco with the media. He blamed himself for the possible loss of his child. He cursed his being. He cursed God and everything in between. If it weren't for his child still in limbo, Michael would have taken his own life as thoughts of suicide held heavy on his mind. Deep down, he was glad that he was not at home.

Michael finally got to sleep around seven in the morning but soon was awakened by Nick as he stumbled into the kitchen. Nick made his apologies and looked on as Michael stared out the window in silence. Nick was lost himself; he knew not how to help his friend cope with this tragic event. He didn't know what to say or do. He, too, sat and shared Michael's silence.

Day 9

There was still no sight of Michael. Reporters were still assuming that Michael Bishope remained in the hospital at his wife's side. A million-dollar reward from one of the tabloid rags was being bandied around for the first photo of Michael Bishope with his comatose wife. A matching million-dollar reward was out there for the first photo of Michael Bishope's baby, dead or alive.

The crowd was even smaller now; even the reporters were not out as they once were. Trouble in the Middle East called many of them away to other news. A few steadfast pro-life and pro-choice warriors remained, some chanting their slogans to the few news cameras that were interested.

*****

Lisa Vach held on to Michael's arm as Dr. Sanji, dressed in surgical scrubs, spoke to him. Michael nodded and remained silent as the doctor informed him of the procedure that he was about to perform. Again Michael nodded and Mrs. Vach gasped and covered her mouth. She wanted to hear none of this, but as Michael's only remaining link to any family, she felt it was her duty to be there for him. She had been so influential in helping Michael's brother, Matthew, raise him after his parents died. She was, in all regards, Michael's second mother. The only mother he knew now. The only one he needed now.

Michael remained in silence, standing in the corridor as the doctor walked away. Nick's parents led Michael over to the bench where they sat in roaring silence, waiting.

Almost two hours had passed before the doctor came back out into the hallway to greet Michael. By the look on Lisa Vach's face, the baby was alive and, although four months premature, healthy from what the doctor could tell. "It's going to be a long process, Mr. Bishope. You will have to bear with us. Patience can be your best friend."

"What about Melissa?" Lisa asked.

"Yes…," Dr. Sanji said as an afterthought and turned to Michael. "You may have a few moments with her before we…ah, before we stop the machines."

Michael looked back at Lisa, who encouraged him to see her one last time before she was pronounced. The doctor led Michael into the cold operating room. As they entered, Michael noticed blood everywhere from the c-section. He instinctively looked around for any sign of the baby in the empty room.

Nothing.

Melissa lay isolated on the cold table under the bright lights. She looked pale white as her chest heaved up and down with the help of the massive machines breathing for her. The tubes going in her mouth and down her throat sickened Michael, and he wanted them removed.

"I'll leave you alone for a moment," said the doctor as he turned and exited the room.

Not exactly sure of what to do, Michael hovered above her a moment. He was frozen with fear. He just stared at his wife lying on the cold medical table. As the tears welled in his eyes, a lump caught in his throat. Michael began crying aloud as he took her lifeless hand into his. He whispered his apologies and asked for her forgiveness. Michael remained slouched over his wife's body as he repeatedly cried for forgiveness.

Dr. Sanji entered the room and walked over to Michael. He touched him on the shoulder and nodded as he made eye contact with the doctor. "We're ready," said the doctor.

Michael nodded and wiped his eyes. He leaned back over and kissed Melissa's cheek. "Go now, my love. You're free," Michael started as he fought back the choke. "Go and find what you have always been looking for." The tears began streaming. "I will always love you, Susan." He kissed her again on the cheek and turned to the doctor, who nodded. Michael turned and walked over to the door, but before he could reach it, the machines stopped. No more lights, no more sound. Michael turned and watched as the last of the air escaped from his wife's body. Dr. Sanji looked at his watch and then up at the clock on the wall. He called the time of death. Michael took one last look at his wife and exited the room.

* * * * *

Even though it was through the glass and he didn't get a very good look, seeing his baby for the first time lifted Michael's spirits. He beamed with joy as he watched the doctors and nurses fuss over the baby Bishope. Mrs. Vach cried over Michael's shoulder as she looked on. She was so happy for Michael, but it was bittersweet. Michael wanted to hold his son and search for Susan and his parents in the baby's eyes.

Michael knew they were not out of the woods just yet. The big fight, from what the doctors had told him, was still in front of him. The next thirty days would answer the unanswered questions of whether or not the baby would survive. Even at this stage of development, the baby was very small, and the doctors were rightly concerned. Michael decided that he was not going to leave the hospital unless it was absolutely necessary. His only concern now, his only motivation in life, was his son fighting for his life on the other side of the glass, four months premature and in critical condition. Michael had to stay.

* * * * *

Almost two weeks later, the baby had his good days and bad days. He had gained almost a full pound. His prognosis was good, and he had been doing very well for the past seventy-two hours. Michael remained in the hallway looking through the glass. He slept, catnaps mostly, on the bench across from the nursery. The nurses had come to know him very well and offered whatever they could, but he politely declined their every offer.

A two-week-old thick beard covered his face, and Michael didn't have it in him to go home and clean up. He didn't want to face the gauntlet of reporters outside the hospital and surely still at his house. But he knew he was going to have to leave tonight anyway, for Melissa's funeral in the morning. Michael was so thankful that Nick's parents took care of all the arrangements.

Before he left that night, a sympathetic nurse took Michael aside and fitted him for a blue surgical gown, gloves, and a mask. She led him into the nursery and watched as Michael held his baby through the clear plastic and cried. He held the baby's tiny fingers and smiled through the tears.

That moment with his son gave Michael the strength to face the world again with new life—and to face the funeral in the morning and return to the hospital with new hope.

* * * * *

After the priest's kind words and beautiful eulogy, Michael was the first and only person to take the podium. He wanted it that way. He wanted nothing out of the ordinary to be said or left unsaid. He wanted all questions to end here. He wanted Melissa to be remembered how he remembered her—loving, warm and always looking at the world through curious eyes. He wanted all her troubles, whatever it was that was tearing her apart, to be laid to rest with her.

Michael looked up. He stood in silence for a moment and gathered his courage as a war of emotion exploded in his mind. Placing a small sheet of paper on the podium, he looked down at the handwritten words. He cleared his throat before he started speaking:

> The universe lies on a path with thee
> Ponder yet, though will I wake

Ponder wake, thou will ignore
Ponder death, yet thou shall see
Ponder life, reflect upon me
Ponder thought, an infinite mirror
The universe lies in the path of thee

Ponder its mirror and reflective gaze
Ponder its sphere in a cloudy haze
Ponder its image so clear and bright
Ponder its thought wrapped around you tight
Ponder you
Ponder me
The universe lies there for thee…

Tears gathered in his eyes as he concluded the words softly. Michael looked back up at the assembled crowd through teary eyes; they were blurred, smeared faces in his vision. He thought he wouldn't be able to make it through the poem without breaking down completely and crying like a baby, but he didn't and was glad for that fact. A thousand questions ran through his mind, but confusion and the ever-present *why* were foremost.

Looking over the crowd, Michael had no idea who half these people were, and at this point, he really didn't care. Michael didn't even care that his lawyer, Tyson Nash, was in attendance, along with a throng of reporters he recognized. None of it mattered anymore. The important thing in his life lay in the lacquered wooden box behind him, but for what reason, he couldn't begin to understand, and it was starting to drive him crazy. He drew blanks and hit roadblocks at every conclusion; nothing made sense to his reasoning.

His life now, his most important thought, was their baby son fighting for his life. Michael felt responsible for all of it. He felt responsible for Susan taking her life. Felt responsible for everything. He wanted to take it all back and wake up from this awful dream. He wanted to give up himself and take his own life and join his love in the hereafter. But he knew he had to march on and hold his head up high for the sake of his child. Perhaps one day there will be an explanation to all of this madness.

For a moment, Michael locked onto Renee's swollen, crying eyes. She understood his sorrows and felt for him as she cried for the death of her friend. Confusing, unanswered questions remained within her mind. She wasn't alone; everybody wanted answers, especially Michael. He couldn't hold her gaze for long for fear of breaking down completely. He shed eye contact and scanned the room, trying to fight off the gathering tears.

A ray of hope came as Michael caught sight of his brother, Matthew. He was sitting in the front row with Renee, Nick, and his parents. Michael felt the love from his family and rejoiced in their sight.

"I am not going to call her Melissa. I never knew Melissa," he said somberly. "She would not have understood what I just said. The poem would mean nothing to anybody but Susan. She would have understood this. She lived for it. It was so much a part of who she was." Michael looked up with a curious expression on his face.

"The stars in the night sky always held a magical fascination to Susan. It was as though she had lost something very important up there, and she searched every night for it. And there was always something special in the way she gazed upon the stars every night. It somehow gave her peace. But she was never completely satisfied. She always wanted to look a little bit longer, just a few more minutes. That was special to me," Michael said with a halfhearted smile.

"That was the Susan I knew. That was the woman I will forever love." Again Michael looked back over the crowd and all the crying faces. He paused to check his emotions. "She's there now, in the stars, where she was most at peace. Perhaps now she can find what she was always looking for," Michael started and wiped the tears from his eyes. "That's where I will find her when I need strength to get through the hard times. This is one of them. She will guide me." Michael lost it and began crying. He hung his head low and dabbed the tears. It was hard for him to continue.

"When you leave here today, I want you to think kindly of Susan. She brought love into my life and made me a better person.

Susan was troubled, but she was not a bad person. She had her reasons for not wanting to have our child. Those of us who knew and loved her are better people for knowing her," Michael said and finally looked out over the crowd. "I want to thank you all for coming," he said and backed away from the podium.

As the crowd slowly filtered out of the room, Nick's parents greeted Michael. Lisa embraced him with a loving, motherly hug. Michael broke down in her arms and cried like a child. Matthew, Nick, and his father gathered around them and held silent. Renee felt like an outsider and remained a short distance away.

*****

Michael didn't return to the hospital right away. He went back to Nick's parents' house to visit with his brother, who couldn't stay long. He was glad to see him but didn't care for the circumstances that brought him out from Boston. Michael missed his brother and hated the fact that they lived so far apart, especially now when he needed him the most.

Michael returned to the hospital later that night under the cloak of darkness. He wasn't surprised to find a frenzy of reporters and protesters chanting and waving signs. Some were for him, and some were against. He didn't care for any of them, didn't care about their cause or what they stood for.

*****

Weeks passed, and Michael remained in the hospital watching his son struggle for life. Michael appeared to have lost a good twenty pounds; he just couldn't bring himself to eat anything. He had lost his appetite and was slowly losing his hope and will to live. Michael waited faithfully. He could scarcely breathe; he felt so much pain. He felt a stern helplessness as he watched the doctors and nurses work with his son, especially when the machines attached to his child screamed and the doctors and nurses rushed in with panicked faces.

Michael would not have made it if Lisa Vach were not there for him. She was his crutch. She comforted him, talked to him as a mother would talk to her grieving son. She brought him food, but even still, he could not bring himself to eat. He loved her and needed her there with him more than he let on.

Three weeks later, and little had changed, though the baby had gained some weight, two more pounds. Time went by so slowly for Michael. Hours melded into an eternity in his wrecked mind as he waited and watched though the glass. The doctors informed him that the weight gain was a very good sign, but it would still take another month before the baby could be moved from the ICU; even that was a hopeful guess.

Michael stood up and kissed Mrs. Vach on the forehead and took the paper bag from her. He walked toward the bathroom.

When he exited the bathroom, his face was cleanly shaven. His face looked frail and on the verge of collapse. Lisa wished he would eat because he didn't look healthy. His clothes barely fit his weakened frame; they hung loose over his thinning shoulders. The burning thoughts and unanswered questions continued their assault on his troubled mind.

As Michael sat on the bench looking through the glass into the ICU, a nurse approached him. She was carrying a clipboard. "Mr. Bishope," she said and sat next to him.

Michael held his gaze through the window on his son. He watched his small chest heave up and down, fighting to draw air into his tiny lungs. He hated all the tubes and wires that were attached to him. It reminded him of Susan. It reminded him of his parents. It reminded him of death.

"Mr. Bishope," the nurse repeated.

Michael slowly turned toward the nurse. "Hi, Anne," Michael said. Her name was AnneMarie, but she liked for Michael to call her Anne. That was reserved for friends only. He had become familiar with most of the hospital staff, and Anne had gone out of her way to make him comfortable.

"I know this is very hard for you right now, but have you thought about the name?" Anne said.

"Yes, I have," Michael replied. Anne looked shocked. She had been asking every day for weeks now, trying to get Michael to give her the baby's name.

"Wow," she said. She wasn't ready to hear that. "What happened?"

Michael looked into her deep brown eyes and studied her face a moment. "Well," he said and paused. "I didn't want to give him a name in case he died. In my twisted mind, I figured it would be easier for me if he didn't have a name. It would be less for me to have to remember," he finished.

Mrs. Vach began crying over Michael's shoulder. That was too much for her to handle. She couldn't stand to see her Michael go through so much turmoil in such a short period of time. He was so young, and he had already lived a lifetime of pain. She couldn't bear the thought of anything else happening to him. She prayed every day and night that the baby would make it through and bring Michael back to life.

"Then I thought, last night actually, what a miracle he really is. I mean, after all I went though and his mother went through, and for him to be alive even now is a miracle itself. And if he were to die now, he shouldn't die without a name. I wouldn't want him to be nameless in heaven."

Anne's eyes watered, and she fought back the pools that were about to run down her face. "Yes, but you shouldn't think about him dying. He's alive, Michael. And so are you," she said through a heavy lump in her throat.

"I realized that last night as I watched him through the glass. It never occurred to me that I would actually see him grow up. I just saw tubes and hoses coming and going from his tiny body. All I could see was death. That's how Susan looked after—" He stopped himself quickly and lowered his head. "Well, you know."

Again she nodded.

"That's the way my parents looked just before they died in the hospital. That's why I couldn't look at it any other way. In my heart, I knew he was going to die because that's all I had ever seen from this situation." Michael's eyes veered off and looked through the glass at his little son.

"But as I watched him last night, I realized that he's a strong kid, a fighter. I watched as the doctors were working on him. I saw his little legs kicking, his arms flailing as if he didn't like what the doctors had done to him. I knew then that this kid was a fighter, and he had a fighting chance. I knew then that I was wrong for the way I had been thinking. I was wrong all along to withhold his name."

The nurse smiled and wiped the tears from her eyes. She could see the new hope in Michael's eyes. It was growing with every word he spoke.

Michael turned back to the nurse. "His name is Luc. Luc Anders Bishope," he said proudly.

The nurse held her smile and placed her hand upon Michael's. "It's a beautiful name. He's going to be a strong child," she said. Looking down at the clipboard, she wrote the child's name on the birth certificate. She placed her hand on his again and smiled. She was happy for this new change in Michael.

32

Three weeks later

The hot September sun bore down on the heads of reporters and the few remaining protesters as they waited the outcome of the hottest story in years: Will the baby Bishope live or die?

Reporters from all over the world filed their stories via satellite back to their respective networks, both here and abroad. There had been nothing, not a single word, from within the hospital regarding the case of the century. Not a quote, not a slip from the staff. Reporters were reduced to interviewing the so-called experts, doctors from other hospitals, and that had already been played out and was getting old. They interviewed protesters, pro-life and pro-choice, but none of them had anything new or exciting worth reporting. The monotony and doldrums were taking its toll on everybody. Reporters were becoming frustrated. They were stuck in this hotbox of nothingness on orders from their bosses.

*****

The baby gained another two pounds in these few weeks that passed like an eternity. His prognosis was good, and the doctors gave him a 70 percent chance of survival. They just needed to see how much weight he gained in the next few weeks before they could raise his percentage.

Michael was elated with the news. He appeared to be a different person altogether. He had started eating again and gained a few pounds himself. His face was cleanly shaven as he peered through the glass with new life in his eyes. Lisa Vach remained at his side and tried to encourage him with every word, with every touch in a motherly way. She loved him as her own son.

Michael was glad she was there. He needed her strength to get him through this. Needed her encouragement. And for a moment, he wondered if he had ever told her how much she meant to him. He was sure he had at some point, though he couldn't exactly recall when.

With an excellent prognosis, this was the beginning of a whole new life for Michael. A life with the child he fought so hard for. Michael lived for the day when his child looked up at him with curious eyes and difficult questions. Michael would deliver love, kindness, hope, and understanding. He would never paint his son's mother in a bad light, only love. Michael vowed that his son would never know of the dark, troubled heart his mother once knew. In the future, when he thought of his mother, Luc would come to know and feel a warm sensation of love in his heart, comforting thoughts in his mind, and an overwhelming feeling of love for someone he would never know.

Michael would go on turning the unwritten page with each new day and slowly and carefully fill in the blanks as he moved through time. He would again reinvent himself in his son's eyes, in his son's hope and love. He would carefully shield his son from the burning questions that still lingered—they would always linger. They haunted him now and would so forever.

With a new light burning in Michael's eyes, the hospital staff approached him. They informed him that they had received mail for him. He was surprised to learn that he received mail at the hospital. He was floored when they further informed him that the hospital was receiving hundreds of thousands of letters and mail addressed to him and for the baby Bishope. He was astonished when they led him into a room almost filled with white postal duffel bags that were overflowing with letters and boxes addressed to him and his son.

Though he didn't open but a handful of letters, he found a full mix of emotions circulating within him. People from all over the world sent letters of encouragement and love. People sent money in US green backs and other more colorful world currency. He was shocked. They sent gifts for the child—teddy bears, stuffed animals, and all sorts of fury things.

They sent letters of hate and told of certain demise, but most of them were encouraging. The few hate or threatening letters were turned over to the police. It would take him weeks, if not months, to go through all this mail, especially with more coming every day. He vowed he would return all the money sent to him with a thank-you note.

Michael continued turning the page day after day and filled in the blank pages with new hope as each day offered new possibilities and hope for his child. Young Luc Bishope was growing stronger every day.

Then came the greatest day in his new unwritten book. Michael was admitted into the ICU and was finally, for the first time after over three months, able to hold his son in his arms. Michael cried as he held his son so gently in his arms. Nurses cried. Mrs. Vach cried watching through the glass.

"He's going to make it," he said through falling tears. A brilliant smile swept across his face. "He's going to make it," he repeated.

"Yes, he is," replied a young nurse as she wiped the tears from her own eyes.

Michael moved carefully over to the chair and slowly sat with his baby in his arms. Michael held him with pure love and tenderness he imagined his father once did with him. He was overjoyed with emotion. How he wished his father were still alive to see this, to see his grandson—oh, how proud he would have been. Then, as if on cue, his son opened his eyes and gave Michael the first of many curious stares. Michael's eyes filled with more tears as he held his baby's curious gaze. He had his mother's bright-green eyes. That was the first thing he noticed. Would they haunt him? Not a chance! He would love them, just as he loved hers. He will eternally cherish his son's resemblance to his mother. Michael will forever be reminded of Susan each time he looks at his son. He couldn't have asked for a more beautiful baby.

Michael's elation soared as new life filled his senses. His baby would live; he would grow in his presence. Michael would be there for his every first—his first step, his first words, his first day of school, and his first baseball game. From death came life, a beautiful life. A life he would cherish and love for the rest of his.

One week later

The head pediatric physician who had cared for baby Luc from birth finally informed Michael that it was time to take his son home. They planned his discharge for the following day. He said it with the soft, courteous manner of a first-year resident. Michael didn't notice or care about the doctor's approach; he was exhilarated with the news. His mind started racing; images accosted him, good and bad. *The baby will be at home. It's a fresh start and a new life*. He would watch his son grow.

The media! A frown quickly swept across his face as the doctor walked away down the corridor. Michael returned to his seat in the waiting room.

Sitting in the waiting room a short while later with Nick and his parents, Michael was approached by Anne, the young nurse he was most familiar with. She was standing next to a sharply dressed man in a dark suit. Anne introduced him as Scott Spencer, the head of operations for the hospital. Michael shook his hand briefly as Anne addressed him.

"We think we have a way for you to escape the media," Anne said.

Michael glanced at Nick, then back toward Anne.

"We're going to fly you out, Mr. Bishope," Scott said. "We're going to fly you by a medical helicopter to a hospital in the valley, where you can have a car waiting for you. There's absolutely no way anybody can follow you. You will have complete anonymity."

Michael glanced with a smile at Nick and his parents for their thoughts on the idea. They all nodded. Nick was smiling. It was a great plan. Michael turned back to Scott Spencer and listened as he laid out the groundwork.

Everything was falling into place. Mr. and Mrs. Vach had already arranged an apartment for Michael close to their home. They didn't want Michael burdened by the reporters who were still gathered at his house. Mrs. Vach wanted him to be close to their home so she could help him and try to keep him out of the spotlight. Michael was happy with the idea. He knew he couldn't go home now, and perhaps not at all. Nick's parents also arranged to have a car waiting for Michael at the sister hospital in the valley.

* * * * *

The flight was a little over fifteen minutes between hospitals. Michael was overjoyed being out of the hospital and on his way to a fresh start. He relished the sight of the great expanse of the city spread out beneath him. The sun was so warm and appeared to be more brilliant than ever above the sprawling city. Michael loved this vantage point. But he was most thankful he didn't have to walk the gauntlet of reporters that still lingered in front of the hospital. He knew they were still in front of his house awaiting his arrival. He wondered how long they would wait. A smile creased his face with the thought.

* * * * *

Nick watched from the parking lot below as the helicopter slowly approached and landed on the roof of the six-story hospital building. He made his way into the hospital to greet his friend.

Mrs. Vach was already in the top floor waiting room as Michael walked in and handed the baby over to her. Lisa handed him a brown paper bag and kissed him on the cheek. Mrs. Vach immediately left with the baby and a nurse into the elevator. Michael was placed in a wheelchair and carted into another elevator. In the elevator, Michael reached into the bag and removed a wig, a hat, and glasses for his cloak. The nurse placed him in a hospital gown and strapped a standard ID tag around his wrist.

As Mrs. Vach exited the hospital with the baby, her husband Dale helped her into the car and drove away without raising an inkling of suspicion from any bystanders. Nick guided Michael's wheelchair out of the hospital and to his car, where, for effect, he helped him into the vehicle. It was a great plan; nobody gave them a second glance. Nobody followed; and Michael could, at least for a while, live in peace.

* * * * *

Entering the apartment, Michael noticed how well stocked it was. Apparently, the Vachs had been busy. Michael walked slowly through the apartment, looking over the landscape. Lisa Vach sat on the couch cradling the baby in her arms. A warm smile crossed her face when their eyes met. Michael continued moving through the apartment, past the new baby crib and the four-month supply of diapers. The apartment was stocked with everything he would need for a month. The refrigerator was stocked with food, and so were the cupboards and counters.

Michael recognized some of the furnishings as his own—and his television, though he couldn't quite figure out how Nick got it out of his house without being followed. He wanted to sleep. He just wanted to lie down and let his new life slowly sink in. He didn't know where each day would take him from here, but he knew that wherever it took him, he would face it head-on. He would face it as a single father. He moved quietly into the lone bedroom and over to the small bed where he sat on its edge. Michael blew a sigh of relief.

Without realizing it, he had lain back on the bed. *My God, what have I done?* he thought as it all sank in. With that, he was out like a light, sleeping like he watched his baby sleep in the ICU. A short time later, Mrs. Vach came in and covered him with a blanket. She would stay with Michael until he was back up on his feet, until he was ready to be alone and start living again.

* * * * *

Reporters scampered for position as three hospital staff members approached the podium that was set up off to the side of the main entrance. This was their big break, their giant scoop, their networks' lead story on the eleven o'clock news.

The three staff members were all dressed with a white doctor's coat, and they stood quietly at the podium. This was going to be a onetime thing, and they waited until everybody was in place. They wanted this farce to be over and all the intrusive people and cameras to vacate the hospital grounds.

Hospital staff, patients, and visitors had been harassed with questions and photos on a daily basis, both coming and going from the hospital. Some staff members were even followed home by reporters, trying to pay them off for information on Michael or the baby Bishope. One nurse was even offered half a million dollars for a picture of the baby Bishope by one of the tabloid papers. She fought against her conscience but finally declined and informed her bosses at the hospital.

The hospital spokesman stepped up to the mic and addressed the reporters. "I would like to read a brief statement, whereafter we will not be taking any questions," he said into the microphone. Shouts, screams, and rapid-fire questions came from the reporters. The spokesman waited for silence before he continued. When he did, he informed the media and essentially the entire world that Michael Bishope was no longer at the hospital. That he and his baby had already left and were at a secluded location where they will remain for an indefinite period of time. He informed them that the baby was born premature but was very healthy when he was released, and his prognosis was outstanding. He concluded with, "Mr. Bishope is a private person and wishes to live in peace. He asked that you all respect his privacy. He would like to put all of this behind him and work on healing and raising his child," said the spokesman. "Thank you all for your time, and as I mentioned, this hospital will not be addressing questions from the media at this time," he said and stepped away from the podium.

Reporters were outraged. They wanted answers; they wanted their story. They hurled questions and shouts at the spokesman as he walked back to the hospital with his two colleagues. Police moved in before it got out of control.

It wasn't long before the police quieted the crowd and moved the reporters off the hospital grounds. They drove away in cars and news vans, and none of them were happy about it. But now was just the start of the game: the quest to be the first to find Michael and his baby. Old contacts—city-, state-, and nationwide—would soon be contacted by hundreds of reporters hoping to catch a lead on the whereabouts of Michael Bishope.

*****

Michael woke with burning questions. They invaded his sleeping dreams, and they wouldn't leave his mind. The questions had been dancing between his ears for weeks, but now they were intensified. He was so focused on the questions in his mind he had forgotten exactly where he was. He looked around the darkened room with curiosity and worry. Then it dawned on him. This was home. This tiny one-bedroom apartment not far from the pimps and prostitutes on Van Nuys Boulevard was home. He smiled with a slight laugh. *Back to from where I started*, he thought. It sure was a long way down in scale from his Brentwood pad.

As his eyes adjusted in the darkness, his stare fell upon a large cardboard box in the corner. With curiosity, Michael moved across the room quietly toward the box. He opened the box and realized that it was full of Susan's belongings: her jewelry, books, and diaries. Michael gasped and quickly shut the box and looked around as if he were committing an illegal act. His heart pounded slightly as he backed away from the box.

When Michael came out into the small living room, he found Lisa sleeping on the couch and the baby sleeping peacefully in the crib. Michael smiled as he stood and watched his baby sleep.

Michael was inspired with love, especially after thinking how close his son came to never being born. He vowed to be the best father he could be and to give his son everything he needed to grow up into a stable and strong man. He knew inside that he was going to spoil this kid rotten, and he didn't care. He wanted to spoil him with all the things he wanted as a child himself. Michael's stolen childhood was going to be lived through his child, and as far as Michael was concerned, young Luc Bishope was going to love every minute of it.

It was Michael's turn to cover Mrs. Vach with a blanket. And as he did, he understood how taxing this whole ordeal must have been on his surrogate parents. He could remember when he spent the night at Nick's house as a child and how Mrs. Vach would wake up at the drop of a feather to check on the kids. But now she just lay there on the couch, sleeping in her exhaustion. He was so thankful for her in his life.

Michael stayed awake through the night, mostly watching his baby, holding his tiny fingers while he slept. He wanted his son to feel the touch of his hand and bond with him as much as possible. He was going to love being a father to this child.

Lisa Vach didn't wake up once, not even when the baby cried. Michael took care of the baby then, changing the diapers and rocking him back to sleep. But as the hour hand hit five in the morning, Michael was slightly startled as somebody or something brushed against the front door. His heart began to race. He thought the worst. He had been found by the media, and they were about to move in for the kill.

Michael moved slowly and ever so quietly across the room and over to the door. He peered carefully through the peephole. The coast was clear. He waited a minute and looked back out. He slowly opened the door and found the morning edition of the *Los Angeles Times*. He smiled and picked it up and shut the door behind him. His smile was lost immediately when he read the headline: Where Is

Michael? The text stood out strong above a large black-and-white photo of Michael exiting the courthouse.

Michael walked back into the room as he read the article. He moved into the kitchen where he placed the paper directly into the trash can. He did not want or need to be reminded of his situation. And the questions came, fast and furious. Why? Why did this happen? Who was he actually married to? What were her secrets? As hard as he tried, he could not escape the questions.

One month later

The Santa Annas were blowing across the valley as they do every fall. Those nasty winds always gave Michael severe headaches as a child. He still didn't care for them, but it wasn't the Santa Anna winds that were giving him the headaches; it was the questions that were bearing down on him. That, and he had not once left the apartment. He was going a bit stir crazy. Cabin fever was setting in, and he was not handling it well. He wanted to rip open Susan's box and examine its contents. He wanted answers!

Lisa Vach came every day and stayed for hours, usually cooking both lunch and dinner for Michael. She brought baby food, groceries, and other essentials. And next week when Luc had his first doctor's appointment, Mrs. Vach would be the one taking the baby. Michael would remain at home, alone with his unanswered questions.

Michael spent most nights sleeping on the couch next to the crib. He loved watching Luc sleep and struggle with curiosity. He could watch him for hours without moving himself. He loved holding him, feeding him, changing his diapers. He loved watching him cry, and he especially loved when his baby smiled. It was the most brilliant smile he had ever seen. Michael was in love with the fact that he was a father. He was looking forward to all the things he and his son would do together.

He remained on the couch watching his baby night after night. He could easily have moved the crib into the bedroom, but he didn't. Michael just wasn't used to Susan not being in bed with him, and he wasn't ready to sleep without her. He had a fear of being alone in the bedroom. He had a fear of Susan's belongings in the box and what secrets they might tell. But again he wanted answers, though he just couldn't bring himself to open the box and go through her personal things no matter what the circumstances. After all, they were her belongings.

But those damn burning questions would not leave him alone! They were constant and excruciatingly painful at times.

Michael moved slowly through each day with a mix of emotions tearing at the cloak of his mind. The days became longer for him and more confusing as more palpable questions tore through his mind. How did things get so screwed up? he thought. Why did this happen? What was her dark secret that she was so willing to kill and die for? Michael was perplexed and outraged at the entire situation. Outraged as to why she would take her own life. Perplexed with questions as to what had happened to her that caused her to break down. He agonized over the fact that she almost killed this precious baby he loved so much.

Nights became sleepless for him as he stared aimlessly into the night with no direction, no focus. He was losing focus of himself, and he knew he had to do something fast. He was not about to let his son down, not for a minute. He knew he needed to address these questions before he could move on and raise his son. He needed to know why, no matter what the consequences were.

* * * * *

As Lisa exited the apartment with Luc for his first doctor's appointment, Michael turned and walked across the room toward the bedroom. He took a deep breath before he entered.

Opening the box, Michael pulled out Susan's most recent diary and carefully opened it to page 1 and started reading. He sat there for hours reading page after page, diary after diary. At times he smiled with a loving memory; other times he became angry. Yet he continued reading and digging for clues. Michael stopped a moment and rolled his eyes, searching for something in his mind. He found it, but appeared bothered by its conclusion. He shrugged off the troublesome emotion and returned his eyes back to the page. Michael rose up on his haunches. His brow folded as he read. "He'll kill me," he read aloud from the page. "Who? Who are you talking about, Susan?" Michael said aloud.

Another hour passed, and he was so in tune with his reading he didn't hear Mrs. Vach walk into the apartment. Only after she called out for him did he mark the page and put down the diary and put it back into the box.

Michael walked into the living room and over to Lisa, where he took his baby out of her arms.

"I forgot how much work this is," she said. "I had my hands full with Nick."

"I can imagine," he replied sarcastically. "How'd it go?"

"Everything is fine," she replied. "The doctor would like to see him again in six weeks."

Michael nodded and began rocking Luc in his arms.

Lisa set her purse and diaper bag on the floor and let out a sigh of relief as she sat on the couch. She looked exhausted. She focused on Michael as he began pacing the floor with the baby, rocking him in his arms. He looked deeply troubled, and she sensed it. A long, heavy silence hung between them.

Then, "Are there any swamps in the Midwest?" Michael asked.

"What?" she asked with a confused look. Her brow wrinkled, and her eyes narrowed. What an odd question, she thought.

"I mean, you're from the Midwest, Kansas, right?"

"Yeah."

"And Dale is from Nebraska?"

"Yes."

"So have you ever heard of any swamps in either of those states?" he asked as he continued pacing the floor.

"I have never heard of any swamps in the Midwest," she replied.

"That's what I thought," Michael said with his back turned toward her.

"Swamps are generally in the southern states: Florida, Mississippi, and Louisiana."

"None in Iowa?"

"No, I wouldn't think so. Why?" Lisa asked.

"Susan. She came from the Midwest. That's what she told me. Iowa, she said." He continued pacing at a more vigorous pace.

She studied him with curious eyes as he paced with the baby in his arms. "All right, what's going on, Michael?" she asked. She knew him too well. It was her mother's intuition taking over and telling her something just wasn't right.

"I don't know. Something just doesn't seem right," he replied. "Susan said her mother used to take her out at night to look at the stars. She said they would get away from the city lights, so they would go to the swamp. They used to listen to the voice of the swamp," he said. "She was fascinated by the stars, you know?" he said as an afterthought. "She loved watching the night sky," he said quietly to himself. "Susan could sit there all night until the sun came up and never look at anything else. And I could never look at anything but her. It was one of those things about her that made me love her so much," he finished and held his steady pace on the floor.

"I know you loved her very much."

Michael stopped in his tracks. "I still love her," he said forcefully.

"I know honey," Lisa replied. She gestured with her hand for Michael to sit next to her on the couch. He sat with a sigh.

"I mean, if she came from the Midwest," he said with a confused expression, "then how could she have gone to the swamps?"

"I don't know, Michael. Maybe it was while they were on vacation, or maybe—" She paused, not really wanting to finish her thought.

"Or maybe what?" he demanded.

"Perhaps I shouldn't."

"Yes, you should. It's all right, Lisa."

"Maybe she lied. Maybe she didn't come from the Midwest at all."

Michael looked off her gaze and peered toward the empty wall. The baby began struggling in his arms. "I kind of had the same feeling myself," he said. "But why would she lie to me about that? I mean, that is such an insignificant thing."

"Maybe not to her."

"Maybe."

"I don't know, Michael. People do things for different reasons. Maybe she was trying to forget where she came from. Maybe she was running from something," Lisa said.

Michael let her suggestion resonate in his mind. "Yeah, maybe. But from what? What could be so bad that it causes you to lie to your husband?"

"Perhaps we'll never know."

Perhaps just wasn't good enough! Michael had to know. He nodded and let the strong silence build between them as his mind mulled over every word. Young Luc protested with a few murmurs of his own. Michael's eyes softened and fell upon his child. He kissed his forehead and began rocking him.

The uncomfortable silence held strong for another moment. Then, "I've been reading her diaries," he said as he turned toward Lisa.

Lisa gave him a queer look. "Well, I can't say I blame you," she started. "You really haven't appeared yourself these last few weeks. You've been distant and somewhat cold. I knew there was something on your mind," said Mrs. Vach. "It would drive me crazy too. Did you find anything?"

Michael shed eye contact as he gently rocked his baby. "I don't know," he started and paused. "Just more questions. More frustration. A lot of things in her diaries just don't add up with what she told me." Michael paused a moment. "There was one thing in there that troubled me. She wrote, 'He would kill me if I ever had a baby.' That's why she wanted to abort our child, because she thought somebody was going to kill her if she gave birth, but who and why? What would cause her to think like that? It doesn't make any sense. Surely she wasn't talking about me," Michael finished with a baffled look.

Lisa held his intent stare. She knew she couldn't give him the answers he had been searching for. "I'm sure she wasn't talking about you, Michael," Lisa said politely.

"Then what was that all about? She was in fear that somebody was going to kill her if she had the baby. That's just absurd to think that."

"I know this is a confusing time for you—"

"And reading those damn diaries made it even more so. I just don't know what to do," he said with defeat in his voice.

"I don't know what to tell you, Michael. I don't know how to begin to give you the answers to what you read. I'm sure she was greatly disturbed herself, being pregnant and all. That does a lot to a woman, you know," she started and placed her hand on his arm. "I just know you're a special person, and you have a tremendous soul, a strong soul. You have been through so much in your young life, losing your parents, losing your wife, and almost losing your son. That's almost too much for anyone to deal with in a lifetime. But as strange as it sounds, everything happens for a reason, and when the time comes, you'll know what to do. Just trust your soul," she said with a warm smile. She wanted to somehow divert his attentions.

Michael smiled back and placed his hand on hers.

She held her smile. She wished she could do more for him, but this was a very troublesome situation already, and she really had no idea how to handle it. "I'm going to start dinner," she said as she got up from the couch and moved toward the kitchen.

* * * * *

Later that night, after Mrs. Vach went home. The baby was sleeping peacefully in the crib. Susan's box of mysteries sat at the foot of the couch, where Michael lay reading from the diaries in the dim light of the room. His quest for understanding, for peace of mind, drove him and focused his mind with sharpened resolve. He had to find the answers.

A little past midnight, Michael finished the last of the diary books. He was almost where he started—nowhere! More images accosted his psyche. Michael lay back on the couch trying somehow to piece this puzzle together. What could he do? An idea came to him, and he sprang from the couch and moved across the room to the computer where he pulled up the internet.

Michael began typing in various commands and thoughts but came up with nothing. He was becoming more frustrated with the dead ends. He was desperately searching for a road called conclusion. It seemed the more he searched, the closer he got to the answers, the more important they became to him. He felt as though something was on the line. There was more at stake than just his burning curiosity.

He searched the internet through the night, only stopping to change the baby and stop him from crying. He loved holding his baby and took any opportunity to bond with him, even just changing his diapers.

After taking a break early the next morning to tend to the baby, Michael returned to the computer. The morning sun blazed through the kitchen window and onto Michael's face. He took no notice; he was even more determined to find what he so searched for. His efforts so far had produced no results.

Then an idea flashed across the screen of his mind. He leaned back over the computer and keyed a few commands. After he found the internet phone book, Michael keyed in Susan's maiden name, Carriere. She must have relatives out there somewhere, he thought. Surely they could shed some light on her situation. What a great idea, he thought. He just wished he thought of it earlier.

After a few seconds, the results flashed across the screen. Michael smiled. He finally had results. Exactly what those results would provide was yet to be determined.

The name *Carriere* came up in several states, from Santa Monica, California, all the way to Boston and everywhere in between. But the largest group was located in New Orleans, Louisiana. *What is New Orleans? It's Mardi Gras, of course*, he thought. *It's legend, myth. It's the mighty Mississippi. It's old, and I'm sure it has swamps.* He looked off the computer screen a moment as he formulated the thoughts in his mind. A twisted shiver rocked him from the inside out. "That's it!" he said aloud.

Michael picked up the phone and started calling all the Carrieres in the New Orleans area. And after two hours of trying, he actually got through to only one person, and they knew nothing of Susan. All the other numbers he had went unanswered. He was becoming frustrated. Michael decided to call every number he had in the country. He was bound and determined to find a living relative of Susan's.

Hours later, Mrs. Vach walked through the front door at 5:30 p.m. Michael had, for the first time in hours, just hung up the phone. He called and spoke with every Carriere across the country, save for the handful in New Orleans. His frustration deepened, though he had a hunch he would find something in the Big Easy.

Through the night and the following day, he tried endlessly to reach those few people in New Orleans, but with no luck. He decided to shoot for the moon and obtain the answers firsthand. But how? Michael knew what he must do. He must go to New Orleans and find out what he needed to know. He needed to finally put this behind him and start living his life.

But how was he going to get there without being accosted by reporters, without being seen and recognized by hundreds, if not thousands, of people at the airport? It didn't take him long to come up with a plan. He called in a favor with his old boss, Larry Moranville, the network head of KNRQ and one of the greatest guys Michael had ever known.

Michael had a great relationship with Larry and thought this plan might work. He spent a good hour on the phone with Moranville in New York. He had explained his situation and let Moranville suggest what came next. Michael knew he would, and they arranged the whole thing for the following day.

* * * * *

The following day, Lisa and Nick led Michael out of the apartment. He was dressed in the same disguise he used at the hospital. They got into a waiting car and drove away. It wasn't a long drive, perhaps six blocks to the Van Nuys airport where the KNRQ private jet waited just off the runway.

As Mrs. Vach pulled the car to a stop near the jet, Michael held and kissed his son goodbye.

"You know, Michael, maybe this isn't such a good idea. People are complicated. They have layers of buried past that they might want to keep buried. If you pull away the layers, you may not like what you find," Lisa said with a concerned expression.

"I don't like it already. I need this, Lisa. I need to know. I feel like whatever I find needs to be found for some reason. It's important," Michael said. "It's really important," he repeated.

Lisa nodded. "I understand."

Michael kissed his baby. "Take good care of him," Michael said.

"You know I will. I took good care of you, didn't I?"

Michael smiled. "Yes, you did. Thank you," he said as tears filled his eyes. "I love you."

"Oh, honey, I love you too," she replied and embraced him. "Now go and find what you are looking for."

Breaking from the embrace, Michael nodded and kissed his son again. He smiled once more and headed toward the waiting jet.

* * * * *

Michael was surprised to see Larry Moranville himself sitting back in the recliner, waiting for Michael to board. Like it or not, Larry was taking this flight with him.

"Larry! I didn't expect to see you make the trip all the way out here," Michael said as he reached out and shook Larry's hand.

Larry pulled the cigar out of his mouth as Michael sat in the leather recliner next to him. "I wanted to talk to you, Mike. I thought the flight to New Orleans would give us a chance to iron things out," Larry said as he stuck the cigar back into his mouth. Michael had his suspicions of what Larry wanted from him.

Larry picked up the phone. "We're all set, Jack," Larry said into the phone.

Michael looked around the interior of the lavish jet. "Wow," he said aloud as the cockpit door opened. An older man dressed in a white pilot's uniform walked out and over to the open door. The pilot pulled the door close and returned to the cockpit.

"Nice, huh?" Larry mumbled.

"Yeah, not bad," Michael replied, looking around his surroundings.

"Bathroom's up there," Larry said, pointing. "Hell, it's even got a bedroom in the back."

"I guess I should have taken more company trips," Michael said as his eyes fell back on Moranville. "So how's the gout, Larry?"

"It's kicking my ass. I can barely walk at times."

"You have to stop eating all that crap, Larry. Too many hundred-dollar lunches," he said with a smile.

Larry smiled as the jet started rolling. "I always liked you, Mike. You never kissed my ass, and that's a rare thing in this business. You always told it how it is. That's why Chandler never liked you, you realize that?"

"I never really knew what was up his ass," Michael replied.

"Prepare for takeoff," the pilot said over the intercom.

"Buckle your seat belt," Larry said as he strapped himself in. Michael followed his lead.

* * * * *

Michael peered out the window as they rose high into the air. He loved watching the ground fall away below each time he flew. It was amazing to him how little everything appeared from this vantage point. Man's innovations and technology melding away with the brown stain of earth.

Once they hit cruising altitude, Larry escaped into the bathroom. Michael gave himself a tour on the spacious jet. He was eying the bar when Larry came out of the bathroom. "You want a drink, Mike?" Larry asked as he approached him.

"No thanks," Michael replied. "I was admiring the plane. It's beautiful."

Larry poured himself a straight whiskey as Michael returned to his seat. "You know why I came, don't you?" Larry asked as he sat next to Michael.

"I have my suspicions."

"I make no secret of what I want, Mike. I want you back," Larry said sternly. "Frankly, you didn't have my permission to quit," he said with a smile. "You're the best damn executive producer we have in any state, and I can't let you go without a fight."

"I can't come back, Larry. At least not right now," Michael replied.

"Well, I'm a tenacious motherfucker, and I have a lot of patience. I'll find your door again," Larry said. "I'll find it soon."

"I know you will, Larry. It wouldn't be like you not to," Michael said with a smile. Michael sighed; he didn't really want to talk about business. Larry picked up on Michael's emotion. "I just need to get away from the news game for a while. Especially now, with the baby and all."

Larry nodded. He understood completely, and as far as Larry was concerned, Michael was still working for him. Larry wondered if faced with the same situation, he himself would want to come back either. "I kind of figured you would say that. Counted on it actually," Larry said and reached over the side of the recliner into his briefcase. He pulled out a manila envelope and handed it to Michael. "Your severance package."

Michael started to protest, but Larry cut him off with a quick wave of his hand. "I insist!" he said firmly. "It's two years' salary, although technically, you're still on the payroll. You don't have my permission to quit just yet," Larry said with a smile.

Michael looked pleadingly at Larry and then pulled out the check. "A million dollars?" Michael protested. Shock was more like it. "I make under three hundred a year."

"I know what you make. So I rounded up. I can do that," Larry said with a shrug of his shoulders. "There's also one hundred thousand dollars of company stock in your son's name. We really didn't have his name, so you can fill that in later." Larry finished.

Michael was floored. He didn't know what to say. He paused in stunned silence. "His name is Luc," he said finally, almost as an afterthought.

"That's a fine name. Luc Bishope. I like it," Larry said with an approving nod and a great smile.

Michael was still too moved to speak. He had saved his money well over the years and had a nice little nest egg for a rainy day.

Michael knew the rain had already started, and it was raining hard lately. He had not worked in some time now, and his nest egg was shrinking bit by bit, so this would surely help him start a new life wherever he wanted. It would give him the time he needed with his son before he went back to work. That's what Michael wanted, to be at home with his son until he was old enough to start school, and thanks to Larry, he could do exactly that. He leaned back in the chair and let it all sink in.

*****

Before Michael exited the jet, Larry stopped him. "You keep in touch, Mike. Like I said, I want you back with the company," Larry started. "I want you running a station of your own."

Michael nodded.

"I want you to know something, Mike. If you come back to any major market in the country, you pick the city, and I'll guarantee you a yearly salary that matches that check I handed you, and that's not including bonuses. That, plus you will run the station and answer only to me," Larry said.

"That's a…generous offer, Larry, but like I said, I need to get away for a little while. I'd like to watch my son grow up. I'm all he has," Michael said and reflected a moment. "He's all I have," he said softly.

"You're a good man, Mike. There's not many left like you. You let me know where you're at and when you're ready to come back," Larry said as he reached out his hand.

Michael gladly took his hand into his. "I will, Larry. But right now my plans are to spend time with my son."

Larry nodded. "I understand, and take your time. You're still on payroll."

"Yeah, you don't have to do that."

"Yes, I do." They held each other's stare for a moment, and then Larry tailed off. "Hey, listen, Mike. I just wanted to say that I am sorry for what happened to you. I'm sorry for people like Frank Chandler and for what we did to you."

"You're a friend, Larry. You didn't do anything to me. You've always been good to me, and I appreciate it. As far as Chandler, he's an asshole. I never liked him. He and other people in the media are bloodsuckers. It's their job, and if he wouldn't have basted me, somebody else would have. Like I said, it's their job. I should know. It was my job too."

Larry nodded. He always liked Michael's straightforwardness. Michael was old school, just like him; that's why he so embraced him. "Well, you take care, Mike. And you stay in touch. I want to hear from you."

"You got it, Larry. And thank you for taking care of me," Michael said. "I'm proud to call you my friend."

"I'm proud to be your friend." Larry nodded with a smile. He let Michael's handshake slip from his hand.

Michael turned and exited the jet and walked to the waiting car.

33

Beholding the sights and smells of the great city of spirits fascinated Michael as he peered from the back window of the moving car. He watched as the vast expanse of the Grand River flowed slowly toward the Gulf of Mexico. The beautiful architecture and old-world feel of the city reminded him of some European cities he once traveled through and loved so much. He was mesmerized with the feel of the city. Its voice spoke to his core, just like the old cities of Europe once did. This place would forever be etched into his memory banks and stored alongside those of his beloved Europe, mental notes to be recalled at a later date and time for inner salvation and peace.

Michael craned his head and pulled focus on the driver and watched as he picked up the phone and keyed in the number. "I have the package. Five minutes out," he said into the phone.

Michael's brow wrinkled as he looked on with curiosity as the driver pulled the car to a stop on a side street.

The driver turned around to face Michael. "Mr. Bishope, we're going to deliver you to a side entrance of the hotel so you won't be recognized. You will be met there by a member of our staff and taken directly to your room. We have already checked you in under Larry Moranville," he said. "He hired my security team."

Michael was surprised—first that Larry had gone to such extremes and, second, that he was being escorted by a security team. "Thank you very much, but I don't want or need a security team," Michael replied.

"Sir, my team was hired to get you safely to and from the hotel without being recognized. What you do after, that is up to you. My job is not over until the day you leave New Orleans, where I will again take you to the airport." With that, the driver turned back and started back up the street.

"I'm surprised Larry gave you my name," Michael said from the back of the car.

"He didn't, sir. I recognized you right off the plane. And be assured, sir, you have my full confidence. Along with that of my team who might recognize you," the driver replied. "We're all ex-special forces, and discretion is our best asset."

"Thank you," Michael said and broke his gaze. He picked up the street scene as the sights painted the canvas of his mind moving by out his window. He smiled as they passed a streetcar, something he thought native to Europe and San Francisco. This city, this life, this aura, this essence in the air was breathtaking to him. If he found nothing else here, he would surely come to once again find himself in this magical city. Perhaps it was the reason he came here in the first place, to find himself. There slowly came a long-lost sense of peace to Michael's fractured heart.

Michael remained on the balcony looking over the life-filled street below as the reddish hues of dusk strained over the western horizon. The vivid image brought with it the clear memories of the glorious sunsets over the Pacific Ocean he loved so much. Michael stayed out of view as the bellhop set his dinner on the table where a tip awaited him. The man left the food and exited the room. Michael remained on the balcony watching the effects of the sun's last light on the grand city.

A strange mix of aromas came to him in the open air on the balcony. This was New Orleans. The smell of the river and jasmine mixed with the many flavors rising from the restaurants below came into his senses. Michael closed his eyes and took in the essence of the great city. Leaving the balcony window open, Michael returned to the room to eat his dinner.

The hotel room was brilliantly splattered with the colors of Mardi Gras—purple, gold, and green. Michael loved it, loved the old feel the room had. The whole city, the hotel, and even this room seemed to be in another time altogether. He already loved this town.

Having spent quite a few hours on the phone trying to contact the people on his list with no luck, Michael decided he was going to explore other possibilities. He was going to venture into the city and go to the addresses he had on every Carriere in town. He didn't care how long it took. He had all the time in the world, and he was not leaving until he had some answers, some peace of mind.

*****

Michael wore a baseball cap and dark sunglasses as he exited the hotel through a side exit. He found himself in a darkened alleyway. He took off the glasses and focused his eyes in the dark. He looked to his left and saw a busy street a short distance away. But as he started walking, he quickly became startled when a stranger suddenly appeared out of the dark.

Instinctively, Michael jumped and took a defensive pose, ready to pounce on any advance the stranger might make. Michael's heart was racing with adrenaline. Instead, the stranger stayed in the shadows. Michael could barely make out the features of the man's face in the darkness. The man pointed and began talking to Michael in a strange language.

Michael was tripped with confusion as the man almost started ranting in a foreign tongue. Michael shook his head, not exactly understanding this man's incoherent jabbering. But there was an uncanny familiarity about the man's appearance, something that sent Michael searching deep into the recesses of his mind.

Michael followed the man's gaze and shrugged his shoulders. When he turned back to look at the stranger, he was no longer there. He looked around his surroundings, peering to the end of the alley. No doors or windows, no exits. The stranger seemed to have disappeared right in front of his eyes.

Michael shook his head and started to the street ahead. He couldn't get past the fact that he recognized the man, but just couldn't place from where he knew him. He turned and gave one last look back into the darkened alley but saw nothing.

As Michael approached the busy street, he lifted the dark sunglasses back to his face. With his cloak intact, he merged into the flowing crowd on the street. He wore his baseball cap low and his head lower, anything to avoid being recognized by anyone. That was the last thing he needed, a media frenzy here in the Big Easy.

Moving down Bourbon Street, Michael passed just outside one of the many garish nightclubs. The sound coming from within spoke directly to his sense of curiosity. He had heard so much about the famous nightlife in New Orleans and wanted to experience everything he could.

Jazz painted the evening air as he continued moving through the night. Strange and inviting aromas were everywhere; each melded with the other and mixed on their way to the heavens. It was such a delight to Michael's senses. The beat of the city was something he thought not possible in this country. It was energy, it was animation, and it was mystery. It was exactly what he needed, a break from reality. He was beside himself and overjoyed with his surroundings, the sights, the smells and sounds of this amazing place.

"Excuse me," he said as he turned the corner and ran smack into a pedestrian on the street. Michael thought nothing of it and continued walking. The man he ran into stood there on the street corner and watched Michael as he walked away. There was something in the man's stare. Then it came to him, and he started walking after Michael.

"MICHAEL!" the man shouted quickly, hoping to jolt a startled response out of him.

Michael heard the man's shout echo through the streets. He fought the urge to turn in recognition of his name, but he continued walking.

So did the man.

A short distance later, under a sprawling oak tree, the man caught up to Michael and stopped him by grabbing his arm. Michael turned to face the man.

The man smiled. "It is you," he said with a smile. "Mr. Bishope, a lot of people are looking for you." The shit-eating smile remained heavy on the man's face. "Well, if this ain't my lucky day."

Michael said nothing; he wasn't about to play into this man's game. His eyes were seething with anger behind his dark glasses.

"Why are you in New Orleans?" the man asked.

Michael said nothing and just stared at him.

"Mr. Bishope, it would be in your best interest to talk to me," he said.

Michael grabbed him by the arm and roughly pushed him up against the oak tree. "Who are you? And what the hell do you want from me?" Michael said.

"My name is Dave Bader. I am a reporter here in town," he said, still in Michael's grasp.

Michael let him go. "I have nothing to say," Michael said. He turned and started walking along the sidewalk. Dave Bader followed a short distance behind him.

"Mr. Bishope, you can talk to me now, or I can make your stay here in the Big Easy very uncomfortable," Bader said, still following Michael.

Michael stopped and turned quickly. "Can't you guys just leave me alone and let me live in peace?" Michael almost shouted.

"No," he replied, shaking his head.

Michael thought about it a moment. "Look, I implore you not to run any story you think you might have," Michael said

"Why?"

"That's my business. It's the reason I'm here."

"Running this story is my business. That is why I am not going to let you slip off into the night. What kind of reporter would I be?"

"One with compassion!" Michael replied quickly.

"There's no room for compassion in the news game. You of all people should know that," he said. "Look, talk to me. You're going to have to talk to somebody eventually. Why not me now? Get it out of the way and move on with your life."

"No, I won't. Not yet."

Bader looked at him with interest. There was something going on here, and Bader wanted to see where he was going.

"What would you say if I asked you to wait a few days and let me see what I dig up here?" Michael asked pleadingly.

"I'd say you're crazy."

Michael smiled and stepped forward. "Look, what's your story here, that you found me? So what? What kind of story is that, especially if I say nothing?"

"I could splash your name across the AP wires," Bader threatened.

"Yes, you could do that, or you could wait, and I will guarantee you an exclusive story. A much larger story than just finding me. You have my word. I won't talk to anyone else but you."

"Yes, but in the meantime, you still remain on the streets and are a very recognizable person. If I don't break this story now, another reporter will surely see you as I have, and I will be shit out of luck on the biggest story of the year."

Michael sighed in frustration and turned away from the reporter a moment. Then turned back. He took the long silence to formulate some sort of plan in his mind. "Again, I implore you, don't do anything just yet. Give me some time. That's all I ask," Michael said with pleading eyes.

"What will you give me?" Bader asked.

Michael pulled his room key from his coat pocket and handed it to Bader. "My word is as good as this. Now you know where I'm staying. You can go there now and snoop around if you want, and we can talk later tonight. You can wait for me and start your interview then. Just give me the time I need before you run anything. Please," Michael begged.

Bader held the key in his hand a moment, then handed it back to Michael. "Okay," he started. "But I don't need your room key. I would like to meet with you later tonight," Bader said as he reached into his wallet and pulled out his business card and handed it to Michael. "Home and cell is on the back."

Michael took the card and looked back up. "Thank you."

"If I don't hear from you tonight, I will go with what I have in the morning. And by noon tomorrow, an army of reporters will be gathered outside your hotel room."

"You will hear from me tonight. You have my word," Michael said and reached out his hand. Dave extended his hand. They shook.

"Thank you," Michael said.

"Get out of here before I change my mind," Bader replied.

Michael nodded and pulled his hand away, then turned and walked away.

"This story better be worth it!" Bader called after Michael.

*****

The night deepened, and the sounds of New Orleans engulfed Michael as he walked down a darkened street in a run-down part of town. The neighborhood was grungy but still had the old-world feel Michael loved so much. He knew it was just the poor part of town that every city has. As run-down as it seemed, Michael found so much beauty in the sights he beheld. Some of the older eighteenth- and nineteenth-century homes held a magical charm.

Quite often, Michael found himself stopped in front of the wrought iron fences outside these treasures of New Orleans, just staring at the splendor of their beauty. He imagined living in one of these relics of the past and how much Susan would have loved it. He looked at the large banana tree in the side yard. The grounds were unkempt, growing wild, yet somehow very beautiful. Rose of Montana vine laced itself around the faded white and peeling Corinthian columns and moved up near the shuttered windows.

The house was dirty, wild, and unlived-in. Michael loved it. He even entertained the thought of buying it and restoring its beauty. He then looked down at the paper in his hand and realized that he came here for a reason. He turned away from the magnificent house and continued walking back down the street.

Houses came smaller and more run-down as he walked. Some of the houses appeared to be lived in, but they were little more than one- and two-room shacks with dirt yards. The mostly white faces of their exteriors hadn't seen paint in years. Very little shrubbery behind the rusted wrought iron fences. Michael didn't care much for this part of town. It lacked the charm and decadence of the old neighborhood from which he just came.

Michael stopped on the street corner and looked through the broken fence, bars missing and bent at another house so similar in appearance to the ones he had passed all along the street. Only this house was on a massive lot and had a little more shrubbery and weeds on its mostly dirt yard. There stood what appeared to be another house or a small shack behind and off to the side of the dilapidated house.

This was the house he was looking for, the one in front, the shitty-looking house with all the character of an abandoned building in Nazi Germany during the war. He moved slowly across the yard and over the rocks and potholes toward the front door. The old wood under his boots creaked and groaned as he moved up the few steps below the porch. Michael moved and stepped over the hole in the porch to the left of the door.

He knocked, and as he did, a strange sensation swept over his body. His senses became amplified. A presence was near, or right there with him. He could feel someone looking at him, watching him intently. The hairs on the back of his neck stood on end. The goose bumps that spread all over his body cried for mercy. He knocked again, but nobody appeared to be home.

Michael turned and moved away from the house, vowing to return at a later time. As he left, he watched his back and looked around carefully. He gave another glance at the small house behind this one. It was very dark, no sign of life. Suddenly Michael stopped in his tracks. His heart began pounding as he thought he saw somebody watching him through the window. He thought he watched the curtains close in the darkened room of the back house. In his mind, he saw a dark figure behind the dirty glass window.

Michael shook his head and played it off to his nervous imagination. He turned and walked across the yard toward the street. He came to a busy intersection and hailed a taxi.

Michael covered a great deal of the city and returned to his hotel room before midnight. He didn't find what he was looking for but was able to cross four names off his list. Tomorrow he would dare to venture out in public during the daytime to try and reach the people he missed tonight.

Michael opened the French doors and moved out onto the balcony. The soft breeze swept the thin curtains gently into the room.

Michael listened to the voice of the city, telling its sordid little secrets to those listening. Michael closed his eyes and let the night envelope him as he leaned on the iron handrail of the grand balcony.

A thought suddenly came to him, and true to his word, Michael picked up the phone and called the number on the back of the reporter's card. Bader answered right away and informed Michael that he was in the lobby. Michael invited him up to the room and ordered room service for them both. They talked until the wee hours, and Dave Bader was soon to be the envy of all the reporters. He was going to have the exclusive of a lifetime. How it ended, he did not know. But from what he learned, he felt the conclusion would be worth the wait. He also felt a strong kinship with Michael.

Bader left the room around four in the morning. They agreed to meet again the following night. Michael had become used to the late hours, and even at this hour, the city was still buzzing with life below his open room. He wanted so much to go down and have a drink in one of the famous nightclubs on Bourbon Street and listen to the jazz until the sun came up. But he knew he couldn't take the chance of being recognized, not yet anyhow. He remained focused and on course with what he needed to do.

* * * * *

Moving carefully through the muggy gray New Orleans day, Michael was careful not to be recognized by anybody he might pass on the street. He couldn't rent a car under his name without drawing attention to his whereabouts, so Michael was reduced to walking, taking taxis, or the streetcars.

Avoiding the foot traffic on Bourbon Street, Michael headed in the other direction out of the alley. He again wondered about the strange incident he encountered the night before in the darkened alley. He still tried to place the face he knew he recognized but still couldn't place from where he knew it. It was a joke, Michael thought. It never happened. It was just my tired, wild imagination seeing things that just weren't there.

Michael handed a few dollars to the taxi driver as he exited the car and started walking down the street. The more he saw of this town, the more he loved everything about it. The buildings, the houses, the Garden District, the splendid, grand churches that reminded him of the Romanesque-style churches in Southern Germany and especially the steepled church in Rättvik, Sweden.

This place, this vision, this smell brought him back to the great cities of Europe. It brought a new life back to his soul and new hope to his dreams. This place was restoring Michael's will to live and carry on.

Michael slowed his pace as he walked down the narrow street between the two beautiful churches: Saint Alphonsus with its stained glass windows and old-world feel, and Saint Mary's with all its statues of the saints and grand arches. Everywhere he went was a reminder of a place he had been somewhere far, far away in another land in another time.

Having lingered in front of the two beautiful churches longer than he should have, he continued walking toward his destination, a small apartment complex around the corner. Or so he thought. It turned out to be three blocks away.

Talking to the older lady at the door, Michael learned that she knew nothing of Susan or Melissa or any family here in town. She was sorry she couldn't help Michael, who thanked her and left in frustration. He was running out of options.

Moving down the street, he realized the familiar surroundings. He looked up at the same house he beheld in darkness the previous night. It was even more of an eyesore in the dreary daylight. But Michael still envisioned purchasing the house and renovating its historical beauty. He decided to go back to the house that gave him the creeps the night before. It was just down the street from what he could tell.

Daylight, as gloomy as it was, painted the house in a different light as he approached. It was the worst house on the street. More dilapidated than he was able to see the prior night. The pecan tree in the front yard was half burnt; its trunk and limbs were like black coal. Trash and empty alcohol bottles were piled up in the yard. The wood on the steps and on the exterior walls of the house were rotting. Windows were broken out, and plywood covered two of the side windows.

Again Michael had a strange feeling that he was being watched. Goose bumps came again as he stepped onto the porch. Michael paused and gathered his composure. Even in the daylight, he could not see anybody around the house or in the yard. But that didn't stop the creeped-out feeling that he had in his gut. He turned back to the door and was careful to step over the hole in the porch. He knocked and waited. No sound from within. He knocked again and waited.

Nothing.

Michael looked down at the sheet of paper in his hand: two more names and addresses. Michael sighed and moved across the yard and onto the street where he turned and took a long, hard look at the house. There was just something about it, something he couldn't place. Something just didn't fit.

Michael turned as a car pulled into the driveway of the house two doors down. He walked over to the heavyset older black woman as she exited the car. The woman sighed and lifted her large purse over her shoulder. When she retrieved the single brown bag of groceries from the front seat and shut the door, Michael approached her.

"Excuse me, ma'am," Michael said cautiously.

The lady jumped slightly and latched onto her purse. The lady gave him the once-over with narrowed eyes. "What you want, mista?" she asked as she continued studying his face. She felt cornered and had an uncomfortable disposition.

"I'm sorry to bother you, but I wonder if you know anything about the people who live in that house on the corner," he said, pointing. The old woman followed his point but kept a stern eye on Michael. She did not trust anyone in this neighborhood. Her eyes promptly returned to Michael.

"Naw. Folks 'round here keep to themselves mostly. Don't know none a' my neighbors," she said. "Say, don't I know who you is?" she asked.

"I just have one of those faces, ma'am. I'm nobody, really."

She didn't buy it. She was sure she had seen him somewhere before, but just couldn't place it. She let out a slight grunt as she continued scrutinizing him with her eyes. "Like I say, I don't know anybody 'round here. Now wait a minute. Now that I think on it a spell, he done been there in dat house 'bout as long as I been here."

"How long is that, ma'am?" Michael asked slowly. He felt that she was leery of his presence and was careful not to alarm her.

"Oh, goin' on 'bout thirty years now," she said. She craned her head in the direction of Michael's asking. "Come ta think on it, used to be a woman dat lived there too. Don't know if she was his wife or what. Like I says, I don't know nothin' 'bout nobody 'round here," she finished.

"But somebody lives there now, right?"

"Yes, I see him come and go once or twice."

"Do you know if there was ever a daughter, a young girl, who ever lived there?" Michael asked with heightened interest.

"Mista, I don't know, an' I don't wanna know!" She was irritated. She started backing away from him, moving slowly toward the house. It, too, was a run-down shack like all the other houses in the area. She quickly rifled for her keys.

Michael hung his head. "Well, thank you for your time," he called after her. "I won't bother you again." Michael turned and began moving down the cracked and graffiti-covered sidewalk. The old woman watched him as he disappeared around the corner.

*****

The day was turning fast, and the smell of rain held heavy on the breeze coming off the river. Michael pushed slowly toward a main street where he could flag down a taxi.

It didn't start with a few drops. It started raining in a torrential downpour, catching Michael off guard. He looked up at the falling rain. It didn't matter to him; it had been raining in his soul for months. He kept his steady pace toward the main street ahead.

As he hailed a taxi, the thunder and lightning came with a mighty roar. It was unlike any other he had witnessed before in California.

The lightning spread in a brilliant white flash across the entire sky, one after the other. Michael counted six lightning strikes within two minutes. And the thunder from Thor's hammer repeatedly pounded the city with tremendous base. Michael had never heard such a noise. Nothing could compare to this spectacular light-and-sound show from the heavens above.

Walking into the darkened alley in the pouring rain, Michael made his way to the side door of the hotel. As he was about to grasp the door handle, he stopped and turned to the strange sound of music playing from somewhere in the alley. Michael moved deeper into the darkness but saw nothing. He moved closer to the street, thinking the music came from one of the clubs on Bourbon Street, but it wasn't. It was coming from somewhere in this alley. As he further searched out the location of the music, Michael became aware of its tune. He had heard it before, but where?

After covering the alley from Bourbon Street all the way to the dead end, Michael started back for the door of the hotel. But the opiate had already begun to run its course; the tune was locked within him, repeating itself in his mind. Where the hell had he heard that tune before? he thought as he moved toward the staircase at the end of the long corridor.

Picking up the phone, Michael called the reporter Dave Bader and informed him that he was going to check out two more leads later; and if he couldn't get a hold of anyone, he was going to return to Los Angeles in the morning. Michael told him that he felt as though this was a wrong turn in coming here and that he's probably not going to find the information he's been looking for, and it was all a waste of time. Besides, he wanted to get back to his son. Michael agreed to meet him later and hung up.

The damp breeze blew the sheer curtains back into the hotel room like a ghostly whisper. Michael moved back over to the bed and plopped down in its soft folds. As he did, he sat bolt upright and realized where he had heard that tune before, but didn't believe it himself. It was the same tune he and Susan had heard in Germany on their honeymoon. And now that he thought about it, the stranger he met, or thought he met, in the alley the other night was the same guy who was playing the guitar and singing the song that night in Berlin. Michael couldn't believe it, didn't want to believe it. It was too far out of the realm of reality for him to grasp. Nonetheless, goose bumps ran the length of his spine.

Again he shook off both episodes to his tired imagination playing tricks on him. He smiled and lay back down on the bed. He listened to the rain and thunder of the Southern night. Jazz music from the clubs below danced with the raindrops as they fell heavy onto the balcony. Michael started dozing off to the soft, rhythmic thumping of the rain beating against the balcony outside, but the same tune woke him abruptly. It would not leave him alone.

He finally got up from the bed and again readied himself for another venture into the city. Two more addresses he needed to check out. Two more people he desperately needed to talk to.

Sins of the Father

THE RAIN continued holding strong in the Southern night. Dark and windy, a fitting night for the city of spirits to let its demons slip from its grasp. Blazing lightning and roaring thunder continued on its eastward course.

The taxi dropped Michael just down the street from his destination. He wanted to walk by the house he found so degraded and yet so interesting. If it was to be his last night in this beautiful city, he wanted to experience and remember some of the things that fascinated him so much, and this house did.

And he felt it coming.

Michael stopped in front of the house and looked up at its fractured facade. It was still something to behold, even through all of its years of neglect. He latched onto the wrought iron fence and looked through the bent and rusty bars. He wondered why he found it so fascinating. Michael looked around at his surroundings, first left, then to his right, then up at the sky. No more rain. A shiver ran through his body. There was something in the air that spooked him;

he could feel it in the pit of his stomach. Michael took one last look at the grand house and turned—

Michael yelled and jumped! He was startled and flailed uncontrollably back into the iron fence, hitting his head against the bars.

An old black woman stood not two inches from Michael in his path, and she was just staring at him with evil eyes. She appeared out of the darkness and looked larger than life. She was a very big woman.

Michael reached up and felt the lump growing on the back of his head and tried to focus on the old lady, but something just wasn't right about her.

"I knew you's comin'. I knew it fo' a' long time, boy," said old Mabel Toullier. Her spooky eyes pierced right through Michael as he stood with confusion.

"Excuse me?" Michael replied. That's what it was—her eyes!

"I knows the evil ya lookin' fo'," she said. Her voice, the way she spoke, sent chills through his body. Her eyes—Michael remained focused on her eyes—petrified him with fear and wonder. Now he got it: she only had one eye. Her left eye was pure white and almost glowed iridescent, like a dim bulb, no pupil. He couldn't take his gaze off her eyes.

"I'm looking for—"

"I knows what ya lookin' fo' boy! You's lookin' fo' young Melissa's daddy! He a baad man, I tell ya."

"She doesn't have a father. He died when she was just a girl," Michael protested.

"He alive!" she said with an unearthly emphasis. "He evil, and he alive in dat house which you been at twice now. You don't wait fo' nobody dis time. Ya go in an' fine what ya need, boy," she said. Her voice cut through him. She was a different sort than he had ever met. Of course, she fit right in with the legends of this beautiful city.

"Her father is still alive?" he asked with a confused facial expression etched perpetually onto his face. Then it occurred to him: Susan confessed to him when he last saw her. She admitted that her father was alive. He remembered that she told him that she lied and how sorry she was about it. How could that have slipped his mind? He thought.

"He still alive," she said just above an unintended whisper. "Her mama's dead, an' I know he kilt her." Old Mabel continued staring at him with her one eye.

Michael nodded. He no longer noticed her strange eyes. "Susan—uh, Melissa mentioned something like that once," he replied as he lowered his head. His heart began pounding in his chest as he thought of the possibilities that lay ahead.

"You's go now an' bring peace to 'em," she said. "Ya make every'ting right now, ya hear?" she finished. It felt like a threat to him, the way she spoke. He felt intimidated.

Michael leveled his eyes onto her for a moment. He nodded and shed eye contact as he started walking slowly away from old Mabel Toullier. His limbs began shaking, making it hard for him to steady his slow stride. So many thoughts trembled in his mind with their confusing direction.

"Ya bring peace to 'em all, boy!" she called after him. She watched as Michael walked down the street toward the house. "Time fo' justice now," she said softly to herself. "Time fo' justice," she repeated slowly with a slight sense of pleasure.

Michael wasn't sure, but he could swear he heard the old lady chanting something as he walked farther down the street.

* * * * *

Michael's heart began pounding as he neared the house. This time, he felt as though he would finally come away with some answers. The old lady knew something and somehow instilled a confident faith in Michael. It was no accident that she appeared like that. *She led me here*, he thought.

Michael knocked on the door and waited with a thumping in his chest. He could not slow it; it came hard and heavy, just like his breathing.

No reply.

His heart began racing even faster. He felt his rage boil, and he again knocked, a little harder this time, a little louder.

Nothing.

Michael became furious and began pounding hard on the front door. He needed the answers from the person who lived here, and he wasn't going away without them. He continued pounding, harder and harder until he pounded so hard the front door clicked and jarred opened slightly. Michael's breathing stopped entirely as he peered through the cracked door into the darkened house. *Did I do that?* he thought.

"Hello?" he called out.

Nothing. No accommodating voice. No welcoming sound from within the darkness staring back at him. A wicked chill pushed through him.

Instinctively, Michael pushed the door open wide and looked in. "Hello," he said again.

No reply.

There was darkness all around him. His heart pounded. His legs and hands shook violently.

A strange howl blew as eerie sound across his senses. Michael turned and peered past the yard and into the street, where his sight fell upon the motionless trees. The night was strangely still and calm, completely motionless and devoid of sound. Michael gave way to another spook he let himself feel when he realized that the sound he heard appeared to have come from within the house.

Michael stood in the doorway a long moment, thinking. Trying to work up the courage for his next move, if he dared.

Shaking.

A strange mix of fear and anger raged within him. "Hello," he again shouted, much louder this time. He turned and examined his surroundings. Not a person around. The wind was gusting, pushing the trees wickedly back and forth, but it was doing so without the eerie sound. The whole world was mute and unaware. Michael started having second thoughts about this whole thing.

He finally decided to throw the dice and enter. He closed the door behind him and moved into the darkness of the house. He was immediately assaulted by the awful smell of alcohol and urine—and the wretched smell of rotting eggs. "Hello!" he yelled.

Nothing.

Feeling his way through the darkness, he found himself moving into another room. It was cold in the house, very cold. This room was even colder. Michael felt through the darkness with his hands extended out in front of him, searching for the light switch on the wall. Amazingly, he didn't run into or kick anything, except for an empty bottle, which made very little noise. When the lights came on, he found himself in the doorway of the kitchen, from which came the smell of rotting eggs. It was a disgusting place, trash and rotting food everywhere. Empty alcohol bottles on the floor and counter. The trash can was overflowing onto the dirty almost-black floor. Cockroaches scampered for cover as the lights came on in their playground.

A burly rat scurried for his darkened hiding spot in the wall. Michael became nauseated by the smell and sight of the disgusting kitchen. He made a motion as if he were going to throw up, but thankfully stopped before he added to the floor. He couldn't escape the strong smell of urine. Where the hell was it coming from?

Michael made a mental note of the door next to the 1960s-style refrigerator and moved quickly out of the kitchen and back into the room from which he came.

This room was a little less messy than the kitchen. There was an immense collection of empty alcohol bottles all over the floor. Michael made a mental note of the things he beheld. The smell, the dirty couch near the front window, the old video camera on the tripod near the newer-looking television. There was another couch near the television, and it appeared to be forty years old. There were holes and stains all over its fabric. A host of videotapes lined neatly on top of the old VCR. Michael shook his head and moved toward the hallway leading to the back of the house.

He flipped on the light switch in the hallway and continued moving slowly. He pushed open the first door on his right and turned on the light. More cockroaches ran for cover in the disgusting bathroom. There was a constant sound of water dripping from the faucet.

Heavy brown water stains painted the once-white porcelain sink. He examined the room and shut the door to the awful stench that came from within. He didn't even want to think about that horrendous smell.

He turned and looked at the door across the way. It had a latch for a padlock that was absent from the door. Michael found it strange but opened the door anyway. No light. But from the dim light in the hallway, Michael could see the room was filled with trash that was knee-deep and more empty bottles. He couldn't imagine any one person could drink this much alcohol in one lifetime. He shook his head and closed the door and moved to the room at the end of the hallway.

Placing his hand on the doorknob, Michael opened the last door and quickly searched for the light switch and flipped on the light. A bare lightbulb hung in the center of the heavily water-stained ceiling. More cockroaches and another large rat ran for cover. This room was also a mess, but not the war zone he had just witnessed. As he moved deeper into the room, Michael saw only one empty bottle in the room, Jack, the familiar Old No. 7, and it was sucked dry. Michael moved near the wall and examined the contents that sat on top of the old dresser. There was nothing of any interest to him.

As he turned, he took note of a handgun stashed haphazardly under the bed. He moved to the side of the bed and slid the gun out with his foot. It was a snub-nose .38 special. He wasn't about to handle the weapon and leave his fingerprints. Who knows the history of the gun, and Michael didn't want to find out the hard way. He pushed it back where he found it with his foot. He shrugged and made his way back to the door.

Michael paused at the doorway and sighed. He really didn't know what he was looking for, and he didn't know what the hell he was thinking coming in here. He could be arrested like a common criminal, like the hundreds of other criminals he covered so many times on the news. That wasn't him. He was about to make a mad dash out of this shithole and back to Los Angeles tonight.

But taking one last look into the room before he killed the light, something caught his eye. He quickly turned the light back on and moved around the bed where he found the gun. He moved a stack of adult newspapers and uncovered three books he recognized. They were the same style and color as some of Susan's diaries. Michael's pulse came rapid. His chest tightened, and he held his breath.

Carefully and slowly with his finger, Michael slid the top book closer to the dim light and moved out of its shadow. His heart quickened as he opened the book and read the name *Melissa's Diaree Book*. It was written in a child's print across the white page.

Michael quickly picked up the book and started examining the inner pages. His mouth parted slightly and was held agape. His face showed the horrors of the daily entries made by a child, his wife, long ago. He read on.

The first page in a child's writing:

> DeAr diAree
>
> I got hurtited today AgAin from my dAddee. He touchedid me Again tooday. Tooday… He did it touchdid it me with the thing where he makes pp. he touchedid it to my but but where I make nummer 2. It hurted so bAd that I don't not like that like he said I wood like that. It wAs not good At one bit.
>
> I Miss my mommee.
>
> MelissA.

"Jesus Christ," Michael said aloud as he finished the page. His heart began racing, thumping. He was appalled, and a look of anger spread quickly across his face. He turned the page and continued reading the diary. The following pages were just text, simple entries with no names attached and written by other people, it seemed. Melissa's alters, he thought. He looked on the page with worry and anger. The frantically scribbled words and emotions troubled him deeply.

A rage boils within my soul. I want to tear the flesh from those who have harmed me. To tear the eyes from their skulls, one at a time so they kan watch in horror.

Why has my daddee done this to me? He said he wood kill me if I…if i…who cares anyway? My greatest dream now is to die…!

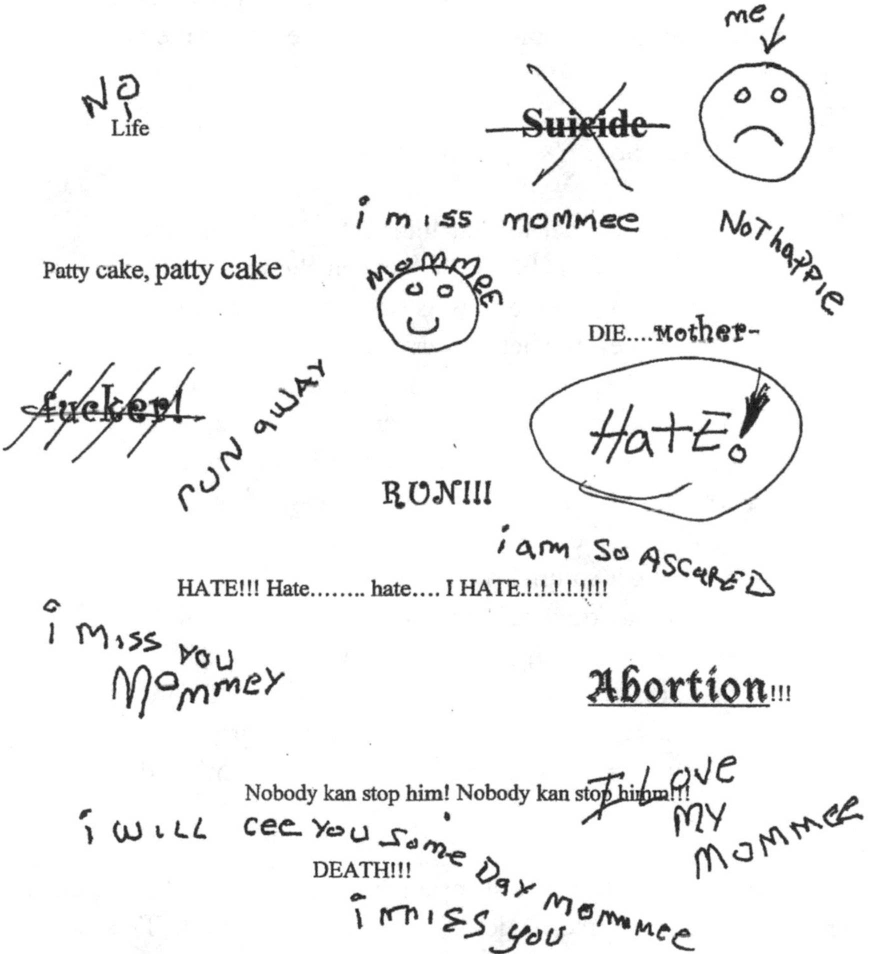

"My God!" Michael said aloud. What was he supposed to make of any of this? He was just as lost and confused as whoever wrote this horrible text. He knew, though, that this was tied directly to Susan. To the reason she was so insistent on having an abortion. To the reason she killed herself.

One thing he knew for sure, he was pissed! He also wanted to tear the eyes from the person responsible for these horrors. He was quickly forming an idea of who was responsible for these horrors to his beloved Susan. Without realizing it, Michael had lowered himself and sat on the filthy, stained bed. He continued reading.

> DeAr whoever!
>
> I, me, she, we felt like A fugitive from the mysteries of the human labyrinth she wAs trying to piece together. She wAs stained with violence. I tried to escape her patterns, escape his patterns. She tried escaping from the familiar grooves of my everyday life. The outer world is so overwhelmingly frightening, but the inner world in which we live is deadly. I am so overwhelmed and confused. She is so close to the edge.
>
> She is so unclean…
>
> I was the greAt mistake of herself. A child born to the wrong parents, born into a world of darkness and torture and unspeAkable acts. She must always remember what I kannot forget.
>
> Don't cherish anything! Not after him! And don't ever…

Just like that, the text stopped midsentence, as if the person writing was interrupted. Michael appeared confused. This surely wasn't the writing of a young child as in the first page. Nor did it contain such violent and unusual writing. He wasn't sure what this page meant nor who wrote it. These pages seemingly came from many different people. But he knew enough to know they all belonged to Susan and that they all lived in her head. Nothing made sense. Everything was jumbled and out of place. Was there meaning in the random order in which the confusing text lay on the page?

Michael peeled his eyes away from the book a moment and stared at the dirty wall shown in the dim light. He hadn't noticed the holes that were bashed into the wall. He imagined the violence it took to create such a crater in the wall. Michael held his stare on the hole in the wall as his mind raced through a multitude of scenarios. In his mind, the jigsaw puzzle was coming together, and the rage continued within him and was bubbling just beneath the surface. Michael sighed and returned his eyes to the next page for further exploration.

Deer diary,

I am so worried about my deerest friend. I fear that somebody is sexually touching her. I think it is her father, but I just don't have the heArt to ask her or confront him. I kan always tell when something has happened, when somebody has touched her, she is always ice cold, she won't talk to mee and she cries the whole night, and she'll never turn the lights on.

It's sooo dark…

I am soo saddened and I fear that there is just nothing I kan do to help her. I feel so powerless in this existence. How kan I escape and give her the help she needs? How kan I cross over and give her the strength thAt I don't even have myself? What am I supposed to do to help her from in here?

I just kan't sit back here and watch her have to go through anothEr abortion. I kan't sit back and watch her cry for a week straight. I just kan't sit back and wAtch her slowly die. I wish she

> would just run, far, far away and break free of that asshole she calls a father!
>
> Macy...

"Macy?" Michael said. He looked bewildered, but he knew that name. He knew it well.

This book was full of confusing and twisted emotions. Susan must have been to hell and back—to have such deranged thoughts and emotions. Michael began to see a distinct pattern in the words. In a rage, he slammed his fist hard into the bed. His chest tightened, and he was ready to explode. For the first time since he was a child when his parents were killed, he wanted to hurt someone. He wanted to bash the life out of the person who stole the life from his beloved Susan.

Michael turned through the following pages, but they lay mostly blank, some scribbles here and there, but nothing of any importance. Michael placed the book on the dirty sheets of the bed and picked up the next book. He flipped open to a page that threw him for a loop. There were dark eerie sketches and scratches throughout the page. An upside-down pentagram burned into the paper like a cattle brand on the hide of a cow. *Death, murder, cunt, bitch, 666, kill, beautiful blood, father*—all scribbled onto the paper.

Michael's brow folded.

"My God," he said. "What the hell was going on with you?" Michael picked up another book and flipped open to the first page, but it was blank. He flipped through a few more pages until he found another entry. He hated reading just how broken down Susan really was, but on the other hand, he couldn't stop himself. He needed as much information, as much evidence as he could gather. Perhaps then, he could justify what he was going to do to the bastard responsible. Somebody was going to pay—of that Michael was sure.

He turned the page, hoping against hope to escape the darkness that was so heavy on every page. He had to press on. He needed the answers that would allow him to bury the past and move on with his life.

When he started this journey, he hoped he would find answers, but he never thought he would find anything this dark and sinister. *There really is a whole world of insanity out there*, he thought. And he was infuriated that this insanity has so harshly touched his life.

Dear Diary,

Well, the time has come. He's gotten me pregnant again for the last time. This is the third time. How kan he do that, it makes me sick! He's my father! I want to kill him! I want to kill him tonight while he's sleeping. I want to hurt him like he hurts me. I want him to bleed like I have bled at his hands so many times. If I can gather enough courage, I will do it. I swear to god, I will kill him tonight when he passes out drunk.

Either way, I am leaving for Kalifornia tomorrow after the abortion. I know where he hides his money, and he'll never see it or me again!

He promised he would kill me anyway if I ever had a baby, and I believe him. He'll find me and kill the baby. He would hunt me like an animal and kill me and dump me in the swamp with my mommy. I know he killed her.

I'll never be safe. I am so afraid of him. I have no choice. Either kill him or leave. Because as long as he is alive, I will never live in peace, and I will never have a baby of my own…

I Miss you mommy

Melissa…

Michael was dazed. He slowly lowered the book into his lap. His breathing escalated in with his brewing rage. His eyes narrowed with seething anger.

And the bough had broken.

Michael snapped.

He screamed and threw the book across the room. He jumped up from the bed in a violent rage and began destroying the room. He kicked a hole in the wall. Knocked over the dresser and kicked it into splinters. He threw the empty bottle through the window. Glass exploded and fell in and out of the room. He flipped the old bed over and ripped the door completely off its hinges, all while screaming bloody murder.

Michael stopped and held still in the doorway trying to quiet his rage. He looked around the room like a lunatic. His wild eyes were full of insane thoughts. As he was searching his mind for some sort of conclusion, his eyes fell on the handle of the gun near the bed.

Michael tilted his head and focused on the gun. His breathing slowed as he moved over and picked up the weapon. He held it up and checked for bullets. He found his conclusion. He slipped the weapon into the front of his pants. He looked around the shattered room and gathered up all of Susan's diaries.

Michael left the light on in the room as he exited and moved into the living room. He placed the diaries on the dirty coffee table in front of the old rotting couch. He looked like a caged animal searching for an escape through the bars as he paced the room, somehow trying to formulate a plan of action. He wanted more information, something that would justify his equally twisted thoughts. For good measure, he kicked a few more holes in the walls in the living room.

Michael moved into and back out of the kitchen several times. Back and forth he paced, in and out of the kitchen like a madman. Into and back out of the bedrooms with no particular reason other than burning off steam, trying to quash his rage before it got the better of him.

As he moved back into the living room, he paused a moment near the couch to catch his breath and slow his heart. He wasn't all that comfortable with the violent thoughts that were tripping his mind. He looked down at the diaries a moment, and then he looked away. His eyes fell on the dark television screen. He yelled and quickly drew the handgun from his jeans and pointed it at the television screen. But as he was about to pull the trigger, his eyes caught the sight of the videotapes lined neatly on top of the VCR. Michael lowered the gun and slowly moved closer to the television and started to examine the videotapes, reading the handwritten text on their spines:

Melissa Alone
Melissa with Daddy
Melissa with Friends
Melissa in Chains

Again Michael's pulse quickened as he pulled the first tape from its jacket. As the television heated up, Michael placed the first tape into the VCR and moved back a few steps and backed into the coffee table. He flipped the table over, clearing it of its debris and sat on it as the video started playing.

The picture was completely dark at first. A child's voice came from a very dark place. Michael could almost smell its dingy, musty odor. There was a certain eerie feel to the darkness, one that must have scared the hell out of a child. Though the voice came clearer, Michael still couldn't make out what the child was saying.

Michael heard footsteps on the concrete floor move away from the camera, but he couldn't see anybody in the picture.

Michael turned and glanced into the kitchen a brief moment, then looked back at the television. He heard the distinct sound of an old door squeaking on its hinges as it opened. There came light into the darkened room from above. A shadow moved away and faded into the light from above.

Again Michael turned and looked into the kitchen. He could almost hear the footsteps tapping across the floor as if it were in real time.

Michael drew back to the screen with blazing eyes. With the new light, he could barely make out the figure of a young girl. She was definitely naked, and she appeared to be horrified and shaking violently. Michael moved closer to the screen for a better look. Michael quickly moved back in shock when he realized that this young child was not only naked, but she was also tied in chains to the chair in what looked like a basement. He turned and took a long look into the kitchen. He could almost hear the voices coming from the basement—terrified voices, taunting voices.

For the longest time, nothing happened on the tape. The naked child sat quietly in the chair, and she wasn't moving. Michael thought she were dead. He hit the fast-forward button and waited. As the tape started again, he still found the girl was limp, as if she were beaten. But then she moved slightly as if she were startled by something. The child looked around in the darkness, searching for what was coming next. She could hear him up in the kitchen above her. She was terrified of what was coming next. She knew this wasn't over, that he was coming back to finish the job. A strange series of facial expressions shook the child, one after the other, all different. Michael found it odd, the manner in which the child moved.

Then she looked to her right. "Who are you?" the child asked. She appeared panicked and quickly looked up at the light from above and feared the worst. He was coming back.

"I heard you crying," the voice replied. "I'm Macy, and I want to be your friend."

"You kan't be here!" the child said with urgency. The desperate, pleading look on her face stared past the camera.

Michael was filled with goose bumps. That terrified look on the child's face really spooked him. He felt her agony, though he couldn't imagine what she had been through.

"But I wanna be your friend," the child replied strangely. Michael stared at the picture of the little girl carefully. It appeared that she was talking to herself in dissimilar voices. Michael found it strange.

"I don't have any friends," the child replied. "I'm not allowed."

"Well, why not? That's silly."

Yes, she was talking to herself in two different voices. He was sure of it. And the child bore a strong resemblance to Susan. He didn't want to believe it, but in his heart, he knew it was her. It was no wonder Susan didn't believe in God. She lived her whole childhood in hell.

"Will you just go away!" the child called out in the darkness. She spoke in anger, but did so very quietly, so as not to alarm anybody from above.

"Okay, but I'm gonna come back because I wanna be your friend," the child said in another voice, Macy's voice.

Melissa looked around the darkened room and let out a sigh of relief when she realized that she was once again alone. After a moment, Melissa began humming. Then softly singing an old nursery-school ditty. "Patty cake, patty cake, baker man. Bake me a cake as fast as you can." Michael looked around the room as she repeated the chorus. The tape ended with the child repeating "Patty Cake" over and over again in desperation, as if calling for somebody to hurry up and come to her rescue. She sounded like a broken record stuck on the same verse.

Michael pulled the tape from the VCR, but before he viewed the second tape, he moved into the kitchen.

He didn't hesitate as he passed through the dirty, scummy kitchen and moved directly to the door and kicked it open. The door broke in half, and the part still attached swung open. It squeaked just as it had in the tape.

Michael was hit like a punch with the staunch odor of mildew and wetness and the strong smell of piss. He stood in the doorway looking into the darkness below and the wooden steps leading down. Michael searched for a light but found none. He moved slowly down the steps until he lost the light. He peered through the darkness as his eyes adjusted to the dismal light. It was the same place as in the tape; Michael was sure of it. He could no longer stand the strong odor of urine. He wondered just how long that little girl was down here and how many times she had no choice but to urinate where she could.

Michael moved back into the living room and placed the second tape into the VCR. The tape showed the same girl, much older now, maybe twelve or thirteen, he thought. And he knew for sure that this girl was Susan. Again she was naked and tied to the chair; only this time she was also blindfolded. She was chanting "Patty Cake" over and over again before the tape went to black-and-white snow.

Michael tried, but he couldn't imagine how lost this young child was. He was angered and wanted to destroy this house and whoever lived here. He wanted to tear apart the first person who walked through the door.

As he reached out to remove the tape, another part of the video started playing on the screen. Michael moved back for a better look. It was Susan, and now she was about sixteen, he thought. Again she was naked, but she lay cowering on the dirty wet basement floor in bright light. She appeared to be in absolute terror. Michael could clearly see dark-purple and green bruises on her back and legs. Somebody really worked her over.

Just when she thought the worst was over and the beating was done, she was completely humiliated from her tormentor as a thin stream of obvious liquid came raining down on her naked body. The voice in the dark grunted as he shook out the last drops. The young girl appeared as if she were going to throw up as a tremendous gag built in her throat.

Now Michael understood where the strong smell of piss came from, and he was livid!

"—and I mean it! Fuck, you piss me off!" a man's voice shouted in the room. The man then cleared his throat with a loud belch.

The young girl flinched in terror as she lay on the concrete floor. "I'm sorry, I'm sorry," she quickly repeated as she folded herself in half, moving into the fetal position. Her head remained near her knees to soften any blows that might be coming.

Yeah, that was definitely Susan, he thought. It was absolutely her voice. The fact that he was absolutely sure made him even more enraged with the actions on the screen.

"—you hear me girl? If you ever have a baby, I'll kill you dead! Not only will I kill you, I'll kill yer baby first, so's you can watch, so's you can see just what you're gonna get next," the man's voice raged.

"Yes, Daddy. I'm sorry, Daddy. I will never have a baby, Daddy. I promise!"

"I'll kill ya. Ain't no matter where ya at. I'll find ya, an' I'll kill ya dead! Ya got that?" he shouted.

"Yes, Daddy. I'll never have a baby, Daddy, never! I promise. I don't want you to kill me. I know you will," she said. She was so scared she would say anything just to make him stop.

"Now you get to the clinic tomorrow, an' you get rid of dat baby yer carryin'! An' I don't wanna hear dat yer pregnant again," he said.

"Yes, Daddy," she said apologetically.

There was another long pause in the action on the tape. Michael could hear Susan's father's breathing escalate from behind the camera. "Now why don't ya come on over here an' make yer daddy happy," he said in a sick low grunt. "Ya knows how I like it."

Without hesitation, Susan moved from her position and crawled across the floor. She remained on her knees as she looked up at the camera as the man grunted.

That was it for Michael. He couldn't stand to see his Susan like that—naked, abused, and humiliated. He couldn't imagine what an animal her father was to force her to do such awful things. How could any man do something so horrific to his own child, to any child for that matter! Michael was outraged.

He removed the tape from the VCR and sat back down on the couch. His anger quickly gave way to tears he cried for his beloved wife. For the pain she lived through all those years of her youth. It was no wonder why she snapped. With all those suppressed memories flooding back into her mind at once, Michael thought. He understood now why she was so insistent about having an abortion. She was in fear she would be killed. Michael understood now and forgave her. He loved her so much. He knew who was responsible. He had his answers. The only remaining question on his mind was what he was going to do about it.

* * * * *

Michael turned off all the lights and sat on the couch in the living room. A neat stack of videotapes lay on the coffee table next to Susan's diaries. Michael waited in the darkness with the handgun tightly in his hand. So many horrific images assaulted his mind. He just couldn't escape those horrible scenes on the videotapes. He was sure they would haunt him forever. Oh. how he wished he had never seen them.

And he waited…

Another hour passed, then two. Michael remained on the couch and was strangely calm. He had ice water running cold through his veins. He resolved himself to the fact that he was going to wait here until somebody came into the house, anybody, he didn't care who it was. He didn't care if he had to wait here another day or another week. Michael wanted vengeance, he wanted justice, and somebody was going to pay!

As the three o'clock hour approached, Michael was becoming quite drowsy; his eyes drooped heavily from lack of sleep. He wasn't far from a long overdue slumber. He was startled by the sound of rattling bottles outside the house. Michael's heart leapt into action, pumping at a rapid pace, but he didn't move a muscle. He remained poised, ready for anything. He felt the adrenaline course through his body. Then the sound of a man pissing came from what sounded to be right outside the front door of the house.

Again Michael didn't move. Whatever was going to happen, it was going to happen in here where he could control the situation.

Michael waited.

A moment later, the front door of the house swung open, and a short man staggered into the house. Michael couldn't make out any of his features in the darkness, only that he was stinking drunk. Michael didn't figure he would be any other way. He slammed the door behind him and started moving across the dark room toward the kitchen. He tried to pocket his keys, but dropped them on the floor. He didn't give them a second glance and kept staggering in the dark room.

Michael flipped on the light, and the man stopped in his tracks and was swaying slightly in his drunken stupor. He pulled focus on Michael's anger-laden face. The man's eyes narrowed.

"What the fuck are ya doin' in my house?" he shouted through slurred speech. Spittle sprayed everywhere when he spoke.

Michael took a long and hard look at the man. Yeah, it was the same man as in the videotapes, Michael was sure of it, though he had changed quite a bit. If Michael would not have been in such a rage, he would have laughed at the sight of this man swaying before him. He was much shorter then he thought he would be, almost comical-looking. He had a stained dirty-blue T-shirt that barely covered his large stomach, and he had gray thinning hair and a bad comb-over.

Michael was expecting more of a domineering man, somebody with strength. But then he realized that this man's strength only came at the hands of a young child who couldn't fight back. Michael shook his head.

"I'm here to kill you, you son of a bitch!" Michael replied calmly. His eyes were cold and lifeless. Vengeance would be his. Nothing else mattered to him anymore. This man took everything from him, and now he was going to pay.

The man's eyes narrowed. He was ready to pounce on Michael but stopped when his bloodshot eyes caught the sight of the gun in Michael's hand. The man held up his hands slightly, showing Michael his palms. "I don't want no trouble, mister. I don't even know who you is or what's ya want."

"You're a disgusting human being," Michael said with anger.

"What'd I do to ya? Who the fuck are ya? Why you in my fuckin' house?"

"You might say I was your son-in-law, though it makes me sick to my stomach to even say it. You're a pig!" Michael shouted in anger.

The man took a step back, totally confused by that statement. He began shaking his head slightly, denying any knowledge of Michael's suggestion. The man stumbled and fell to his knees. Michael moved over, and the gun became more visible as he moved closer to the man.

"You ruined my life, you motherfucker!" Michael shouted as he held the gun against the man's head as he cried for mercy. He cried like a terror-filled child, sobbing. Michael found it fitting how karma came to life right in front of his eyes.

The man tried to plea for mercy, but Michael cut him off.

"I know what you did, you son of a bitch! I saw the tapes!" Michael shouted. "Now you're going to die!" he said as he pulled back the hammer of the gun.

Michael shoved the barrel of the gun into the man's face. "Say it! Say it!" Michael shouted.

The man refused to say anything and continued crying, drooling from his mouth. Snot bubbles came from the man's nose.

Michael pulled the gun away from his face and punched him square in the nose, sending the man sprawling to the floor. "Say it!" Michael shouted again and shoved the gun back in the man's face.

The man spat at him from the floor. Michael tossed the gun aside and pounced on him. He punched him several times in the face. Blood was coming from the man's mouth and nose, but Michael continued pummeling the man, punching him over and over again. Finally, the man fell onto the floor. Blood was pouring from his face.

Michael stood over him with clenched fists. He tried to imagine how many times he made Susan bleed and if his actions were justified. For good measure, Michael punched him a few more times before he retrieved the gun.

The man spat blood from his mouth and wiped his face as he looked up at Michael, who was standing over him. "You gonna kill me one way or another, ain't ya?" the man asked. He knew his time had come, and he seemed to have lost any will to live.

"You're going to pay for what you took away from me," Michael said. "For what you took away from Melissa."

"Fuck you!" the man shouted.

Michael punched him again, square in the face. The man fell back and hit his head on the floor.

"Say it!" Michael shouted.

The man rose up a bit, but was still sprawled on the floor.

"Say it, who are you?" Michael shouted.

"I'm her daddy. I made the tapes," he said and spat again on the floor. "Are ya happy now? Did ya git what yea come fer?"

Michael wasn't happy. He certainly wasn't expecting him to admit to anything. Michael didn't know what to say. He stood there, somewhat shocked.

"Ya gonna kill me now?" the man asked as he watched Michael slowly back away from him.

Michael was almost paralyzed, lost in thought. His mind was racing, searching for the right answers. He didn't want to throw his life away, and he certainly didn't want this man to get away with everything he had done. But what was he going to do?

"Why don't ya just kill me!" the man shouted.

Michael appeared startled and snapped from his slight trance. He looked back down at the man on the floor. Michael's eyes were dead and filled with evil intent. He held the gun to the man's head and pulled back the hammer. "No. I'm not like you," Michael replied with a hateful scowl.

The man looked shocked. He had resided himself to the fact that he was finally, after all these years, going to pay for the sins of his actions. He wanted to die.

"That girl was crazy in the head. She talked to people who just weren't there. Ya know what I mean? She was downright nuts!" the man said, trying to goad Michael into finally doing away with him. It was as if he wanted somebody to end his misery.

Michael wasn't having any part of it.

The man decided to push his luck. "She was a much better fuck when she was ten. I didn't have no trouble with her back then," he said with cold eyes and a twisted smile on his sick and bloody face. His eyes were cold. "Then she started getting pregnant, an' I ain't gonna have no crazy nutjobs like her runnin' 'round here." He kept his eyes on Michael, who was seething with anger. The man sensed his dazzling conclusion was at hand, and Michael would put an end to his miserable life with a single shot.

Michael jumped onto the man and started pounding him into oblivion. He continued punching him in the face and head even after he was knocked out cold.

Michael fell back on his knees and began crying. The man lay lifeless in front of him on the floor, bleeding heavily from his face. Michael hoped he had not killed him and waited for any sign of life. It soon came when the man moved slightly. Michael continued watching as he wiped tears from his own eyes.

Michael sat there for twenty minutes as the man lay on the floor. Then as he looked over at the video tapes, Michael rose to his feet and moved over to the coffee table and stood over it. He turned and picked up the gun and emptied all the bullets. He placed the gun on the coffee table, leaving one single bullet on top of the television set.

The man moved again slightly, and for good measure, Michael leveled another devastating blow to the man's face. He was knocked out cold. Michael was thankful the man was out cold; his hands were sore as hell, and he was sure he had at least one broken bone, if not more.

Michael picked up all the videotapes and Susan's diaries and headed out the front door. Michael didn't hesitate. With the videotapes in his arms, he ran through the darkness and falling rain.

* * * * *

Michael waited by the pay phone in the pouring rain after calling Dave Bader for a ride. He covered the videotapes under his shirt as he waited.

Michael was soaking wet when he got into Dave's car. Michael told him to go to the police station immediately. Michael began telling Bader the whole sordid story as he drove. Bader was in shock, not only at what Michael was saying but also for the fact that he was going to have the exclusive of a lifetime. He was thankful that he started the tape recorder just before Michael entered his car.

* * * * *

Walking into the police station, Michael and Dave walked over to the front desk. When the desk sergeant looked up, he recognized Michael straight away. "Hey, you're that guy on television," he said to Michael. A slight starstruck smile crossed his face.

"Michael Bishope," his commanding officer said over his shoulder as he approached from the back room. "What can I do for you, sir?" he asked.

Michael told him of his case with his wife, which the officer already knew about. He began to tell him the story of finding her father and what he had done. "These are for you," Michael said and handed him the stack of videotapes. "I implore you to look at these right away!" Michael said with a strong sense of urgency.

"Yes, you should look at these now!" Bader added with a heavy emphasis.

"Here's the address where you can find the son of a bitch." Michael handed him a slip of paper and watched as the officer looked on with curiosity.

The officer looked a bit baffled as he glanced at the tapes. He nodded at Michael's pleading glare. "I'll go have a look," he said and exited into the back room. Dave pulled Michael aside and continued asking him more questions; he wanted the complete story.

Michael kept his word to the reporter and willingly answered all questions. Michael always kept his word no matter what the situation. That was the one thing he remembered his father teaching him, how important it was to keep your word. It was a little piece of his father he could always hold on to.

With the reporter jotting down every note Michael let slip, Michael knew that he would finally have closure with this part of his life. He looked forward to seeing his child. He missed and loved him so much.

It didn't take long before the same police officer came out of the back room. Only this time he appeared to be livid, almost in a state of rage. A handful of equally enraged police officers followed him. The lead officer quietly said something to the desk sergeant, who looked shocked. He immediately got on the radio and called patrol cars into action.

Michael reached out and stopped the lead officer, grabbing his arm as he stood. "I'm going with you," Michael said. The officer's stare went right through Michael as if he were a clean pane of glass. This man had snapped and was ready to kill.

"No!" the officer said coldly.

"I wasn't asking," Michael said quickly as he tightened his grip on the man's arm. "I am going with you!"

The officer's expression softened somewhat. He couldn't imagine the hell Michael must have been going through. "You ride with me, but you stay in the car! Got it?"

"Yes, sir," Michael replied and followed the group of officers out of the station.

Dave Bader wasn't about to miss any part of this story. He followed in his own car.

* * * * *

When they arrived with a convoy of police cars, there were already four other police cars in front of the house. It was a scene Michael had witnessed many times before covering the news, though he had never really been this close to the action. He wasn't sure if he was that comfortable being this close. But he needed to be here.

Red-and-blue lights flashed all over the gaudy neighborhood, painting the houses red and blue. Michael saw police officers taking cover behind cars and trees with their guns drawn, pistols and shotguns. The rain continued falling through the red-and-blue lights with an eerie strobing effect. The dirt driveway was now slushy brown mud.

Michael learned that he was driving with the police captain and was again ordered to remain in the car before the captain exited to take charge of the operation.

Michael watched the captain take hold of a bullhorn in the falling rain and approach the house. The car's windshield wipers continued sliding across the windscreen, giving Michael a clear sight of the action.

Perhaps he should have not left the gun in the house, he thought. But he wasn't thinking straight himself when he left. Suddenly Michael regretted his action. He felt as though he should warn the police, but it was too late.

As the captain keyed the bullhorn, a gunshot exploded from within the house. The captain ducked for cover behind the car. Other police officers readied themselves for action, some diving in the mud behind cars.

Michael dove to the floor of the police car. A moment later, Michael peered over the dashboard and through the window of the police cruiser. Nothing came from the house. It was silent.

Police began moving about, staying covered. Michael wanted to get the hell out of the car. He didn't want to hear another shot, and he certainly didn't want to be in the vicinity when and if another shot rang out. But following orders, he remained where he was.

For the next hour, there was no movement by the police officers. SWAT was already in position and was slowly moving closer to the house. They were about to enter.

Michael finally exited the police car and backed away from the action, far away. Dave Bader pulled him over to the side, and they watched the action with a small group of people who ventured out of their houses just before dawn.

A flash grenade exploded inside the house—just before the SWAT team quickly entered the house with their weapons drawn, ready to kill any threat.

Michael and Bader looked on.

The police on the street waited and moved about in anticipation.

The captain was on a walkie-talkie with the SWAT team.

Waiting.

Then the call came from within the house. The captain turned to his officers. "All clear," he shouted. The officers holstered their weapons.

Michael and Bader approached the house but was stopped by a rookie cop near the iron gates on the edge of the property.

"I think he's dead," a SWAT officer said to a uniformed officer as he exited the house. He continued moving toward the street as another SWAT officer ran from the house yelling.

"Get an ambulance! He's still alive!" he shouted.

Michael and Bader exchanged looks. Michael knew that justice, if not already served, was going to be served. He was sure of it.

A wave of commotion followed. Police officers moved in and out of the house with flashlights.

Melissa's father was taken away on a stretcher and loaded into a waiting ambulance. Michael could see only that there was a bandage on his head. He saw no blood, only the dry blood on his face.

Police began carrying his personal belongings out of the house. The first was the television set and the VCR. They were loaded into a police car. Other belongings, things Michael didn't notice when he was in the house, were taken from what he thought was the basement. The basement was too dark for him to see anything. He wondered what other information he could have come up with if he only had a flashlight down there. He was very curious to know what was down there, but it was too late for that. He was sure the police would not be so forthcoming with that information, not even to him.

Michael later found out that it was just a flesh wound, and Melissa's father would survive to stand trial. Michael knew then that justice would be served and that he did the right thing. And he would make it a point to be at the trial to make sure this man got what he deserved.

* * * * *

As the dawn slowly started breaking through the dim light of the dark clouds, Michael peered toward the back house around the side of Melissa's house. Michael asked to borrow a flashlight from an officer and walked around back. Michael approached the house cautiously and shone the light onto the front porch. He found old Mabel sitting on the porch in a rocking chair, and she was in complete darkness.

Right then, it came to him. He knew that she had been there, on that porch, watching him each time he came there. He knew he felt someone watching him. He felt it in the pit of his stomach. He moved closer to the old wooden steps of the porch. "Thank you for your help," he said to the old woman sitting on the porch.

She looked right through him with both eyes clearly visible. 'Boy, I don't know ya," she replied with a slight hint of anger.

Her tone bothered him. Michael looked at her with confusion. He focused back on her eyes. She had both eyes unlike earlier.

Michael took a step back. He was confused. He knew he had spoken with her, with this woman who had only one eye. She was the reason he had all his answers, good or bad; he had what he came for.

"Excuse me, ma'am, but you and I spoke earlier tonight, just down the street," he said, pointing.

"Boy, I ain't never talked ta you! I ain't never seen you afore in my life! You's white folk don't make no sense ta me. I's stay clear of all ya'all," she replied.

No matter what she said, Michael knew in his heart that she led him here and that they had spoken just down the street. He held her harsh gaze for a moment. He nodded. "Okay. Well, sorry to bother you then," he said as he slowly backed away from the porch.

Old Mabel nodded. She smiled a secret smile as Michael walked back to the front of the house where all the police were gathered.

When Michael returned to the front of the house, the police captain asked him to stick around. He said he needed to ask him some questions before he left. He wanted him to remain in the city for a few more days of questioning, but Michael wanted to get back to Los Angeles to see his son. He would agree to return, but he was leaving soon.

*****

It was after nine in the morning when the police finally finished questioning Michael. The rain had stopped, but the skies were threatening to burst at any moment. Dave Bader waited until they were through. So did the growing mass of reporters who had gotten wind of Michael Bishope's involvement. But only one reporter was getting the exclusive, and he also wanted closure on his once-in-a-lifetime story.

Michael remained and was leaning against the police car, looking at the house. He wondered what could have been if Melissa had been left alone as a child' and encouraged to grow. He wondered what would have been if she had only told him about her life. But he knew that she would have never told anybody, especially him, and he understood why. He wanted to believe she could have had a better life. He wished so much that he would have somehow been able to see this earlier and somehow put an end to all this madness.

Michael understood why Susan developed altered personalities, and he didn't blame her. Any child would have, being put in the same awful situation. He loved her; he always would. He would speak fondly of her to their son. Their son would always remember his mother in a good way. Michael would make sure of that.

* * * * *

Dave Bader offered Michael a ride back to his hotel, be he declined the offer. Michael wanted to walk in the rain and clear his head. Dave understood and dropped him off a few blocks away from the reporters, leaving Michael alone in the falling rain. Michael counted at least eight police cars in front of the house as they left. This chapter of his life was now closed as far as he was concerned.

He would return for the trial, but he would not return here, not to this house where his wife's life was taken. This place was the start of her death. She started dying inside long before he had ever met her. He wanted nothing more to do with this part of town, not even the house he was so fascinated with. He would walk by it without a second glance. He just wanted to walk and feel the rain cleanse his soul.

Michael later found out that Susan's father had no living relatives, and the house, all paid for, was his. But Michael wanted no part of its sordid history and asked Dave Bader to auction it off and donate the money to an abused children's foundation.

Michael made arrangements for his return to Los Angeles and stayed in his hotel room the whole day, sleeping mostly. He needed it. He hadn't been sleeping right in months, only an hour or two each night. He slept like a baby. He slept through the torrential rain and thunder that exploded like cannon fire throughout the city.

And Michael slept...

34

As the headline story broke across the country and around the world the following morning, Michael landed back in Los Angeles as the reporters and news crews were heading to New Orleans in droves. Michael was glad to be back home. He wished that the private jet would finally come to a stop so he could burst from the plane and run to his child, who was waiting with Mrs. Vach.

The reunion with his son was joyous for Michael. He remained outside the car, holding his son in his arms as Mrs. Vach looked on. She was happy for him. Happy that he found what he was looking for, happy that he was back where he belonged, with his son, with his family. He vowed to never leave his son again, no matter what the circumstances.

* * * * *

It wasn't until well after Melissa's father's trial, almost a year later, that Michael told Mister and Mrs. Vach what had happened in New Orleans. They too were appalled. It took Michael a while to open up to them, but he needed to keep it a private matter until he knew the man's fate. Michael took comfort in the fact that the man would die in prison.

Back in New Orleans, when Michael attended the trial, he gave numerous interviews to the media and sold the book rights. He was only looking out for his son's future. All the money was going to go to him anyway. Michael was still weighing film offers, though he wasn't sure if that was exactly what he wanted at the time.

Since his return to Los Angeles, the press corps had pretty much left him alone, though he still got an occasional reporter wanting to do a follow-up story.

For years, Michael would be recognized wherever he went. People would always want to know about his son and ask all sorts of uncomfortable questions. Michael still wanted to remain a private person. He felt as though he needed to remain so for his son's sake. He wanted to protect him from the prying eyes of the cold world. He knew firsthand how damaging it could be.

As young Luc grew into his second year, Michael knew it was time to leave the city where he grew up. He didn't want his son to grow up with all the gangs and crime that were so prevalent there. It was getting worse all the time.

For years, Michael had wanted to leave the area and start fresh somewhere else, somewhere near a good river where he could teach his son to fly-fish and have a chance at a better life. And this was his opportunity. He was heading back to live with his brother, Matthew, for a while, just outside Boston until his house was built next door in Connecticut. He had taken Moranville's offer and agreed to run the New York station of KNRQ. Michael bought a piece of land in Southern Connecticut, and he would commute into the city three days a week to run the station.

The land he bought was perfect and beautiful. The closest neighbors were almost a half a mile away. It had a stream running through the property where he could teach his son how to fly-fish and how to grow up in a peaceful country atmosphere. It was a place where he could spend long summer days with his son outside and sit on the porch in the evenings. He wanted the simple life for his son, whom he loved so very much.

Michael and Luc settled into their new home nicely. And the small town nearby was wonderful and charming. The town accepted Michael and his son as one of their own. No questions, no stares, just downright acceptance, and Michael loved it. Michael took his son to the diner every Saturday afternoon for lunch. Then they walked through the town to get an ice cream before they returned home to watch the sun set in the evenings.

* * * * *

For a good year or two, Tyson Nash was the most sought-after lawyer in Los Angeles. He appeared back on the Larry King show three times. He was on *Oprah* once and a score of local shows. He was now a major player in the legal field. At present, he was representing a famous actor charged with shoplifting from an equally famous Beverly Hills department store. It was the second star Nash represented, and Nash still loved the spotlight.

It was one year later, as Michael was about to shut off the television for the night, that he caught another glimpse of Tyson Nash on the television screen, though he didn't catch the entire story. It appeared that Nash was in a world of trouble himself. Michael flipped through the channels but found no mention of the breaking story out of Los Angeles. He figured he'd read about it in the morning paper. Or not…

* * * * *

Michael stood in the open doorway looking at his son. He was so strong and so big now, and Michael was so proud. He was growing by leaps and bounds, and his curiosity was undying. But lately he had been asking about his mother. It was a time Michael knew was coming. He knew he couldn't keep it a secret forever. He decided it was time and moved over to the bed where his son was sleeping.

Michael sat on the edge of the bed and leaned over and kissed his son on the forehead.

Young Luc stirred and looked through squinted eyes at his father. "We going fishing now, Daddy?" he asked.

Michael smiled. He loved to hear his son call him daddy. What a wonderful feeling that was to him. "No, son, it's still nighttime."

Young Luc looked around the room, then finally out the window. "Oh," he said with another glorious look of confusion on his face.

Michael loved those curious looks his son got when things didn't make much sense to him. Michael smiled.

"Luc, I wanted to talk to you about your mother," Michael said.

Young Luc snapped to attention and rubbed his eyes. "Okay," he said and looked up at his hero, his father, who was about to tell him all about his mother…

* * * * *

Luc fell asleep that night with a feeling of love from a mother he never knew. And he woke the following morning with a happiness Michael had never seen. It fit him.

As they walked down to the river, each carrying a fishing pole, young Luc looked up at his father. "Daddy, tonight after dinner, can we stay up late and look at the stars?"

Michael stopped and looked down at his son.

Luc smiled back, though he didn't know why.

"Sure, son. We can look at the stars tonight."

They walked off down to the river and spent the lazy day as buddies in the grand realm of Mother Nature.

About the Author

Steve grew up in Simi Valley, CA and has lived in Sweden, Germany, and Australia. He now lives in Texas. Steve has traveled extensively throughout the United States and also lived in Las Vegas, NV, Arizona, Connecticut, Mississippi, New York City, and New Jersey twice or thrice and not necessarily in that order. Needless to say, travel is a big passion that he loves so much. He has dreams of moving to a beautiful log home in the North East, Vermont, New Hampshire, Maine, or somewhere that receives an abundance of snow. The fresh, white mantle painted on the virgin horizon has always held a deeply profound meaning to Steve and that's where he wants to spend the rest of his life, waiting for the winter's first snowfall and cold winter nights sitting by the fireplace.

Having worked as a government operations director for security and surveillance companies, Steve has worked all over the United States as well. One of Steve's favorite jobs was as a postproduction coordinator at 20th Century Fox back in the 90s. That job and the proximity to the film industry started his passion in writing screen plays back then. Steve sold two scripts in the film industry and optioned two others. None of which ever went into production.

Steve is also a foodie. He loves cooking especially for other people. Whenever in a new city, state, or town he tries to explore all the restaurants featured in Guy Fieri's Diners, drive-ins, and Dives. To date, Steve has been to about sixty eateries featured on the show and book. He wants a 1500 square foot kitchen complete with a coal fire pizza oven in his log home with a fireplace and loft in the kitchen. *A Fathers Voice* is Steve's fourth book, including a children's book he wrote while living in Germany.

CPSIA information can be obtained
at www.ICGtesting.com
Printed in the USA
LVHW030956010321
680243LV00037B/386